CONTEMPORARY ISSUES
in
HEALTHCARE
LAW and ETHICS

Third Edition

CONTEMPORARY ISSUES
in
HEALTHCARE
LAW and ETHICS

Third Edition

Dean M. Harris

Health Administration Press, Chicago
AUPHA Press, Washington, DC

AUPHA
HAP

Your board, staff, or clients may also benefit from this book's insight. For more information on quantity discounts, contact the Health Administration Press Marketing Manager at (312) 424-9470.

11   10   09   08   07   5   4   3   2   1

Library of Congress Cataloging-in-Publication Data

Harris, Dean M., 1951–
    Contemporary issues in healthcare law and ethics / by Dean M. Harris.—
3rd ed.
        p. ; cm.
    Includes bibliographical references and index.
    ISBN 978-1-56793-279-9 (hardcover : alk. paper)
    1. Medical care—Law and legislation—United States—Popular works.
    2. Medical ethics—Popular works. I. Title.
    [DNLM: 1. Delivery of Health Care—legislation & jurisprudence—
    United States. 2. Ethics, Medical—United States. 3. Insurance, Health—
    legislation & jurisprudence—United States. W 32.5 AA1 H313c 2007]
    KF3825.Z9H37 2007
    344.7303'21—dc22

                                                                    2007012262

The paper used in this publication meets the minimum requirements of American National Standard for Information Sciences—Permanence of Paper for Printed Library Materials, ANSI Z39.48-1984. ∞™

Acquisitions editor: Audrey Kaufman; Project manager: Gregory Sebben; Cover designer: Chris Underdown.

Health Administration Press
A division of the Foundation
    of the American College of
    Healthcare Executives
One North Franklin Street
Suite 1700
Chicago, IL 60606
(312) 424-2800

Association of University Programs
    in Health Administration
730 11th Street, NW
4th Floor
Washington, DC 20001
(202) 638-1448

Dedicated to
Deborah McLaughlin Harris

CONTENTS

DETAILED CONTENTS

LIST OF FIGURES

LIST OF PROBLEMS

PREFACE TO THE THIRD EDITION

With this third edition, the book has been changed in two important ways. As always, the primary motivation for revising a book on healthcare law and ethics is to update the material and provide more current information about a broad range of issues. The third edition includes information about several important developments, such as decisions by the U.S. Supreme Court about the liability of health plans and physician-assisted suicide. In addition to discussing the Terri Schiavo case, the third edition addresses current issues in the law and ethics of human reproduction, such as emergency contraception, the federal Partial-Birth Abortion Ban Act, and the Supreme Court's decision upholding that Act. There is an expanded and updated discussion of medical malpractice reform and legal requirements to report medical errors, as well as updated material on the obligations to provide emergency care and to make healthcare services accessible to persons with limited English proficiency. Other updates include the new Medicare prescription drug law and a federal case involving the HIPAA privacy rules. Finally, new material has been added about the ongoing effort to promote universal health insurance coverage.

The second major change in the third edition is a change in emphasis and focus. At the time of the first and second editions, the healthcare industry and the rest of the country were preoccupied with the issues and problems of managed care. HMOs and other managed care organizations were using strict methods of utilization review in an effort to reduce healthcare costs, and there was a severe backlash against managed care. Some of the most important legal issues before Congress, the Supreme Court, and state governments at that time involved objections to managed care techniques and proposals for managed care reform.

Since then, many things have changed. Congress has become concerned with matters other than managed care, and the public backlash has forced third-party payers to tone down some of their techniques of cost containment. Not surprisingly, healthcare costs have increased significantly in the past few years. Now people are much more concerned with the cost and availability of health insurance than with the techniques of cost containment. The problem of the uninsured is back on the "radar screen" (where it should have been all along). As many companies outsource jobs, eliminate benefits, and go bankrupt, people are now very worried about the continued availability of health insurance coverage.

For all of these reasons, the third edition adds a new final chapter on health insurance and the ongoing effort to achieve universal coverage. Instead of building toward the ultimate issues of managed heathcare, the new third edition builds toward the ultimate issues of providing and extending health insurance coverage. The topics in that new final chapter are (1) state regulation of insurance companies and HMOs; (2) the problem of extending access to coverage; and (3) state efforts to achieve universal health insurance coverage. This chapter includes material on the 2006 Massachusetts law on healthcare reform and health insurance coverage, as well the litigation in federal court over Maryland's 2006 Fair Share Health Care Fund Act.

ACKNOWLEDGMENTS

I am grateful to many people for their assistance with various aspects of this project. I particularly appreciate the support and encouragement of Dr. Peggy Leatt, chair of the Department of Health Policy and Administration, UNC School of Public Health. In addition, I am grateful to my colleague, Dr. Bruce Fried, for his encouragement and advice.

I want to thank my research assistants, Kerry Burleigh, Ryan Lee, and Jocelyn Fina. I am also grateful to the staff at Health Administration Press for their hard work throughout the entire process.

Most important, I thank Deborah, David, and Devon Harris for their patience, good humor, and support.

THE ROLE OF LAW IN THE U.S. HEALTHCARE SYSTEM

1

USING THE LAW TO PROMOTE OUR POLICY GOALS AND ETHICAL PRINCIPLES

The study of law is more than simply memorizing a list of activities that are illegal, such as Medicare fraud or price-fixing. It is more than memorizing the penalties for particular violations, such as the number of years in prison one can receive for a class B felony or the fine for driving 50 miles per hour in a 35 mile per hour zone. It is more than trying to remember the names of court cases or the citations to statutes and regulations. Instead, law is a policy discipline and a social science.

Moreover, the law is not cast in stone, but is subject to change. For hundreds or perhaps thousands of years, people have reconsidered and changed the rules that govern their activities. In a democratic society, we have the power to make further changes in the laws by which we live. Therefore, as students and scholars of law, we not only study the current state of the law, but also what we think the law should be. In particular, we consider how we can use the law to accomplish our goals of public policy.

We begin this type of analysis by identifying a practical problem. For example, we may want to focus on discrimination, violence, environmental pollution, or inadequate access to healthcare services. Then, we try to figure out how to use the law and the legal system to solve that particular problem by creating a new law or by changing an existing law.

"There Ought to Be a Law!"

When we talk about reforming the healthcare system, we are really saying we should change the laws that regulate that system. For example, if we think health insurance companies should be required to provide coverage for people without regard to their health status, we are really arguing for a change in the law that governs the operation of insurance companies. If we think health maintenance organizations should be required to authorize potentially lifesaving care for patients dying of cancer or should be held liable in damages for the harm caused by their refusal to authorize care, we

3

are really arguing in favor of laws that would make those changes to the existing rules of law. In fact, those proposed changes to the law are at the heart of the ongoing debate in Congress and state legislatures about patients' rights and managed care reform. Thus, when we say we want to reform the healthcare system to achieve our policy goals, what we really are saying is, "There ought to be a law."

Coming to this conclusion is the relatively easy part. The harder—and more interesting—part is figuring out what kind of law to create and what that law should provide. Several alternatives will arise, and each will have its own advantages and disadvantages. The task is to choose the alternative that will be most effective and most efficient in achieving the particular policy goal.

The first alternative to consider is whether the problem can best be handled by means of a single federal law or a series of separate state laws. As discussed in Chapter 2, one of the underlying themes of healthcare law and policy is determining the appropriate roles for the federal government and state governments in regulating healthcare providers and third-party payers. Each level of government has its own legal powers and its own practical advantages. The federal government has the power to create laws that establish uniform standards throughout the country and has greater resources than the states to finance and enforce its laws. The states, however, may be more aware of and responsive to local needs and may be able to experiment with new approaches for which a national consensus has not yet developed. Of course, regulation by one level of government does not necessarily preclude regulation by the other, and many activities are subject to overlapping regulation by federal, state, and even local authorities.

In addition to choosing local, state, or federal law, an approach or combination of approaches to using the law must be selected as a way to solve a particular problem. For example, several different approaches to using the law as a means of promoting quality of patient care and reducing medical errors are available. Under a regulatory approach, a governmental body would prohibit certain activities or require that those activities only be performed under governmental supervision. One example of this regulatory approach is licensure of healthcare professionals, in which state governments prohibit unqualified persons from practicing and provide governmental supervision over persons who are permitted to practice. A different approach would be to create or recognize a private right of action on the part of an injured patient to sue the healthcare provider who caused the injury for monetary damages. In a combination of these different approaches, our legal system attempts to promote quality of care by requiring a physician to obtain a license to practice medicine from a state licensing board, but it also permits an injured patient to sue the licensed physician for medical malpractice in a civil action. A third approach would be to use the government's power as a large-scale buyer of healthcare services to impose legal requirements on those health-care facilities and professionals who elect to serve the beneficiaries of government payment programs.

Once we decide on the best approach or combination of approaches, the next step is to decide where to draw the line between lawful and unlawful conduct. It may be obvious that certain really bad conduct should be against the law and that certain really good conduct should be lawful. However, most activities in the real world fall somewhere in the middle. In creating a law, we have to draw a line and say that everything on one side of the line is lawful and everything on the other side is unlawful. As a matter of fundamental fairness, that line must be clear and understandable, so that people will have fair notice of what is prohibited and will be able to conform their behavior to the requirements of the law.

In deciding where to draw the line, we want to choose the point at which the law will be most effective in stopping the bad conduct without inhibiting socially useful activities. If the rules of law are too weak, they will not be effective in achieving the policy goal. If the rules are too restrictive, however, they will be impractical to follow, difficult to enforce, and prohibitively expensive for society as a whole. We also need to avoid, or at least minimize, the unintended consequences that are almost certain to occur when we create a new law or revise an existing law. Thus, the challenge is to create or revise a law that will accomplish our policy goals in an effective manner with a minimum of adverse consequences.

Ethics in the Healthcare Field

When people talk about ethics in healthcare, they may be speaking about a variety of topics, including bioethics, professional ethics, and business or organizational ethics. Depending on the context, this book will address each of these different aspects of ethics in the healthcare field.

Sometimes the term "ethics" is used to refer to the moral quandaries of bioethics, such as defining the extent of a patient's right to refuse treatment or the right to a natural death. We might conclude, for example, that a competent adult patient should have the right to refuse a lifesaving blood transfusion on the grounds of religious belief. Under those circumstances, an individual's right to religious freedom may outweigh society's interest in keeping its members alive. However, if the patient's death would leave the patient's child as a ward of the state, we might conclude that the interests of society should take precedence over the rights of the individual. In either case, our view of the appropriate ethical solution is *not* a question of what is required or allowed by the laws of the state. Rather, our view of what is right and wrong is an expression of our moral philosophy and our beliefs about the proper relationship between the individual and society.

In other situations, the concept of ethics in healthcare is used to refer to the professional standards of medical practitioners, such as the Principles of Medical Ethics adopted by the American Medical Association (AMA). These principles do not have the force of law and do not purport to dictate how society as a whole should resolve difficult questions of morality. Rather, the AMA's Principles of Medical Ethics only set forth the standards of ethical conduct for physicians.

For example, the current debate over physician-assisted suicide involves several aspects of healthcare ethics. Wholly apart from the legal issue of criminal prosecution for causing the death of another human being is the ethical issue of whether causing the death of another person is morally right. In addition, there is a separate issue of professional ethics regarding whether a member of the medical profession should participate in the suicide of a patient. In that regard, the AMA Council on Ethical and Judicial Affairs has stated that physicians should *not* assist terminally ill patients in committing suicide, whether or not suicide is justifiable in a moral sense or permissible under the laws of the state.[1] This example shows the importance of distinguishing among the legal, moral, and professional issues in this type of debate and clarifying how the term "ethics" is being used.

Aside from the moral issues of bioethics and the professional standards of medical ethics, the term may be used to refer to business or organizational ethics in the context of the healthcare industry. As one author has explained, "[b]usiness ethics is the study of how personal moral norms apply to the activities and goals of commercial enterprise."[2] As in any other business, each organization in the healthcare industry must determine what it considers to be appropriate conduct for its officers and employees. The Joint Commission (formerly the Joint Commission on Accreditation of Healthcare Organizations), for example, requires accredited facilities to operate in accordance with a "code of ethical business and professional behavior."[3] Moreover, because of the unique importance of healthcare, organizations in the healthcare industry and the people who work in those organizations have additional ethical duties to the people and communities they serve.

The Relationship Between Law and Ethics

Contrary to popular notions, the law is not totally separate from ethics. In fact, the rules of law are based on ethical beliefs that are commonly held in our society. These basic ethical principles include respect for individual autonomy, beneficence (helping others), nonmaleficence (not harming others), and justice or fairness.[4] Regardless of whether these ethical duties are derived from religious faith, natural law, or a social contract, these principles form the basis for the legal rules of our society. For example, the legal prohibitions against violence and theft are expressions of the ethical principle of nonmaleficence.

In some cases, however, these ethical duties require us to do more than what is currently required by law. As discussed in Chapter 11, U.S. law generally imposes no duty to help a stranger in distress, even though most people believe an ethical obligation exists to do so. Therefore, it is reasonable to ask at this point why the law does not always go as far as ethics in requiring particular conduct.

Creating rules of law to implement the principle of nonmaleficence, such as prohibiting one person from attacking another or stealing the property of another, is relatively easy. Members of our society generally agree that attacking other people in any way or stealing any amount of their money or property is morally wrong. In contrast, it is more difficult to create rules of law that would require us to help others, in accordance with the ethical principle of beneficence.

No consensus can be reached on precisely how far each of us should be required to go in giving our time and money to help other people, or how much sacrifice and risk we should be required to incur in doing so. In addition, it is very difficult to develop clear rules in advance that would put people on notice of how much help they are required to provide to others to avoid violating the law. If we cannot reach a consensus or draw clear lines between lawful and unlawful conduct, we cannot hold people legally liable for failing to act as we would have preferred.

The disparity between ethical principles and legal obligations can be particularly acute with regard to providing healthcare services to people in need. According to the President's Commission for the Study of Ethical Problems in Medicine and Biomedical and Behavioral Research, society has a moral obligation to provide access to an adequate level of healthcare for all of its members, even though there is no comprehensive legal right to healthcare at the present time.[5] Under these circumstances, the ethical duty of beneficence requires us to do more than is currently required by law. In the meantime, we can also work to change the law in ways that would provide greater access to care.

This dynamic interaction between healthcare law and ethics can be seen in the tragic case of a 15-year-old boy who died outside the door of Ravenswood Hospital in Chicago. On May 16, 1998, Christopher Sercye was playing basketball when he was shot twice in the stomach. His friends helped him get to the bottom of the entrance ramp of the private hospital's emergency department, but Christopher collapsed outside the door. Although his friends and police officers pleaded with hospital employees to help him, the emergency department employees refused to leave the building because of hospital policy. Eventually, a police officer took Christopher in a wheelchair to the emergency department, where he died. Later, the director of the Illinois Department of Public Health spoke to the *Washington Post* about this tragic case:

"It's important for people in healthcare to be first and foremost care-givers and not lawyers," complained John Lumpkin, director of the Illinois Department of Public Health, whose office mailed letters to that effect to all hospitals licensed by his regulatory agency. "First and foremost, you do what's right for the patient. There is no legal obligation for them to provide care outside their doors but morally we would expect them to do the right thing."[6]

In fact, if Christopher was on the hospital's property, the hospital was legally obligated to provide the necessary emergency care. In 1986, Congress enacted the Emergency Medical Treatment and Active Labor Act, which is also known as the Consolidated Omnibus Budget Reconciliation Act antidumping law.[7] That law requires all hospitals that have an emergency department and participate in the Medicare program to provide certain emergency services, regardless of a patient's ability to pay. The law applies to any individual who "comes to the emergency department."[8] Under regulations that had been issued by the U.S. Department of Health and Human Services (HHS), a person was considered to have come to the emergency department if he was "on the hospital property."[9] Therefore, if Christopher was on the property of the hospital, the hospital was legally required to provide emergency services.

As a result of this incident, Ravenswood Hospital changed its policy. In addition, without admitting that it did anything wrong, the hospital paid $40,000 in a settlement with the HHS Office of Inspector General (OIG).[10] Morality may have required more than the law in that case, but it does appear that some legal obligations were already in effect at that time.

These events also caused HHS to clarify or change the law on a prospective basis. In its amended regulations, HHS explicitly provided that the hospital property includes "the entire main hospital campus . . . including the parking lot, sidewalk, and driveway."[11] In addition, HHS defined the term "campus" to include areas within 250 yards of the main hospital buildings.[12] These amendments remind us that we have the ability to change the law over time to become more consistent with our ethical principles.

In the meantime, the OIG, which reached the settlement with Ravenswood Hospital, is encouraging all healthcare organizations to adopt effective compliance programs. According to the OIG, those compliance programs should not be limited to ensuring compliance with the law, but they should also be designed to encourage ethical business behavior.[13] Each healthcare organization should strive for a standard of ethical behavior that exceeds the current requirements of law. In addition, each organization should encourage its officers, employees, and trustees to consider the ethical implications of their decisions and should develop policies and systems that encourage people to act in the best interest of the patient and of society in general.

In figuring out how to do "the right thing," you should *not* begin your analysis by asking what the law requires you to do. That would be like letting the tail wag the dog. Instead, determine what act or decision would be the most ethical. Then, find a way to do that in a manner that complies with the law and minimizes the risk of liability. In addition, you may decide that advocating a change in the law is necessary to encourage or require people to act in an ethical manner.

The Goals of this Book

One of the goals of this book is to help you to stay out of jail and reduce the risk of civil and criminal liability. In fact, you *can* be sent to prison for breaking some of the laws in the healthcare industry, such as those against price-fixing and Medicare fraud. In addition, healthcare providers can be held liable for millions of dollars in damages. From a positive perspective, it is important to know what the laws permit you to do, and not merely what the laws prohibit.

However, memorizing every one of the potentially applicable laws or creating a complete list of legal "dos and don'ts" is impossible. Even if that could be done, it would not be particularly helpful, because laws change every day with the issuance of new statutes, regulations, and court decisions.

Moreover, legal consequences depend on the unique facts of each particular case, and every case is different. For example, we may know that factors A, B, and C would make an arrangement between a hospital and a physician lawful, but that factors X, Y, and Z would make it unlawful as a violation of the Medicare antikickback law.[14] The problem is that your situation will never be exactly like A, B, and C or exactly like X, Y, and Z, but rather will be somewhere in the middle. Under these circumstances, the lawyer's job is to analyze the particular set of facts, apply the rules of law to those facts, and form a professional opinion or prediction as to whether a court or government agency is likely to find your facts more similar to A, B, and C or to X, Y, and Z. In fact, that is precisely what lawyers are trained to do.

In contrast, managers and healthcare professionals need to learn how to identify situations that raise potential legal issues. In that way, they will begin to develop a good intuitive sense for avoiding legal problems and for knowing when to consult their lawyers. Therefore, another goal of this book is to help managers and healthcare professionals learn how to identify potential legal problems that they are likely to encounter in the healthcare industry.

Another important objective is to understand how legal rules have changed over time and how they continue to change to promote the underlying goals of an evolving public policy. As discussed earlier, the laws regulating the U.S. healthcare system are the result of the collective desire of society to change the previous laws for reasons of policy and ethics. By studying the underlying policy goals and ethical principles, you can gain a better understanding of the existing laws that regulate the healthcare system. Moreover, by understanding the policies on which the laws are based, it will be easier to recognize a situation that raises a potential legal issue. In other words, you will be able to <u>recognize</u> when something *should* be <u>against</u> the law.

It is important to understand what the law currently requires of participants in the healthcare field, but that alone is not sufficient. It is also important to understand how to change the law. In that way, you will be able to achieve your policy objectives, promote your ethical standards, and make progress toward the common goal of healthcare reform.

Notes

1. Council on Ethical and Judicial Affairs, American Medical Association, "2.211," in Council on Ethical and Judicial Affairs, *Code of Medical Ethics: Current Opinions with Annotations* (Chicago: American Medical Association, 1996–1997).
2. L.L. Nash, *Good Intentions Aside: A Manager's Guide to Resolving Ethical Problems* (Boston: Harvard Business School Press, 1990): 5.
3. Joint Commission on Accreditation of Healthcare Organizations, "New Standards Seek to Protect Integrity of Clinical Decision Making," *Joint Commission Perspectives*, Jan./Feb. (1997): 18–19.
4. National Commission for the Protection of Human Subjects of Biomedical and Behavioral Research, *The Belmont Report: Ethical Principles and Guidelines for the Protection of Human Subjects in Research*, DHEW Pub. No. (OS) 78–0012 (Washington, DC: U.S. Government Printing Office, 1978). [Online report; retrieved 5/18/07.] http://ohsr.od.nih.gov/guidelines/belmont.html.
5. President's Commission for the Study of Ethical Problems in Medicine and Biomedical and Behavioral Research, *Securing Access to Health Care: A Report on the Ethical Implications of Differences in the Availability of Health Services*, no. 5, vols. 1–3 (Washington, DC: U.S. Government Printing Office, 1998).
6. J. Jeter, "Chicago Cringes at Teen's Death; Hospital Wouldn't Treat Gunshot Victim 35 Feet From Its Door," *Washington Post*, May 20, 1998, A2.
7. Emergency Medical Treatment and Active Labor Act of 1986 (EMTALA), 42 U.S.C. § 1395dd (2005).
8. *Id.* § 1395dd(a).
9. 42 C.F.R. § 489.24 (2001).

10. L. Meckler, "Ravenswood Hospital is Fined $40,000 in Boy's Death," *Chicago Sun-Times*, March 13, 1999, 4.

11. Office of Inspector General; Medicare Program; Prospective Payment System for Hospital Outpatient Services, 65 Fed. Reg. 18,434, 18,548 (April 7, 2000).

12. *Id.* at 18,538 (adding a new 42 C.F.R. § 413.65).

13. See Publication of the Office of Inspector General Compliance Program for Hospitals, 63 Fed. Reg. 8,987, 8,988 (Feb. 23, 1998).

14. 42 U.S.C. § 1320a–7b (2000).

THE AMERICAN LEGAL SYSTEM

Who Makes the Laws, and Who Changes the Laws?

In some societies, the law is simply what the king, chief, dictator, or high priest says it is. However, in the U.S. system, laws are created by the legislatures, courts, and administrative agencies.

Under the doctrine of separation of powers, the legislative, executive, and judicial branches of government perform different functions. Moreover, each branch of government creates laws in different ways. The judicial branch makes laws by deciding particular cases brought before the court. In deciding the case, the judge may not merely do what she thinks is right, just, or fair in each individual case. Instead, the judge is required to decide each case in a manner consistent with the legal precedents that were established in similar cases. That body of precedents is known as the *common law*.

As it is developed by the courts, the common law is constantly changing. The court's decision in each new case is added to the preexisting body of precedents and thereby becomes a part of the common law. Moreover, courts have the power to change the common law to accommodate the changing values and policies of our society. For example, at one time a traditional common-law doctrine of charitable immunity provided that non-profit hospitals could not be held liable for negligence. However, courts in many states decided that charitable immunity was no longer appropriate because of changes in the nature of hospitals and the ability to purchase insurance. Therefore, some courts acted on their own to change the law in their respective states, without the need for any action by the legislative or executive branches.

Of course, legislatures have the power to enact their own sets of laws, which are referred to as *statutes*. The legislature that enacted a statute has the power to change it by adopting an amendment or by repealing the old statute and enacting a new and different statute. Moreover, a statute enacted by the legislature will take precedence over a rule of the common law. Therefore, if the judicial branch is unwilling to change a traditional rule of the common law, the legislature in that jurisdiction may take action on its own to change the law by enacting a statute.

For example, the rules that apply to medical malpractice suits have been developed over many years by the courts of each state as rules of the common law. However, state legislatures in many states became convinced that malpractice awards against healthcare providers should be limited, and they enacted tort reform statutes, which changed the common-law rules. In California, the state legislature enacted a statute known as the Medical Injury Compensation Reform Act, which imposed a maximum limit or "cap" on the damages a patient could recover for pain and suffering in a medical malpractice case.[1] Because statutes take precedence over common law, judges in California were obligated to follow the new statute, even if they thought it was unwise as a matter of public policy or unfair as applied in a particular case. When a statute exists that applies to the facts of the case, the court is required to decide the case in accordance with that statute. If there is any question about the meaning of that statute, the court must interpret it in a way that will carry out the intent of the legislature.

However, in one situation a court has the power to overrule a statute, although that power is rarely used. If the court determines that a statute is unconstitutional, it is not limited to merely carrying out the intent of the legislature. For example, a court might rule that a state statute imposing a cap on malpractice damages violates the state's own constitution and therefore cannot be enforced.[2] Thus, legislatures can supersede the common law by enacting a statute, but courts retain the important power to declare that a statute is unconstitutional.

Because of the complexity of government regulation, legislators have neither the time nor the expertise to develop all of the details of the law. Therefore, legislatures create administrative agencies and delegate authority to the agencies to develop the specific requirements of the law. For example, Congress enacted statutes to establish the Medicare and Medicaid programs and set forth the broad outlines of those programs, but it delegated authority to the secretary of the U.S. Department of Health and Human Services (HHS) to develop many of the details. Similarly, state legislatures enacted statutes to require healthcare facilities and practitioners to obtain licenses before providing services in the state and created administrative agencies or licensing boards with the authority to license and regulate the providers.

In addition to enforcing the laws passed by the legislature, administrative agencies make laws of their own. Through a process referred to as *rulemaking*, agencies adopt rules or regulations, such as the Medicare regulations of HHS, that flesh out the details of the regulatory scheme established by the legislature. If the agency's regulations are within the scope of its statutory authority from the legislature, and if the agency followed the appropriate rulemaking procedures, its regulations have the force of law. In addition, through the process of *adjudication*, the agencies decide individual cases that arise under the regulatory scheme and thereby make a type of administrative "common law." For example, when a medical licensing board conducts a hearing to consider whether to revoke a physician's license, the board's decisions in prior cases may provide a set of precedents for resolving the pending case.

Under the doctrine of exhaustion of administrative remedies, a person who objects to the action of an agency must go through the agency's own internal process of administrative review before challenging the agency's action in court. Once the agency has completed its process of internal administrative review, a person who is dissatisfied with the final decision may seek judicial review of the agency's action in the courts.

Ordinarily, courts will defer to the judgment and expertise of the agency and will uphold the agency's decision if it is supported by substantial evidence in the record as a whole. Thus, it is difficult to obtain a reversal of an agency's decision, especially when the issue involves the agency's judgment or disputed questions of fact. Nevertheless, the court may reverse an agency's final decision if the agency failed to follow all of the procedural requirements, such as providing notice of its intended action and properly adopting all of the rules on which an agency's decision was based. Therefore, a challenge to agency action by means of judicial review is more likely to prevail on issues of legal procedure than on the substantive merits of the agency's decision.

By reviewing the decisions and regulations of the agency, the court will provide a safeguard against arbitrary action. Under the doctrine of separation of powers, each branch of government provides checks and balances against the other branches and contributes to the ongoing development and refinement of the law. Separation of powers can be seen among the three branches of state government, as well as among the three branches of the federal government.

In addition, an important relationship, called "federalism," exists between the 50 state governments and the federal government. Under the Supremacy Clause in Article VI, Clause 2 of the U.S. Constitution, laws enacted by the federal government are the supreme law of the land and take precedence over any contrary provisions of state law. For example, the federal government has chosen to regulate employee health plans under the federal Employee Retirement Income Security Act of 1974.[3] As a result of this clause in the Constitution, state laws on the same subject are often preempted—or displaced—by the federal law. Although the Supremacy Clause provides for federal preemption of state laws, the Tenth Amendment to the U.S. Constitution reserves certain powers to the states.

In the healthcare field, one of the underlying issues of law and policy is determining what should be regulated by the federal government as opposed to state government. For example, some people have argued that the laws should be changed to give the federal government a more active role in controlling medical malpractice litigation and regulating the licensure of healthcare professionals. However, others believe states should continue their traditional role in governing those particular issues. Similarly, some people have argued that the federal Medicaid law should be changed to allow the states more flexibility in operating their own Medicaid programs, whereas others believe we should retain the law that provides minimum federal standards for all state Medicaid programs. Other examples include whether we should regulate managed care organizations at the state or federal level and whether we should have one uniform federal law of patient privacy or different state privacy laws that could exceed the federal standards. As indicated by these examples, the appropriate roles of the federal and state governments will be a recurring theme in the analysis of healthcare policy and law.

Substantive Areas of Law

Important distinctions must be made within the overall framework of the law, such as the difference between civil and criminal law. The category of criminal law refers to wrongs against society as a whole, even if the wrong consists of harming an identifiable member of society. Regardless of whether the victim pursues a private claim for damages against the perpetrator, society has been wronged by a violation of its criminal law. Therefore, society may impose punishment in the form of fines, imprisonment, or, in some places, execution.

Of course, strict procedures have been established for determining a person's guilt or innocence in a criminal case, such as the constitutional right to trial by jury. Moreover, the accused cannot be forced to testify against himself, and the prosecution is required to prove the guilt of the accused beyond a reasonable doubt. A criminal case will be prosecuted by a district attorney in state court or a U.S. attorney in federal court and will be described by a caption such as "*People v. Jones,*" "*[state name] v. Jones,*" or "*U.S. v. Jones.*"

The healthcare field is experiencing a trend toward expanding the application of criminal law to healthcare facilities and practitioners. Historically, criminal law has been used to prohibit abortion, and criminal penalties are still in effect for performing abortions not authorized by law. In addition, criminal law has been used for many years to prevent the unlicensed practice of medicine. In 1889, a West Virginia statute prohibited the unlicensed practice of medicine, and the U.S. Supreme Court upheld a criminal conviction for violating that statute.[4]

However, the modern trend has been to expand the application of criminal laws to other types of conduct by healthcare providers. In cases of Medicare fraud and abuse, providers are subject to criminal prosecution and not merely civil or administrative remedies. In addition, criminal law has been applied against providers in several cases involving harm to their patients. For example, Dr. Gerald Einaugler, a New York physician, was convicted of the crimes of reckless endangerment and willful neglect of a patient.[5] In another case, a Wisconsin district attorney charged a laboratory company with homicide for alleged recklessness in reading Pap smears, which apparently caused the deaths of two women.[6] The Michigan attorney general brought a criminal case against a nursing home company for charges that included alleged patient abuse and alteration or destruction of medical records.[7] Although each of these cases is unique, together they appear to indicate a trend toward greater use of criminal charges against healthcare practitioners and organizations.

Despite this increase in the use of criminal law, most legal issues in the healthcare field still involve matters of civil law, such as contracts or torts. A civil case involves the private rights and obligations of specific parties. For example, if Mrs. Jones attacked Mr. Smith, the victim (Smith) could sue the attacker (Jones) in a civil suit for battery and seek monetary damages as compensation for losses, such as pain and suffering, medical expenses, and lost wages. The civil case would be captioned "*Smith v. Jones*," which means Smith is the plaintiff who filed the suit and Jones is the defendant who is being sued. As a civil case, it would be pursued by Mr. Smith and his attorney, rather than by a public prosecutor. To prevail, Mr. Smith would not need to prove his case beyond a reasonable doubt. Rather, Mr. Smith would merely need to prove that the greater weight of the evidence (i.e., more than 50 percent) is in his favor.

Many civil cases are based on a *contract*, which is a voluntary agreement between two or more parties. If people fail to meet their obligations as set forth in a contract, which is referred to as breach of contract, the court may use the power of government to force them to pay monetary damages to the other party to the contract.

In the healthcare industry, contracts are used to construct buildings, purchase equipment and supplies, hire administrators, and sell services to patients and third-party payers. Some of the specialized types of contracts in the healthcare industry are physician recruitment contracts, management contracts for operating a facility, exclusive contracts to provide medical coverage for a department of a hospital, and preferred provider contracts with managed care organizations. In addition, the physician–patient relationship is based on a contract, which may be in writing or implied from the actions of the parties.

In contrast, a *tort* is a wrong committed by one person against another, without the need for any contract between the parties. For example, a driver who carelessly injures a pedestrian has committed a wrongful act, even though the driver had no preexisting contractual relationship with the pedestrian. Regardless of whether the state elects to prosecute the driver for a criminal offense such as reckless driving, the injured pedestrian may sue the driver for monetary damages in a civil action under the law of torts. Similarly, if a physician fails to meet the applicable standard of care in providing services to a patient, the patient may sue the provider for medical malpractice, which is based on the tort of negligence.

State and Federal Court Systems

Each state has its own system of courts, and the federal courts constitute a separate system. Within each system, the most important distinction is between the trial courts and the appellate courts.

A trial court determines the facts of a particular case, such as which driver caused an accident. If a jury is involved, its members will determine the facts, and the role of the trial judge will be limited to controlling the proceeding, instructing the jury about the law, and ruling on objections made by the lawyers. Alternatively, many cases are tried by a judge without a jury, in which case the judge will act as the finder of fact and the judge of the law.

Although trial courts are often referred to as "lower courts," they have important powers that cannot be exercised by the so-called "higher courts." The higher courts are referred to as appellate courts because they hear appeals from decisions of the lower courts. The appellate courts are higher in the sense that they have the power to reverse decisions of the lower courts, and they may establish legal precedents that are binding on the lower courts within their territorial jurisdiction. However, the appellate courts do not have the authority to conduct their own trials and cannot even hear a case until it has been heard or rejected by the lower court.

When a higher court considers an appeal, it does not conduct a new trial or listen to the witnesses. An appeal is a review of documents in the record and transcripts of the prior testimony, together with the written and oral arguments of the lawyers for each side. The purpose of the appeal is to determine whether the trial judge made errors of law in conducting the trial, such as mistakes in instructing the jury or ruling on the admission of evidence. The appellate court may affirm, reverse, or modify the decision of the trial court. In some cases, the appellate court may determine that the trial judge's mistakes were sufficiently serious to require a whole new trial of the case. In that event, the appellate court cannot conduct the new trial, but rather must send the case back to the lower court for retrial.

In the federal system, the trial courts are called federal district courts. There are 89 federal district courts in the 50 states, and some of the larger states have several districts. For example, the state of Illinois has three: the Northern District in Chicago, the Southern District in East St. Louis, and the Central District in Springfield. In addition to the federal district courts, there are some specialized federal courts such as tax court and bankruptcy court.

At the appellate level, the federal system has 13 intermediate appellate courts. These include 12 regional courts of appeals with jurisdiction

over particular geographic areas, or "circuits." In addition, the U.S. Court
of Appeals for the Federal Circuit has nationwide jurisdiction over appeals
in particular kinds of cases, such as trademarks, patents, and international
trade. The highest court in the federal system is the U.S. Supreme Court.

State court systems have a similar structure, with trial courts and
appellate courts, although the names of the courts vary widely. For example, the Supreme Court of California is the highest court in that state, but
the Supreme Court of New York is the trial court in that system. New
York's highest court is the Court of Appeals, which is the name of the intermediate appellate court in North Carolina. Some states refer to their trial
courts as superior courts, district courts, or circuit courts, and some states
have specialized courts for probate, juvenile, and family law cases. To evaluate the significance of a court decision, it is crucial to understand the level
of the court that rendered the decision.

In one sense, the authority of federal courts is more limited than the
authority of state courts. State governments have substantial power over
matters that occur within their states, and state courts have general jurisdiction over cases in their respective states. In contrast, the powers of the
federal government are limited by the U.S. Constitution, even though federal law is the supreme law of the land. Thus, federal courts may only exercise jurisdiction in particular types of cases.

To understand the decision of a federal court, the first step is to determine why the federal court had jurisdiction of that particular case. For example, federal courts have jurisdiction over cases arising under federal statutes.
If a patient claims that a hospital failed to provide emergency medical services as required by the Consolidated Omnibus Budget Reconciliation Act's
antidumping law,[8] which is a federal statute, the patient may sue the hospital in federal court, as discussed in Chapter 11. Similarly, many cases involving Medicare, antitrust law, and employment discrimination arise under federal statutes and therefore may be filed in federal district court.

Aside from federal statutes, another basis for federal court jurisdiction is the protection of rights under the U.S. Constitution. Sometimes
people believe their state government has violated their rights under the
federal constitution. The Fourteenth Amendment to the U.S. Constitution
provides that no *state* may "deprive any person of life, liberty, or property,
without due process of law; nor deny to any person within its jurisdiction
the equal protection of the laws."[9] Therefore, a person may ask the federal
court to order the state government to stop violating the person's rights
under the federal constitution.

That is the context in which the U.S. Supreme Court addressed the
issue of abortion in the famous case of *Roe v. Wade*.[10] Jane Roe is the fictitious name of a woman who was unmarried and pregnant and who wanted
to obtain an abortion in Texas. The legislature of the state of Texas had
enacted statutes that made obtaining an abortion a crime, except when

necessary to save the life of the mother. Because Ms. Roe did not fit within that exception, the criminal statutes enacted by the state prevented her from obtaining an abortion.

According to Ms. Roe, the state of Texas was violating her rights under the U.S. Constitution, including her right of personal privacy. Ms. Roe filed a case in federal court against the district attorney of Dallas County, who was an official of the state. Specifically, she asked the federal court to prevent the state official from enforcing the state's criminal abortion statutes. In its decision, the U.S. Supreme Court agreed that the Texas criminal abortion statutes violated Ms. Roe's rights under the U.S. Constitution.

In this type of case, it is important to recognize the limited nature of a federal court's decision. In *Roe v. Wade*, the U.S. Supreme Court did *not* purport to decide the ethical issue of abortion. Nor did the federal court decide any issues of Texas law, which can only be decided by the courts of that state. Moreover, the U.S. Supreme Court recognized that the state of Texas and other states may continue to prohibit abortion under some circumstances. Because the role of the federal courts in this type of case is limited to deciding the constitutional issues, the decision of the federal court will be limited to those issues.

Another example of the limited role of the federal court in this type of litigation involved the termination of treatment for Ms. Nancy Cruzan.[11] In that case, Ms. Cruzan had been injured in an automobile accident and was in a persistent vegetative state. Her parents wanted to terminate her artificial nutrition and hydration. However, she had never made any formal advance directive and had not expressed her desires clearly with regard to continuing or terminating life-sustaining treatment. The highest state court in Missouri had refused to order nutrition and hydration to be terminated because there was no clear and convincing evidence of the patient's desires, as required by Missouri law. Thus, Ms. Cruzan's parents asked a federal court to order the treatment terminated.

Under those circumstances, the federal court had no authority to determine whether Ms. Cruzan's case had met the requirements of Missouri law. The highest state court in Missouri had already determined that there was no clear and convincing evidence, and an issue of Missouri law could only be decided by the state courts of Missouri. Therefore, the only issue for the U.S. Supreme Court in that case was whether Missouri's requirement of clear and convincing evidence violated Ms. Cruzan's rights under the U.S. Constitution. After hearing the case, the U.S. Supreme Court merely held that Missouri's requirement did not violate the U.S. Constitution. That was a limited ruling in accordance with the limited role of the federal courts.

In addition to cases involving federal statutes and constitutional rights, federal courts have jurisdiction to hear cases between citizens of different states. Thus, federal courts may decide cases involving contracts or torts, provided that the dispute is between citizens of different states. For example, the federal court could decide a medical malpractice case, provided that the patient and physician are citizens of different states.

At the time the U.S. Constitution was adopted, a concern arose that citizens of one state would not be treated fairly in the courts of another state. For example, if a citizen of Georgia had to sue a citizen of Vermont in the state court of Vermont, the plaintiff from Georgia might be treated as an outsider in the Vermont courtroom, and the local defendant might have a "home court advantage." Therefore, the U.S. Constitution permits the Georgia plaintiff to sue the Vermont defendant in federal district court, although the federal court will be located within the state of Vermont.

This authority of the federal court is referred to as "diversity jurisdiction," because the federal court may only hear the case if a diversity of citizenship exists between the parties. When the federal court hears a case under its diversity jurisdiction, it acts as if it were a court of the state. Therefore, the federal court would apply the statutes and common law of that particular state rather than the federal law.

The Process of a Civil Lawsuit

Regardless of whether a civil suit is filed in state or federal court, the process for handling the case will be essentially the same. Although there are some variations in the civil procedure of each state and between state and federal procedure, one basic format is used for civil cases in almost every U.S. jurisdiction.

The plaintiff generally begins the case by filing and serving a complaint, and the defendant files and serves an answer (see Figure 2.1). After an exchange of information, known as *discovery*, takes place, a trial, post-trial motions, and appeals may ensue. Under some circumstances, the court may terminate the case on legal grounds at an early stage of the proceedings. Many cases are also resolved by some type of negotiated settlement before the entire process is completed.

The Plaintiff's Complaint and Summons

The *complaint* is a document that sets forth the basis for the plaintiff's suit. It begins with a caption identifying the parties and the court, and then it tells the plaintiff's side of the story in numbered paragraphs. Finally, the complaint asks the court to grant particular types of legal relief, such as ordering the defendant to pay monetary damages or issuing an injunction against some action by the defendant.

The plaintiff will file the complaint in the office of the clerk of court and will serve a copy of the complaint on the defendant. In addition, the plaintiff will serve a *summons*, which officially notifies the defendant of the

FIGURE 2.1
The Process
of a Civil
Lawsuit

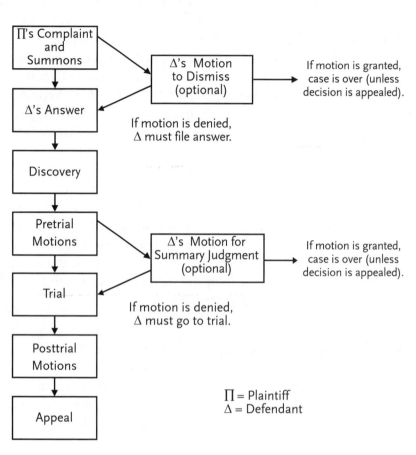

Π = Plaintiff
Δ = Defendant

suit and the deadline for the defendant to respond. It is important to distinguish between the functions of filing and service. To file a document, it must be delivered to the office of the clerk by hand or by some other permissible means, and it will be stamped as received with the date and time by the personnel in that office. In contrast, a document is served by delivering it to the opposing party or to an authorized agent by handing it to them or by some other manner permitted by law.

The Defendant's Answer or Motion to Dismiss

The defendant ordinarily responds to the complaint by filing and serving an answer, which contains the same caption as the complaint. In the answer, the defendant is required to admit or deny each of the numbered paragraphs of the complaint or state that the defendant lacks sufficient knowledge to be able to admit or deny that particular allegation. In addition to denying the factual allegations, the answer may set forth defenses, which are legal reasons why the plaintiff would not be entitled to recover damages from the defendant. Thus, denials are disputes about the facts alleged in the complaint, whereas defenses raise issues of law. The answer may also include a counterclaim by which the defendant asserts her own claim against the plaintiff. Finally, the answer will request particular types of relief from the court, such as dismissing the complaint or requiring the plaintiff to pay the defendant's costs.

As indicated in Figure 2.1, the defendant may take the optional step of filing a motion to dismiss the plaintiff's complaint. A motion is simply a request for a particular action from the court. Obviously, the defendant would like the case to be thrown out as soon as possible to avoid the time and expense of further litigation and the possibility of losing at trial.

However, the factual disputes between the parties, such as who is telling the truth, cannot be resolved until the trial. Therefore, in a motion to dismiss, the defendant is *not* disputing the factual allegations in the complaint. Rather, for the purpose of the defendant's motion to dismiss, all of the facts alleged by the plaintiff in the complaint are assumed to be true.

In a motion to dismiss, the defendant argues that, *even if* all of the plaintiff's allegations were true, the plaintiff could not win the case as a matter of law. For example, the complaint may disclose on its face that the plaintiff waited too many years to file the suit, and therefore the claim is foreclosed by the statute of limitations. Under those circumstances, even if all of the plaintiff's allegations were true, the plaintiff could not prevail and the case should be dismissed before wasting any more time and money.

Similarly, a case should be dismissed if the allegations of the complaint do not constitute a legally valid claim. For example, a plaintiff who was born with severe birth defects might try to assert a claim against a physician or laboratory for alleged negligence in genetic testing or counseling of the plaintiff's parents. Under that theory, if the plaintiff's parents had been properly tested and advised, they could have obtained an abortion, in which case the plaintiff would have never been born and would have never suffered the terrible birth defects. In some states, courts would allow the plaintiff to pursue a claim for negligence or malpractice under those circumstances. However, some states refuse to recognize a claim for "wrongful life." If the particular jurisdiction does not consider wrongful life to be a legally valid claim, the plaintiff could not prevail, even if all of the allegations are assumed to be true. Therefore, the court would grant a motion to dismiss and would terminate the case unless the claim is reinstated by a higher court on appeal.

If the court denies the defendant's motion to dismiss, that does not mean the plaintiff wins the case. Rather, denial of the motion merely means the case will not be dismissed at that point, and the defendant will be required to file and serve an answer in the manner described previously.

Discovery

In the movies and on television, trials appear to be won at the last minute with the help of a secret document or surprise witness. In reality, few surprises occur in a civil trial.

Long before the trial begins, each side has the right to obtain information about the other side's witnesses, exhibits, and arguments. In addition, each side has the right to question the other side's witnesses under oath in advance of the trial. The process of exchanging information before trial is referred to as *discovery*.

Each party is required to disclose information before the trial for several reasons:

1. The process of discovery reduces the element of surprise. Although surprise is dramatic and exciting, civil litigation is not a game. Rather, the process is a serious search for truth, and that search is advanced more by disclosure than by surprise. By being well prepared for trial, each side will be able to introduce its best evidence and make its best arguments.
2. Pretrial discovery helps speed up the trial and avoids wasting time while the judge and jury are present. Each party can distill its case down to the most important issues and evidence and avoid lines of questioning that turn out to be unproductive.
3. The discovery process may facilitate settlement of the case without the need for a lengthy and expensive trial. If each side knows the strengths and weaknesses of the other side's case, it can analyze the likelihood of success, the risks of trial, and the value of the claims for purposes of settlement.

Several methods are used for pretrial discovery, including depositions, written interrogatories, and requests for production of documents. Each party has the right to choose the methods it wishes to use and may use all of those available. In a deposition, lawyers have the opportunity to question opposing parties or their witnesses under oath. In addition, parties may be required to provide relevant documents and answer written interrogatories with regard to the issues in the case. As an ethical matter, parties and their lawyers must respond honestly and provide the documents to which the other party is entitled. Moreover, the court can impose legal sanctions such as fines for failure to respond to discovery in good faith.

Pretrial Motions

After conducting discovery and before beginning the trial, a party may file a motion to obtain an advance ruling on the admissibility of particular evidence. In addition, either party may file a motion for summary judgment to limit the issues at trial or resolve the case without the need for a trial.

In a motion for summary judgment, the moving party argues that there is no genuine issue of material fact for determination at a trial, and the moving party is entitled to judgment in its favor as a matter of law.

A motion for summary judgment is different from a motion to dismiss. In a defendant's motion for summary judgment, the allegations of the plaintiff's complaint are *not* assumed to be true. Rather, the plaintiff is required to come forward with a written forecast or preview of the evidence that it would introduce at trial in support of each of its allegations. For the plaintiff to prevail at trial, it would have to introduce some evidence on each of the essential elements of its claim. Those elements are specified by the substantive law that governs the particular type of claim, such as the law of contracts or the law of torts. If the plaintiff cannot show any evidence on one of the essential elements of its claim, even after completing discovery, a trial would be futile, and the court would grant the defendant's motion for summary judgment.

For example, to win a suit for medical malpractice, the plaintiff must be able to introduce some evidence on all four of the essential elements of a negligence case: duty, breach of duty, causation, and damages. Even if the plaintiff could prove the first three elements, there could be no recovery without at least some evidence that the plaintiff suffered damages. If the plaintiff cannot produce any evidence of damages, the defendant should not be required to endure the time and expense of a trial that the plaintiff cannot possibly win. Therefore, the defendant makes a motion for summary judgment.

If the court grants the defendant's motion for summary judgment, the case is over unless that decision is reversed on appeal. However, if the court denies the defendant's motion for summary judgment, that does *not* mean that the plaintiff wins the case. Rather, it merely means the case will not be terminated at that stage, and a trial must be held to determine the facts.

The Trial

All of the documents and other exhibits that a party wants to use at trial must be listed and provided to the other party before the trial begins. Similarly, each party must provide a list of the witnesses it may call to testify at the trial.

Each party will have the opportunity to make an opening statement, introduce evidence, call witnesses to testify on direct examination, question the witnesses for the other party on cross-examination, and make a closing argument. The plaintiff has the burden of proof with regard to each of the essential elements of its claim. Finally, the judge will instruct the jury by explaining the law that applies to the case, and the jury will retire to deliberate and make its decision. As discussed previously in connection with the role of a trial court, the purpose of a trial is to determine the facts. If no jury is used in a particular case, the judge will act as the finder of fact as well as the judge of the law.

Posttrial Motions

After a decision has been rendered, the losing party has the right to ask the trial judge to reject the decision of the jury and substitute a different decision in favor of the losing party. In addition, the losing party may ask the judge to reduce the amount of damages awarded by the jury or order a new trial of the case. Even if the trial judge is unlikely to grant these motions, they may be made by the losing party as the next step before filing an appeal to a higher court.

The Appeal

As discussed earlier in connection with the role of an appellate court, the appeal is not a new trial. Rather, it is a review of the written record and transcript of testimony from the trial court, together with the written briefs and oral arguments of the lawyers for each side.

The purpose of the appeal is not to reevaluate the facts, but rather to determine whether the trial judge made errors of law in conducting the trial or ruling on particular issues. For example, the party that lost the trial may argue that the trial judge had incorrectly instructed the jury about the law or made erroneous decisions to admit or exclude certain items of evidence. Some errors in a trial are so minor that they would not have affected the outcome of the trial, and those are described as "harmless errors." However, if the appellate court decides that the trial judge made serious errors of law, the appellate court may reverse the decision of the trial court or grant the losing party an entirely new trial.

Notes

1. Cal. Civ. Code § 3333.2 (West 1997).
2. See, e.g., *Lucas v. United States*, 757 S.W.2d 687 (Tex. 1988).
3. Employee Retirement Income Security Act of 1974 (ERISA), 29 U.S.C. §§ 1001 *et seq.* (2005).
4. *Dent v. West Virginia*, 129 U.S. 114, 128 (1889).
5. *People v. Einaugler*, 208 A.D.2d 946, 618, N.Y.S.2d 414 (N.Y. App. Div. 1994), *aff'd, Einaugler v. Supreme Court of the State of New York*, 109 F.3d 836, 839–841 (2d Cir. 1997).
6. E. Felsenthal, "Chem-Bio Charged with Homicide over Pap Smears," *Wall Street Journal*, April 13, 1995, B4.
7. M. Moss, "Criminal Probes Target Abusive Nursing Homes," *Wall Street Journal*, May 28, 1998, B1.

8. Emergency Medical Treatment and Active Labor Act of 1986 (EMTALA), 42 U.S.C. § 1395dd (2005).

9. U.S. CONST. amend. XIV, § 1.

10. 410 U.S. 113 (1973).

11. See *Cruzan v. Director, Missouri Department of Health*, 497 U.S. 261 (1990).

HOW TO CONDUCT LEGAL RESEARCH

A certain mystique that is justified in some respects and unjustified in others surrounds the complexities of legal research. Using the techniques of legal research to locate a particular court decision, statute, regulation, or bill is easy. In that situation, you are looking for something specific that you already know exists. For example, you have read about the decision of the U.S. Supreme Court in *Cruzan v. Director, Missouri Department of Health*,[1] which was discussed in Chapter 2. Now, you may want to find a copy of the actual opinion of the court to read yourself. After completing this chapter, you will have a working knowledge of the skills required to find that case, as well as other types of legal materials.

However, it is important to recognize that there is a different type of legal research that is beyond the scope of this book. As discussed in Chapter 1, lawyers are trained to apply the law to the facts of a particular case and to reach a conclusion as to the likely consequences of a particular situation. In performing that analysis, lawyers need to identify *all* of the sources of legal authority that might apply to a particular situation or else perform sufficient research to determine with confidence that there is no controlling legal authority.

For that purpose, merely finding a case that deals with the particular subject, such as the *Cruzan* case, would not be sufficient. Rather, it would be necessary to find *all* of the applicable precedents under the common law of a particular jurisdiction and determine whether and to what extent those common-law rules have been changed by subsequent cases, modified by statutes, or affected by constitutional decisions. If an applicable statute exists, it would be necessary to identify *all* of the judicial opinions that interpret the statute or address its constitutionality, as well as any regulations that supplement the statutory requirements.

Obviously, that type of comprehensive legal research requires extensive training, experience, and judgment and ordinarily should be left to the professionals. Nevertheless, nonlawyers can learn to use legal research techniques to locate and obtain important materials, such as cases, statutes, regulations, and proposed legislation. To learn how to find these materials, the first step is to understand the citation format by which legal materials are identified, labeled, and categorized. The next step is to learn how to find the materials in the easiest possible way.

As your skills improve, finding documents and information will become easier. Like a treasure hunt, it can be both frustrating and gratifying. So, happy hunting!

Understanding Legal Citation Form

As in other disciplines, the law has developed a standardized method of identifying and labeling every law; this method is referred to as *citation form*. Every case, statute, and rule can be distinguished from every other by means of its label. Moreover, for those who have learned to read the "secret code," the labels provide a great deal of information about the particular law. For example, the label will indicate the type of law, the identity of the court or legislature that adopted the law, and the date on which it was adopted. Most important, the labels provide the easiest way to find a particular law, regardless of whether you are using books in a library or doing computerized research on the Internet.

Citations to Case Law

Citations to cases begin with the identification of the plaintiff and defendant from the caption of the case, such as *Roe v. Wade*. Ordinarily, the plaintiff is listed first. However, in some jurisdictions, the defendant is listed first in an appellate decision if the defendant filed the appeal.

After the identification of the parties, the citation identifies the court that decided the case by reference to a particular set of books, which are called *reports* or *reporters*. For example, the *United States Reports* (abbreviated "U.S.") contain only the decisions of the U.S. Supreme Court. Thus, the identity and level of the court that decided the case can be determined by reference to the particular set of reporters mentioned in the citation.

In addition, the citation will include a volume number before the abbreviated name of the reporter and a page number after that abbreviated name. Specifically, the first number is the volume of that reporter in which the court's opinion can be found, and the subsequent number is the page on which the opinion begins. For example, the citation to *Roe v. Wade*, 410 U.S. 113 (1973), indicates that the opinion can be found in the *United States Reports*, which means that the case must have been decided by the U.S. Supreme Court. The citation also indicates that the opinion can be found in volume 410 of that reporter and begins at page 113. Finally, the date of 1973 in parentheses at the end of the citation is the date on which the court rendered its decision.

In addition to the official *United States Reports*, which are published by the federal government, decisions of the U.S. Supreme Court are published commercially in the *Supreme Court Reporter* (abbreviated "S.Ct.") and the *Lawyer's Edition* (abbreviated "L.Ed."). Regardless of the publisher, the abbreviation of the reporter will be preceded by the volume number and followed by the page number at which the court's opinion can be found.

Decisions of a federal court of appeals are published in the *Federal Reporter*, which is simply abbreviated as "F." Because so many volumes of that reporter have been published, the publisher began a second and third series, which are abbreviated "F.2d" and "F.3d," respectively. The inclusion of a case in any series of the *Federal Reporter* will indicate that it was decided by a federal court of appeals but does not indicate which one decided the case. Therefore, the citation includes a parenthetical notation that identifies the particular court, such as the U.S. Court of Appeals for the Ninth Circuit, as well as the date of decision.

For example, the case of *Spain v. Aetna*, which is discussed in Chapter 16, is cited as *Spain v. Aetna Life Insurance Company*, 11 F.3d 129 (9th Cir. 1993), *cert. denied*, 511 U.S. 1052 (1994). This citation indicates that the case can be found in volume 11 of the third series of the *Federal Reporter* and begins at page 129. It was decided by the federal Court of Appeals for the Ninth Circuit in 1993. The term "*cert. denied*" indicates that, after the decision by the Ninth Circuit in 1993, the U.S. Supreme Court refused to hear the case in 1994. Because the U.S. Supreme Court refused to hear the case, the decision of the court of appeals is still the law within the geographic boundaries of the Ninth Circuit. However, no conclusion can be drawn about the view of the Supreme Court from its decision to deny "cert." in a particular case. The Supreme Court only accepts a small percentage of the cases that are filed, and its decision not to hear a case does not necessarily mean that it agreed with the decision of the lower court.

Decisions of the federal district courts are reported in the *Federal Supplement*, which is abbreviated as "F.Supp." or "F.Supp.2d." To identify the particular district court that rendered the decision, the parenthetical notation containing the date will also contain an abbreviation for the court. For example, "S.D.N.Y." is the federal district court for the Southern District of New York. The citation to *Owens v. Nacogdoches County Hospital District*, 741 F.Supp. 1269 (E.D. Tex. 1990) indicates that the case was decided by the federal district court for the Eastern District of Texas in 1990.

State court decisions are reported and cited in similar fashion. The official reporters are identified by the abbreviation of the state, such as "Mass." or "Va." In addition, there are unofficial reporters for state court decisions within a particular region, such as the *Pacific Reporter* ("P." or "P.2d") or the *North Eastern Reporter* ("N.E." or "N.E.2d"), and there are unofficial reporters specifically for California ("Cal.Rptr." or "Cal.Rptr.2d") and New York ("N.Y.S." or "N.Y.S.2d"). Sometimes a citation will include a parallel cite, which indicates where to find the case in the unofficial as well as the official reporter.

Regardless of which reporter is used, the citation will indicate the level of the state court that rendered the decision, such as a trial court, an intermediate appellate court, or the highest court in the state. For example, a famous medical malpractice case is cited as *Darling v. Charleston Community Memorial Hospital*, 211 N.E.2d 253 (Ill. 1965), *cert. denied*, 383 U.S. 946 (1966). The first parenthetical notation contains the date of decision and the abbreviation of a state, which in this case was Illinois. The abbreviation of a state without any other letters indicates that the decision was rendered by the highest court of that state. In contrast, a citation to "Ill. App." would indicate that the decision was rendered by an appellate court, which is *not* the highest court in Illinois.

Citations to Statutes and Regulations

Federal statutes are enacted as public laws by a particular session of Congress and can be identified by their public law (Pub. L.) number. For example, the National Organ Transplant Act was enacted in 1984 by the 98th Congress. It was the 507th public law passed by that session of Congress. Therefore, the law may be identified and cited as Pub. L. No. 98-507 (1984).

After public laws are enacted, they are compiled into the *United States Code* (U.S.C.), which is a codification of statutes by title and section (§). For example, the National Organ Transplant Act was codified in Title 42 of the U.S.C., which contains many of the federal statutes relating to public health and welfare. An important provision of that act, which prohibits buying or selling human organs, was designated as section 274e of Title 42 and may be cited as 42 U.S.C. § 274e.

For easier reference, the sections of the U.S.C. are divided into subsections, which are labeled by letters in parentheses, such as subsection (a) of § 274e. However, it is extremely important to distinguish a letter that is part of the *section* from a letter that indicates a *subsection*. To include additional sections in the U.S.C. or to squeeze new sections in between existing sections, Congress may add a lowercase letter *without parentheses* after a number as the designation for a new section of the Code. For example, Title 42 has a § 274, as well as § 274a, 274b, 274c, 274d, and 274e, each of which are separate sections and not merely subsections of section 274. Thus, the prohibition against buying or selling human organs in the National Organ Transplant Act is codified as § 274e, not subsection (e) of § 274. Similarly, the definitional section of the federal Medicare statute is 42 U.S.C. § 1395x, not § 1395(x), but there is also a subsection (x), which is labeled as 1395x(x).

Another aspect of U.S.C. section numbering that tends to irritate people is the use of multiple letters as additional code sections. In addition to § 1395x, the Medicare law contains a separate § 1395xx, although mercifully § 1395xx is not long enough to have its own subsection (x). After filling up § 1395x, 1395y, and 1395z, the Code will begin a new series of sections as 1395aa, 1395bb, and so forth. Similarly, after using up § 1395zz, the next available section number would be 1395aaa. In each case, these duplicated letters are *not* in parentheses, and therefore they signify separate sections, *not* subsections.

The final point on section numbering in the U.S.C. is to recognize that sections of the Code are *not* the same as sections of the act by which Congress adopted the statute. For example, provisions of the Medicare and Medicaid laws are often referred to as specific sections of the Social Security Act. However, those section numbers of the act are not the same as the section numbers of the U.S.C. in which those provisions have been codified.

At the state level, statutes are also enacted as public laws, session laws, or acts and are later codified into titles and sections. For example, in 1989 the legislature of the state of Maine enacted statutes on the legal effect of clinical practice guidelines in medical malpractice cases. Those statutes were adopted as Chapter 931, § 4 of the laws of 1989 and were later codified in Title 24, § 2971 through 2979 of the Maine Revised Statutes Annotated.

Like statutes, regulations of the federal and state governments, which are often referred to as "rules," are codified after their adoption. Federal regulations are published first in the daily *Federal Register* (Fed. Reg.) in proposed or final form. If the regulations are adopted, they will be codified in the *Code of Federal Regulations* (C.F.R.), which is categorized by title, part, and section. For example, the safe harbor regulations under the Medicare/Medicaid antikickback law were published on January 29, 1992, in volume 57, page 3330 of the *Federal Register* and are codified at 42 C.F.R. § 1001.952. Similarly, regulations of state government will be codified in the state's administrative code and can be identified and located by means of their citation.

How to Find Legal Materials in the Easiest Possible Way

There are lots of difficult ways to find legal materials, but the goal of legal research is to save time by finding those materials with as little effort as possible. Finding things the easy way depends on what you are looking for and what you already know.

Regardless of whether you are using sets of books in a library or researching online, finding a statute, regulation, or case is fairly easy if you already have the citation in the form described earlier. If you do not have the citation, you will need to search by the name of a party to the case, the date of a statute or regulation, the subject of the law, or some other means.

One alternative is to search for materials in the bound sets of federal and state reporters, statutes, and regulations at a law library in your area. As always, the easiest way to search is by means of the citation. However, if you do not know the citation to the case, but you know the name of one of the parties, you should be able to find the citation by using the volume that contains the alphabetical tables of cases for the courts in that particular jurisdiction. Similarly, the bound sets of statutory codes usually have index volumes, and so does the *Code of Federal Regulations*. In using these index volumes, you may need to be creative and try different words to describe the topic for which you are searching. For example, statutes that regulate pig farming for the protection of public health might be listed under pigs, hogs, swine, animals, farm animals, or some other term.

After you have located a statute in a bound volume, be sure to check for any subsequent amendments in the supplement or "pocket part," which will be located in the back of the bound volume or in an adjacent paperback volume. If all else fails, you can politely throw yourself on the mercy of the nice people at the library's reference desk.

Many people find it difficult to get to a law library and may prefer to search for legal materials online. Some companies offer useful proprietary services for computer-assisted legal research, but they can be unavailable, complicated, or expensive. Therefore, the following discussion focuses on information that is available to the public on the Internet and easily accessible without charge. As with any type of research, online legal research requires creativity, and the optimum techniques will vary depending on the type of material for which you are searching. In particular, different techniques and different sites can be used for federal and state legislation, regulations, and cases.

Most important, the goal is to avoid reinventing the wheel. Before you begin your research, try to figure out who has looked up this information before and where you can find the results of their research. For example, the authors of a treatise on healthcare law, such as *Health Law* by Furrow et al.,[2] would have already identified most of the important cases, statutes, and regulations on each specific topic. The names of those cases should be listed alphabetically in a table of cases in the front or back of the treatise, together with the citation of each case, and a treatise may also include tables of statutes and regulations. Similarly, an article on a particular subject in a journal or law review may be a good place to start, because it would contain citations to the relevant cases and statutes on that subject. Locating current articles in free online services may be difficult, but you can find articles on particular subjects through an index in a law library, a proprietary database, or an online catalog. Articles and treatises may contain a useful explanation of the law on a specific subject, but it is important to remember that the law may have changed since the date of publication.

You need not duplicate others' efforts by starting from scratch. In fact, even Sir Isaac Newton attributed his success to "standing on the shoulders of giants."[3]

Federal Legislation

Fortunately, the Library of Congress has developed an excellent system for obtaining legislative information on the Internet. The system is called "Thomas," in honor of Thomas Jefferson, who believed in the importance of an educated population. The site is located at thomas.loc.gov and is an excellent gateway to statutes and pending legislation.

Each session of Congress lasts two years. For example, the 107th session was held in 2001 and 2002. For the current session of Congress, you can find pending bills by searching with a word or phrase or, if you know it, by the number of the bill. In searching by bill number, each number is preceded by the letter "S" for Senate bills and "H" or "HR" for bills in the House of Representatives.

After a particular session of Congress has adjourned, you can still use Thomas to locate legislation from that session. For example, Representative Pete Stark (D-CA) introduced a bill in the 105th Congress with a working title of "No Private Contracts to Be Negotiated when the Patient Is Buck Naked Act of 1997." On the Thomas home page, follow "Bills, Resolutions," then choose "Search Bill Summary, Status," and select the 105th session of Congress. Search for the bill by word or phrase. By inserting the phrase "buck naked" in the "word/phrase" window, you will find, not surprisingly, that only one bill pending in Congress contained that phrase exactly as entered, and that bill was H.R.2784. You can read a summary of the bill, obtain information about its history and status in the legislative process, and even read the text of the bill. In addition, "Bill Summary and Status" provides links to any reports of Congressional committees that considered the bill. That type of report is part of the legislative history and can help in understanding the intent of Congress in enacting that particular law.

Even if you do not know the title or number of a bill, you could find that bill by reference to its sponsor. Under "Bill Summary & Status" for the 105th Congress, you could "Try the Advanced Search" and look under "sponsor" for Congressman Stark in the alphabetical listing of members of the House of Representatives. Among the summaries of the bills sponsored by Congressman Stark in that session of Congress, only the summary of H.R.2784 refers to "private contracts during periods in which the patient is in an exposed condition."

If a bill was enacted into law, you can find it through Thomas by the public law number. For example, the Health Insurance Portability and Accountability Act of 1996 was enacted in the 104th Congress as Public Law No. 104-191. On the Thomas home page, select "Public Laws," and then select the 104th session of Congress. Next, choose to "view" the range of Public Laws that includes 104-191. By clicking on the H.R. link—in this case H.R. 3103—you can obtain information about the law, including a summary and the text of the legislation. In addition, there is a link to the Latest Report of the Conference Committee (House Report 104-736).

Once a public law has been codified as part of the U.S.C., you can find it by using its U.S.C. citation. If you do not know the citation, one approach is to use a secondary source, such as a health law treatise or an article, as a search aid. Once you know the citation to a federal statute in the U.S.C., you can use the free online service of FindLaw at www.findlaw.com. On the FindLaw home page, select "Laws: Cases & Codes," and then "US Code." From there, it is easy to search the U.S.C. by filling in the title and section number in the appropriate boxes.

Another way to find a federal statute in the U.S.C. is on the web site of the U.S. Government Printing Office (GPO) at www.access.gpo.gov. Select "GPO Access" (ignoring the drop-down menu), follow the "United States Code," and search by subject. For example, if you search for the subject of "organ transplants" in the U.S.C., you would find several statutes on that subject, including 42 U.S.C. § 274e, which prohibits the purchase or sale of human organs. However, at the present time, it may be difficult to find a federal statute by means of its citation on GPO Access. Therefore, if you know the citation, it is easier to locate the federal statute by using the title and section boxes on FindLaw.

Federal Regulations

For federal regulations, GPO Access is helpful and easy to use. GPO Access has a quick link to the "Code of Federal Regulations." With that link, you can select "Retrieve CFR Sections by Citation" and fill in the boxes for the title, part, and section of the regulation. Similarly, there is a quick link from GPO Access to the *Federal Register*. You can use the browse feature to read a particular issue of the *Federal Register* by selecting the year and then the specific date. In the table of contents at the beginning of each issue, you can find the regulations and notices that were issued by each federal agency in the alphabetical list.

Another way to obtain federal regulations in the healthcare field is from the web sites maintained by specific agencies of the federal government. For example, the web site of the Centers for Medicare & Medicaid Services (formerly the Health Care Financing Administration), retrieved at cms.hhs.gov or cms.gov, contains information about relevant statutes and regulations, as well as extensive information about the Medicare and Medicaid programs. Similarly, the web site maintained by the Office of Inspector General of the U.S. Department of Health and Human Services, oig.hhs.gov, contains reports, notices, advisory opinions, fraud alerts, and information about compliance programs. Finally, the Federal Trade Commission (FTC), at www.ftc.gov/bc/healthindex.htm, provides access to a great deal of information about antitrust issues in the healthcare field, including the Statements of Antitrust Enforcement Policy in Healthcare, advisory opinions, and summaries of the FTC's enforcement actions in the healthcare industry. These government web sites are updated frequently and are extremely useful.

Federal Cases

The best ways to find federal cases in free online services include searching FindLaw at www.findlaw.com or Cornell Law School's Legal Information Institute at www.law.cornell.edu. In FindLaw, from the "For Legal Professionals" tab, you can click on "Cases & Codes," and then choose the Supreme Court, a federal court of appeals, or a federal trial court. For example, under "US Supreme Court—Opinions & Web Site," you can use the boxes to search by citation or by the name of a party, such as "Cruzan." When you search by the name of a party, you may need to experiment with some variations or abbreviations of the name.

Online services might not include the decisions of lower federal courts that were issued before a certain date. However, these services are usually improved and expanded over time.

State-Law Materials

State statutes, regulations, and court decisions may be obtained in several ways, but not all state materials are available online at this time. Many state courts, legislatures, and agencies maintain their own web sites that provide easy access to information and documents. Although there are limits to what can be obtained, these state government sites are certainly good places to start.

In addition, on the FindLaw home page, you can select "Jurisdictions" and choose a particular state. Then, select "Primary Materials—Cases, Codes and Regulations" to find the state statutes, regulations, and court decisions. If you are searching California law, the statutes are listed under "Laws: Cases & Codes." On Cornell Law School's home page, you can select "Law by Source or Jurisdiction," then "State Law" from the drop-down menu, and then "Listing by Jurisdiction" to choose a particular state. In that way, you can find court decisions, statutes, and administrative regulations for that state.

Over time, more legal materials will become available to the public in free online services. In addition, new methods may be developed to help you find legal materials in the easiest possible way.

Notes

1. 497 U.S. 261 (1990).
2. See B.R. Furrow, T.L. Greaney, S.H. Johnson, T.S. Jost, and R.L. Schwartz, *Health Law*, 2d ed. (St. Paul, MN: West Group, 2000) (an abridgment of the same authors' *Health Law*, Practitioner Treatise Series).
3. A. Partington (ed.), *The Oxford Dictionary of Quotations*, rev. 4th ed. (New York: Oxford University Press, 1996): 493.

MANAGING AND REGULATING THE HEALTHCARE SYSTEM

THE LEGAL STRUCTURE AND GOVERNANCE OF HEALTHCARE ORGANIZATIONS

This chapter explains the different ways in which healthcare organizations may be established and describes the advantages and disadvantages of each type of legal structure. In addition, the chapter addresses the rights and responsibilities of the people who manage and oversee healthcare organizations, such as the officers and directors of healthcare facilities.

In the wake of recent corporate and accounting scandals, renewed attention is being paid to issues of organizational ethics, accountability, and fiduciary duties of officers and directors. Although most of those scandals involved industries other than healthcare, many of the same legal and ethical issues apply to healthcare facilities and even to nonprofit organizations. From a legal perspective, the obligations of officers and directors are derived from the law that governs the particular type of organization, such as business corporation law, nonprofit corporation law, or the law applicable to public bodies. Those laws are discussed in this chapter in regard to each type of healthcare organization.

In addition, officers and directors of healthcare organizations have ethical obligations to manage their facilities for the benefit of their communities. The underlying values of healthcare extend beyond economic efficiency and maximizing profit. Regardless of the type of legal structure, those who manage and oversee healthcare organizations should always remember that they are the stewards of some of society's most important assets.

Healthcare Providers as Legal Entities

Healthcare facilities may be owned and operated by a variety of legal entities. Some of these entities are public, governmental bodies and others are private, nongovernmental organizations. There are two types of private healthcare facility: those owned by investors and those owned by charitable or religious organizations. In developing and operating a facility, providers may choose from a variety of organizational forms, such as a for-profit business corporation, a nonprofit corporation with members, or a nonprofit corporation with a self-perpetuating board. Each form of legal organization has advantages and disadvantages for the healthcare provider and for society as a whole.

Different legal rules and obligations apply to each type of entity. In evaluating the obligations of a healthcare facility, the first task is to determine the type of legal entity that is involved in the particular case. This task may be complicated by the fact that some healthcare facilities are hybrid organizations. For example, a government-owned hospital might be managed by a private corporation, or it might be leased to a for-profit or nonprofit corporation that actually operates the facility. In those cases, evaluating legal obligations is more complex and depends on the applicable laws as well as the terms of the management contract or lease.

Historically, most hospitals have been owned by units of government or private, nonprofit corporations. Recent years have seen a significant trend toward for-profit ownership of hospitals and the development of for-profit hospital chains, but most hospitals are still owned by public or nonprofit entities. In contrast, the vast majority of skilled nursing facilities or nursing homes are owned by for-profit corporations. Although some skilled nursing facilities are operated by nonprofit hospitals or religious organizations, most are owned and operated by for-profit chains. Similarly, most of the large psychiatric hospital systems are owned and operated by for-profit companies, although there are many public psychiatric hospitals and psychiatric units of public hospitals. In the field of home health, the industry is dominated by large, for-profit chains and franchises, although some home health agencies are operated by hospitals, public health departments, or nonprofit organizations. Physicians and other individual practitioners may operate as sole proprietors or in partnership with others, but many physicians are now shareholders or employees of a professional corporation or a similar legal entity.

Public Healthcare Facilities

Government-owned providers are often referred to as "public" facilities. Many hospitals and other healthcare facilities are owned and operated by units of local government, such as counties, cities, hospital districts, hospital authorities, and local public health departments. However, it is not only local governments that can own and operate healthcare facilities. One of the largest hospital systems in the country is operated by the federal government through the U.S. Department of Veterans Affairs. Many states operate public psychiatric hospitals as well as large teaching hospitals at state universities.

Governmental ownership provides several advantages from the viewpoint of the operator of a public healthcare facility. First, a public facility may receive direct financial support from a government agency. In addition, the facility will be exempt from income taxes and property taxes and is eligible to receive tax-deductible donations. Therefore, individuals and corporations may be more willing to donate money or property to the facility, because the donor can claim a tax deduction for the donation.

In addition, a public facility can raise money for construction or new equipment by issuing tax-exempt bonds. In that type of financing, people and institutions lend money to the facility by purchasing the bonds, and the facility promises to pay the money back to the bondholders, with interest, over a long period. Because the bonds are tax-exempt, the bondholders will not have to pay federal income tax on the interest they receive on the bonds. Therefore, they will be willing to lend the money to the public facility at a lower rate of interest, which is a significant advantage to the facility. Although a public facility can raise money by tax-exempt bond financing, it cannot raise money by selling shares in the facility to members of the public, which is referred to as equity financing.

A public healthcare facility will be subject to a high degree of public oversight and control. If the facility is operated directly by a unit of government, the administrators of that facility will be appointed by government officials and may also be removed by those officials. If the public facility has a board of trustees, the board of the facility is probably appointed in whole or in part by a governmental body such as an elected board of county commissioners. Ordinarily, the board meetings of a public healthcare facility are open to the public and the news media under the state open-meeting law. In addition, most of the public facility's records, other than medical records of individual patients, may be available to the public and the media under the state public-record law. The funds of a public healthcare facility are generally considered to be public funds, and thus may be subject to laws that restrict a government agency's use and investment of the public's money. The employees of a public healthcare facility are public employees, and therefore probably cannot be terminated for cause without lengthy and complex proceedings. Finally, the powers of a public facility are limited to those set forth in the statute or resolution by which it was created, and that statute or resolution may limit the activities of the facility or prohibit expansion into other geographic areas.

From the perspective of the facility's managers, this type of public oversight and control may be seen as a hindrance, particularly if partisan politics are allowed to interfere in the operation of the facility. However, from the point of view of the citizens in the community, public oversight and control of *their* healthcare facility may seem advantageous and appropriate. Most important, many public facilities have a legal obligation to provide access to care for people in their communities, and public oversight may help to ensure that this obligation is fulfilled.

For-Profit Corporations

For-profit or "investor-owned" facilities are usually established as business corporations under state corporation law. As explained by Chief Justice John Marshall of the U.S. Supreme Court in 1819, "corporation is an artificial being, invisible, intangible, and existing only in contemplation of law."[1] Thus, a corporation is a legal being or entity, and it exists as a person in the eyes of the law.

As a legal entity, a corporation is distinct from its owners, who are referred to as shareholders. A corporation could be owned by a single person, in which case the corporate entity would survive after the death of its sole shareholder. Moreover, a corporation has its own rights and responsibilities. A corporation can own property, enter into contracts, borrow money, and hire employees. In addition, it is required to pay taxes, can be held liable for damages under the civil law of contracts or torts, and can be fined by the government for violating the criminal law.

Another important aspect of a corporation is that its owners have limited liability for the entity's debts. Specifically, a corporation's debt is the obligation of the corporation and *not* the obligation of the shareholders, even if it has only one shareholder. If the corporation cannot pay its bills and goes out of business, the shareholders may lose all of their investment in the corporation. However, as a general rule, the creditors cannot make the shareholders pay the corporation's obligations.

Another advantage of the corporate form is that organizational control and decision-making authority are clearly set forth in the state corporation law and the documents that created the corporation. Even if there are many investors, a structure will be in place for making decisions, as well as a mechanism for changing who gets to make the decisions.

Thus, the corporate form is a very efficient way to pool the efforts and resources of many people, raise capital, conduct operations, and avoid personal liability. To raise capital, for-profit corporations may borrow money, but not by means of tax-exempt bond financing. In addition, for-profit corporations may use equity financing by selling shares in the corporation to members of the public. Those who purchase the shares are referred to as shareholders or stockholders. In equity financing, the shareholders would not own any of the assets of the corporation. Instead, the corporation would own all of the assets, and each investor would merely own some percentage of the shares in the corporation. If one of the shareholders decides to sell his shares to someone else, the corporation continues to exist, and no departing shareholder has the right to take away any part of the assets of the corporation.

Corporations are creatures of state law, rather than federal law. The state provides the right to establish a corporation and gives investors the advantage of limited liability. Therefore, to establish a corporation, the organizers must file a document with a particular agency or official of state government. This official is usually referred to as the secretary of state or the commissioner of corporations. The document to be filed is called the articles of incorporation; in some states this is referred to as the certificate of incorporation or corporate charter. That document will set forth the name and purpose of the corporation, as well as other information about the structure, governance, and financing of the corporation. In addition to its articles of incorporation, a corporation will also have a set of bylaws that describe its officers, meetings, and other aspects of its internal operations. To preserve the advantage of limited liability, these corporate formalities must be followed, and the funds of the corporation must not be commingled with the funds of any other person or corporation.

Under state law, a corporation is governed by its board of directors. "[T]he board of directors has the ultimate responsibility for managing the business and affairs of a corporation."[2] The directors have the power to appoint the officers of the corporation, such as the president or chief executive officer. In addition, directors are responsible for overseeing the corporation and making sure decisions are fiscally responsible and in compliance with the law.

Directors have duties to the corporation and its shareholders, such as duties of care and loyalty. These are referred to as fiduciary duties, because they are similar to the duties a trustee owes to the beneficiary of a trust or the duties a guardian owes to a ward. The directors of a corporation are not personally liable for its debts. However, directors can be held liable if they breach their fiduciary duties to the corporation and its shareholders. Under some circumstances, the directors of a healthcare corporation could be held legally liable for failure to ensure that the corporation has an effective program to promote compliance with the law.[3]

Directors have the power to change the management, policies, and direction of the corporation. Therefore, the fundamental issue of corporate control is determining who chooses the board and who can replace the board. In a for-profit corporation, the shareholders elect the directors. As a general rule, each share of common stock entitles the holder to one vote; thus, some shareholders will have more votes than others. If the holders of a majority of the shares are dissatisfied with the decisions of the current board, they may be able to replace the board by electing different directors. Note that the shareholders do not have the right to vote directly for the officers of the corporation; therefore, they cannot simply vote to remove the current management. However, the shareholders can change the management of the corporation indirectly by electing a new board of directors that would appoint a new set of officers to manage the corporation.

Often, a for-profit healthcare facility will be part of a larger organization or "chain" that owns many facilities. In that case, it is possible for all of the facilities to be part of one large corporation. It is more likely, however, that each facility is separately incorporated, in which case the shares of each "subsidiary" would be owned, directly or indirectly, by a "parent corporation."

Healthcare facilities that are owned by for-profit corporations are required to pay income taxes and property taxes. In addition, donors are unlikely to give money to a for-profit facility, because the contribution would not be tax deductible for the donor.

However, for-profit corporations provide some significant advantages to their owners and managers. First, profits may be distributed to the shareholders, and the value of their investment may increase over time. In addition, for-profit corporations may use stock options to recruit and provide financial incentives for employees. For-profit corporations do not need to adhere to the restrictions on the use of public funds or the rules for tax-exempt organizations, which are described later. The employees of a for-profit facility are not public employees, and the facility is subject to less public oversight and control than a government-owned facility. Finally, for-profit hospitals provide less charity care than public hospitals,[4] and they may tend to be located in more affluent communities than nonprofit hospitals.[5] Although these factors may be advantages from the viewpoint of the facility's owners and managers, they could present serious problems from the perspective of society as a whole.

Private, Nonprofit Corporations

In contrast to facilities that are owned by governmental bodies or business corporations, many hospitals and other healthcare facilities are owned by private, nonprofit corporations. These organizations are not operated for the purpose of generating a profit, but they are private entities as opposed to agencies of government. Therefore, these private, nonprofit organizations and the facilities they own are not subject to the same degree of public oversight and control as facilities owned by the government. In most cases, private, nonprofit hospitals are exempt from state open-meeting laws and public-record laws, and their employees are not considered to be public employees.

A nonprofit corporation has no stock and no stockholders. Some nonprofit corporations have members, but many others merely have a self-perpetuating board of trustees. Like the shareholders of a for-profit corporation, the members of a nonprofit are not personally liable for the debts of the corporation.

Under state law, a nonprofit corporation is governed by its board of directors or board of trustees. Like the directors of a business corporation, directors or trustees of a nonprofit organization have fiduciary duties to the corporation, such as the duties of care and loyalty.[6] The board of a nonprofit corporation will appoint the officers, and the officers will hire the employees.

In a nonprofit corporation, the power to elect directors or trustees depends on whether the corporation has members. If it has members, those members elect the directors or trustees of the nonprofit corporation. If the nonprofit corporation has no members, the self-perpetuating board of trustees will simply elect its own successors.

The principal advantage of a nonprofit structure is the ability to apply for exemption from federal and state income taxes, state sales taxes, and local taxes on the ownership of property. In addition, a tax-exempt, nonprofit facility may solicit charitable contributions that will be tax deductible for the donors. Like a public healthcare facility, a private, nonprofit facility may raise money by means of tax-exempt bond financing, but it may not use equity financing through a sale of shares.

To create a private, nonprofit organization, the first step is to create a nonprofit corporation under the state's nonprofit corporation law. That alone does not make the organization exempt from federal and state taxes, however; thus, the organizers must take the second step of applying for tax-exempt status under federal and state tax law, including Section 501(c)(3) of the Internal Revenue Code.

Under Section 501(c)(3), the tax-exempt organization must be organized for a charitable purpose, such as providing healthcare services to the public, and must be limited to that charitable purpose by its articles of incorporation. A tax-exempt organization may not be organized or operated for private benefit, but rather must provide a benefit to the community.[7] Moreover, none of the net earnings may inure to the benefit of any private individual. Finally, the articles of incorporation should expressly provide that, if the organization is dissolved, the assets will be distributed to another tax-exempt organization or to an agency of government.

Nonprofit corporations often make a "profit" in the sense that they have an excess of revenues over expenses. However, that profit must be used to carry out the charitable purposes of the organization and *cannot* be distributed to the members, trustees, or any other private parties. Paying reasonable salaries to officers and employees does not violate the rules against inurement or private benefit. Tax-exempt hospitals may even use some types of incentive compensation arrangements, provided that the compensation arrangement is consistent with the organization's exempt purposes and does not encourage an executive to act in a manner that conflicts with those purposes.

A private, nonprofit corporation will not be subject to the restrictions that apply to the use and investment of public funds. However, a nonprofit organization will be subject to the requirements of Section 501(c)(3) and must use caution to avoid losing its valuable tax-exempt status. In particular, tax-exempt organizations must carefully review those legal requirements before engaging in such transactions as joint ventures, physician contracts, executive compensation arrangements, and unrelated business activities.

In the past, the only sanction available to the Internal Revenue Service (IRS) for abuse of those rules was to revoke an organization's tax-exempt status. Yet because that sanction is so drastic, it was seldom used. Therefore, Congress amended the law in 1996 to authorize the IRS to impose so-called "intermediate sanctions" without revoking an organization's tax-exempt status.[8] Under the amended statute, the IRS may impose taxes on certain individuals, such as officers or directors of a tax-exempt organization, if the organization provides an excessive economic benefit to those individuals.

Many private, nonprofit healthcare facilities provide substantial amounts of charity care, especially if the community has no publicly owned facility. However, some nonprofit facilities provide much less charity care and operate in a manner that is similar to that of for-profit facilities. Currently, the IRS does not require tax-exempt hospitals to provide charity care as a condition of maintaining their tax exemption.[9] Although tax-exempt organizations must operate for a charitable purpose, the IRS's position is that promoting health and providing a benefit to the community are sufficient as charitable purposes. Thus, a nonprofit hospital can maintain its tax exemption if its emergency department provides care to everyone, regardless of the ability to pay, and if the hospital provides services to everyone in the community who is able to pay. Some people argue that tax-exempt hospitals should also be required by law to provide charity care and demonstrate their benefit to the community.

Although the federal IRS does not require hospitals to provide charity care, some state legislatures have enacted statutes that require tax-exempt, nonprofit hospitals in their states to provide a specific amount or percentage of charity care, or to provide information to state officials about the hospital's benefit to the community. In addition, some state officials and private lawyers have challenged tax-exempt, nonprofit hospitals on various grounds, such as their levels of charity care, collection practices, prices charged to uninsured patients, and use of their charitable assets.[10] As one commentator has noted, these legal challenges have made charity care a more visible issue and may cause nonprofit hospitals to change their practices, even if the legal challenges are unsuccessful in court.[11]

PROBLEM 4.1: ALTERNATIVES FOR DEVELOPING A HOSPITAL

Jefferson County has never had a hospital. To obtain acute-care services, residents have to travel 20 to 30 miles to a hospital in an adjacent county. For many years, the civic leaders have talked about building a hospital and, for more than ten years, the board of county commissioners has been putting its annual budget surplus in its "hospital fund." At the present time, the county commissioners have accumulated $25 million in cash, which is earmarked for a hospital, but the commissioners have been informed that $100 million will be required to build and equip a hospital of the appropriate size.

The county commissioners have considered several proposals for developing a hospital:

1. Establish a public hospital to be owned and operated by the county. Under this plan, the county would use the $25 million in the hospital fund as a down payment and would finance the remaining $75 million by tax-exempt bonds. Once the building is completed, the county would hire an administrator to run the hospital. Commissioner Green likes this idea, because she has a nephew who needs a job and thinks running a hospital sounds like a lot of fun.

2. Establish a nonprofit corporation and have the county make a grant of $25 million to the nonprofit corporation for the purpose of building a hospital in the community. The nonprofit corporation would use bond financing for the remaining $75 million in capital cost. Once construction is completed, the hospital would be operated by the nonprofit corporation. If the non-profit corporation ever dissolved or ceased to operate the hospital, it would have to return the entire $25 million grant to the county. Commissioner Blue is strongly opposed to this proposal. According to Commissioner Blue, if everything in the county, including the new hospital, were to be destroyed someday by nuclear war, the county would not be able to get back any of the money that it gave to the nonprofit corporation. Commissioner Brown thinks Commissioner Blue is an idiot.

3. Establish a for-profit corporation that will raise $100 million by selling shares in the new corporation to investors on the open market. This alternative was proposed by Commissioner Black. Because of his success in business, he believes private enterprise can build and operate the hospital in the most efficient manner. Under his proposal, the county will use the $25 million in its hospital fund to buy one-fourth of the shares in the new for-profit corporation. Therefore, the county will be a minority shareholder, but will probably be the largest single shareholder in the new corporation. Commissioner Green, who wants the county to build and operate the hospital itself, is opposed to the idea of using a for-profit corporation because of a concern for the uninsured and indigent people in the community.

As you might expect, the board of commissioners has been unable to agree on a proposal, and at the last meeting they almost came to blows. Therefore, the chair has appointed a committee to study the issue and report back at the next meeting. In turn, the committee has hired you as a consultant and wants your advice as to the best alternative for the county. The best alternative might be one of the aforementioned three proposals, some combination of those proposals, or a completely different proposal. Before evaluating each alternative, please fill in the chart showing the advantages and disadvantages for each type of legal structure (Chart 4.1). Then, make a written recommendation to the county explaining your reasoning.

Incidentally, as they say on television, this story is purely fictional, and any resemblance to real persons, living or dead, is purely coincidental.

Recent Issues and Trends

In response to the pressures of cost containment and managed care, many healthcare facilities have joined forces with other providers to improve their competitive position. By merging or affiliating with other providers, healthcare facilities may be able to reduce their costs for producing each unit of service through economies of scale. In addition, combined facilities may be able to purchase equipment and supplies at lower prices through volume discounts and improve their bargaining power with large-scale buyers by providing a full range of services at a reasonable cost in a broad geographic area.

Under these circumstances, a significant trend has been seen in the healthcare industry toward consolidation of hospitals and other providers by means of merger, acquisition, and other types of affiliation. Some of these consolidations have involved the acquisition of public or nonprofit hospitals by large, for-profit corporations. In addition, some nonprofit hospitals have merged or combined with other nonprofits to create large multihospital systems, which may be under the ultimate control of a single nonprofit holding company.

Aside from these alliances among similar institutions, a trend has emerged toward consolidation or affiliation among different types of providers to establish integrated delivery systems. Some hospitals have purchased physician practices or joined with physicians on the medical staff to create physician–hospital organizations (PHOs), which sell a combined package of hospital and physician services. Other affiliations have combined healthcare providers and payers into integrated organizations that perform multiple functions. From a legal perspective, significant issues are raised by the formation and operation of these alliances, networks, and integrated delivery systems, including the issues of antitrust law that are addressed in Chapter 9.

Not all alliances between healthcare providers are as complete or as permanent as an acquisition of assets or the formation of a multihospital system. Sometimes providers will enter into limited arrangements for specific purposes while retaining their independent existence. For example, providers may enter into contracts with other providers to obtain particular

Issue	Public	Private, Nonprofit	Private, For-Profit
Exempt from income taxes	✓	✓	✓
Exempt from property taxes	✓	✓	✓
Eligible for tax-deductible donations	✓	✓	✓
Able to use tax-exempt bond financing	✓	✓	✓
Able to use equity financing		✓	✓
Able to use employee incentives of stock options		✓	✓
Subject to public oversight and control	✓	✓	✓
Subject to public employment laws	✓		
Obligated to provide charity care	✓	✓	✓
Subject to restrictions on use of public funds	✓		
Subject to IRS rules for 501(c)(3) corporations		✓	✓

CHART 4.1

Pros and Cons of Each Organizational Form for Healthcare Facilities

services that are available only at one of the facilities. In addition, many healthcare facilities have entered into contracts for management of the entire facility for a specified period of time. Under a contract, each party merely obligates itself to perform the tasks set forth in the agreement.

Similarly, a joint venture allows two or more healthcare providers to work together on a particular project, but they retain their independent existence and remain independent competitors for all other purposes. For example, two hospitals may form a partnership or corporation for the sole purpose of jointly owning and operating a magnetic resonance imaging facility or home health agency, but the two hospitals would continue to exist as separate entities in all other respects. Also, as already discussed, a hospital and the physicians on its medical staff could establish a PHO to sell a combined package of physician and hospital services. This type of joint venture could be structured as a corporation, partnership, or other entity, and would be owned jointly by the hospital and the physicians.

In another important trend, some public and nonprofit healthcare organizations, including hospitals, health maintenance organizations, and health plans, have converted to for-profit status. Like the acquisition of a public or nonprofit facility by a for-profit corporation, these conversions raise complex issues of corporate law and important issues of public policy. In one study, for example, researchers concluded that "public hospitals that converted to for-profit status showed a significant decline in the level of uncompensated care they provided."[12]

Finally, new forms of business organization have been developed in recent years, such as the limited liability company (LLC). As in other industries, some healthcare providers have elected to organize or reorganize themselves under one of these new forms of legal structure. The characteristics, advantages, and disadvantages of these new forms of business organization are discussed in the sections that follow.

Purchase of Public and Nonprofit Facilities

The acquisition of one entity by another may raise various issues of corporate, tax, securities, and antitrust law, as well as a variety of regulatory issues. If the entity to be acquired (the "target") is a public or nonprofit healthcare facility, additional issues will arise as a result of the public or nonprofit status of the target. Therefore, the nature of the target will affect the structure of the transaction and the issues that must be addressed.

Under state corporation law, the principal methods of acquiring a corporation are merger, acquisition of stock, and acquisition of assets. A merger is a statutory procedure to combine the assets and liabilities of two corporations in which one corporation survives and the other ceases to exist. In a stock acquisition, the buyer purchases the stock, as opposed to the assets, of the target company. Technically, the purchaser of stock is not buying anything from the target company itself, but rather is buying the stock directly from the stockholders of the target company. This acquisition technique could not be used to purchase a public hospital, because a public entity has no stock and no stockholders. Moreover, the government may not sell a department or agency, such as a public hospital or health department, just as it may not sell the police department or fire department.

However, the government may sell police cars, fire trucks, firehouses, and other *assets* of a government agency. Thus, a buyer could use an asset acquisition to purchase a public hospital by paying the governmental body for the land, buildings, equipment, and other property of the hospital. In an asset acquisition, the purchaser buys all or substantially all of the assets directly from the target company as opposed to its stockholders. After the asset acquisition of a public hospital, the governmental body no longer operates the hospital facilities, and it uses the proceeds from selling the facilities to carry out its other public functions.

In selling the assets of a public hospital, the governmental body may be required to comply with state statutes that explicitly regulate the sale of public hospitals or more general state statutes that regulate the sale or disposition of any public property. Moreover, in determining the value of the assets and selecting a buyer, public officials must act in the public interest as opposed to their own personal interest. For example, a federal investigation was launched in 1995 to determine whether a public hospital executive had undervalued the assets of the hospital to encourage a for-profit chain to buy the hospital and give the executive a job.[13]

The sale of a private, nonprofit hospital raises many of the same issues. Like a public hospital, a nonprofit has no stock. Therefore, the sale of a nonprofit hospital is often structured as a sale of assets. The nonprofit corporation would not be required to comply with state statutes on the sale of public hospitals or the disposition of public property. However, some states have enacted statutes that regulate the sale of private, nonprofit hospitals. In addition, the directors or trustees of a nonprofit corporation are required to meet their fiduciary duty to the corporation by making sure that it receives fair market value for the sale of its assets.

As shown in Figure 4.1, ABC, Inc. is a for-profit corporation that wants to buy the hospital assets of the nonprofit XYZ, Inc. Note that ABC is not acquiring any stock in XYZ, because XYZ has no stock. Rather, ABC will purchase all or substantially all of the assets of XYZ and must pay XYZ the fair market value of its assets. After selling its assets to ABC, XYZ will continue to exist as an independent, nonprofit corporation and will not become a subsidiary of ABC. However, XYZ will no longer own the assets of the hospital, and its sole remaining asset will be the proceeds of the sale. Theoretically, XYZ could dissolve and distribute its money to another nonprofit corporation or to the government. However, the more likely scenario is that XYZ will become a nonprofit foundation. Instead of being in the business of operating a hospital, XYZ will be in the business of giving away money to carry out its charitable purposes.

Like the directors and officers of a business corporation, the trustees and officers of a nonprofit corporation must put the interests of the organization ahead of their personal interests, particularly in responding to a proposed change in control.[14] After an acquisition, the acquiring entity will often terminate the executives and board members of the target and replace them with people designated by the acquiring entity. Even in a nonprofit organization, executives and trustees may react negatively to a proposed acquisition that would have the effect of removing them from their current positions. In other situations, executives of the target may be unduly influenced to support a proposed acquisition because of lucrative job offers from the acquiring entity.[15] Under these circumstances, the fiduciary duties and ethical obligations of officers and trustees require them to disclose

FIGURE 4.1
Asset
Acquisition
of a
Nonprofit
Hospital

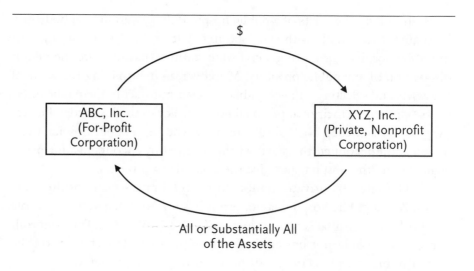

their conflicts of interest, obtain independent advice, and make decisions in the best interest of the nonprofit corporation.

The asset acquisition in Figure 4.1 would be even more complicated if some of the executives or trustees of the nonprofit XYZ were also directors, officers, or shareholders of the for-profit ABC. In that case, a conflict of interest would exist that might result in the assets of the nonprofit XYZ being sold to ABC for less than fair market value. To protect against this conflict of interest and self-dealing, XYZ should obtain an independent valuation of its assets, and the sale should be approved by trustees who have no personal interest in the transaction.

If a nonprofit hospital is being acquired by another nonprofit hospital or by a nonprofit hospital system, the acquisition could be structured in different ways. For example, one nonprofit hospital can acquire or combine with another by using the structure of a nonprofit membership corporation with only one member.[16] The target hospital would amend its articles of incorporation to become a nonprofit membership corporation of which the sole member would be the acquiring hospital. As the sole member of the target hospital, the acquiring hospital would effectively control the activities of the target. Alternatively, the parties could create a nonprofit holding company that would be the sole member of *both* of the nonprofit hospitals. By making the two nonprofit hospitals "sister companies" under the control of a common "parent," this alternative would avoid the negative connotation that one hospital was "acquired" by the other. Another alternative for a transaction between two nonprofit corporations is to amend the target's articles of incorporation to give the acquiring party authority to appoint directors of the target or approve particular decisions by the target.

In the 1980s, many nonprofit hospitals went through corporate reorganizations to establish nonprofit parent companies with control over various nonprofit and for-profit subsidiaries. Each of those subsidiaries performs a particular function, such as hospital services, long-term care, home health, ownership of real property, or other business activities, that may be taxable or tax-exempt. In addition, the nonprofit parent company may be used as a vehicle for acquiring other healthcare facilities and developing a multihospital system.

In recent years, state attorneys general have challenged some actions by nonprofit hospitals and systems, such as proposed affiliations and attempts to close a facility and consolidate services. Some cases have involved issues of nonprofit corporation law, such as whether court approval is required for certain amendments to the articles of incorporation or changes in corporate structure.[17] In other cases, state attorneys general have relied on the law of charitable trusts and their traditional authority to protect the assets of a charitable trust.[18] This type of challenge may result in a settlement or a decision to abandon the proposed transaction.

Conversion from Nonprofit to For-Profit Status

In contrast to the sale of a nonprofit's assets, conversion is a process to change the nature of the corporation from nonprofit to for-profit status. Originally, the assets of the nonprofit were dedicated to charitable purposes, and the articles of incorporation prohibited the use of those charitable assets for the benefit of any private party. Some states, such as California and Florida, developed a procedure to amend a nonprofit's articles of incorporation to change the organization into a for-profit business corporation.

Under that procedure, the amendment to the nonprofit's articles of incorporation must be submitted to a state official for approval, and approval will be granted only if an important condition is satisfied. Specifically, the nonprofit corporation must donate an amount of money equal to its current net worth to a different charitable organization. In that way the value of the nonprofit's assets will still be used for charitable purposes.

In Figure 4.2, XYZ, Inc. is a private, nonprofit corporation that owns and operates a hospital. As a nonprofit, XYZ has no stock, and its assets are dedicated by its articles of incorporation to purely charitable purposes. Subject to the approval of a state official, XYZ would transfer an amount of money equal to its current net worth to LMNO, Inc., which is a new nonprofit corporation established for that purpose. Thus, XYZ would *not* transfer the land, buildings, or equipment of the hospital to LMNO, but rather would transfer an amount of money equal to the net worth of XYZ at the time of conversion. Once XYZ amends its articles of incorporation to become a for-profit corporation, it would be able to raise all or part of that money by selling shares to investors in the market for equity financing.

After the conversion of XYZ, LMNO will not own or operate a hospital. However, LMNO will have a substantial amount of money and will

FIGURE 4.2
Conversion
from
Nonprofit to
For–Profit
Status

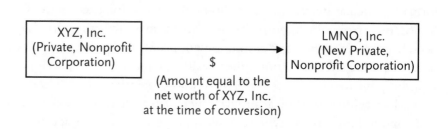

In this type of conversion, the most important issue is accurately determining the net worth of the nonprofit organization. If the net worth was underestimated, an insufficient amount of money would be transferred to the new nonprofit corporation to carry out the charitable purposes. Moreover, the shareholders of the for-profit corporation would obtain an inappropriate windfall. In the past, instances have occurred in which the net worth of a nonprofit corporation was underestimated.[19] In response, state officials have become more vigilant in scrutinizing these transactions, and some states have enacted additional legislation to regulate this type of conversion.[20] Similar issues arise when Blue Cross and Blue Shield plans attempt to convert from nonprofit to for-profit status, although those conversions may take a variety of different forms.[21]

Joint Ventures Between Nonprofit and For-Profit Organizations

Sometimes a nonprofit, tax-exempt hospital enters into a joint venture with a for-profit corporation. In that situation, the nonprofit corporation must make sure that it is operating exclusively for a charitable purpose and that the benefit to the for-profit corporation is only incidental. If the nonprofit hospital fails to meet these conditions, it could lose its tax-exempt status under Section 501(c)(3).

This issue becomes particularly acute in a so-called "whole hospital joint venture." In that type of arrangement, a nonprofit hospital and a for-profit corporation may form an LLC in which each party has an ownership interest. The for-profit corporation would contribute certain assets to the jointly owned LLC. The nonprofit would contribute all of its operating assets, including the hospital, to the LLC, and the LLC would operate the hospital.

One advantage of the whole-hospital joint venture is that it raises additional funding for hospital operations. However, the arrangement raises serious concerns of public policy.[22] The assets of a nonprofit hospital may only be used to carry out the organization's charitable purposes and not to benefit the for-profit partner to the whole-hospital joint venture. For that reason, some of these proposed joint ventures have been challenged by state attorneys general under charitable trust law and other legal doctrines. Another policy concern with whole-hospital joint ventures is that the parties may be using the format of a joint venture in an attempt to avoid the obligations of state laws that regulate the sale of nonprofit hospitals or the conversion to for-profit status. Finally, the whole-hospital joint venture appears to be a way to effectively give the for-profit corporation an equity interest in the operation of the hospital without giving up the nonprofit's tax-exempt status. In 1998, the IRS issued a Revenue Ruling with regard to whole-hospital joint ventures.[23] According to the IRS, the ability of a nonprofit organization to keep its tax-exempt status will depend on the specific facts of each particular case.

From a policy perspective, we must ensure that a change in control of a nonprofit hospital, by whatever means, does not adversely affect the use of its assets for charitable purposes. As the techniques of acquisition become more complex, our legal system must develop new ways to protect the interest of the public and ensure that legal formalities are not used to evade regulatory requirements.

New Forms of Business Organization

As discussed previously, one important advantage of the corporate form is that investors have limited liability for debts of the entity. For the goal of avoiding personal liability, a corporation would be preferable to a general partnership, because general partners are personally liable for debts of the partnership. However, partnerships have a significant advantage in that they are treated more favorably than corporations for purposes of federal tax law. In fact, federal tax law creates a disincentive to choosing a corporation as a form of doing business.

In a corporation, profits are taxed at the corporate level. After paying taxes, the corporation may distribute a portion of the profit to its shareholders in the form of a dividend. Then, the profits are taxed again at the individual level when the shareholder receives the dividend. In that way, the federal government has taxed the profits twice; this is referred to as double taxation. In contrast, partnerships are not taxed as entities. Rather, all of the tax consequences simply flow through to the partners, who pay the tax once at the individual level.

These laws create conflicting incentives and disincentives in choosing the most advantageous form of business organization. As indicated in Figure 4.3, for the goal of limiting personal liability of investors, the corporation is the most advantageous form and the general partnership is the least desirable form. However, for the goal of minimizing federal taxes, the

FIGURE 4.3
The
Spectrum of
Conflicting
Goals

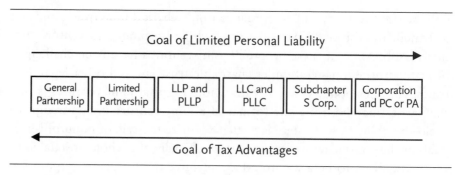

Goal of Limited Personal Liability

| General Partnership | Limited Partnership | LLP and PLLP | LLC and PLLC | Subchapter S Corp. | Corporation and PC or PA |

Goal of Tax Advantages

general partnership is the most advantageous form and the corporation is the least desirable form.

Under these circumstances, it is not surprising that the law has developed some hybrid forms of business organization in an attempt to achieve the best of both worlds. One such hybrid organization is called the "Subchapter S corporation," which provides the limited liability of a corporation and the tax advantages of a partnership. However, there are significant restrictions on the use of a Subchapter S corporation that make it unavailable in many situations, such as limitations on the number and type of permissible shareholders. Another hybrid form of organization is the "limited partnership," in which some of the investors are referred to as limited partners. The limited partners are entitled to limited liability as if they were shareholders of a corporation. However, to form a limited partnership, at least one general partner must bear unlimited liability for debts of the entity. Moreover, to maintain limited liability, a limited partner may not participate in the management of the organization.

In recent years, new hybrid forms have been developed, such as the LLC and the limited liability partnership (LLP). An LLC is like a corporation in terms of its limited liability, but it is taxed like a partnership. In addition, an LLC is more flexible than a Subchapter S corporation with regard to the limits on investors. An LLP is taxed like a general partnership, but it may register with the state government to avoid personal liability of the partners under some circumstances.

Finally, there are specialized legal entities for professionals, such as physicians, who want to limit their liability by conducting business in a corporate form. Many states had a traditional prohibition against the practice of medicine by corporations. Therefore, state legislatures enacted statutes to explicitly authorize the practice of medicine in the corporate form. These professional corporation laws may require registration with the state medical licensing board and usually limit the ownership of shares in the professional corporation to persons who are licensed to practice medicine in that state. Often, physicians will establish their private practice as a professional corporation or professional association under those specific state laws. In similar ways, physicians in some states may organize their private medical practice as a professional limited liability company (PLLC) or a professional limited liability partnership (PLLP).

Notes

1. *Trustees of Dartmouth College v. Woodward*, 17 U.S. 518, 636 (1819).
2. *Quickturn Design Systems, Inc. v. Shapiro*, 721 A.2d 1281, 1291 (Del. 1998).
3. See *In re Caremark International, Inc.*, 698 A.2d 959, 970 (Del. Ch. 1996).
4. See generally R. Kuttner, "Columbia/HCA and the Resurgence of the For-Profit Hospital Business," *New England Journal of Medicine*, 335 (1996): 362, 446.
5. E.C. Norton and D.O. Staiger, "How Hospital Ownership Affects Care for the Uninsured," *Rand Journal of Economics*, 25(1) (1994): 171–185, at 172 ("for-profit hospitals may be skimming off the cream by locating in well-insured areas").
6. See generally N. Ono, "Boards of Directors Under Fire: An Examination of Nonprofit Board Duties in the Health Care Environment," *Annals of Health Law*, 7 (1998): 107–138.
7. See, e.g., *Geisinger Health Plan v. Commissioner*, 985 F.2d 1210, 1217 (3d Cir. 1993) ("a nonprofit hospital will qualify for tax-exempt status if it primarily benefits the community").
8. See Taxpayer Bill of Rights 2, Pub. L. No. 104-168, § 1311, 110 Stat. 1452, 1475 (1996) (codified at 26 U.S.C. § 4958 (2006)).
9. See J.R. Horwitz, "Why We Need the Independent Sector: The Behavior, Law, and Ethics of Not-for-Profit Hospitals," *UCLA Law Review* 50(6) (2003): 1345–1411, 1382–84; T.L. Greaney, "New Governance Norms and Quality of Care in Nonprofit Hospitals," *Annals of Health Law* 14 (2005): 421–436, 427 ("One of the most remarkable aspects of federal tax-exempt organization law is the absence of any specific requirement of charity care in IRS enforcement in the hospital sector.").
10. See Greaney, *supra* note 9.
11. *Id.* at 427–428 ("Regardless of their chances for success in litigation, these cases have focused the attention of the regulators, legislatures, and the public on the quantity of charity care provided and the billing and collection practices of nonprofit hospitals.").

12. K.R. Desai, C.V. Lukas, and G.J. Young, "Public Hospitals: Privatization and Uncompensated Care," *Health Affairs*, 19(2) (2000): 167–172, at 170.

13. A. Gerlin, "Hospital in Florida Is Focus of Probes Tied to Scuttled Bid by Columbia/HCA," *Wall Street Journal*, May 8, 1995, B10.

14. See generally C.T. Moran, "Why Revlon Applies to Nonprofit Corporations," *The Business Lawyer*, 53 (1998): 373–395.

15. See "Ethics & the CEO," *Hospitals and Health Networks*, January 20, 1998, 28–34.

16. See D.A. Reiser, "Decision-Makers Without Duties: Defining the Duties of Parent Corporations Acting as Sole Corporate Members in Nonprofit Health Care Systems," *Rutgers Law Review*, 53 (2001): 979–1026.

17. See, e.g., *Nathan Littauer Hospital Association v. Spitzer*, 734 N.Y.S.2d 671 (N.Y. App. Div. 2001), *motion for leave to appeal denied*, 744 N.Y.S.2d 762 (N.Y. 2002) (rejecting claim by New York attorney general that court approval was required for charter amendments in an affiliation of two nonprofit hospitals).

18. See D. Bellandi, "The Watchdogs Are Biting: State Attorneys General Asserting Authority over Not-for-Profit Hospitals," *Modern Healthcare*, January 29, 2001, 22.

19. See Moran, *supra* note 14, at 373 (describing the conversion of a nonprofit health maintenance organization for about $38 million followed by a public offering of the company the next year that was valued at $150 million).

20. See U.S. General Accounting Office, *Not-for-Profit Hospitals: Conversion Issues Prompt Increased State Oversight*, Letter Report, GAO/HEHS-98-24 (December 16, 1997).

21. See, e.g., *Blue Cross and Blue Shield of Missouri v. Nixon*, 81 S.W.3d 546 (Mo. Ct. App. 2002) (state officials challenged the transfer of assets to a for-profit subsidiary).

22. See Ono, *supra* note 6, at 133 (in a challenge by the state attorney general, a Michigan court held that a nonprofit hospital's joint venture violated its charitable purpose).

23. See Rev. Rul. 98-15, 1998-12 I.R.B. 6.

GOVERNMENT REGULATION OF PUBLIC HEALTH AND HEALTHCARE SERVICES

Federal and state governments play important roles in protecting the public health and regulating the healthcare system. As discussed in Chapter 2, one of the underlying themes of healthcare law and policy is deciding what activities should be regulated by the federal government as opposed to the government of each state. Each level of government has its own powers and responsibilities, and each relies on its own sources of legal authority.

State authority to promote public health and regulate healthcare providers is based on the police power, which is the traditional authority of the state to protect public health, safety, and welfare. "According to settled principles the police power of a State must be held to embrace, at least, such reasonable regulations established directly by legislative enactment as will protect the public health and the public safety."[1] Under the police power, states may require individuals to be vaccinated against disease[2] and may prohibit individuals from providing healthcare services without obtaining a license from the state.[3]

In contrast, the federal government's authority over health and healthcare is based primarily on the power of Congress to regulate interstate commerce. For example, the National Organ Transplant Act,[4] which was discussed in Chapter 3, prohibits the sale of human organs *provided* that the sale affects interstate commerce. The concept of interstate commerce is usually interpreted very broadly, and courts have held that a wide range of activities can affect interstate commerce. For example, the U.S. Supreme Court held that interstate commerce can be affected by growing wheat on your own land for your own personal consumption.[5] In the healthcare field, the Supreme Court held that an alleged conspiracy to prevent the construction of a local hospital would substantially affect interstate commerce by reducing the interstate flow of supplies, insurance payments, financing, and management fees.[6] Therefore, most activities in the healthcare system would be found to have an effect on interstate commerce and could be subject to federal regulation on that basis.

Aside from its power to regulate interstate commerce, the federal government can effectively control many aspects of healthcare through its conditional spending power. Under that power, Congress may require states to enact particular laws as a condition of federal aid to the states.[7] If a state objects to the condition, it is free to turn down the federal money. For example, the U.S. Supreme Court held that Congress has the power to require states to enact certificate-of-need (CON) laws as a condition of federal grants, even if that type of law would violate the state's own constitution.[8] Similarly, the federal government provides Medicaid funding to states that are willing to enact medical assistance programs that meet specific federal requirements.

In addition to placing conditions on grants to the states, the federal government uses its power as a large-scale buyer of healthcare services to impose conditions directly on healthcare providers that choose to participate in the Medicare program. Although participation in the Medicare program is a practical necessity for most healthcare providers, it is technically voluntary. Therefore, the Medicare program may use voluntary participation as a jurisdictional hook to impose requirements on providers, even if those requirements could not be imposed as a regulation of interstate commerce. The federal government also uses voluntary participation by skilled nursing facilities in the Medicare and Medicaid programs as a way to impose requirements for protecting patients' rights in those facilities.

Some activities may be subject to federal and state regulation at the same time. As discussed in Chapter 2, federal laws are the supreme law of the land, and they supersede contrary provisions of state law. In enacting a federal statute, Congress might explicitly provide that the federal law preempts all state laws on the same subject. In other situations, Congress might explicitly permit states to adopt additional requirements to regulate the same activities as the federal statute, provided that the state laws do not interfere with the federal regulatory scheme. Under those circumstances, the federal law would establish a "floor" of minimum requirements that must be met throughout the country, and individual states could impose higher requirements within their respective jurisdictions if they so desire. Sometimes Congress does not clearly state its intent with regard to federal preemption of state authority, and those situations often result in litigation to determine whether the federal law preempts a particular law of the state.

In the healthcare system, federal and state regulation can be used to accomplish several important goals:

1. to protect the public health by preventing and controlling communicable disease and protecting the public against bioterrorism,
2. to promote the quality of healthcare services provided by facilities and individual practitioners,
3. to reduce healthcare costs and promote access to care, and
4. to protect consumers in the market for health insurance and other types of coverage.

The first three of these goals of government regulation are addressed in this chapter. The fourth goal of protecting consumers in the market for health insurance is addressed in Chapter 17.

Government Regulation to Protect the Public Health

Under their police powers, state governments are responsible for traditional public health functions such as promoting sanitation and controlling communicable disease.[9] State legislatures may delegate power to administrative agencies at the state level and may authorize municipalities or local boards of health to exercise specific powers. For example, states may authorize local public health officials to investigate instances of communicable disease and to isolate or quarantine persons who pose a danger to the public health. States also require healthcare professionals to report outbreaks of communicable disease to state or local agencies, even though that may require a breach of patient confidentiality. In fact, the federal privacy rule that was adopted under the Health Insurance Portability and Accountability Act contains an explicit exception to permit healthcare providers and other covered entities to disclose individually identifiable health information to public health officials for such purposes as disease control and surveillance.[10] Aside from the federal privacy rule, state laws may authorize disclosure of otherwise confidential information and provide immunity from liability for those who make reports in compliance with the law.

In contrast to the active role of the states, the federal role in traditional public health functions has been more limited. However, the terrorist attacks on the World Trade Center and the Pentagon on September 11, 2001, and the subsequent anthrax attacks may require reconsideration of the respective roles of state and federal governments in protecting the public health.[11] No simple solution can be offered about the best way to allocate authority and coordinate the efforts of government agencies in responding to a bioterrorist attack.[12] As experts have pointed out, state and local officials are in the best position to identify and respond to an outbreak,[13] but bioterrorist attacks are likely to extend beyond the boundaries of an individual state and may fall within the federal government's authority to protect national security.[14]

One of the most interesting developments in this area has been the drafting of a model law for consideration by state legislatures. To ensure that states will have the legal authority to respond effectively to bioterrorism, the Centers for Disease Control and Prevention and other organizations asked experts in public health law to prepare a model act,[15] known as the Model State Emergency Health Powers Act.[16] The December 21, 2001, version of the model act is a "draft for discussion" rather than a final document for wholesale adoption by state legislatures.[17] Thus, legislatures in many states have considered and adopted statutes on these issues, but have not necessarily incorporated all of the suggested provisions of the model act.[18] In fact, important issues must be considered and policy decisions must be made before adopting this type of law. Aside from the appropriate roles of the state and federal governments, as already discussed, these issues include the appropriate role of law enforcement authorities in responding to a public health emergency, rationing of scarce resources in an emergency, criteria for declaring a state of emergency, and proper balance between governmental powers and civil liberties during an emergency.[19]

The issue of preserving civil liberties during a public health emergency has been a source of significant controversy. One prominent author has criticized the model act on the grounds that "draconian quarantine measures would probably have the unintended effect of encouraging people to avoid public health officials and physicians rather than to seek them out."[20] However, other experts, including the principal authors of the model act, have defended their balancing of state power and individual liberty.[21] The drafters have argued that the model act provides more protection of individual rights than many of the earlier state laws, and they have pointed out that "compulsory power has always been a part of public health law, because it is sometimes necessary to prevent or ameliorate unacceptable threats to the common good."[22]

Government Regulation for Quality of Care

One of the most important issues in healthcare law is determining whether to rely on government regulation, industry self-regulation, market competition, or some combination of those methods as a means of achieving policy goals.[23] In America's free-market economy, competition ordinarily improves the quality and reduces the price of goods and services for the benefit of the consumer. For example, in the healthcare industry, competition may promote quality and reduce costs as providers compete among themselves for managed care contracts. It is doubtful, however, that competition alone could ensure the quality of healthcare services. Most consumers lack the specialized knowledge required to evaluate the quality of medical care, and they often have little choice in selecting their providers.

Another possible way to ensure quality in the competitive marketplace is through the tort liability system of medical malpractice. Theoretically, the tort liability system should publicly identify the bad providers and drive them out of business as a result of damage awards, settlements, and higher premiums for malpractice insurance. In addition, the threat of malpractice liability should serve as a deterrent by causing other providers to be more careful. However, the tort liability system does not necessarily identify negligent providers or drive them out of business. As discussed in Chapter 10, even though a small number of patients receive large damage awards, most patients who are injured as a result of negligence never even file a claim. Therefore, we cannot rely solely on the medical malpractice system to ensure the quality of healthcare services in the competitive marketplace.

Under these circumstances, the remaining alternatives to promote the quality of care are government regulation or industry self-regulation. The advantage of government regulation is that a disinterested party will establish the rules and inspect the providers. However, some providers resent the interference by government agents and argue that government bureaucrats and inspectors have less expertise than people in the healthcare industry.

As an alternative, some healthcare providers favor industry and professional self-regulation. Examples of self-regulation include medical peer review and the voluntary accreditation of facilities by the Joint Commission, which is a private, nongovernmental organization. Under industry and professional self-regulation, people with substantial knowledge and experience will establish the standards and inspect the providers. However, there may be a lack of oversight by a truly disinterested party. In fact, some people believe allowing healthcare providers to regulate one another is like "letting the fox guard the chicken coop."

For these reasons, our legal system uses a combination of government regulation and industry self-regulation as a means of promoting the quality of care. As a policy matter, the issue is not whether to choose one extreme or the other. Rather, the issue is deciding where to draw the line between government regulation and industry or professional self-regulation, or perhaps choosing which strategy is appropriate for which problem. If we decide that we want a particular activity to be subject to government regulation, the further issue of whether the activity will be regulated by the state or the federal government must be settled. That choice between state and federal control will affect not only the selection of the regulatory agency but also the method of regulation. As already discussed, state and federal governments impose different types of regulation and rely on different types of legal authority as the basis for their regulation.

For many years, people involved in the healthcare system have tried to figure out ways to improve the quality of care and promote patient safety. Many different approaches may be used to improve quality, such as research, training, technology, continuous quality improvement, and clinical practice guidelines. In addition, the law can be used in several ways as a means to promote quality of care.

Merely enacting a statute that requires all healthcare professionals and facilities to provide high-quality care or face the consequence would not be effective. Unfortunately, it is not as simple as that, but some measures may be taken. We may be able to enact laws to require conduct we think will promote quality of care, such as requiring minimum levels of nurse staffing in healthcare facilities or requiring hospitals to use a computerized system for entering physician orders. We could also adopt new laws or change existing laws to provide incentives that encourage particular conduct, such as encouraging medical peer review by providing immunity to participants in the peer-review process or encouraging the use of clinical practice guidelines by making compliance with guidelines a defense against a claim of medical malpractice. Another alternative is to adopt laws that prohibit or discourage conduct we think would be detrimental to the quality of care.

When considering each of these alternatives, however, it is important to remember that the proposed legal intervention is not an end in itself, but merely a means to an end. We also need to recognize our limitations and proceed with caution in using the coercive power of the law to require healthcare professionals and organizations to do things we *think* are likely to promote quality of care. Like evidence-based medicine, research on the effect of healthcare laws would be useful in determining the likely benefits and costs of proposed legal interventions.

One proposed legal intervention would require healthcare facilities to report medical errors to a government agency at the state or federal level. In 2000, the Institute of Medicine (IOM) issued its influential report, *To Err Is Human,* stating that up to 98,000 people are killed every year by medical errors in U.S. hospitals.[24] As part of that report, the IOM recommended that Congress establish a system, similar to the existing one in the airline industry, for reporting adverse events in the healthcare industry. The IOM also recommended adopting *mandatory* reporting of adverse events that cause serious harm or death and *voluntary* reporting of less serious events to help identify weaknesses in the system.

Others, however, have questioned whether a system that works in the airline industry would work as well in the healthcare industry.[25] In addition, healthcare providers are concerned that patients or their lawyers could obtain copies of the medical error reports for use in malpractice cases. Despite these concerns, several states have enacted laws to require some type of mandatory reporting, and those laws may provide some protection against disclosure of patient-identifiable information.[26] At the federal level, Congress has considered some bills that would make reporting mandatory,[27] but it has not enacted a federal requirement for mandatory reporting. As discussed in Chapter 10, Congress has provided some degree of confidentiality for information that is voluntarily provided to certain safety organizations.[28] Another way in which the law is used to promote quality of care is the system of licensure for healthcare professionals and facilities. As discussed in the next section, licensure is not the same thing as accreditation or certification, and it is important to distinguish among those different methods of promoting the quality of care.

Licensure of Individual Healthcare Professionals

State governments use their police power to protect the public health, safety, and welfare by prohibiting individuals from providing healthcare services without a license from the state. In fact, practicing medicine without a license may be punishable as a violation of the criminal law.[29] In addition to using the criminal law, each state regulates the practice of medicine and other health professions by means of state licensing boards, such as a board of medical examiners. As one commentator has explained, the justification for regulating practitioners is "market failure, in particular, a failure caused by lack of information in the hands of consumers and the inability of consumers to understand such information as was available to them."[30]

Unlike a state medical society, which is a voluntary professional association, a licensing board is an official agency of state government. Because of the need for expertise in evaluating professional competence and ethics, state licensing boards are composed primarily of members of the particular profession. However, these boards act with the power of the state and are subject to the same statutory and constitutional restrictions that apply to the actions of government. State licensing boards are required, for example, to comply with due process of law by giving fair notice and an opportunity to be heard before taking adverse action on a license.

Professional licensing boards operate under state statutes, which are referred to as practice acts. Although minor differences are seen in each state and for each profession, all of these practice acts are developed with a common structure. First, the practice acts prohibit the unlicensed practice of a particular healthcare profession within the boundaries of the state. Then, each profession's act defines the practice of that profession by reference to specific types of activities or in relation to the activities that constitute the practice of medicine. Often, the act will provide a series of exceptions, so that a person will not be unlawfully practicing that profession if she is lawfully practicing a different healthcare profession within the bounds of her license. In addition, the practice act will create a board with the power to grant, deny, suspend, and revoke licenses in accordance with the standards and procedures set forth in the act and the rules adopted by the board. As a state agency created by the legislature, the board has only those powers that the legislature delegated to the board by statute. Finally, the act will specify the procedures for administrative appeal and judicial review of the board's licensing decisions.

Professional licensure can be used in a positive way to promote the quality of care and protect the public health. However, it can also be abused as a means of preserving the status quo in situations where medical doctors have a lucrative monopoly over the performance of certain functions. State licensure may be used to prevent competition from other professionals or innovation by practitioners of different methods of treatment such as homeopathic medicine. In addition, some people believe nurses and other allied health professionals are capable of safely performing many of the functions that are currently limited by law to licensed physicians, and therefore state licensure interferes with efforts to reduce healthcare costs and increase access to care. Finally, some people argue that medical licensing perpetuates an outmoded system of gender bias against the predominantly female profession of nursing.

As part of its comprehensive proposal for healthcare reform, the Clinton administration tried to limit the power of the states with regard to professional licensure. Specifically, the administration's proposal would have prohibited states from imposing restrictions on the practice of any category of healthcare professionals unless those restrictions are justified by the training and skill of those professionals.[31] By proposing federal preemption of state licensure restrictions that are not "justified," it appears that the Clinton administration would have left the ultimate evaluation of those restrictions to the federal courts. However, that reform proposal was not enacted, and the licensure of healthcare professionals remains under the control of the states.

One of the most interesting issues in professional licensure is determining the type of conduct that would justify revocation of a license. According to a 1990 report on state medical boards by the U.S. Department of Health and Human Services (HHS) Office of Inspector General (OIG), "the great majority of disciplinary actions taken by the State boards concerns the improper use of drugs or alcohol—be it inappropriate prescribing, unlawful distribution, or self-abuse."[32] Even if the abuse of alcohol or drugs occurred outside the context of medical practice, as in driving under the influence, that conduct may justify revocation of a license to practice medicine. As one court explained in upholding a board's disciplinary action,

> the state can impose discipline on a professional license only if the conduct upon which the discipline is based relates to the practice of the particular profession and thereby demonstrates an unfitness to practice such profession. . . .
>
> Convictions involving alcohol consumption reflect a lack of sound professional and personal judgment that is relevant to a physician's fitness and competence to practice medicine. Alcohol consumption quickly affects normal driving ability, and driving under the influence of alcohol threatens personal safety and places the safety of the public in jeopardy. . . .
>
> Driving while under the influence of alcohol also shows an inability or unwillingness to obey the legal prohibition against drinking and driving and constitutes a serious breach of a duty owed to society. . . .

In relation to multiple convictions involving driving and alcohol consumption, we reject the argument that a physician can seal off or compartmentalize personal conduct so it does not affect the physician's professional practice. . . .

Substantial legal authority provides that conduct occurring outside the practice of medicine may form the basis for imposing discipline on a license because such conduct reflects on a licensee's fitness and qualifications to practice medicine. . . . A physician who commits income tax fraud, solicits the subornation of perjury, or files false, fraudulent insurance claims has not practiced medicine incompetently. Nonetheless that physician has shown dishonesty, poor character, a lack of integrity, and an inability or unwillingness to follow the law, and thereby has demonstrated professional unfitness meriting license discipline. . . .[33]

Thus, boards may impose discipline for conduct outside the bounds of the traditional physician–patient relationship, but some issues on the scope of a board's power remain undecided. State boards might have the authority to revoke the license of a physician for giving improper testimony as a medical expert witness in a malpractice case.[34] Moreover, as discussed in Chapter 16, at least one state licensing board has taken disciplinary action against a physician for a utilization review decision that was made when the physician was medical director of a managed care organization.

Licensure of Healthcare Facilities

State governments also use their police power to promote quality of care in healthcare facilities by requiring facilities to obtain a license to operate. In fact, licensure laws for healthcare facilities are similar to practice acts for healthcare professionals, although the regulatory body for facilities is usually a traditional administrative agency rather than a board composed of professionals.

Licensing statutes will prohibit a facility from operating without a license; identify the state agency with the authority to grant, deny, suspend, or revoke a license; and provide procedures for disciplinary action, administrative appeals, and judicial review. In addition to the procedures for licensure, the statutes usually authorize the agency to adopt rules for operating a facility, such as requirements for staffing, record keeping, policies, and safety standards.

Under their licensing authority, state agencies have the power to inspect facilities and take disciplinary action. For relatively minor infractions, the agency might impose a fine or require the facility to submit a plan of correction. In more serious cases, the agency might suspend admissions to the facility or even revoke the facility's license. If the matter involved injury to a patient, an adverse licensure action may have negative consequences for the facility in future malpractice litigation. Therefore, even if the agency's disciplinary action is not severe, the facility may contest the agency's decision through the process of administrative appeal and judicial review.

At this juncture, it is appropriate to remind you that although this chapter focuses on laws specific to the healthcare industry, healthcare facilities are also subject to general laws that apply to all individuals and organizations. For example, as employers, healthcare facilities and medical practices are subject to labor laws that regulate matters such as minimum wage, overtime pay, employee benefit plans, and discrimination. These laws are beyond the scope of this book, but information about them is available on the web site of the U.S. Department of Labor at www.dol.gov.

Accreditation of Healthcare Facilities

Unlike licensure of facilities under the police power of the state, accreditation is a voluntary process of industry self-regulation. The most prominent accrediting organization for healthcare facilities is the Joint Commission, which is a private, nongovernmental organization controlled by the healthcare industry. The Joint Commission has developed detailed standards for the operation of healthcare facilities, and it surveys each participating facility on a periodic basis.

Although Joint Commission accreditation is voluntary, about 80 percent of hospitals participating in the Medicare program are accredited.[35] In addition to being an indication of quality and a method of self-improvement, Joint Commission accreditation may provide two important benefits for a facility. First, hospital licensing agencies in most states rely on Joint Commission accreditation for the purpose of licensure. In those states, the hospital may send its Joint Commission survey report to the state hospital licensing agency, and the state will accept that report for licensure without a separate survey by a state inspector. As a second benefit of Joint Commission accreditation, accredited hospitals are automatically *deemed* to meet most of the requirements for participating in the federal Medicare program,[36] avoiding yet another duplicative survey.

Although the deemed status of accredited hospitals is advantageous for the facilities, it raises an important issue of public policy. In effect, most state licensing agencies and the federal Medicare program are saying that if the facility is good enough for the industry's own program of self-regulation, it is good enough for the government agencies. In other industries in which human lives are at stake, allowing companies to exempt themselves from regular government inspections merely by producing a "seal of approval" from their own industry association would be inconceivable. Yet that is the way in which our society relies on industry self-regulation for acute-care hospitals, and some people believe the system works extremely well.

Certification of Healthcare Facilities for the Medicare and Medicaid Programs

In contrast to voluntary accreditation by the Joint Commission and mandatory licensure by the state, certification of healthcare facilities refers to the process of acceptance for participation in the Medicare and Medicaid payment programs. Therefore, certification is an exercise of the government's power as a buyer, rather than its power as a regulator.

Although Medicare is a federal program, many of the survey activities are performed by state agencies under contract or other arrangement with the federal government. As already discussed, facilities that are already accredited by the Joint Commission are deemed to meet most of the requirements for Medicare certification. Therefore, the 20 percent of Medicare-participating hospitals that are *not* accredited go through the governmental process of certification by state agencies acting on behalf of the federal government.

A certified facility will have a written provider agreement with the program, which is a type of contract, and the facility must comply with the conditions of participation. If the facility fails to comply with all of the applicable requirements, the Medicare program could terminate the provider agreement, which would prevent the facility from treating Medicare patients. As discussed in Chapter 8, the federal HHS OIG also uses its authority under the law of Medicare fraud and abuse to promote quality of care in participating facilities. As part of the settlement in some cases of fraud and abuse, the OIG has required healthcare organizations to implement a system of quality improvement as well as make changes to their system of financial controls. The OIG's authority over Medicare fraud and abuse is not limited to facilities that are surveyed by state agencies on behalf of the federal government, but applies as well to facilities that are deemed acceptable by virtue of their Joint Commission accreditation.

It is important to recognize that the term "certification" has a very different meaning for individual practitioners than it does for facilities. For physicians, certification is granted by one of the independent, nongovernmental organizations that are known as medical specialty boards, and similar systems are in place for other types of healthcare professionals. When used in that sense for individual healthcare professionals, certification is a voluntary, nongovernmental process of professional self-regulation. Thus, healthcare professionals are subject to government regulation in the form of licensure under the police power of the state and professional self-regulation by means of specialty board certification. In addition, healthcare professionals are subject to government supervision as participants in federal payment programs and professional self-regulation in the credentialing process for medical staff membership and clinical privileges, as discussed in Chapter 7. In a similar manner, healthcare facilities are subject to government regulation in the form of state licensure, industry self-regulation by means of voluntary accreditation by the Joint Commission, and government supervision as participants in federal payment programs. In these ways, our legal system promotes quality of care by a unique mix of government regulation, industry and professional self-regulation, and free-market competition.

Government Regulation of Diversified Organizations

A trend toward diversification is being seen in the healthcare industry, which has blurred some of the traditional distinctions among different types of entities. As discussed in Chapter 4, providers such as hospitals and physicians are joining together to form diversified organizations, which offer a combined package of services. In addition, healthcare providers are performing functions that traditionally were performed by insurance companies and health maintenance organizations (HMOs).

In some cases, organizations of providers are taking on risk by agreeing to provide services for a group of people at a predetermined price. Depending on the need for services and the cost of providing those services, the providers will make a profit or suffer a loss. The providers may describe their arrangement as a preferred provider organization or a physician–hospital organization. However, they are performing a function that is similar in some ways to that of an insurance company or an HMO. As a policy matter, the public has an interest in making sure that the provider organization is financially responsible, so that it will be able to provide the services for which payment has already been made. Therefore, a provider organization that takes on actuarial risk poses a regulatory challenge for society.

A similar regulatory challenge is posed by diversification at the other end of the provider–payer spectrum. Insurance companies and self-insured employers, which had originally limited their activities to paying for healthcare services, are now establishing their own networks of providers. Although they are regulated only as payers, they may also be participating in the delivery of healthcare services, which was a function formerly reserved to the providers. As payers and providers from each end of the spectrum diversify toward the middle, our society must address the important question of how those hybrid entities should be regulated.

A system of government regulation is based on fitting each activity into a defined category and applying rules that are appropriate for that category. However, if something has characteristics that fit into more than one category, a decision must be made as to whether it should be licensed and regulated in one category, the other category, both categories, or perhaps an entirely new category for that new type of entity.

A historical example of this phenomenon is the HMO, which pays for care and also provides or arranges for care. Although it provides or arranges for care through licensed physicians, the HMO is not really a medical practice under the authority of the professional licensing board. Furthermore, although it performs a payment function, it is not really an insurance company. Therefore, it was necessary to adopt laws to create a new regulatory category for HMOs.

Like the HMO, other types of hybrid organizations are found in the modern healthcare marketplace. Many of these entities perform diversified functions and do not fit into the traditional boxes of healthcare regulation. As with the other regulatory issues discussed, the legal and policy challenge is to find ways to protect the public interest without imposing excessive regulatory burdens that would stifle competition and innovation.

Government Regulation for Cost Containment and Access

CON laws prohibit the development of new healthcare facilities and services unless the provider can demonstrate to the satisfaction of state officials that the proposed facilities and services are needed. In most states, government officials have the power to decide which facilities may be built and which services may be provided by each facility. Thus, CON regulation goes to the very heart of the ongoing debate between government regulation and free-market competition as the best method of achieving policy goals in the healthcare field.

Purposes and Effects of CON Laws

CON laws may have an effect on the quality of care, although the nature of that effect is subject to debate. For some highly specialized services, a limitation on the number of providers may promote quality by ensuring that all authorized providers will perform a sufficient volume of procedures to develop and maintain their proficiency. Some evidence indicates, for example, that hospitals that perform a large volume of open-heart surgery procedures have better results, in terms of mortality rates, than programs that perform a small number of procedures. However, in other ways, CON regulation may have an adverse effect on the quality of care by preventing some facilities from acquiring state-of-the-art equipment. Moreover, by reducing the level of competition, CON regulation limits the need for healthcare providers to compete with each other on the basis of quality.

Economic Theory Supporting CON Laws

Although CON laws may have an effect on quality, the primary goals of CON regulation are cost containment and access. In regard to cost, the economic theory of CON regulation is that the law of supply and demand does not operate normally in the healthcare field.[37] In most industries, an increase in the supply of goods and services or an increase in the number of competing sellers would cause prices to go down as sellers competed among themselves for business. However, some people believe an increase in the supply of healthcare services or an increase in the number of competing providers would cause prices to go up rather than down.

Under that economic theory, the healthcare industry does not respond to normal competitive forces. If healthcare services are covered by insurance, the consumer is insulated from the cost and does not have to make economic decisions about purchasing those services. In addition, most consumers do not have the specialized knowledge to determine their need for healthcare services or to compare the relative cost and quality of each alternative. Consumers tend to purchase whatever services are recommended by their physician, provided those services are covered by the consumer's insurance plan. Under these circumstances, most consumers do not shop for the lowest price among healthcare providers.

Therefore, providers do not have to compete for the business of consumers on the basis of price. Even if the supply of healthcare services were to increase, providers would not need to cut their prices as they would in an ordinary competitive market. In fact, as the number of providers increases, healthcare providers might even need to increase their prices to compensate for a reduction in volume at each facility.

As an oversimplified example, assume that Hospital A has the only magnetic resonance imaging (MRI) scanner in the area. If it costs Hospital A $1 million per year in operating costs for the MRI service, and if Hospital A provides 1,000 MRI procedures per year, Hospital A would charge $1,000 per procedure to break even. However, if Hospital B obtains an MRI scanner in the same area and provides half of the local procedures (500 procedures), Hospital B would have to charge $2,000 per procedure ($1 million annual operating cost divided by 500 procedures = $2,000 per procedure). Moreover, Hospital A would have to raise its charge from $1,000 to $2,000 per procedure to spread its costs over a smaller number of procedures or else perform additional procedures that might be unnecessary. This type of scenario leads some people to believe society should replace competition with government regulation of the supply of healthcare services and facilities. Hence, there is a need for CON laws.

However, a serious question remains as to whether the economic theory of CON regulation is valid. That economic theory was developed in the 1960s and 1970s, when providers encountered little price competition, and the Medicare program paid hospitals on a retrospective cost-reimbursement basis. Under that system of Medicare reimbursement, hospitals had a perverse incentive to build expensive facilities, even if they were not really necessary. Arguably, government regulation was necessary to control the supply of facilities and equipment. However, as discussed in Chapter 8, Medicare now pays hospitals on the basis of prospectively determined prices rather than retrospectively determined costs. Under the new system, hospitals no longer have an incentive to maximize their costs, but instead will seek to reduce their costs to maximize net revenue.

In addition, under managed care, providers now compete on the basis of price for preferred provider contracts. That bargaining process may restrain healthcare costs and prices without the need for government regulation of supply. Even if the economic theory of CON regulation was correct at the time it was developed, it might be invalid as applied to a system of prospective payment and managed care. Moreover, empirical research does not prove that CON laws have significantly reduced healthcare costs, and those states that eliminated CON regulation did not experience significant increases in costs after their laws were repealed.[38]

Supply/Demand Theory Supporting CON Laws

Another argument in favor of CON regulation is that restraining the supply of healthcare facilities is the best way—or perhaps the only way—to prevent healthcare providers from performing unnecessary services. Under this theory, the demand for services by patients and physicians is not the same as the actual need for those services. Moreover, the demand for additional services will go up whenever the supply of available facilities increases.[39] Therefore, government should determine the true need for new facilities, allow only those facilities to be built, and rely on physicians in those facilities to ration the limited resources to the most appropriate patients.[40] This rationale for CON regulation can be criticized on several grounds. First, it is paternalistic for government officials to decide what people really need, as opposed to what patients and their physicians really want. Moreover, it is probably unrealistic to think government officials have the ability to determine what people really need. If physicians are really performing unnecessary procedures, other ways exist to deal with that problem, such as utilization review, peer review, and professional discipline. Finally, in light of the existing problems of insurance coverage and access to care, it is doubtful that all providers would allocate their limited resources to patients with the greatest need.

Other Justifications for CON Laws

Despite these criticisms, CON laws may be justifiable on other grounds as a method of promoting access to care.

1. State officials may be able to require applicants for a CON to provide a particular level of indigent care or service to Medicaid patients as a condition of approval.
2. When more than one applicant is competing for a single CON, the state agency could choose the applicant that is most likely to provide access to care.

3. The state could promote geographic access by limiting the development of new facilities to areas with the highest level of need.
4. CON laws can promote access by protecting public hospitals from competition for the paying patients they need for their financial survival.

Public hospitals and some nonprofit hospitals provide a great deal of care to the indigent, which is a financial loss to the facility. They need the revenue from insured patients to offset the loss and remain financially viable. If a for-profit facility were opened in the same area, it would take away many of the paying patients and leave most of the indigent patients to the public hospital. That practice is referred to as "cream-skimming." To combat this practice, CON laws may be necessary to protect the financial viability of public hospitals, regardless of whether the economic theory of those laws is valid.

The System of CON Regulation

In 1974, the federal government decided to encourage CON laws by enacting the National Health Planning and Resources Development Act.[41] That federal statute provided funding to state governments on the condition that states enact CON laws that comply with federal standards. Initially, almost all states enacted CON laws. However, the federal statute was repealed in 1986, and some states eliminated or reduced their CON requirements.

Nevertheless, more than half of the states currently impose CON regulation for some types of facilities and services.[42] In some states, efforts to repeal CON laws have met with strong and successful resistance by existing providers who like being protected from competition.[43] In addition, it is possible that state governments use CON laws to limit their expenditures for Medicaid by restricting the number of nursing home beds for which the Medicaid program would be obligated to pay.

In an unregulated market, competing sellers decide what services to offer and where to offer them. However, in a system regulated by CON laws, state officials decide where facilities may be built, who may build them, and what services may be offered in those facilities. In some ways, the healthcare industry under CON regulation resembles the centrally planned economy of the former Soviet Union. However, other U.S. industries, such as public utilities and automobile dealerships in some states, have similar regulatory barriers to market entry.

Where CON laws exist, they are not limited to public facilities or facilities that receive government funds. Moreover, CON laws are not limited to services provided to publicly insured patients, such as those covered by Medicare and Medicaid. Rather, CON laws apply to private and public facilities, and they apply to services provided to commercially insured and self-paying patients, as well as to patients who are publicly insured.

Therefore, CON laws limit what a private organization may do with its own land, buildings, money, and patients.

However, CON regulation does not require government approval for the continued operation of existing facilities, equipment, and services. The state CON agency can protect existing facilities from competition by refusing to grant a CON to a potential competitor but ordinarily cannot take away an existing facility's CON, even if the facility is underutilized. Therefore, the CON system has a bias in favor of existing providers, which have received what amounts to a permanent franchise from the state.

Under these circumstances, the attitude of existing providers and their managers is ambivalent. When CON laws prevent them from developing new facilities or offering new services, they tend to complain bitterly about intrusive overregulation by the government. However, when someone proposes to compete in their geographic area, they insist that CON laws should be aggressively enforced to prevent "needless duplication" of healthcare facilities and services, which would be bad for society as a whole.

Under a system of CON regulation, the first issue is whether a CON is needed for a particular project. By their terms, CON statutes only apply to specific types of facilities, equipment, and services. In some situations, a CON would be required only if the project involves a capital expenditure or annual operating cost that exceeds a threshold specified in the law. However, some activities will require a CON regardless of the capital and operating expense.

Providers may attempt to structure or describe their projects in ways that will avoid the time and expense of applying for a CON. For ethical as well as legal reasons, providers must be honest in making representations to the state CON agency with regard to the costs and nature of a project. In the meantime, the provider's competitors may argue that the project should be subject to CON review. The competitors will insist, of course, that they are opposing the project out of concern for the interests of society as a whole and not because of any desire to protect their existing market shares. Eventually, the CON agency will have to determine whether the project is subject to CON review.

Sometimes healthcare facilities and their advisers are successful in finding a loophole to avoid CON review. Then, the state CON agency may attempt to close that loophole for the future by amending its regulations or by seeking an amendment to the statute. Eventually, the facilities and their advisers will find a new loophole and the process will begin all over again in a never-ending game of "cat and mouse" between the regulated industry and the regulators.

The Medical Arms Race

In addition to dealing with an agency of government, providers often fight among themselves for valuable CONs, in what has been referred to as the "medical arms race." Although state laws differ, the basic regulatory pattern is divided into two separate processes: one for statewide health planning, and one for the review of specific CON applications.

The health planning process involves conducting an inventory of existing facilities and services in each geographic area of the state and determining the future need for each type of facility and service. These determinations of need are made without regard to any particular applicant and result in allocations for which anyone may apply. For example, a state might determine that a need exists for 30 new skilled nursing facilities, ten new home health agencies, and three new ambulatory surgery facilities in particular counties or regions of the state. Those needs would be reflected in a state health plan or state regulations, which allocate particular numbers of facilities for future CON reviews.

In some states, the allocations and determinations of need are made by the Statewide Health Coordinating Council (SHCC), which may include representatives of provider associations, public officials, and consumers. If providers want to develop facilities or services in the near future, they may ask the SHCC or other state officials to recognize the need for the proposed facility or service and make an allocation for a future CON review. However, other providers may urge or lobby the SHCC not to allocate any new facilities or services that might compete with them in the future. As one court explained, adopting and amending the state health plan is a quasi-legislative process of rulemaking, whereas reviewing individual CON applications is a quasi-judicial process of adjudication.[44]

Allocations are usually based on some quantitative-need methodology, including projections of future population, incidence rate for a particular disease, historical and anticipated rates of utilization, and capacity of existing and proposed facilities. State officials use these methodologies to calculate the precise number of beds, operating rooms, machines, or facilities that supposedly will be needed at a particular time in the future. However, these methodologies may be based on gross estimates and assumptions that can be manipulated to achieve a particular result. For example, a state could choose assumptions for its need methodology that would result in an allocation of fewer nursing home beds and thereby limit its Medicaid expenditure for nursing home services. Thus, it is possible that states could use the health planning process to ration care by limiting the number of beds, machines, and facilities to a level for which their citizens are willing to pay. Moreover, to the extent that quantitative methodologies are based on historical utilization, they may understate the need because of disparities in the number of procedures provided in the past to women and members of minority groups.

Regardless of whether the allocations are based on scientific methodology, politics, or budgetary considerations, they play a crucial role in the

CON review process. Under some state laws, the need determinations in the state health plan are conclusive, and providers can only apply for a CON for facilities or services that are allocated by the plan. Other state laws are more flexible, however, and give applicants an opportunity to try to prove a need for more facilities or services than the number identified in the plan.

Ordinarily, all of the applications for a particular service in a particular area will be reviewed on a competitive basis as part of a single "batch" or review cycle. Depending on the state's procedure, opportunities may be provided for a public hearing and written comments about the pending applications. Eventually, the CON agency will decide whether to approve, deny, or conditionally approve the application on the basis of review criteria set forth in the state statute and regulations. In addition to general statutory criteria, such as need, access, and financial feasibility, many state agencies have adopted specific regulations to set forth quantitative criteria for particular services and equipment. These quantitative criteria are designed to ensure sufficient utilization of the proposed service or equipment and to prevent adverse effects on existing providers. Unless the state law provides an exception, a CON application must be consistent with *all* of the general and specific criteria to be approved.

After the CON agency has made its initial decision, a disappointed applicant or other affected party has the right to an administrative appeal. When all administrative remedies have been exhausted and the agency has made its final decision, a party may request judicial review in the courts. In some states, CON litigation can be very time consuming and expensive. However, cases are often settled between the state agency and an applicant or among the competing applicants. For example, a settlement may provide for the approval of an application subject to specified conditions.

After a CON is awarded, providers will have some continuing obligations. First, a CON holder will be required to develop and operate the facility or service in accordance with the representations in its application. Second, the holder must comply with any conditions the state agency imposed on the award of the CON, such as providing a specified level of care to the indigent or charging specified rates.

Depending on the particular state law, these obligations may apply to a future buyer of a facility that obtained a CON. Therefore, a prospective buyer should use due diligence before purchasing a healthcare facility to determine whether the buyer will inherit legal obligations as the new owner and operator of the facility. Moreover, some states prohibit the transfer of a CON or require the agency's prior approval for a transfer. Finally, if a facility fails to comply with the law, the agency may have the authority to withdraw the CON.

Problem 5.1: CON for Open-Heart Surgery

To whom it may concern:

Jackson County Hospital needs your help!

As chief executive officer of Jackson County Hospital, I am issuing this request for professional assistance. We have a big problem, and we are willing to pay whatever is necessary to any outside consultants who can help us solve this problem. Alternatively, I would be happy to offer the full-time position of executive vice president of the hospital to anyone who can solve this problem for us.

The problem is that we desperately need to establish an open-heart surgery service at the hospital, but the state government denied our application for a certificate of need (CON). There is still time to appeal the decision of the state agency, but I do not know whether we would have a good case. Even if we file an appeal, I do not know whether we could convince the state agency or a court that we comply with all of the regulations for granting a CON.

Please review the enclosed facts and regulations, which set forth all you need to know to help us with this problem. Then, please write your answers to the questions that are attached to this memorandum. Your response must be no more than three double-spaced pages. I look forward to reading your answers and to rewarding the best responses.

The Facts

Jackson County Hospital (County) is a 400-bed, general, acute-care hospital in a medium-sized city, owned and operated by the county of Jackson. County offers most types of sophisticated healthcare services, including MRI, lithotripsy, neonatal intensive care, and cardiac catheterization. However, County does not provide open-heart surgery and must refer all patients for open-heart surgery to other hospitals.

County's primary competitor is Doctor's Hospital, which is the only other hospital in Jackson County. Doctor's Hospital, a private, nonprofit hospital with only private rooms, is the hospital of choice for most of the commercially insured patients in the area. However, Doctor's provides very little care for the indigent. Most of the uninsured patients and Medicaid patients in the area are treated at County.

Doctor's developed an open-heart surgery service about eight years ago when there were fewer regulatory restrictions on acquiring medical equipment and developing new healthcare services. At the present time, Doctor's has the only open-heart surgery service within a 100-mile radius of the city in which Doctor's and County are located.

County desperately wants to develop an open-heart surgery service for several reasons. First, the new service would generate revenue to support other operations of the hospital. Second, to attract more commercially insured patients for all of its services, County needs to change its image as a "second-class hospital" that lacks the modern facilities and equipment that are available at Doctor's. Third, because County cannot perform open-heart surgery on those patients who require it, physicians are reluctant to refer patients to County for other cardiac services, such as cardiac catheterizations. Fourth, County has had difficulty in obtaining preferred provider contracts with managed care organizations because it is unable to provide the full range of services the patients may require. For all of these reasons, County's top strategic goal is establishing an open-heart surgery service.

However, County has been unable to obtain approval for an open-heart surgery service under the state's CON law. Although County applied for a CON, its application has just been denied by the state CON agency.

THE STATE CON REGULATIONS FOR OPEN-HEART SURGERY SERVICES

Following are the state CON regulations that apply to County:

SECTION .1700—CRITERIA AND STANDARDS FOR OPEN-HEART SURGERY SERVICES AND HEART-LUNG BYPASS MACHINES[45]

1713 Definitions

The following definitions shall apply to all rules in this Section:

(1) "Capacity" of an open-heart surgery room means 400 adult-equivalent open-heart surgical procedures per year. One open-heart surgical procedure on persons age 5 and under is valued at two adult open-heart surgical procedures. For purposes of determining capacity, one open-heart surgical procedure is defined to be one visit or trip by a patient to the open-heart surgery room for an open-heart operation.

(4) "Open-heart surgery service area" means a geographical area defined by the applicant, which has boundaries that are not farther than 90 road miles from the facility, except that the open-heart surgery service area of an academic medical center teaching hospital designated in 10 NCAC 3R. 3050 shall not be limited to 90 road miles.

(5) "Open-heart surgery services" is defined in G.S. 131E-176(18b).

(6) "Open-heart surgical procedures" means highly specialized surgical procedures which:

    (a) utilize a heart-lung bypass machine (the "pump") to perform extracorporeal circulation and oxygenation during surgery;

    (b) are designed to correct congenital and acquired cardiac coronary disease; and

    (c) are identified by Medicare Diagnostic Related Group (DRG) numbers 104, 105, 106, 107, and 108.

(7) "Open-heart surgery room" means an operating room primarily used to perform open-heart surgical procedures, as reported on the most current hospital licensure application.

(8) "Open-heart surgery program" means all of the open-heart surgery rooms operated in one hospital.

(9) "Primary open-heart surgery service area" means a geographical area defined by the applicant, which has boundaries that are not farther than 45 road miles from the facility, except that the primary open-heart surgery service area of an academic medical center teaching hospital designated to 10 NCAC 3R. 3050 shall not be limited to 45 road miles.

1715 Required Performance Standards

The applicant shall demonstrate that the proposed project is capable of meeting the following standards:

(1) each open-heart surgery room shall be utilized at an annual rate of at least 50 percent of capacity, measured during the twelfth quarter following completion of the project;

(3) a new or additional heart-lung bypass machine shall be utilized at 200 open-heart surgical procedures per year, measured during the twelfth quarter following completion of the project;

(5) each existing open-heart surgery program in each facility which has a primary open-heart surgery service area that overlaps the proposed primary open-heart surgery service area operated at a level of at least 80 percent of capacity during the 12-month period reflected in the most recent licensure form on file with the Division of Facility Services.

THE STATE AGENCY'S DECISION TO DENY COUNTY'S APPLICATION

The state agency recognized that County would provide access to the medically underserved and that its project would be financially feasible. However, the state agency denied the application because the agency believed County failed to meet some of the quantitative criteria set forth in the regulations.

1. Nonconformity with § 1715(1)

First, the state agency found that County's projected utilization of open-heart surgery procedures did not meet the level required by the regulation at § 1715(1). In its CON application, County proposed to develop only one open-heart surgery room. In addition, County made the following quarterly projections of adult and pediatric (aged 5 years and younger) open-heart surgery procedures for the first 3 years (12 calendar quarters) of operation after completion of the project.

Quarter	Adult Open-Heart Procedures	Pediatric Open-Heart Procedures
1	5	1
2	8	1
3	11	1
4	14	1
5	17	2
6	20	2
7	23	3
8	26	3
9	29	3
10	32	4
11	36	4
12	40	5

In its decision, the state agency found that County's application was non-conforming with the regulatory criterion at § 1715(1), on the grounds that County's projected utilization was less than 50 percent of capacity measured during the 12th quarter after completion of the project. The state agency reasoned that the capacity of one open-heart surgery room is defined by the regulation at § 1713(1) as 400 procedures. Therefore, 50 percent of capacity would be 200 procedures. The regulation at § 1715(1) requires a projected utilization of at least 50 percent of capacity (200 procedures) but allows the projected utilization to be measured by annualizing the utilization that was projected for the 12th quarter of operation. Therefore, the applicant must project a utilization of at least 50 procedures during the 12th quarter of operation because that would annualize at 200 procedures, which is 50 percent of the capacity of 400 procedures. In this case, the agency found that County projected a total of only 45 procedures in the 12th quarter, which failed to meet the requirement of § 1715(1).

2. Nonconformity with § 1715(5)

In addition, the state agency found that the level of historical utilization at Doctor's existing open-heart surgery program was not high enough to permit approval of another open-heart surgery program in the same geographic area under the agency's regulation at § 1715(5). Not surprisingly, the administrator of Doctor's had opposed the County application for a CON on the grounds that there was no need for an additional open-heart surgery service in the same geographic area.

Because Doctor's is located in the same city as County, it is clear that Doctor's primary open-heart surgery service area overlaps County's proposed primary open-heart surgery service area. In fact, Doctor's is the only facility whose primary service area overlaps County's proposed primary service area for open-heart surgery. During the 12-month period reflected in the most recent licensure form that Doctor's filed with the Division of Facility Services, Doctor's performed a total of 610 adult open-heart surgery procedures and 20 pediatric open-heart surgery procedures in its open-heart surgery program, which consists of two open-heart surgery rooms.

In its decision to deny the County application, the state agency found that County's application was nonconforming with the agency's regulatory criterion at § 1715(5). Specifically, the agency found that Doctor's existing open-heart surgery program had not operated at a level of at least 80 percent of capacity during the 12-month period reflected in its most recently filed licensure form. As discussed earlier, Doctor's open-heart surgery program had two open-heart surgery rooms. Therefore, the state agency reasoned that, pursuant to the regulation at § 1713(1), the capacity of each of Doctor's open-heart surgery rooms was 400 procedures and the total capacity of Doctor's open-heart surgery program was 800 procedures. Therefore, according to the agency, the regulation at § 1715(5) required Doctor's to operate at a level of at least 640 procedures, which is 80 percent of the capacity of 800 possible procedures. Because Doctor's had only operated at a level of 630 procedures in the past year, the agency reasoned that Doctor's had not operated at 80 percent of capacity and County's application for a CON could not be approved.

3. Nonconformity with § 1715(3)

Finally, the state agency found that County's application was nonconforming to the regulation at § 1715(3) because County's proposed new heart-lung bypass machine would not be used at a rate of 200 procedures per year as measured during the 12th quarter. As discussed, County projected to perform a total of only 45 procedures during the 12th quarter, which would annualize at 180 procedures, rather than the 50 procedures needed to annualize at the required level of 200 procedures.

QUESTIONS

1. Was the state agency correct in finding that County's application was nonconforming with the criterion at § 1715(1)? Why or why not?
2. Was the state agency correct in finding that County's application was nonconforming with the criterion at § 1715(5)? Why or why not?
3. On what basis could County argue that it is conforming with the criterion at § 1715(3)? On what basis could the state agency argue that County's application is nonconforming with that criterion? In your opinion, which side has the more persuasive argument? Why?
4. If County's application is not conforming with all of the current regulations, what could County do in an effort to develop an open-heart surgery program?

Notes

1. *Jacobson v. Massachusetts*, 197 U.S. 11, 25 (1905).
2. *Id.*
3. *Dent v. West Virginia*, 129 U.S. 114, 128 (1889) (upholding conviction for violation of West Virginia statute that prohibited unlicensed practice of medicine).
4. 42 U.S.C. § 274e (2006).
5. *Wickard v. Filburn*, 317 U.S. 111, 127–28 (1942).
6. *Hospital Building Co. v. Rex Hospital Trustees*, 425 U.S. 738, 744 (1976).
7. See generally *South Dakota v. Dole*, 483 U.S. 203 (1987).
8. *North Carolina ex rel. Morrow v. Califano*, 445 F. Supp. 532, 534 (E.D.N.C. 1977), *aff'd mem.*, 435 U.S. 962 (1978).
9. See L.O. Gostin, *Public Health Law: Power, Duty, Restraint* (Berkeley: University of California Press; New York: The Milbank Memorial Fund, 2000): 47–51.
10. 45 C.F.R. § 164.512(b) (2006).
11. See, e.g., W.E. Parmet, "After September 11: Rethinking Public Health Federalism," *Journal of Law, Medicine & Ethics*, 30(2) (2002): 201–211.
12. See, e.g., J.G. Hodge, "Bioterrorism Law and Policy: Critical Choices in Public Health," *Journal of Law, Medicine & Ethics*, 30(2) (2002): 254–61.
13. Parmet, *supra* note 11, at 201.
14. Hodge, *supra* note 12, at 258.
15. See *id.* at 254–55.
16. The Center for Law and the Public's Health at Georgetown and Johns Hopkins Universities, "The Model State Emergency Health Powers Act," Draft as of December 21, 2001. [Online report; retrieved 1/30/07.] www2a.cdc.gov/phlp/docs/msehpa2.pdf.
17. See G.J. Annas, "Bioterrorism, Public Health, and Civil Liberties," *New England Journal of Medicine*, 346(17) (2002): 1337–1342, at 1340 ("No one any longer considers the act a 'model.' Instead, it is now labeled a 'draft for discussion.'").
18. The Center for Law & the Public's Health at Georgetown & Johns Hopkins Universities, "Model State Emergency Health Powers Act: Legislative Status Update." [Online report; retrieved 1/30/07.] www.publichealthlaw.net/Resources/Modellaws.htm #MSEHPA.
19. Hodge, *supra* note 12, at 255.
20. Annas, *supra* note 17, at 1340.

21. L.O. Gostin, et al., "The Model State Emergency Health Powers Act," *Journal of the American Medical Association*, 288(5) (2002): 622–628.

22. *Id.*

23. See generally T.S. Jost, "Oversight of the Quality of Medical Care: Regulation, Management, or the Market?" *Arizona Law Review*, 37 (1995): 825–868, at 859 ("The deficiencies of the market and of management insure the existence of a continuing legitimate role for quality regulation.").

24. See L.T. Kohn, J.M. Corrigan, and M. Donaldson (eds.), *To Err Is Human: Building a Safer Health System* (Washington, DC: Institute of Medicine, 2000).

25. See, e.g., L.I. Palmer, "Patient Safety, Risk Reduction, and the Law," *Houston Law Review*, 36 (1999): 1609–1661, at 1638 ("Advocates for patient safety have offered solutions from the airline industry without noting how different health care is from the airline industry in terms of both organization and surrounding legal structure.").

26. See, e.g., 40 Pa. Cons. Stat. § 1303.313(a) (duty of medical facilities to report serious events to government officials, but without any information that would identify the individual patient); *id.* at § 1303.311(a) (certain documents are not discoverable or admissible in evidence).

27. See, e.g., proposed Stop All Frequent Errors (SAFE) in Medicare and Medicaid Act of 2000, S. 2378, 106th Cong. (2000) (bipartisan bill would have established mandatory reporting by providers with confidentiality for the reported information).

28. Patient Safety and Quality Improvement Act of 2005, Pub. L. No. 109-41, 119 Stat. 424 (2005).

29. See, e.g., *Michigan v. Rogers*, 641 N.W.2d 595 (Mich. App. 2001) (upholding prosecution of a "natural doctor" who used a machine to diagnose a child with ear problems as having a tapeworm, a bacteria, and a brain aneurysm).

30. Jost, *supra* note 23, at 827.

31. See Health Security Act, H.R. 3600, 103rd Cong. § 1161 (1993).

32. U.S. Department of Health and Human Services, Office of Inspector General, *State Medical Boards and Medical Discipline*, OEI-01-89-00560 (August 1990): 15.

33. *Griffiths v. Superior Court*, 96 Cal. App. 4th 757, 769–72 (Cal. App. 2002), *review denied*, 2002 Cal. LEXIS 3826 (2002).

34. See e.g., *In re Lustgarten*, 629 S.E.2d 886 (N.C. App. 2006).

35. U.S. Department of Health and Human Services, Office of Inspector General, *The External Review of Hospital Quality: The Role of Medicare Certification*, OEI-01-97-00052 (July 1999): 1, 6.

36. See 42 U.S.C. § 1395bb (2006).

37. See generally L.H. Wolfson, "State Regulation of Health Facility Planning: The Economic Theory and Political Realities of Certificates of Need," *DePaul Journal of Health Care Law*, 4 (2001): 261–314.

38. C.J. Conover and F.A. Sloan, "Does Removing Certificate-of-Need Regulations Lead to a Surge in Health Care Spending?" *Journal of Health Politics, Policy & Law*, 23(3) (1998): 455–481.

39. See B.R. Furrow, et al., *Health Law:* 2d ed., Hornbook Series (St. Paul, MN: West Group, 2000): at 29 ("the demand for care will always expand to the limits of the supply.").

40. *Id.*

41. See Pub. L. No. 93-641, 42 U.S.C. §§ 300k–300n-6 (repealed 1986).

42. See Furrow, *supra* note 39, at 32 and n.3. See also American Health Planning Association, "Brochure for 2006 National Directory." [Online document; retrieved 2/1/07.] www.ahpanet.org/national_directory.html (listing 37 states with CON programs as of 2006).

43. See, e.g., K. Greene, "Nonprofit Hospitals Win in Georgia," *Wall Street Journal (Southeast Journal),* March 19, 1997, S3.

44. See *Adventist Healthcare Midatlantic, Inc. v. Suburban Hospital, Inc.,* 711 A.2d 158, 166–68 (Md. 1998).

45. N.C. Admin. Code tit. 10, r. 3R.1700 (2002). Updated regulations located today at N.C. Admin. Code tit. 10A, 14C.1701 and 14C.1703 (2006).

PROTECTING THE PRIVACY OF MEDICAL INFORMATION

Most patients do not want providers to disclose their medical information to other people, except as specifically authorized by the patient. Disclosure of personal information could be harmful or embarrassing to him, especially if it is disclosed to the patient's employer, insurance company, neighbors, spouse, or former spouse. However, more than merely preventing harm or embarrassment to a person is at stake in confidentiality issues.

Inappropriate disclosure of medical information could harm the public health and reduce the quality of care by making people unwilling to provide necessary information to their healthcare providers. If patients had to worry that personal information would be disclosed to others, they would not provide the candid information that practitioners and facilities need to provide appropriate care. Even worse, people might refrain from seeking necessary treatment out of fear that information about them would be disclosed. Therefore, the underlying goals of medical privacy are to encourage patients to seek appropriate care and to confide fully in their healthcare providers. In these ways, confidentiality should improve the quality of care and promote public health.

From an ethical perspective, the privacy of medical information is based on the ethical principle of autonomy or self-determination. Patients have the right to control the disclosure of their own medical information and the right to condition their consent to treatment on the provider's promise to maintain confidentiality. In addition, improper disclosure of private information could harm the patient and thereby violate the ethical principle of nonmaleficence. Finally, to the extent that confidentiality promotes quality of care and public health, it is consistent with the ethical principle of beneficence.

Healthcare professional organizations have recognized these ethical principles and adopted the obligation of confidentiality in their own codes of ethics. In accordance with the traditional Hippocratic Oath, the Principles of Medical Ethics of the American Medical Association (AMA) encourage physicians to "safeguard patient confidences and privacy within the constraints of the law."[1] Similarly, the *Code of Ethics* of the American College of Healthcare Executives provides that healthcare executives have the responsibility to "[w]ork to ensure the existence of procedures that will safeguard the confidentiality and privacy of patients or others served."[2] Other professional organizations have adopted similar principles for their members.

In some ways, the problem of medical privacy has become more acute now that data are stored on computers and transferred electronically among practitioners, facilities, and third-party payers. As former U.S. Department of Health and Human Services (HHS) Secretary Donna Shalala put it, "[g]one are the days when our family doctor kept our records sealed away in an office file cabinet. Patient information is now accessed and exchanged quickly."[3] It is certainly true that electronic storage and transmission of data increases the extent to which information can be disseminated as well as the possibility of improper disclosure.[4] However, it is important to keep these technological changes in perspective and avoid undue nostalgia for the supposed "good old days," which probably never existed. In fact, the concept of a historical golden age of individual privacy, before the advent of computers, is something of an illusion. In these supposed good old days, when Americans lived in small towns or discrete urban neighborhoods, everyone knew everyone else, and everyone knew everyone else's business. Of course, the family doctor dutifully kept everyone's medical records secure and confidential, but if someone had a medical problem such as mental illness or alcoholism, everyone else in the community would have known about it.[5]

Aside from dealing with changes in information technology and new systems of healthcare financing and delivery, another major problem in protecting privacy is preventing employers from misusing medical information about their employees. This problem is caused by the peculiar U.S. system of health insurance, in which many people obtain coverage for themselves and their dependents through their place of employment. People with employment-based coverage want their employer or its agent to pay their medical bills but do not want their employer to look at their medical bills. Under this system, the employer or its agent has a legitimate reason to review medical bills and medical records to determine the appropriateness of payment. However, employers should not be allowed to use this personal health information to make other employment-related decisions, such as hiring and promotion. It is interesting to note that the same anachronistic system of employment-based coverage that causes so many problems in the availability and continuity of coverage also causes problems in protecting the privacy of medical information. Nevertheless, as others have pointed out, the alternative of a single-payer system of health coverage would pose a different and perhaps more serious threat to privacy by providing the medical bills and medical records of all citizens directly to the government.[6]

Despite the importance of protecting medical privacy, some situations occur in which the public interest requires that information be disclosed, even without the consent of the individual patient.[7] To prevent epidemics, for example, we want physicians to report communicable diseases to public health authorities. We also want healthcare providers to report gunshot wounds and suspected cases of child abuse to designated agencies, despite the consequent breach of confidentiality. In addition, the use and disclosure of medical records may be necessary to provide appropriate treatment and to conduct important medical and pharmaceutical research. Therefore, the issue of public policy is not merely a question of how to provide the maximum protection for individual privacy. Rather, it is a question of how to provide sufficient protection for individual privacy without interfering too much with other public needs, such as public safety, communicable disease control, medical treatment, and healthcare research.

State and federal governments have attempted to balance these conflicting policies when developing their laws on the privacy and disclosure of medical information. Historically, the role of the federal government in this area was somewhat limited, and most aspects of patient privacy have been subject to the laws of the states. Since 1996, however, the federal government has begun to play a major role in patient privacy through the enactment of the Health Insurance Portability and Accountability Act (HIPAA) and the adoption of the federal HIPAA privacy rule. Although it is very detailed, the federal privacy rule does not totally preempt the field of patient confidentiality. Rather, state laws will continue to apply when they impose higher standards than the federal rule and when they deal with issues that are not addressed in the federal rule. Therefore, it is still necessary to consider both the federal privacy rule and the laws of the individual states.

State Laws on Privacy of Patient Information

Historically, the confidentiality of patient information has been governed by the laws of the individual states. Those state laws, however, have been referred to as "a patchwork of State laws and regulations that are incomplete and, at times, inconsistent."[8] The state laws are different in many respects from one state to the next, and laws in some states provide more privacy protection than those in other states. Moreover, even within each individual state, confidentiality laws do not provide comprehensive protection for the privacy of medical information.

Many state privacy laws are provider specific in the sense that each law only applies to information in the possession of a specific type of provider. For example, most states have statutes or common-law rules of evidence that prevent physicians from having to disclose patient confidences on the witness stand, unless the patient waives the physician–patient privilege. Those same states may have separate statutes or regulations that apply to the patient records maintained by hospitals, other healthcare facilities, health departments, pharmacies, insurance companies, and health maintenance organizations (HMOs). Ordinarily, those provider-specific laws do not protect the confidentiality of information once it has been transferred to a different type of entity.

Many state laws are disease specific as well, in that they only apply to records that indicate a particular diagnosis or treatment for a particular disease. For example, some states have specific statutes or rules that protect the records of AIDS or HIV-positive patients. Other states provide special protection for genetic information as a way to prevent discrimination on the basis of those characteristics. States also have laws that require providers to report communicable diseases and regulate the use of the reported information. However, those state laws are often limited to the specific diseases that are identified by name in the statutes or regulations.

State laws may also provide a legal remedy for unauthorized disclosure of confidential information. One of the inherent obligations of the provider-patient relationship is to preserve the confidences of the patient. Subject to certain exceptions, providers have a duty to refrain from disclosing information about their patients. In addition, practitioners and facilities have a duty to exercise reasonable care to prevent disclosure by their employees and must take reasonable steps to prevent unauthorized access to patients' records by third parties. If these duties are breached, the practitioner or facility could be held liable for damages under the laws of the state. As one court explained,

> [w]e repeat here our earlier finding that a doctor who makes an unauthorized divulgence of confidence should respond in damages.
>
> Any time a doctor undertakes the treatment of a patient, and the consensual relationship of physician and patient is established, two jural obligations (of significance here) are simultaneously assumed by the doctor. Doctor and patient enter into a simple contract, the patient hoping that he will be cured and the doctor optimistically assuming that he will be compensated. As an implied condition of that contract, this Court is of the opinion that the doctor warrants that any confidential information gained through the relationship will not be released without the patient's permission. Almost every member of the public is aware of the promise of discretion contained in the Hippocratic Oath, and every patient has a right to rely upon this warranty of silence. The promise of secrecy is as much an express warranty as the advertisement of a commercial entrepreneur. Consequently, when a doctor

breaches his duty of secrecy, he is in violation of part of his obligations under the contract.

When a patient seeks out a doctor and retains him, he must
admit him to the most private part of the material domain of man.
Nothing material is more important or more intimate to man than
the health of his mind and body. Since the layman is unfamiliar
with the road to recovery, he cannot sift the circumstances of his
life and habits to determine what is information pertinent to his
health. As a consequence, he must disclose all information in his
consultations with his doctor—even that which is embarrassing,
disgraceful or incriminating. To promote full disclosure, the medical profession extends the promise of secrecy referred to above.
The candor which this promise elicits is necessary to the effective
pursuit of health; there can be no reticence, no reservation, no
reluctance when patients discuss their problems with their doctors.
But the disclosure is certainly intended to be private. If a doctor
should reveal any of these confidences, he surely effects an invasion of the privacy of his patient. We are of the opinion that the
preservation of the patient's privacy is no mere ethical duty upon
the part of the doctor; there is a legal duty as well. The unauthorized revelation of medical secrets, or any confidential communication given in the course of treatment, is tortuous conduct which
may be the basis for an action in damages.[9]

In accordance with these principles, patients have filed claims against
providers for unauthorized disclosure to the patient's employer, spouse,
and others. In one particularly egregious case, the patient's treating physician allegedly made an unauthorized disclosure about the patient's medical condition and use of prescription drugs to the patient's former spouse,
who was also a physician.[10] Then the former spouse used that information
against the patient in their pending legal dispute over custody of their children. In that case, the Supreme Court of Washington held that the patient
could state a valid claim against the treating physician for unauthorized
disclosure under the general state statute for medical malpractice, because
the treating physician had made the disclosure in the context of providing
healthcare services to the patient.[11]

In other situations, however, healthcare providers may be held legally
liable for failing to disclose confidential information about a patient who
poses a danger to others. For example, in *Tarasoff v. Regents of the University
of California*,[12] the patient had told his therapist that he intended to kill a
particular person, and subsequently did so. In a suit by the parents of the
victim, the court held that the therapist should have warned the intended
victim, even though it would have required disclosure of confidential information. As explained by the court in that case,

We recognize the public interest in supporting effective treatment of mental illness and in protecting the rights of patients to privacy . . . and the consequent public importance of safeguarding the confidential character of psychotherapeutic communication. Against this interest, however, we must weigh the public interest in safety from violent assault. . . .

We realize that the open and confidential character of psychotherapeutic dialogue encourages patients to express threats of violence, few of which are ever executed. Certainly a therapist should not be encouraged routinely to reveal such threats; such disclosures could seriously disrupt the patient's relationship with his therapist and with the persons threatened. To the contrary, the therapist's obligations to his patient require that he not disclose a confidence unless such disclosure is necessary to avert danger to others, and even then that he do so discreetly, and in a fashion that would preserve the privacy of his patient to the fullest extent compatible with the prevention of the threatened danger.

The revelation of a communication under the above circumstances is not a breach of trust or a violation of professional ethics. . . . We conclude that the public policy favoring protection of the confidential character of patient-psychotherapist communications must yield to the extent to which disclosure is essential to avert danger to others. The protective privilege ends where the public peril begins.[13]

In addition to balancing the public policies in that case, the court attempted to establish a standard to guide practitioners in determining when disclosure is required.

When a therapist determines, or pursuant to the standards of his profession should determine, that his patient presents a serious danger of violence to another, he incurs an obligation to use reasonable care to protect the intended victim against such danger. The discharge of this duty may require the therapist to take one or more of various steps, depending upon the nature of the case. Thus it may call for him to warn the intended victim or others likely to apprise the victim of the danger, to notify the police, or to take whatever other steps are reasonably necessary under the circumstances.[14]

As the court pointed out, disclosure of patient information under these circumstances is consistent with the AMA's Principles of Medical Ethics.[15] In fact, the current version of the AMA's Fundamental Elements of the Patient-Physician Relationship provides that "[t]he physician should not reveal confidential communications or information without the

consent of the patient, unless provided for by law or by the need to protect the welfare of the individual or the public interest."[16]

Under these circumstances, healthcare providers may be held liable
under state law for improperly disclosing patient information or for improperly failing to disclose patient information. The legal duties to disclose and
not to disclose will depend on the specific facts of each particular case.
Depending on the facts, disclosure of patient information may be prohibited, required, or permitted at the option of the provider. In addition,
providers must comply with the requirements of federal law as discussed
in the next section.

Federal Law and the HIPAA Privacy Rule

Before 1996, federal involvement in the field of patient privacy was limited to a few specific areas. Federal law restricts the disclosure of treatment
records for alcoholism and substance abuse.[17] In addition, federal law provides rules for conducting research with human subjects in institutions that
receive federal support, including a requirement for "adequate provisions
to protect the privacy of subjects and to maintain the confidentiality of
data."[18] Of course, federal law also regulates the confidentiality and disclosure of records in the possession of federal agencies.[19]

The most significant federal involvement in patient privacy began in
1996 when Congress enacted HIPAA.[20] In that statute, Congress recognized that electronic transmission of health information could improve the
efficiency of the healthcare system,[21] but it also recognized the importance
of protecting "the privacy of individually identifiable health information."[22]
Therefore, Congress required the secretary of HHS to adopt various standards for electronic exchange of information, such as standards for transactions, data elements, and code sets; a standard unique health identifier;
electronic signatures; and the security of health information.[23]

With regard to privacy, however, Congress took a different approach
to developing federal standards, putting a process in motion with a series
of statutory deadlines.[24] First, Congress directed the secretary of HHS to
make recommendations to Congress within one year on the protection of
privacy, including consideration of individual rights and the appropriate
use and transfer of medical information. In addition, Congress gave itself
three years to enact privacy standards by means of additional legislation.
Under the HIPAA statute, if Congress fails to enact privacy standards by
new legislation within three years, the secretary of HHS is required to adopt
standards for protecting privacy by means of a rule.

The secretary of HHS made her recommendations to Congress on
the privacy of medical information, but Congress was unable to enact additional legislation by the end of the three-year period. Congress did

consider some proposals for additional legislation,[25] but the issues of privacy and disclosure proved to be too complicated and controversial for action by Congress.

Therefore, on November 3, 1999, the Secretary of HHS issued her standards for protecting privacy in the form of a proposed rule.[26] During the public comment period, HHS received 52,000 comments on the proposed rule. After that period, on December 28, 2000, the Secretary issued the final rule.[27] (Although it is referred to as "a rule," it actually is a long and complicated set of rules. When published in the *Federal Register* with three columns of small print per page, the final rule was 31 pages and was accompanied by 336 additional pages of explanatory material from HHS.)

Originally, the final rule was supposed to become effective on February 26, 2001. However, because of an administrative error, it did not become effective until April 14, 2001. Most individuals and organizations that are subject to the rule had to be in compliance by April 14, 2003, although small health plans had until April 14, 2004, to comply. Some healthcare organizations have challenged the validity of the privacy rule on a variety of constitutional and statutory grounds, but courts have rejected those arguments and upheld the validity of the rule.[28]

In the meantime, healthcare providers, payers, researchers, and other organizations devoted their attention and resources to making the procedural and technological changes needed to comply with the rule. Of course, the government and the industry have different perceptions of the burden and different estimates of the cost of complying with the rule. The truth is probably somewhere in the middle of those competing estimates.

In addition to raising concerns about the cost and burden of compliance, many industry organizations argued that the privacy rule would have the unintended and undesired effects of interfering with some healthcare treatment and research. For example, providers complained that requirements for prior written consent by the patient for using or disclosing information could delay necessary medical care. In addition, medical schools and other research organizations argued that strict requirements for the use of individually identifiable data would prevent important medical, pharmaceutical, and healthcare research.

The federal government responded to some of these concerns by making several changes to the final privacy rule. After issuing proposed modifications on March 27, 2002,[29] HHS issued a final rule on August 14, 2002, that modifies the previous final rule.[30] According to HHS,

> [t]he purpose of these modifications is to maintain strong protections for the privacy of individually identifiable health information while clarifying certain of the Privacy Rule's provisions, addressing the unintended negative effects of the Privacy Rule on health care quality or access to health care, and relieving unintended administrative burdens created by the Privacy Rule.[31]

In issuing its August 2002 modifications, HHS made a significant change on the issue of whether to require prior written consent by the patient for using or disclosing information. As discussed previously, some providers had argued that the original requirements for prior consent would cause delays in providing necessary care. Therefore, in the August 2002 modifications, HHS eliminated the requirement for prior written consent in the context of particular functions such as medical treatment. However, HHS enhanced the requirement to provide notice of the covered entity's privacy policies by requiring those providers who treat patients directly to try in good faith to have patients acknowledge in writing that the notice was received.

Several organizations of healthcare consumers and providers challenged HHS's elimination of the requirement to obtain a patient's prior consent for using or disclosing information. However, in that case the federal district court upheld HHS's August 2002 modifications to the HIPAA privacy rule, and the Court of Appeals for the Third Circuit affirmed that decision. Following is an excerpt from the decision of the Court of Appeals in that case.

CITIZENS FOR HEALTH V. LEAVITT, 428 F.3D 167 (3RD CIR. 2005), *CERT. DENIED*, 127 S. CT. 3 (2006) (CITATIONS, FOOTNOTES, AND SOME PARTS OF TEXT OMITTED)

Appellant Citizens for Health, along with nine other national and state associations and nine individuals (collectively "Citizens"), brought this action against the Secretary of the United States Department of Health and Human Services ("HHS" or "Agency") challenging a rule promulgated by the Agency pursuant to the administrative simplification provisions of the Health Insurance Portability and Accountability Act of 1996 ("HIPAA"). Citizens allege that the "Privacy Rule"—officially titled "Standards for Privacy of Individually Identifiable Health Information"—is invalid because it unlawfully authorizes health plans, health care clearinghouses, and certain health care providers to use and disclose personal health information for so-called "routine uses" without patient consent. . . . Citizens challenge subsection (a) as authorizing disclosures that, they contend, violate individual privacy rights.

The District Court granted summary judgment to the Secretary on all of Citizens' claims based on its conclusions that the promulgation of the Privacy Rule did not violate the Administrative Procedure Act [the "APA"], that the Secretary did not exceed the scope of authority granted to him by HIPAA, and that, insofar as the Privacy Rule is permissive and does not compel any uses or disclosures of personal health information by providers, it does not affirmatively interfere with any right protected by the First or Fifth Amendments.

Because we reason to the same conclusions reached by the District Court, albeit under a slightly different analysis, we will affirm.

I. BACKGROUND

The objectionable provision is only one aspect of a complex set of regulations that is the last in a series of attempts by HHS to strike a balance between two competing objectives of HIPAA—improving the efficiency and effectiveness of the national health care system and preserving individual privacy in personal health information.

A. HIPAA

HIPAA was passed by Congress in August 1996 to address a number of issues regarding the national health care and health insurance system. The statutory provisions relevant to the issues in this case are found in Subtitle F of Title II. Aimed at "administrative simplification," HIPAA Sections 261 through 264 provide for "the establishment of standards and requirements for the electronic transmission of certain health information." More specifically, these provisions direct the Secretary to adopt uniform national standards for the secure electronic exchange of health information.

Section 264 prescribes the process by which standards regarding the privacy of individually identifiable health information were to be adopted. This process contemplated that, within a year of HIPAA's enactment, the Secretary would submit detailed recommendations on such privacy standards, including individual rights concerning individually identifiable health information, procedures for exercising such rights, and the "uses and disclosures of such information that should be authorized or required," to Congress. If Congress did not enact further legislation within three years of HIPAA's enactment, the Secretary was directed to promulgate final regulations implementing the standards within 42 months of HIPAA's enactment. The Act specified that any regulation promulgated pursuant to the authority of Section 264 would provide a federal baseline for privacy protection, but that such regulations would "not supercede a contrary provision of State law, if the provision of State law imposes requirements, standards, or implementation specifications that are more stringent than the requirements, standards, or implementation specifications imposed under the regulation."

B. The Privacy Rule

Because Congress did not enact privacy legislation by its self-imposed three-year deadline, the Secretary promulgated the privacy standards contemplated in Section 264 through an administrative rulemaking process. During this process, the Rule went through four iterations: the Proposed Original Rule, the Original Rule, the Proposed Amended Rule, and the Amended Rule. The Original Rule required covered entities to seek individual consent before using or disclosing protected health information for routine uses. Before the Original Rule could take effect, however, the Secretary was inundated with unsolicited criticism, principally from health care insurers and providers, warning that the Original Rule's mandatory consent provisions would significantly impact the ability of the health care industry to operate efficiently. He responded by reopening the rulemaking process. The final result was the Amended Rule—the currently effective, codified version of the Privacy Rule which is the subject of Citizens' challenge here.

The Amended Rule retains most of the Original Rule's privacy protections. It prohibits "covered entities"—defined as health plans, health care clearinghouses, and health care providers who transmit any health information in electronic form in connection with a transaction covered by the regulations—from using or disclosing an individual's "protected health information"—defined as individually identifiable health information maintained in or transmitted in any form or media including electronic media—except as otherwise provided by the Rule. Covered entities must seek authorization from individuals before using or disclosing information unless a specific exception applies. Uses and disclosures that the Amended Rule allows must be limited to the "minimum necessary" to accomplish the intended purpose.

The Amended Rule departs from the Original Rule in one crucial respect. Where the Original Rule required covered entities to seek individual consent to use or disclose health information in all but the narrowest of circumstances, the Amended Rule allows such uses and disclosures without patient consent for "treatment, payment, and health care operations"—so-called "routine uses." "Health care operations," the broadest category under the routine use exception, refers to a range of management functions of covered entities, including quality assessment, practitioner evaluation, student training programs, insurance rating, auditing services, and business planning and development. The Rule allows individuals the right to request restrictions on uses and disclosures of protected health information and to enter into agreements with covered entities regarding such restrictions, but does not require covered entities to abide by such requests or to agree to any restriction. The Rule also permits, but does not require, covered entities to design and implement a consent process for routine uses and disclosures.

Importantly, the Rule contains detailed preemption provisions, which are consistent with HIPAA Sections 1178(a)(2)(B) and 264(c)(2). These provisions establish that the Rule is intended as a "federal floor" for privacy protection, allowing state law to control where a "provision of State law relates to the privacy of individually identifiable health information and is more stringent than a standard, requirement, or implementation specification adopted under [the Privacy Rule]."

II. PROCEDURAL HISTORY

Citizens filed this action on April 10, 2003. In its Amended Complaint, Citizens alleged that the Secretary violated the APA and Sections 261 through 264 of HIPAA in promulgating the Amended Rule, and that, to the extent that the

Amended Rule rescinded or eliminated the need for consent for the use and disclosure of individually identifiable health information for "routine uses," the Amended Rule violated privacy rights protected by the Fifth Amendment and free speech rights protected by the First Amendment of the United States Constitution. Both parties moved for summary judgment, and, after a hearing on December 10, 2003, the District Court granted summary judgment in favor of the Secretary.

On Citizens' APA claims, the Court concluded that the Secretary had adequately informed the public regarding the proposed rulemaking, examined the relevant data, responded to public comments, and provided a reasoned analysis that rationally connected the facts with the decision to rescind the consent requirement in the Amended Rule. Regarding Citizens' claims alleging violations of HIPAA, the Court concluded that the changes in the Amended Rule were reasonably related to the legislative purpose of Subtitle F of the Act, and, because the Amended Rule was promulgated before the Original Rule took effect, the Amended Rule did not eliminate any "rights" created under the Original Rule. Finally, regarding Citizens' constitutional claims, the Court concluded that because (1) neither the First Amendment nor the Fifth Amendment places an affirmative obligation on the State to protect individuals' rights from harm by third parties and (2) the Amended Rule is wholly permissive as to whether covered entities seek consent from an individual before using or disclosing personal health information for routine uses, the Amended Rule did not violate individual rights under either Amendment. . . .

On appeal, Citizens reassert the claims they made before the District Court, that the Secretary, by promulgating the Privacy Rule, (1) unlawfully infringed Citzens' fundamental rights to privacy in personal health information under due process principles of the Fifth Amendment of the United States Constitution; (2) unlawfully infringed Citzens' rights to communicate privately with their medical practitioners under the First Amendment of the Constitution; (3) contravened Congress's intent in enacting HIPAA by eliminating Citizens' reasonable expectations of medical privacy; and (4) violated the APA by arbitrarily and capriciously reversing a settled course of behavior and adopting a policy that he had previously rejected. . . .

A. Fifth Amendment Substantive Due Process Claim

. . . . We begin our analysis with the premise that the right to medical privacy asserted by Citizens is legally cognizable under the Due Process Clause of the Fifth Amendment, although, as Citizens themselves concede, its "boundaries . . . have not been exhaustively delineated." Whatever those boundaries may be, it is undisputed that a violation of a citizen's right to medical privacy rises to the level of a constitutional claim only when that violation can properly be ascribed to the government. The Constitution protects against state interference with fundamental rights. It only applies to restrict private behavior in limited circumstances. Because such circumstances are not present in this case, and because the "violations" of the right to medical privacy that Citizens have asserted, if they amount to violations of that right at all, occurred at the hands of private entities, the protections of the Due Process Clause of the Fifth Amendment are not implicated in this case. We will accordingly affirm the District Court's finding that the Secretary did not violate Citizens' constitutional rights when he promulgated the Amended Rule. . . .

The fact that covered entities are construing the "may use" language as constituting a new federal seal of approval, and may be ignoring state laws regarding protections to be afforded to such information, is regrettable and disquieting. That routine requests for privacy are apparently being ignored by covered entities is even more unfortunate. But our task here is to determine the constitutionality of the Amended Rule, not the propriety of covered entities' actions under state or common law. Because, for all of the reasons stated above, the covered entities' actions that Citizens challenge do not implicate the federal government, we reject Citizens' Fifth Amendment claim.

B. First Amendment Claim

Citizens' First Amendment claim is that the Amended Rule infringes individuals' right to confidential communications with health care practitioners, i.e., a right to refrain from public speech regarding private personal health information. Citizens argue that the effect of the Amended Rule is to chill speech between individuals and their health care practitioners because the possibility of nonconsensual disclosures makes individuals less likely to participate fully in diagnosis and treatment and more likely to be evasive and withhold important information. . . .

Citizens' First Amendment claim fails on the same grounds as their Fifth Amendment claim: the potential "chilling" of patients' rights to free speech derives not from any action of the government, but from the independent decisions of private parties with respect to the use and disclosure of individual health information. For all of the reasons enumerated above, the decisions of the private parties to use or disclose private health information in reliance on the Amended Rule, which may or may not "chill" expression between health care providers and their patients, does not implicate the government in a way that gives rise to a constitutional claim. We will therefore affirm the District Court's grant of summary judgment to the Secretary on Citizens' First Amendment claim.

C. Claims Alleging Violations of HIPAA

In claims based on HIPAA's statutory language, Citizens argue (1) that the Secretary exceeded the regulatory authority delegated by HIPAA because the Act only authorizes the Secretary to promulgate regulations that enhance privacy and (2) that the Amended Rule impermissibly retroactively rescinded individual rights created by the Original Rule and disturbed Citizens' "settled expectations" in the privacy of their health information. We find the District Court's analysis of these statutory claims to be cogent. Citizens argue that the Secretary has eliminated their reasonable expectations of medical privacy retroactively and prospectively and that such action is inconsistent with Congress's intent in enacting HIPAA. However, Citizens' argument that the controlling policy underlying HIPAA is medical privacy and that the Amended Rule wholly sacrifices this interest to covered entities' interests in efficiency and flexibility ignores the Act's stated goals of "simplifying the administration of health insurance," and "improving the efficiency and effectiveness of the health care system." As the District Court aptly explained, HIPAA requires the Secretary to "balance privacy protection and the efficiency of the health care system—not simply to enhance privacy." We thus conclude that Citizens' first HIPAA claim lacks merit.

We also agree with the District Court's finding that the Amended Rule does not retroactively eliminate rights that Citizens enjoyed under the Original Rule or under various laws or standards of practice that existed before the Amended Rule went into effect. Because the Original Rule was amended before its compliance date, "covered entities were never under a legal obligation to comply with the Original Rule's consent requirement." Citizens, therefore, never enjoyed any rights under the Original Rule at all. Nor does the Amended Rule retroactively eliminate Citizens' reasonable expectations based on state law, standards of medical ethics, and established standards of practice because the Amended Rule does not disturb any preexisting, "more stringent" state law privacy rights. Accordingly, we reject Citizens' second HIPPA [sic] claim as well, and will affirm the grant of summary judgment to the Secretary on these claims.

D. APA Claims

Lastly, Citizens challenge the rulemaking process under the APA, contending that (1) the Secretary's rulemaking was arbitrary and capricious ... and (2) the Secretary failed to provide adequate notice of the rescission of the consent requirement of the Original Rule.... Citizens argue that the Secretary acted arbitrarily and capriciously by failing to adequately explain the rescission of the consent requirement, ignoring earlier findings, and failing to respond to public comments.

We dispose of Citizens' argument that the Secretary did not provide adequate notice to the public of his intention to rescind the consent requirement first. On this point, the District Court correctly pointed out that the APA requires a notice to provide either "the terms or substance of the proposed rule" or "a description of the subjects and issues involved." In this case, the Notice for Proposed Rulemaking did both. We will therefore affirm the District Court's grant of summary judgment to the Secretary on this claim.

We also reject Citizens' claim that the Secretary acted arbitrarily and capriciously in promulgating the Amended Rule. Citizens argue that the Secretary acted arbitrarily and capriciously in promulgating the Amended Rule by improperly reversing a "settled course of behavior" established in the Original Rule and adopting a policy that he had previously rejected. When an agency rejects a "settled course of behavior," however, it need only supply a "reasoned analysis" for the change to overcome any presumption that the settled rule best carries out the policies committed to the agency by Congress. Such an analysis requires the agency to "examine the relevant data and articulate a satisfactory explanation for its action including a "rational connection between the facts found and the choice made."'"

Here, the Secretary examined the relevant data, and gave adequate consideration to the large volume of public comments that HHS received during the rulemaking process. The Secretary considered other alternatives and explained why they were unworkable. The Secretary also considered Congress's dual goals in devising the privacy standards, i.e., protecting the confidentiality of personal health information and improving the efficiency and effectiveness of the national health care system.

In sum, the Secretary's decision to respond to the unintended negative effects and administrative burdens of the Original Rule by rescinding the consent requirement for routine uses and implementing more stringent notice requirements was explained in a detailed analysis that rationally connected the decision to the facts. . . . [W]e agree with the District Court's analysis and conclusion that the Secretary's decision was reasonable given the findings and that the Secretary did not act arbitrarily and capriciously in violation of the APA. Accordingly, we will affirm the grant of summary judgment to the Secretary on these claims.

V. Conclusion

For the reasons set forth above, we will AFFIRM the judgment of the District Court.

As a practical matter, the requirements of the privacy rule are very complex. For most requirements, there are exceptions, and often there are exceptions to the exceptions. In general, the rule limits the circumstances in which a "covered entity" may use or disclose "protected health information." The covered entities are health plans, healthcare clearinghouses, and healthcare providers that transmit information by electronic means. This would include health insurance companies, HMOs, the Medicare and Medicaid programs, healthcare facilities, institutional providers, and most physician practices. Subject to certain exceptions, the privacy rule protects health information that identifies an individual or could be used to identify an individual.

Covered entities have many obligations under the rule. First, they have the negative obligation to not use or disclose information except in accordance with the rule. For some purposes, the covered entity must limit disclosure to the minimum amount of information that is necessary to accomplish that purpose. However, there are exceptions to that requirement, and it does not apply to disclosures for the purpose of treatment. If the purpose of the disclosure falls within the definition of "marketing," the rule sets forth additional requirements that must be satisfied.

Covered entities also have affirmative obligations. For example, they are required to establish policies, provide notices, conduct employee training, designate a privacy official and a person to receive complaints, put safeguards into place to protect confidentiality, and retain documents as provided by the rule.

In addition, HHS recognized the need to protect health information when covered entities use the services of other organizations, such as accountants, lawyers, computer technicians, and accrediting organizations. In performing certain functions for the covered entity, those "business associates" would have access to individually identifiable information about the patients or members of the covered entity. However, those other organizations are not included within the definition of covered entity, and they are not subject to direct regulation under the privacy rule. Thus, the privacy rule protects health information in the hands of those organizations by requiring covered entities to enter into specific written agreements with their business associates.

Some providers complained about the burden of renegotiating contracts with all of their business associates by the deadline set forth in the original rule. Therefore, HHS provided some relief in the August 2002 modifications by means of transition rules and sample contract provisions.

Individuals have certain rights under the rule. In general, and subject to various exceptions, individuals have the right to obtain their own health information, request corrections to statements in their medical records, and obtain an "accounting of disclosures" to find out who has received information from their records.

The privacy rule is enforced by the HHS Office for Civil Rights, and there are significant penalties for violating the rule. Civil penalties may be as high as $25,000, and criminal penalties for more serious violations can be as high as $250,000 or ten years in prison. The HIPAA statute does not explicitly provide a private cause of action for patients to seek damages from those who improperly disclose their records. However, creative lawyers may be able to assert claims for civil liability under existing state laws by arguing that the federal privacy rule is the "standard of care" for purposes of state law claims.[32]

If the individual patient is a minor, the parent would ordinarily have the right to consent to treatment on behalf of the minor and obtain the minor's medical information. However, some states have laws that permit minors to consent on their own for treatment of specific conditions such as substance abuse or sexually transmitted diseases. If the minor may lawfully give consent to treatment, state law might prohibit disclosure of information to the parent. This issue has led to conflict between some healthcare providers, who believe privacy will encourage adolescents to seek treatment, and some officials at HHS, who believe parents should have access to medical information about their children, especially with regard to drug abuse and abortion. Under the statutory scheme set forth in HIPAA, this issue is generally governed by the law of the individual state.[33]

The relationship between federal and state law affects other issues as well. Some people believe privacy should be governed by a single federal standard to have uniformity throughout the country. Under that theory, a federal law should preempt or supersede any state law on the subject of healthcare privacy. Others argue that the federal law should merely establish the minimum standard or "floor" for privacy protection, and individual states should be permitted to impose more stringent protections within their individual states. Under that approach, compliance with the federal privacy rule would not relieve covered entities from the obligation to comply with applicable state laws as well. Although it seems desirable to allow states to provide additional protections for privacy if they so desire, serious problems of practicality could arise in subjecting a nationwide system of electronic transactions to different privacy standards in different states. Nevertheless, in the HIPAA legislation, Congress resolved this issue of federalism in favor of greater flexibility for the states instead of nationwide uniformity. Under HIPAA, the privacy rule adopted by HHS does not supersede or preempt state laws that provide a higher level of protection for the privacy of healthcare information.[34]

In connection with its August 2002 modifications, HHS issued a fact sheet that described some of its most important changes.[35] An excerpt from this fact sheet, dated August 9, 2002, follows.

MODIFICATIONS TO THE STANDARDS FOR PRIVACY OF INDIVIDUALLY IDENTIBIABLE HEALTH INFORMATION — FINAL RULE

. . . .

FINAL MODIFICATIONS:

Marketing—The final Rule requires a covered entity to obtain an individual's prior written authorization to use his or her protected health information for marketing purposes except for a face-to-face encounter or a communication involving a promotional gift of nominal value. The Department defines marketing to distinguish between the types of communications that are and are not marketing, and makes clear that a covered entity is prohibited from selling lists of patients and enrollees to third parties or from disclosing protected health information to a third party for the marketing activities of the third party, without the individual's authorization. The Rule clarifies that doctors and other covered entities communicating with patients about treatment options or the covered entity's own health-related products and services are not considered marketing. For example, health care plans can inform patients of additional health plan coverage and value-added items and services, such as discounts for prescription drugs or eyeglasses.

Consent and Notice—The Department makes changes to protect privacy while eliminating barriers to treatment by strengthening the notice requirement and making consent for routine health care delivery purposes (known as treatment, payment, and health care operations) optional. The Rule requires covered entities to provide patients with notice of the patient's privacy rights and the privacy practices of the covered entity. The strengthened notice requires direct treatment providers to make a good faith effort to obtain patient's written acknowledgment of the notice of privacy rights and practices. The final Rule promotes access to care by removing mandatory consent requirements that would inhibit patient access to health care while providing covered entities with the option of developing a consent process that works for that entity. The Rule also allows consent requirements already in place to continue.

Uses and Disclosures Regarding Food and Drug Administration (FDA)–Regulated Products and Activities—The final Rule permits covered entities to disclose protected health information, without authorization, to a person subject to the jurisdiction of the FDA for public health purposes related to the quality, safety or effectiveness of FDA-regulated products or activities such as collecting or reporting adverse events, dangerous products, and defects or problems with FDA-regulated products. This assures that information will continue to be available to protect public health and safety, as it is today.

Incidental Use and Disclosure—The final Rule acknowledges that uses or disclosures that are incidental to an otherwise permitted use or disclosure may occur. Such incidental uses or disclosures are not considered a violation of the Rule provided that the covered entity has met the reasonable safeguards and minimum necessary requirements. For example, if these requirements are met, doctors' offices may use waiting room sign-in sheets, hospitals may keep patient charts at bedside, doctors can talk to patients in semi-private rooms, and doctors can confer at nurse's stations without fear of violating the rule if overheard by a passerby.

Authorization—The final Rule clarifies the authorization requirements to the Privacy Rule to, among other things, eliminate separate authorization requirements for covered entities. Patients will have to grant permission in advance for each type of non-routine use or disclosure, but providers will not have to use different types of forms. These modifications also consolidate and streamline core elements and notification requirements.

Minimum Necessary—The final Rule exempts from the minimum necessary standards any uses or disclosures for which the covered entity has received an authorization. The Rule previously exempted only certain types of authorizations from the minimum necessary requirement, but since the rule will only have one type of authorization, the exemption is now applied to all authorizations. Minimum necessary requirements are still in effect to ensure an individual's privacy for most other uses and disclosures.

The Department clarifies in the preamble that the minimum necessary standard is not intended to impede disclosures necessary for workers' compensation programs. The Department will actively monitor to ensure that workers' compensation programs are not unduly affected by the Rule.

Parents and Minors—The final Rule clarifies that state law, or other applicable law, governs in the area of parents and minors. Generally, the Privacy Rule provides parents with new rights to control the health information about their minor children, with limited exceptions that are based on state or other applicable law and professional practice. For example, where a state has explicitly addressed disclosure of a minor's health information to a parent, or access to a child's medical record by a parent, the final Rule clarifies that state law governs. In addition, the final Rule clarifies that, in the special cases in which the minor controls his or her own health information under such law and that law does not define the parents' ability to access the child's health information a licensed health care provider continues to be able to exercise discretion to grant or deny such access as long as that decision is consistent with the state or other applicable law.

Business Associates—The final Rule gives covered entities (except small health plans) up to an additional year to change existing written contracts to come into compliance with the business associate requirements. The additional time will ease the burden of covered entities renegotiating contracts all at once. The Department has also provided sample business associate contract provisions.

Research—The final Rule facilitates researchers' use of a single combined form to obtain informed consent for the research and authorization to use or disclose protected health information for such research. The final Rule also clarifies the requirements relating to a researcher obtaining an IRB [institutional review board] or Privacy Board waiver of authorization by streamlining the privacy waiver criteria to more closely follow the requirement of the "Common Rule," which governs federally funded research. The transition provisions have been expanded to prevent needless interruption of ongoing research.

Limited Data Set—The final Rule permits the creation and dissemination of a limited data set (that does not include directly identifiable information) for research, public health, and health care operations. In addition, to further protect privacy, the final Rule conditions disclosure of the limited data set on a covered entity and the recipient entering into a data use agreement, in which the recipient would agree to limit the use of the data set for the purposes for which it was given, and to ensure the security of the data, as well as not to identify the information or use it to contact any individual.

OTHER PROVISIONS:

. . . .

Group Health Plan Disclosures of Enrollment and Disenrollment Information— The final Rule allows a group health plan, a health insurance issuer, or HMO acting for a group health plan to disclose to a plan sponsor, such as an employer, information on whether the individual is enrolled in or has disenrolled from a plan offered by the sponsor without amending the plan documents.

Accounting of Disclosure—The final Rule exempts disclosures made pursuant to an authorization from the accounting requirements. The authorization process itself adequately protects individual privacy by assuring that the individual's permission is given both knowingly and voluntarily. The final Rule also exempts from the accounting requirements incidental disclosures, and disclosures that are part of a limited data set. The Rule provides a simplified alternative approach for accounting for multiple research disclosures that includes providing a description of the research for which an individual's protected health information may have been disclosed and the researcher's contact information . . .

Protected Health Information: Exclusion for Employment Records—The final Rule clarifies that employment records maintained by a covered entity in its capacity as an employer are excluded from the definition of protected health information. The modifications do not change the fact that individually identifiable health information created, received, or maintained by a covered entity in its health care capacity is protected health information.

The final Rule also includes technical corrections and additional clarifications related to various sections of the existing rule. The final Rule is designed to ensure that protections for patient privacy are implemented in a manner that maximizes privacy while not compromising either the availability or the quality of medical care.

On July 6, 2001, the Department issued its first guidance to answer common questions and clarify certain of the Privacy Rule's provisions. The Department is committed to assisting covered entities come into compliance with the Rule. Therefore, the Department will update the guidance to reflect the modifications adopted in this final Rule. The revised guidance will be available on the HHS Office for Civil Rights Privacy Web site at www.hhs.gov/ocr/hipaa/.

Notes

1.   American Medical Association, *Code of Medical Ethics, Principles of Medical Ethics*, point IV (2001). [Online document; retrieved

1/18/07.] www.ama-assn.org/apps/pf_new/pf_online-f_n
=browse&doc=policyfiles/E0.00.HTM&&s_t=&st_p=&nth=1&pre
v_pol=policyfiles/HnE/H-525.998.HTM&nxt_pol=policyfiles/E-
1.00.HTM&.

2. American College of Healthcare Executives, *Code of Ethics* (2003).
   [Online document; retrieved 1/18/07.] www.ache.org/
   ABT_ACHE/code.cfm.

3. U.S. Department of Health and Human Services, "HHS Announces
   Final Regulation Establishing First-Ever National Standards To
   Protect Patients' Personal Medical Records," Press Release,
   December 20, 2000. [Online document; retrieved 1/18/07.]
   www.hhs.gov/news/press/2000pres/20001220.html.

4. See Standards for Privacy of Individually Identifiable Health
   Information, 65 Fed. Reg. 82,462, 82,465 (Dec. 28, 2000) ("[T]he
   disclosure of information may require only the push of a button.").

5. *Id.* ("In some ways, this imperfect system of record keeping created
   a false sense of privacy among patients, providers, and others.").

6. D.A. Hyman and M. Hall, "Two Cheers for Employment-Based
   Health Insurance," *Yale Journal of Health Policy, Law & Ethics*,
   (II)(1) (2001): 23–58, at 33.

7. See generally C. Scott, "Is Too Much Privacy Bad for Your Health?
   An Introduction to the Law, Ethics, and HIPAA Rule on Medical
   Privacy," *Georgia State University Law Review*, 17(2) (2000):
   481–529, at 494–95 ("Maine citizens seem to have concluded that
   too much privacy could be bad for their health.").

8. 65 Fed. Reg. at 82,466.

9. *Hammonds v. Aetna Casualty & Surety Co.*, 243 F. Supp. 793,
   801–802 (N.D. Ohio 1965) (applying Ohio law where the jurisdiction of the federal court was based on diversity of citizenship).

10. *Berger v. Sonneland*, 26 P.3d 257 (Wash. 2001).

11. *Id.* at 265–267 (rejecting the treating physician's argument that the
    state medical privacy statute was the exclusive remedy, in which case
    the patient's claim would have been time-barred by failure to meet
    the statute of limitations).

12. 551 P.2d 334 (Cal. 1976).

13. *Id.* at 346–47 (citations and footnotes omitted).

14. *Id.* at 340.

15. *Id.* at 347.

16. American Medical Association, *Code of Medical Ethics*, 10.01:
    Fundamental Elements of the Patient-Physician Relationship.
    [Online document; retrieved 1/18/07.] www.ama-assn.org/
    ama/pub/category/8313.html.

17. 42 C.F.R. §§ 2.1 *et seq.* (2005).

18. 45 C.F.R. § 46.111(a)(7) (2005) (criteria for IRB approval).

19. See Scott, *supra* note 7, at 508.

20. Health Insurance Portability and Accountability Act of 1996, Pub. L. No. 104-191, 110 Stat. 1936 (1996).

21. *Id.* § 261, 110 Stat. at 2021.

22. *Id.* § 264, 110 Stat. at 2033.

23. *Id.* § 262, 110 Stat. at 2021.

24. *Id.* § 264, 110 Stat. at 2033.

25. See, e.g., proposed Medical Information Privacy and Security Act, S. 573, 106th Cong. (1999) [sponsored by Senators Patrick Leahy (D-VT), Thomas Daschle (D-SD), Byron Dorgan (D-ND), and Edward Kennedy (D-MA)]; proposed Consumer Health and Research Technology Protection Act, H.R. 3900, 105th Cong. (1998) [sponsored by Representatives Christopher Shays (R-CT) and Thomas Barrett (D-WI)].

26. Standards for Privacy of Individually Identifiable Health Information, 64 Fed. Reg. 59,918 (Nov. 3, 1999) (proposed rule).

27. Standards for Privacy of Individually Identifiable Health Information, 65 Fed. Reg. 82,462 (Dec. 28, 2000) (final rule).

28. See, e.g., *South Carolina Medical Association v. Thompson*, 327 F.3d 346 (4th Cir. 2003); *Association of American Physicians & Surgeons, Inc. v. U.S. Department of Health and Human Services*, 224 F. Supp. 2d 1115 (S.D. Tex. 2002), *aff'd* 67 Fed. Appx. 253 (5th Cir. 2003).

29. Standards for Privacy of Individually Identifiable Health Information, 67 Fed. Reg. 14,776 (March 27, 2002) (proposed rule; modification).

30. Standards for Privacy of Individually Identifiable Health Information, 67 Fed. Reg. 53,182 (Aug. 14, 2002) (final rule).

31. *Id.* at 53,182.

32. J. Kulynych and D. Korn, "The Effect of the New Federal Medical-Privacy Rule on Research," *New England Journal of Medicine*, 346(3) (2002): 201–204, at 203.

33. See generally, 67 Fed. Reg. at 53,200–201.

34. Health Insurance Portability and Accountability Act of 1996, Pub. L. No. 104–191, § 264(c)(2), 110 Stat. 1936, 2033–34 (1996).

35. U.S. Department of Health and Human Services, *Modifications to the Standards for Privacy of Individually Identifiable Health Information—Final Rule* (August 9, 2002). [Online document; retrieved 1/18/07.] www.hhs.gov/news/press/2002pres/20020809.html.

MEDICAL STAFF MEMBERSHIP AND CLINICAL PRIVILEGES

One of the most important aspects of healthcare law is the relationship between physicians and healthcare facilities or organizations. Under the law of medical malpractice, as discussed in Chapter 10, patients often seek to hold a hospital or other healthcare organization liable for a physician's negligence. Ordinarily, the result in that type of case depends on the precise nature of the relationship between the physician and the institution. That relationship also raises issues under the law of Medicare fraud and abuse. As explained in Chapter 8, federal law prohibits certain types of financial arrangements between healthcare facilities and referring physicians. Finally, as discussed in Chapter 9, there are antitrust law implications in some cases where physicians are prevented from practicing in healthcare institutions.

In the hospital context, the relationship has been based primarily on the physician's request for permission to treat patients at a particular hospital. In recent years, physicians have requested permission to affiliate with other types of healthcare organizations, such as networks, preferred provider organizations, and managed care organizations (MCOs). To be able to treat the patients enrolled in a particular plan, or at least to be able to treat those patients on favorable terms, physicians need to ask the MCO for permission to join its network of "preferred providers."

Inevitably, disputes arise in connection with these new physician relationships, just as they have in the hospital context. An MCO may refuse to allow a physician to join its network, just as hospitals have refused to grant permission for certain physicians to practice at their facilities. In addition, a patient may seek to hold the MCO liable for the negligence of an individual physician, just as patients have sought to hold hospitals liable for the negligence of physicians.

It is not surprising that courts attempt to resolve these new disputes between physicians and MCOs by analogy to the preexisting legal principles, which were developed in the context of physicians and hospitals. Although the factual situations are somewhat different, the issues are essentially the same. The first issue is determining when a healthcare organization may refuse to permit a licensed physician to practice in connection with that organization. In the managed care context, MCOs may have the right to exclude and terminate physicians in the process of selective contracting, as discussed in Chapter 14. In addition, if the organization permits the physician to participate, the separate issue arises of determining when the organization will be held liable for the negligence of an individual physician. The potential liability of MCOs for the negligence of participating physicians is discussed in Chapter 10.

To understand these issues in the new context of managed care, it is necessary to understand the traditional relationship between physicians and hospitals, as well as the legal principles that have been developed in connection with that relationship.

The Relationship Between Physicians and Hospitals

To survive economically and fulfill their respective functions in the healthcare system, physicians and hospitals need each other. Most physicians need to have some access to the facilities of a hospital, even if they see many of their patients in an office setting. In addition to admitting patients to the hospital, physicians may rely on the hospital to perform diagnostic tests on their patients. In many cases, hospitals bear the expense of providing the facilities and equipment physicians need to treat their patients.

At the same time, hospitals need physicians to get patients into the hospital. Except in an emergency, a prospective patient cannot simply walk into a hospital and ask for care. Rather, a patient may be admitted to a hospital only under the authority of a physician or other practitioner who has admitting privileges at that particular facility. Once the patient has been admitted, only a physician or other designated practitioner has the authority to order tests and treatments for that patient.

In establishing a relationship, hospitals and physicians can choose from at least three different types of arrangement:

1. employment,
2. contract, or
3. medical staff membership and clinical privileges.

Employment

The parties could decide to make the physician an employee of the hospital. Historically, only a small percentage of physicians were actually employees of a hospital. Although teaching hospitals employed many physicians, that was not the practice at most community hospitals. In recent years, however, the use of employment relationships has increased somewhat, as hospitals have purchased physician practices and hired the physicians as employees of the hospital or an affiliated organization. Many hospitals also employ "hospitalists" who specialize in caring for inpatients.

In some states, this type of employment arrangement may violate the traditional doctrine that prohibits the corporate practice of medicine. Under that doctrine, only a licensed *individual* may practice medicine, and a corporation may not own or control the practice of an individual physician. Therefore, physicians in those states could not be employees of a corporation such as a hospital. However, even in those states that follow the traditional doctrine, the restriction can usually be circumvented by making the physicians employees of a separate entity or by using a contract instead of an employment relationship.

Contractual Agreement

In a contractual relationship, the physician is not an employee, but rather is an independent contractor. Therefore, the hospital cannot tell the contracting physician how to perform the work, as it could with an employee; it can only require that the physician meet the obligations set forth in the contract. Instead of contracting directly with an individual physician, the hospital might contract with a professional corporation or professional association, which will hire the individual physicians as employees of the professional corporation or professional association.

Frequently, hospitals use contracts to obtain the services of hospital-based physicians (HBPs). HBPs are responsible for providing all of the necessary medical coverage in a particular department of the hospital, such as radiology, pathology, anesthesiology, or emergency. Ordinarily, those hospital contracts are exclusive, and only the contracting physicians may provide services in that particular department for the duration of the contract. This type of exclusive arrangement has several advantages for the hospital, such as convenience in scheduling; quality control; consistency in the use of procedures, equipment, and supplies; and ensuring full-time medical coverage for all patients, including those who are unable to pay for their care.

Medical Staff Membership and Clinical Privilege Status

The third category of relationship is medical staff membership and clinical privileges. In this category, the physicians are not employees of the hospital, and they have not entered into a contract to operate a particular department of the hospital. Rather, they are physicians in the private practice of medicine who have applied for the privilege of admitting and treating their patients at that particular facility. As discussed here, physicians are not automatically entitled to admit their patients to a particular hospital, even if they are licensed to practice medicine in the state. Rather, they must apply for membership and privileges under the criteria set forth in the bylaws of the hospital's medical staff.

Under these circumstances, many of the physicians practicing in U.S. hospitals are not employees of the hospital. However, those nonemployee physicians have the power to make decisions and take actions that will significantly affect the quality of care provided by the hospital as well as its financial viability. As discussed in Chapter 8, hospitals may gain or lose money under the Medicare prospective payment system as a result of treatment and discharge decisions made by physicians who are not employees of the hospital. In addition, as discussed in Chapter 10, a hospital may be held liable for the negligence of a physician who is not an employee of the hospital if it reasonably appears to the patient that the physician was an employee or agent of the hospital. Thus, a hospital's legal liability and financial viability, as well as its overall quality of care, will depend to a large extent on the actions of physicians who are not under the direct control of the hospital, but merely are members of the hospital's organized medical staff.

The Organized Medical Staff

The medical staff of a hospital is not a separate corporation. Rather, it is an association that has its own members, officers, and bylaws and that is also part of the larger hospital organization.

Although the medical staff has a great deal of influence, it is not the ultimate authority in the hospital. As in any corporation, that authority is the board of directors, which is sometimes referred to as the board of trustees or governing board. The governing board oversees the operation of the hospital and is responsible for ensuring that it is operated in a lawful, prudent, and fiscally responsible manner.

Most members of hospital governing boards are neither healthcare professionals nor experts in health administration. In a public or nonprofit hospital, trustees are usually civic leaders with experience in business or charitable activities, as well as respected representatives of various constituencies in the community. If the hospital is owned by a for-profit chain, the governing board is likely to consist of representatives who were designated by the parent company. Of course, the governing board will usually rely on the administrative staff for matters of day-to-day operation and will usually defer to the medical staff on matters that involve professional expertise.

In general, the roles and responsibilities of the hospital's governing board, administration, and medical staff are set forth in the accreditation standards of the Joint Commission. Because of the importance of Joint Commission accreditation, as discussed in Chapter 6, most acute-care general hospitals in the United States have adopted the organizational structure that is set forth in the Joint Commission standards.

Under Joint Commission standards, the organized medical staff is responsible for overseeing the care provided by individual physicians at the hospital.[1] Although the physicians may have their own private practices in competition with each other, they are responsible as a group for overseeing the quality of services provided at the hospital by each individual member of the group.[2] The organized medical staff "reports to and is accountable to the governing body."[3] Specifically, the medical staff is accountable for the quality of care provided to patients of the hospital.[4]

Although the medical staff adopts its own bylaws, the governing body must approve those bylaws before they become effective.[5] However, once they are in effect, they may not be amended unilaterally by the governing body or by the medical staff.[6] The bylaws will describe the internal organization of the medical staff, including the roles of officers, departments, and committees such as the executive committee of the medical staff. In addition, the bylaws of the medical staff will describe the criteria for each category of membership, the obligations of members, procedures for credentialing, grounds for terminating membership and privileges, and procedures for hearings and appeals.

If physicians want to treat their patients at the hospital, they must apply for membership on the medical staff. In addition, they must ask for clinical privileges to provide specific services at the facility. After the application is submitted, it will be reviewed in the process of credentialing, which includes the opportunity for a hearing and appeal.[7] Moreover, physicians must go through the credentialing process at least every two years to be reappointed to the medical staff and obtain renewal or revision of their clinical privileges.[8] Although the medical staff makes recommendations with regard to appointment and privileges, the ultimate decision must be made by the governing body of the hospital.[9]

Under Joint Commission standards, the criteria for medical staff membership and clinical privileges should include, among other things, licensure, competence, and professional performance.[10] In addition, some hospitals require applicants to reside and practice within a certain distance of the hospital and maintain adequate malpractice insurance coverage. Of course, credentialing decisions may *not* be based on race, gender, religion, or national origin. One of the most controversial issues in credentialing is whether hospitals may use the health status of the applicant or staff member as a criterion for membership and privileges. On one hand, it is important to ensure that patients are not harmed by physicians with problems such as substance abuse, mental illness, failing vision, or loss of memory. However, under some circumstances, a physician's mental or physical problem could constitute a disability, and hospitals may not discriminate on the basis of disability. Under Joint Commission standards, the criteria for granting privileges should include documentation of the individual's health status.[11] However, the Joint Commission also recognizes the potential application of the federal law that prohibits discrimination on the basis of disability, and has assured hospitals that it will interpret its standard in a way that allows hospitals to comply with the law.[12] For example, if a physician is HIV-positive or has AIDS, the hospital must determine if that is a legitimate reason to deny, revoke, or restrict the physician's membership and privileges. In attempting to balance the interests of the hospital, its patients, and the infected physician, one approach is to rely on the concept of informed consent. The legal issue is whether hospitals may require HIV-positive physicians to give prior notice to their patients about their medical condition, as a condition of permitting the physician to treat patients at the hospital. In one case, a trial court approved the hospital's action in requiring a surgeon who had AIDS to obtain the specific informed consent of his patients before performing surgery as a condition of restoring his surgical privileges.[13]

Aside from the issue of the applicant's health status, another controversial issue in credentialing is whether to grant privileges to practitioners who are not trained and licensed as doctors of medicine. Ordinarily, nurses do not request staff membership and clinical privileges because they are usually employees of the hospital rather than independent practitioners with their own patients. However, many chiropractors, podiatrists, oral surgeons, psychologists, nurse-anesthetists, and midwives have applied for hospital privileges. Those nonphysician practitioners want the opportunity to use the facilities of the hospital for diagnosing and treating their patients. Some hospitals and physicians have argued that granting membership and privileges to nonphysicians would adversely affect the quality of care provided in the hospital. In response, nonphysicians argue that medical doctors are merely trying to keep out competition and perpetuate their monopoly of hospital services.

Historically, the Joint Commission required hospitals to limit their medical staffs to licensed medical doctors and dentists. This enabled hospitals to use Joint Commission standards as a reason to deny applications from practitioners such as chiropractors and podiatrists. However, after challenges were made under federal antitrust law, the Joint Commission changed its standards to leave the decision up to each individual hospital, subject only to the limits of state professional licensure laws. In addition, the Joint Commission has broadened the category of practitioners who may be given clinical privileges by separating the concepts of staff membership and clinical privileges. According to the Joint Commission's 2006 Comprehensive Accreditation Manual for Hospitals, "[a]pplicants for membership may receive appointment to membership without receiving privileges; applicants for privileges need not necessarily be members of the medical staff."[14]

As already discussed, hospitals often enter into exclusive contracts with HBPs to provide all of the medical coverage in a particular department of the hospital. In those situations, the physician's clinical privileges may terminate upon expiration of the contract, without the need to demonstrate good cause for terminating those privileges. Alternatively, the hospital may permit contract physicians to retain their privileges upon termination of the contract but effectively prevent them from practicing at the hospital by awarding an exclusive contract to someone else.

Denial or Termination of Membership and Privileges

As discussed in Chapter 10, in malpractice cases hospitals can be held liable for allowing an incompetent physician to provide services in the facility. In that type of case, an injured patient—or the estate of a patient—would sue the physician for alleged negligence in diagnosis or treatment and may also sue the hospital for its own alleged negligence in failing to properly screen applicants for clinical privileges. This legal theory of hospital liability is referred to as corporate negligence, and it can also be applied to the decision of a network or an MCO permitting a physician to become a participating provider. Under these circumstances, hospitals and other healthcare organizations have an incentive to be extremely careful in screening and selecting applicants.

However, if the organization denies the application, it may be sued by the disappointed applicant. From the organization's point of view, it is a no-win situation. In effect, the organization has to choose whether it would prefer to be sued by an angry practitioner for allegedly unlawful exclusion or by patients or their estates for allegedly negligent credentialing. From the practitioner's point of view, the denial or termination of privileges would interfere with the ability to earn a living and cause a lifelong injury to professional reputation.

In the past, physicians who had their privileges revoked might be able to get a fresh start by moving to a different part of the country and obtaining privileges at a different hospital. Often, cases of threatened revocation were handled by means of a negotiated settlement. In many of those cases, the physician would voluntarily resign, and the hospital would agree to provide a neutral reference so that the physician could obtain privileges at a different hospital. Although state laws may have required hospitals to report adverse credentialing decisions to the state medical licensing board, those actions were characterized as voluntary resignations, rather than as adverse decisions, to avoid the need to make a report.

Obviously, that system did not address the problem with the physician's abilities, but merely transferred the problem to another hospital and to other patients. Therefore, some states have strengthened their requirements for reporting adverse credentialing decisions to include a voluntary resignation under threat of revocation. In addition, the Federation of State Medical Boards has established a data bank on physician disciplinary actions, and the federal government has established the National Practitioner Data Bank (NPDB) pursuant to a 1986 federal statute.[15] Under that statute, hospitals and MCOs are required to notify the NPDB of adverse credentialing actions against physicians. In addition, insurance payments on behalf of physicians for medical malpractice must also be reported. Information about individual physicians in the NPDB is not available to the public, but hospitals must obtain information from the data bank when physicians apply for clinical privileges and every two years thereafter.

As a mechanism for ensuring patient safety and quality of care, the NPDB has had some serious problems because of the reluctance of healthcare organizations to report incidents to the data bank. According to a report by the U.S. Department of Health and Human Services Office of Inspector General, 60 percent of U.S. hospitals have never reported an adverse action, nor have 84 percent of registered MCOs.[16] As a practical matter, healthcare organizations and physicians have found ways to avoid having to file reports to the NPDB, such as resolving credentialing disputes without a reportable adverse action or making payments in malpractice cases on behalf of the hospital rather than on behalf of the physician.

Despite the weaknesses in the system of reporting to the NPDB, more publicity surrounds disciplinary matters than in the past. As already discussed, some state governments have strengthened their reporting requirements, and state licensing boards are sharing information about disciplinary actions. In fact, some state boards make information about disciplinary actions available to the public on the Internet.

Under this more intensive system of reporting and publicity, it is much more difficult for a practitioner to simply start over in a new location. This has resulted in more protection for the public as a whole. At the same time, the new system increases the economic and professional consequences of an adverse credentialing decision for the affected practitioner. Under these circumstances, it is more important than ever to ensure that every credentialing decision has a legitimate basis, as well as a realistic way to challenge any decision that is improper.

In some cases, hospitals have revoked clinical privileges for valid reasons, such as incompetence, unethical behavior, and alcoholism or other substance abuse. However, some hospitals have also excluded or expelled practitioners to prevent them from competing with the hospital or with existing members of the medical staff.

Moreover, in matters of credentialing, the healthcare industry has a long history of discrimination on the basis of race, gender, religion, and national origin. Before the passage of civil rights legislation, membership on some hospital medical staffs was explicitly limited by discriminatory criteria in the medical staff bylaws. Even after the passage of civil rights laws, some discrimination in credentialing has continued, but it is usually hidden under expressions of purported concern for the applicant's qualifications or ability to work with others. As in cases of employment discrimination, it may be difficult to determine whether a credentialing decision was based on a person's qualifications or on discrimination, in which case the supposed concern for the person's qualifications was merely a pretext. Finally, in the world of complex human relationships, some decisions on employment or credentialing involve a mixture of proper and improper motives.

Judicial Review of Credentialing Decisions

For the reasons already discussed, a legal remedy must be available by which practitioners can appeal an inappropriate denial or termination of their privileges. However, the extent to which credentialing decisions should be subject to review and reversal by the courts is a complex policy issue.

In fact, tension exists between conflicting public policies in this area of the law. On one hand, we want to ensure that practitioners will have an effective right of appeal in cases of improper exclusion. However, we also want to encourage hospitals and their medical staffs to keep out practitioners who would be likely to pose a danger to the public. In almost all cases, those incompetent or unethical practitioners hold licenses from the state, which demonstrates that government regulation alone is not sufficient to protect the public health and ensure the quality of care. Therefore, we need to supplement government regulation with professional self-regulation through the mechanism of peer review. The goal for the legal system is to develop a remedy that will be effective for the aggrieved practitioner without interfering with the important function of medical peer review in the process of credentialing.

Over time, various legal theories have been in and out of favor as possible remedies for allegedly improper credentialing decisions. At first, excluded practitioners argued that they had been deprived of their constitutional right to due process of law. However, that has not been an effective theory in this context for several reasons. The constitutional obligation to provide due process of law only applies to units of government, such as public hospitals, the actions of which are deemed to be the actions of the state. Therefore, a private hospital's denial or revocation of privileges is not subject to the requirement of due process of law. Under current law, a private hospital's receipt of Medicare and Medicaid reimbursement or funding from the Hill-Burton program does not turn the private hospital's actions into "state action."[17]

Finally, for a public hospital that *is* subject to the requirements of due process, the hospital would only be required to show that it provided notice and an opportunity to be heard, as well as some reasonable basis for its decision.

Apart from the constitutional requirement of due process, some states have statutes or common-law doctrines that allow courts to review the credentialing decisions of private hospitals. Most state courts would require some evidence that a fair procedure was used and some reasonable basis for the decision, but the court's review of the hospital's decision would be very superficial. Courts recognize that the procedure for credentialing hearings may be informal, and the hospital is not required to follow all of the procedural requirements of a civil or criminal trial. Moreover, in reviewing the substantive basis for a credentialing decision, courts will ordinarily defer to the judgment of the hospital. As one court has explained,

> No court should substitute its evaluation of such matters for that of the Hospital Board . . . Human lives are at stake, and the governing board must be given discretion in its selection so that it can have confidence in the competence and moral commitment of its staff. The evaluation of professional proficiency of doctors is best left to the specialized expertise of their peers, subject only to limited judicial surveillance . . . In short, so long as staff selections are administered with fairness, geared by a rationale compatible with hospital responsibility, and unencumbered with irrelevant considerations, a court should not interfere. Courts must not attempt to take on the escutcheon of Caduceus.[18]

Under these circumstances, and because of the court's limited standard of judicial review, it is very difficult for excluded physicians to prevail in this type of case. Even if they were driven out for discriminatory or anticompetitive reasons, they were probably given a written notice in advance and some apparent opportunity to be heard. Moreover, the hospital's written decision, which may have been written by the hospital's attorney, is likely to contain a reason that appears to be valid and a recitation of some evidence in support of the decision.

In addition, state and federal governments have provided immunity for most activities in the process of medical peer review. To encourage physicians to express themselves freely in the peer-review process, states have enacted statutes that provide some immunity for participants and confidentiality for their statements and documents. Similarly, Congress has provided immunity from damages for good-faith participation in peer-review activities. That immunity would apply to claims under various legal theories, including the antitrust claims discussed in Chapter 9.

The theory of these state and federal laws is that quality of care requires an effective system of peer review, and effective peer review requires immunity from damages for the participants. In other words, physicians would not participate in the process or provide candid evaluations of their peers unless they were given significant protection against the possibility of damages and the cost of litigation.

Theoretically, these state and federal immunities have exceptions that preserve the possibility of pursuing legitimate claims. In reality, however, it is difficult for a practitioner to obtain effective legal relief, even if the credentialing decision was made for an improper reason. Thus, our society has made the policy decision to promote quality of care by means of professional self-regulation, even though some legitimate grievances by practitioners may not be effectively redressed.

Notes

1. See Joint Commission on Accreditation of Healthcare Organizations, *2006 Comprehensive Accreditation Manual for Hospitals: The Official Handbook* (2006): MS.1.10 [hereinafter *Official Handbook*].
2. *Id*. at MS.2.10.
3. *Id*. at MS.1.10.
4. *Id*. at Elements of Performance for MS.1.10, No. 5.
5. *Id*. at Elements of Performance for MS.1.20, No. 3 ("The governing body approves and complies with the medical staff bylaws."). See also Elements of Performance for MS.4.20, No. 5 (authority of the governing body).
6. *Id*. at MS.1.30 (prohibiting unilateral amendment of medical staff bylaws).
7. See *id*. at MS.4.10–4.70.
8. *Id*. at Elements of Performance for MS.4.60, No. 3 (appointment cannot be longer than two years); Elements of Performance for MS.4.20, No. 4 (privileges cannot last longer than two years).
9. *Id*. at Elements of Performance for MS.4.60, No. 5 ("Membership is recommended by the medical staff and granted by the governing body.").
10. *Id*. at Elements of Performance for MS.4.20, Nos. 3, 6, and 7. See also *id*. at Rationale for MS.4.10 (listing the permissible documentation for credentialing).
11. *Id*. at Elements of Performance for MS.4.20, No. 6. See also *id*. at MS.4.80 (the medical staff's process for handling problems with the physical or mental health of its individual members).
12. *Id*. at Elements of Performance for MS.4.20, Note 2 on page MS-22.
13. *Estate of Behringer v. Medical Center at Princeton*, 592 A.2d 1251 (N.J. Super. 1991).
14. *Id*. at MS-17 (Credentialing, Privileging, and Appointment).
15. See Health Care Quality Improvement Act of 1986, Pub. L. No. 99-660, §§ 421–27, 100 Stat. 3743, 3788–92 (1986), codified as amended at 42 U.S.C. §§ 11131–37 (2005).
16. U.S. Department of Health and Human Services, Office of Inspector General, *Managed Care Organization Nonreporting to the*

National Practitioner Data Bank: A Signal for Broader Concern,
OEI-01-99-00690 (May 2001): 4, 8.

17. See, e.g., *Modaber v. Culpepper Memorial Hospital, Inc.*, 674 F.2d 1023, 1025–26 (4th Cir. 1982).

18. *Sosa v. Val Verde Memorial Hospital,* 437 F.2d 173, 177 (5th Cir. 1971).

THE LAW OF GOVERNMENT PAYMENT PROGRAMS: MEDICARE, MEDICAID, AND FRAUD AND ABUSE

To provide coverage to persons who are elderly, disabled, or indigent, Congress enacted the Medicare and Medicaid laws. The programs that resulted from those laws have caused profound changes in the U.S. healthcare system and have made the federal government the largest buyer of healthcare services.

Since the creation of Medicare and Medicaid in the 1960s, many legal disputes have raised questions about the meaning and intent of the statutes, regulations, and policies that were adopted to implement the programs. In general, those disputes can be categorized as issues of eligibility, benefits, or payment. Eligibility refers to the criteria an individual must meet to qualify as a beneficiary of the program. In contrast, the issue of benefits is a matter of defining the services covered by the program. In other words, assuming that a person has qualified as an eligible beneficiary, what services are covered and to what extent are they covered? The issue of payment refers to the amount of money the program will pay to the facility or practitioner as compensation for providing covered services to an eligible beneficiary, as well as the methodology by which that compensation is determined. A separate set of issues involves fraud and abuse of the government payment programs, such as false claims, kickbacks, and self-referrals, which are discussed in detail in this chapter.

The Medicare Program

Medicare provides health insurance coverage to approximately 40 million people, which makes it the largest health plan in the country. Serious concerns have arisen about the long-term solvency of the program and its ability to meet the needs of the aging baby boom generation. In addition, there has been a great deal of dissatisfaction with the limitations on the scope of Medicare benefits, particularly in the areas of long-term care and prescription drugs. In 2003, Congress responded to concerns about the lack of prescription drug coverage by enacting the Medicare Prescription Drug, Improvement, and Modernization Act (MMA), which is described later.[1] Nevertheless, concerns persist with regard to the costs and extent of prescription drug coverage under Medicare, and Congress has yet to deal with the increasing costs of long-term care.

The Medicare program was established by federal statute, which is referred to as Title XVIII of the Social Security Act. It is a purely federal program administered by the Centers for Medicare & Medicaid Services (CMS), formerly known as the Health Care Financing Administration (HCFA), and is part of the Department of Health and Human Services (HHS).

To implement the program, CMS has adopted regulations, which are contained in the *Code of Federal Regulations* and the *Federal Register*, and has published numerous policy manuals on various aspects of the program. In addition, the federal government enters into contracts with private insurance companies to act as intermediaries or carriers on behalf of the government and enters into contracts with peer-review organizations to review the services rendered to beneficiaries of the program.

At the time the Medicare program was created in 1965, the intent of Congress was merely to provide insurance for elderly persons, not to help the larger community or achieve broader social goals.[2] Over time, Medicare has become a mechanism to support other goals such as care for the indigent, graduate medical education, and healthcare facilities in rural areas.[3] In addition, Congress uses Medicare participation as a "hook" by imposing various requirements on healthcare providers that choose to participate in that government payment program. In 2000, the U.S. Supreme Court concluded that "[t]he structure and operation of the Medicare program reveal a comprehensive federal assistance enterprise aimed at ensuring the availability of quality health care for the broader community."[4]

Medicare Eligibility and Benefits

People may qualify for Medicare if they are over the age of 65 years, are permanently disabled, or have end-stage renal disease. Part A of Medicare primarily covers inpatient hospital services; Part B covers outpatient hospital care, physician services, and some other services and supplies. Although Medicare pays for home health services, the program is restrictive about paying for nursing home care. In the Balanced Budget Act of 1997 (BBA),[5] Congress created Part C of the Medicare program, now known as Medicare Advantage, which allows each beneficiary to choose from a variety of approved managed care plans. Alternatively, beneficiaries may choose to remain in the traditional fee-for-service program under Parts A and B. In the fee-for-service program, beneficiaries have the right to select the provider of their choice.[6] The 2003 MMA has created a new Part D for prescription drug coverage.

Medicare could be described as schizophrenic because it has two inconsistent aspects. In some respects, Medicare resembles an insurance plan, because part of the program is funded by premiums that are paid by beneficiaries. On the other hand, part of the program is financed by payroll taxes and government revenues. Thus, Medicare also resembles a tax-funded social welfare program, which redistributes wealth among different individuals and groups. In general, Medicare is not means-tested; therefore, wealthy retirees can qualify for the program. In fact, some of the beneficiaries have much more income and assets than the workers who are taxed to support the program. Of course, wealthy and middle-class beneficiaries view the Medicare program as a type of insurance for which they insist they already have paid. The MMA takes a significant step toward means-testing by requiring beneficiaries with high incomes to pay more for Part B coverage.[7] As one commentator has pointed out, the move toward means-testing could erode the level of political support for the Medicare program as a whole.[8]

As discussed in Chapter 11, the U.S. Constitution does not require Congress to establish and maintain a Medicare program. In other words, Congress had the authority to create a Medicare program, but it was not constitutionally obligated to do so. In the absence of a constitutional mandate, Congress has considerable flexibility to determine which groups of people to assist and which services to cover. In addition, Congress has the legal authority to change or even eliminate the Medicare program on a prospective basis, regardless of the expectations of beneficiaries or the financial contributions of employees.[9] Of course, eliminating the Medicare program altogether would not be politically feasible and would certainly not be desirable. However, to maintain the long-term solvency of the program, Congress may find it necessary in the future to reform the program in ways that would be detrimental to the interests of beneficiaries, and it certainly has the legal authority to do so.

As one type of fundamental reform, some have argued in favor of changing Medicare to a premium support or voucher system. Under that type of system, the government would not act as an insurer and would not pay the medical bills incurred by beneficiaries. Instead, the government would give beneficiaries a sum of money or a voucher to purchase the coverage of their choice in the private health insurance market. This type of approach would be similar to a defined contribution retirement plan or 401(k) plan, in which the employees make their own investment decisions with the money contributed by their employers. Obviously, changing the Medicare program in that manner would have advantages and disadvantages, and the proposal has been met with strong opposition as well as support. Compounding this issue are political and philosophical disputes about the appropriate roles of government and the private sector.

Medicare Payment Issues

Providers are not legally required to participate in the Medicare program, even though participation may be a financial necessity as a practical matter. Because participation is voluntary, the federal government has broad authority to impose conditions on healthcare facilities and practitioners who choose to participate. In imposing those conditions of participation, the government is acting as a buyer, rather than a regulator. However, the government is a unique type of buyer, because it has the power to fine or imprison healthcare providers who violate its rules.

The Medicare statute explicitly prohibits federal control of the practice of medicine or the operation of healthcare facilities.[10] Nevertheless, courts have allowed the Medicare program to limit the payment of providers and use mechanisms of cost containment.[11] Therefore, the government has the power to limit the rate of payment for each type of service and may impose administrative requirements for receipt of payment.

From the provider's point of view, the relationship with the government may appear to be a contractual arrangement, in which the facility or practitioner performs services for beneficiaries and receives payment from the government for providing those services. However, courts have held that the provider's relationship with the government is more than merely a contract to perform services in exchange for payment. The U.S. Supreme Court has held that providers, as well as patients, are recipients of benefits under the federal Medicare program.[12]

Moreover, by receiving Medicare reimbursement, a healthcare facility becomes a recipient of federal financial assistance and thereby subjects itself to the requirements of additional federal laws.[13] However, the mere receipt of federal reimbursement does not turn any action of a private hospital into an action of the state; therefore, private hospitals are not subject to the same constitutional obligations as government agencies.[14]

Almost any licensed provider may choose to participate in the Medicare program and receive payment for treating Medicare beneficiaries. The methodology for paying each type of provider is set forth by statute and can be quite inflexible. Historically, the program could not pay more to particular providers as compensation for a higher level of quality or efficiency. However, in recent years, the Medicare program has developed some "pay for performance" initiatives and has authorized several demonstration projects to experiment with alternative methods of purchasing services and compensating providers.[15]

Originally, the Medicare program paid hospitals for services rendered to Medicare patients on the basis of retrospectively determined costs. In effect, the government looked at all of the costs that the hospital had incurred during the previous year and then paid the hospital the portion of the costs that was attributable to the treatment of Medicare beneficiaries. This payment methodology required each hospital to prepare detailed cost reports listing each item of cost in each department of the hospital and allocate various overhead costs to particular allowable and nonallowable cost centers. Of course, the government or its intermediaries had to audit those cost reports, and frequent disputes occurred over the amount of reimbursement to which the hospital was entitled.

In addition to being incredibly complex, this system of retrospective–cost based reimbursement was inherently inflationary. For example, if 50 percent of a hospital's patient days were for the treatment of Medicare patients, the Medicare program would reimburse the hospital for approximately 50 percent of the hospital's costs, including the costs of building new facilities and acquiring new equipment. Therefore, the hospital's management and board could build and equip new facilities without much risk, even if the additions were not absolutely necessary, because the government was expected to pay almost half of the cost. Just as taxpayers might be more inclined to make expenditures if they are tax deductible, hospitals had an incentive to spend money and no real incentive to economize.

For that reason, the Medicare program eliminated retrospective–cost based reimbursement of hospitals and replaced it with a new prospective payment system (PPS). Under PPS, a hospital that treats a Medicare patient will receive an amount of money that is determined prospectively (i.e., in advance of treating the patient). The amount of that payment will depend on the patient's diagnosis, which will be placed in one of about 500 diagnosis-related groups (DRGs). Because the payment to the hospital is *not* based on the hospital's costs, the hospital has no incentive to increase its costs as a way of maximizing its Medicare reimbursement.

In fact, the incentive under PPS is just the opposite. If an inpatient remains in the hospital for a long time and receives a lot of expensive tests and treatments, the cost for treating that patient will probably exceed the prospectively determined amount for that DRG, and the hospital will lose money on treating that particular patient. However, if the hospital can treat the patient for less than the DRG amount, the hospital essentially makes a profit on that particular patient. Thus, some people say hospitals now have an incentive to discharge patients "quicker and sicker."

Significantly, a hospital has only a limited ability to control its costs for treating a particular patient. As discussed in Chapter 7, decisions on when to discharge a patient and what services to provide are made by the physician, who is often not an employee of the hospital. Nevertheless, some hospitals have tried to encourage their physicians to discharge Medicare patients as soon as possible and to consider how their decisions regarding tests and treatments affect the hospital financially. Some hospitals have even tried to give their physicians financial incentives to reduce the cost of treatment. However, Congress has prohibited hospitals from paying physicians to reduce the level of services for Medicare and Medicaid patients.[16]

Over the years, Congress has tried to reduce Medicare expenditures by expanding the application of PPS to additional categories of cost and additional types of service. For example, the BBA of 1997 replaced cost reimbursement for skilled nursing facilities and home health agencies with new PPS.

When the Medicare program was enacted, physicians were paid on the basis of "reasonable charges," which were similar to the charge screens used by commercial insurers. Subsequently, Medicare adopted the Resource-Based Relative Value Scale, under which the program pays more for physician services that require a higher level of training and resources. In addition, the Medicare program limits the amounts physicians may charge for services rendered to Medicare patients.

One of the most controversial issues is whether a willing patient may enter into a private contract with a willing physician to pay more than the limit for services that are covered by the Medicare program. For example, if a private insurance company would pay $200 for a particular physician service, and if Medicare would pay only $100 for that service, a physician might decide to not accept any more patients who are covered by the Medicare program and instead devote more time to treating privately insured patients. To obtain the services of that particular physician, some Medicare patients might be willing to pay the $200 out of their own pocket, or at least the incremental difference of $100, assuming they can afford to do so. However, the law severely restricts the ability of Medicare patients and their physicians to enter into that type of contract. Under § 4507 of the BBA, Medicare patients may only contract privately for covered services if the physician agrees not to bill Medicare for any services to any patient for a period of two years. In other words, the only way a physician can privately agree on a higher charge for a covered service is by dropping out of the Medicare program for at least two years, which would be totally impractical for most physicians.

Supporters of private contracting argue that Medicare should not interfere with the free-enterprise system. Moreover, they argue that the prohibition against private contracts denies access to the services of desirable physicians and prevents those who are willing from purchasing services of higher quality. Opponents respond that private contracting would force patients to pay higher fees for physician services, would put elderly patients at a disadvantage in bargaining with their physicians, and would effectively create one Medicare program for the rich and one for the poor.

Out of this debate came at least two pieces of proposed legislation. In the 105th Congress, Senator Jon Kyl (R-AZ) proposed expanding the opportunities for private contracting by sponsoring the Medicare Beneficiary Freedom to Contract Act of 1997.[17] In response, Representative Pete Stark (D-CA) introduced a bill to emphasize the vulnerability of Medicare patients in attempting to negotiate with their physicians. Representative Stark's bill is entitled "A bill to amend title XVIII of the Social Security Act to limit the ability of physicians to demand more money through private contracts during periods in which the patient is in an exposed condition."[18]

Many providers complain that the Medicare program does not adequately pay for services rendered to Medicare patients and that the government has refused to provide appropriate increases in rates of payment. As a political matter, Congress may find it easier to cut payments to providers or reduce the rate of increase in payments to providers, rather than cutting Medicare benefits or increasing taxes and premiums. However, at some point, there is a danger that reductions in provider payments may have adverse effects on quality and access to care, especially if providers are unable to shift their costs to private payers in the competitive system of managed care.

Medicare Managed Care and Part C (Medicare Advantage)

For several years, members of Congress from both political parties have attempted to reform the Medicare program in an effort to use the cost-saving mechanisms of managed care and provide more choices to beneficiaries. Although Medicare had a health maintenance organization program for many years, only a small percentage of Medicare patients were enrolled in managed care plans. In 1997, as part of the BBA, Congress added the Medicare+Choice system as Part C of the Medicare program. Under the 1997 amendments, a beneficiary could remain in the traditional fee-for-service program under Parts A and B or could choose from a variety of qualified Medicare+Choice plans under Part C.

In the 2003 MMA, Congress again revised the Medicare managed care program. Beneficiaries may now choose to join a Medicare Advantage Plan, which is operated by a private company and approved by the Medicare program. In a Medicare Advantage Plan, the beneficiary's premiums and copayments may be lower than in traditional Medicare, and the Medicare Advantage Plan might provide some additional benefits. However, the Medicare Advantage Plan might impose additional restrictions, such as limiting the choice of physicians and requiring approval to consult a specialist. Each beneficiary has the option to remain in the traditional fee-for-service program under Parts A and B and, in fact, that is the default option unless the beneficiary elects to join a Medicare Advantage Plan.

Under traditional fee-for-service Medicare, the government acts as an insurer and bears the risk of having to pay for all of the covered services needed. In contrast, Part C operates somewhat like a voucher system or a defined contribution pension plan. If the beneficiary chooses a Medicare managed care plan, the government will make a specified payment to that plan on behalf of the beneficiary, instead of paying the expenses actually incurred by the beneficiary under Parts A and B. In that way, the government can shift the risk of unanticipated expenses to the managed care plan. In addition to limiting the government's potential liability, the government is in the politically advantageous posture of providing desirable benefits to the voters while forcing the private managed care plans to make the difficult and unpopular decisions on utilization review and denial of care.

The Medicare Prescription Drug Benefit (Part D)

In 2003, Congress enacted the MMA, which creates a new Part D for prescription drug coverage.[19] Beneficiaries are not required to enroll in Part D, but they may choose to enroll by joining a Medicare drug plan or a Medicare managed care plan that includes prescription drug coverage. Medicare drug plans are operated by health insurance companies or other private companies that are approved by the Medicare program. If the beneficiary chooses a Medicare Advantage Plan under Part C, that plan might also include coverage for prescription drugs.

The MMA includes complex rules with regard to alternatives, costs, and coverage. Different plans may have different levels of coverage and different costs. In addition, Medicare prescription drug plans may have a gap in coverage after the beneficiary exhausts the standard amount of coverage and before the beneficiary qualifies for the catastrophic coverage. This gap is referred to as the "doughnut hole."

One of the most controversial issues in the Medicare prescription drug program is whether the federal government should negotiate prices directly with pharmaceutical manufacturers or, alternatively, rely on private drug plans to negotiate with manufacturers. Rather than using Medicare's usual system of government-administered pricing, the MMA prohibits HHS from establishing the prices or formularies under Medicare Part D and participating in those negotiations with manufacturers.[20] In a subsection of the law entitled "noninterference," Congress provided that the Secretary of HHS "may not interfere with the negotiations" between pharmaceutical manufacturers and the sponsors of private prescriptiprtion drug plans.[21]

Some people have objected to the noninterference provision and have argued that the federal government should attempt to negotiate for lower drug prices on behalf of Medicare beneficiaries. On January 5, 2007, Congress began consideration of a bill that would require HHS to negotiate prices with drug manufacturers, "including discounts, rebates, and other price concessions."[22] Although this proposal appears to present a way of reducing costs for the Medicare program, the Congressional Budget Office (CBO) concluded that HHS would not be able to negotiate more favorable prices than those currently available to prescription drug plans. CBO's cost estimate on the proposed legislation follows.

January 10, 2007

Honorable John D. Dingell
Chairman
Committee on Energy and Commerce
U.S. House of Representatives
Washington, DC 20515

Dear Mr. Chairman:

At the request of your staff, the Congressional Budget Office has reviewed H.R. 4, the Medicare Prescription Drug Price Negotiation Act of 2007, as introduced on January 5, 2007. The bill would revise section 1860D-11(i) of the Social Security Act, which is commonly known as the "noninterference provision" because it prohibits the Secretary of Health and Human Services from participating in the negotiations between drug manufacturers, pharmacies, and sponsors of prescription drug plans (PDPs) involved in Part D of Medicare, or from requiring a particular formulary or price structure for covered Part D drugs.

H.R. 4 would require the Secretary to negotiate with drug manufacturers the prices that could be charged to PDPs for covered drugs. However, the bill would prohibit the Secretary from requiring a particular formulary and would allow PDPs to negotiate prices that are lower than those obtained by the Secretary. The bill would also require the Secretary to report to the Congress every six months on the results of his negotiations with drug manufacturers.

CBO estimates that H.R. 4 would have a negligible effect on federal spending because we anticipate that the Secretary would be unable to negotiate prices across the broad range of covered Part D drugs that are more favorable than those obtained by PDPs under current law. Since the legislation specifically directs the Secretary to negotiate only about the prices that could be charged to PDPs, and explicitly indicates that the Secretary would not have authority to negotiate about some other factors that may influence the prescription drug market, we assume that the negotiations would be limited solely to a discussion about the prices to be charged to PDPs. In that context, the Secretary's ability to influence the outcome of those negotiations would be limited. For example, without the authority to establish a formulary, we believe that the Secretary would not be able to encourage the use of particular drugs by Part D beneficiaries, and as a result would lack the leverage to obtain significant discounts in his negotiations with drug manufacturers.

Instead, prices for covered Part D drugs would continue to be determined through negotiations between drug manufacturers and PDPs. Under current law, PDPs are allowed to establish formularies—subject to certain limits—and thus have some ability to direct demand to drugs produced by one manufacturer rather than another. The PDPs also bear substantial financial risk and therefore have strong incentives to negotiate price discounts in order to control their costs and offer coverage that attracts enrollees through features such as low premiums and cost-sharing requirements. Therefore, the PDPs have both the incentives and the tools to negotiate drug prices that the government, under the legislation, would not have. H.R. 4 would not alter that essential dynamic.

I hope this information is helpful to you. The CBO staff contacts for further information are Eric Rollins and Shinobu Suzuki.

Sincerely,
Donald B. Marron
Acting Director
cc: Honorable Joe Barton
Ranking Member

The Medicaid Program

Medicaid is a means-tested, social welfare program that uses tax revenues to provide health coverage for persons who cannot afford private health insurance. Unlike Medicare, which is a purely federal program, Medicaid is operated and funded by both state and federal governments. This situation gives rise to interesting issues of federalism, as well as occasional disputes over the powers and duties of each level of government.

An Exercise in Federalism

The federal Medicaid statute, known as Title XIX of the Social Security Act, was enacted by Congress pursuant to its conditional spending power. By means of that statute, Congress makes an offer to the government of each state. If a state establishes a medical assistance program that meets all of the federal standards, the federal government will provide a large share of the cost of that program in the form of federal financial participation (FFP). In other words, states have the option to establish a medical assistance program, but they are not required to do so. Even though the program is voluntary, every state has established a Medicaid program to obtain its share of FFP.

If a state decides to participate, it is legally required to comply with the federal statutes and regulations, and state agencies are required to submit a Medicaid plan to HHS for approval. Even after the state's plan is approved, the secretary of HHS has the authority to terminate all or part of a state's FFP if the state violates federal requirements. Although the state program must meet minimum federal requirements, states have flexibility in some aspects of their programs, and the federal government may grant waivers of specific federal requirements at the request of a state.

One of the federal standards that some states have sought to avoid is the requirement that beneficiaries are entitled to their free choice of provider. That federal requirement interfered with efforts by state agencies to develop managed care programs for their Medicaid beneficiaries.

Therefore, Medicaid officials in many states had asked the federal government to waive the requirement for free choice of provider. In 1997, Congress simplified the process by enacting § 4701 of the BBA, which allowed states to put most Medicaid beneficiaries into managed care programs without requesting a federal waiver.

Some people think the federal government should give the states even more flexibility to design and operate their own medical assistance programs without having to meet federal requirements or request a federal waiver. In 1995, the Republican-dominated House of Representatives passed a bill to change Medicaid to a block-grant system, under which the federal government would provide funding for the individual states to operate their own medical assistance programs.[23] However, the Democratic minority in Congress argued that eliminating federal standards would have an adverse effect on Medicaid beneficiaries. Eventually, the bill containing the Republican block-grant proposal was vetoed by President Clinton, but that did not end the dispute over the appropriate role for the federal and state governments in the Medicaid program.

With regard to enforcement, the federal Medicaid statute makes it clear that the Secretary of HHS has the ability, by threatening to reduce or terminate federal funds, to compel state Medicaid agencies to comply with federal laws. However, disagreements have occurred over whether Medicaid beneficiaries and providers have the right to sue state Medicaid agencies in federal court to require a state to comply with federal statutes and regulations.[24] The mere fact that a federal law exists on a subject does not necessarily mean individuals have a private right of action as a means of enforcing that law.

Eligibility for Medicaid

As a social welfare program, Medicaid eligibility is restricted to persons with limited income and assets. Some people are considered to be categorically eligible for Medicaid because they fit within certain categories of persons on public assistance. In the past, persons receiving cash payments under the Aid to Families with Dependent Children program were categorically eligible for the Medicaid program, as were disabled persons who received payments under the Supplemental Security Income program. However, the 1996 welfare reform legislation abolished the Aid to Families with Dependent Children program, substituted the new Temporary Assistance for Needy Families program, and made categorical eligibility for Medicaid more complicated.

Medicaid eligibility is limited to U.S. citizens and to those immigrants who fit within the category of "qualified aliens." Thus, undocumented aliens are generally not eligible for Medicaid, but there is an exception for emergency treatment, including labor and delivery. In addition, Section 6036 of the Deficit Reduction Act of 2005 requires states to document the citizenship status of Medicaid applicants and recipients, and requires participants to prove their citizenship status with documentary evidence.[25]

In addition to qualification for Medicaid as "categorically needy," some people may qualify for Medicaid as "medically needy" if they have very high medical expenses. For example, people with chronic conditions may spend so much money on medical care that they "spend down" to the poverty level, in which case they may qualify for Medicaid.

Similarly, many residents of nursing homes will exhaust all of their resources and thereby qualify for Medicaid. Most Americans do not have long term–care insurance, and most health insurance policies will not pay the cost for room and board in a nursing home, which can be extremely expensive. In addition, the Medicare program is restrictive about paying for nursing home care. Therefore, even if people enter nursing homes as private, paying residents, they may quickly exhaust their remaining funds, at which time the Medicaid program may become responsible for their expenses. For this reason, Medicaid is not merely a program for recipients of public assistance. It is also a way of paying the nursing home costs for many middle-class retirees, instead of imposing those costs on their own adult children.

Some people go so far as to transfer their remaining assets to other family members as a way to qualify for Medicaid, a practice that raises several legal and ethical issues. Some people believe it is unethical for wealthy retirees to give substantial assets to their adult children and then apply for Medicaid when they have no more resources. However, others respond that people who worked hard and paid taxes for 40 or 50 years ought to be able to leave some of their money or property to their families, without having every penny dissipated for nursing home care. As a legal matter, people who transfer assets for less than fair market value within a certain number of years before entering a nursing home and applying for Medicaid may be disqualified for nursing home benefits for several years.[26]

Medicaid Benefits

As in other aspects of the Medicaid program, states have some flexibility on the issue of which benefits to cover, provided that the states meet the basic requirements established by federal law. In fact, federal law specifies services all states must cover, services states may cover at their option, and services states may not cover at all with funds from the Medicaid program. If a state chooses to do so, it may offer certain optional services, such as eyeglasses, and the state will receive FFP for the cost of those optional services.

The minimum federal requirements are different for the categorically needy and the medically needy.[27] In addition, special service requirements are in place for eligible beneficiaries under the age of 21 years, for whom the state is required to provide "early and periodic screening, diagnostic, and treatment services," or EPSDT.[28] For children's health advocates, the EPSDT requirement may also provide a mechanism to obtain important services that would otherwise be unavailable as a result of limitations on specific services.[29]

In regard to required services, the federal regulation at 42 C.F.R. § 440.230(c) provides that a state "may not arbitrarily deny or reduce the amount, duration, or scope of a required service . . . to an otherwise eligible recipient solely because of the diagnosis, type of illness, or condition." In other words, a state Medicaid agency may limit a service on the basis of medical necessity, but it may not provide less coverage on the basis of the particular type of illness. For example, the Iowa Medicaid agency decided that it would not pay for sex-change operations, on the grounds that they are never a medically necessary treatment for the condition of transsexualism. However, a sex-change operation, which is also known as sex reassignment surgery, is the only available treatment for that condition. Therefore, a federal court of appeals ruled that Iowa was arbitrarily denying services to Medicaid beneficiaries solely because of the diagnosis, type of illness, or condition.[30] Even though Iowa may want to use its limited Medicaid funds for other purposes, federal law provides that Iowa cannot deny required Medicaid services on the basis of the patient's condition, which in that case was transsexualism.

Obviously, that type of case raises difficult policy issues of how to allocate limited financial resources, as well as interesting issues of federalism. Similar issues have arisen in cases seeking Medicaid funding for expensive organ transplants.[31] In those cases, a state's refusal to pay for the transplant may cause the death of an identifiable child or adult. Instead of paying for the transplant, however, the state could use that money to provide healthcare services to hundreds of people. Those unidentified people may go without care if the federal government forces the state to use its Medicaid funds to pay for the transplant. Aside from the ethical issue of determining the "right" thing to do are separate issues of determining who should make the decision and how the decision should be made.

Several years ago, the state of Oregon squarely addressed these difficult questions by requesting a federal waiver as a demonstration project for its state Medicaid program.[32] In addition to using the techniques of managed care, Oregon wanted to avoid the federal requirements on the broad scope of covered services and procedures. First, Oregon used a public process to prioritize different procedures in terms of their cost and benefit and then decided to cover only those procedures that ranked above a particular cutoff point on the list. With the money Oregon would save by not covering low-ranking procedures, it would expand Medicaid eligibility to many more people in the state. Obviously, that proposal required a waiver from the federal government. Among other problems, it might constitute a denial of service solely because of the type of illness or condition, which would violate federal Medicaid law. Moreover, there were some initial concerns that the Oregon plan might discriminate against disabled persons, in violation of the Americans with Disabilities Act, by refusing to cover procedures that are needed by persons with disabilities. Eventually those concerns were resolved, and the federal government granted the Medicaid waiver. In doing so, the federal government took an important step toward state flexibility in the Medicaid program and permitted an interesting experiment in rationing care.

With regard to services states may *not* cover, the federal law known as the Hyde Amendment generally prohibits the states from using Medicaid funds to pay for abortions. Thus, states have the option to use their own non-Medicaid funds to pay for lawful abortions but ordinarily may not use Medicaid funds, which include a large percentage of FFP.

As discussed in Chapter 13, abortion at an early stage of pregnancy is a lawful procedure, which state governments may not prohibit or prevent. Therefore, some people have argued that the government is required to pay for that lawful procedure, especially because the government pays for prenatal care, delivery, and other pregnancy-related services. However, the U.S. Supreme Court has rejected that argument and has held that the government may prohibit the use of Medicaid funds to pay for abortions. In other words, the government cannot stop a woman from choosing to have an abortion at an early stage of pregnancy, but the government is not obligated to pay for the chosen procedure. As the Supreme Court has explained:

> [I]t simply does not follow that a woman's freedom of choice carries with it a constitutional entitlement to the financial resources to avail herself of the full range of protected choices . . . although government may not place obstacles in the path of a woman's exercise of her freedom of choice, it need not remove those not of its own creation. Indigency falls in the latter category. The financial constraints that restrict an indigent woman's ability to enjoy the full range of constitutionally protected freedom of choice are the product not of governmental restrictions on access to abortions, but rather of her indigency.[33]

In addition, the Supreme Court reasoned that Congress has a legitimate interest in protecting potential life; therefore, Congress may give financial incentives to women on Medicaid to encourage them to choose childbirth over abortion.[34] Although many people would disagree with the Supreme Court's reasoning, it is currently the law of the land. However, some state supreme courts have held that there is a right to public funding of abortion under their state constitutions.[35]

Medicaid Payment Issues

Because of budgetary limitations and increasing costs, states have tried to reduce Medicaid payments to healthcare facilities and practitioners, or at least reduce the rate of increases in those payments. As discussed previously in connection with the Medicare program, there is a danger that reducing payments to providers may cause problems in quality and access to care. In 1998, one of the largest nursing home chains in the country threatened to withdraw from the Medicaid program at many of its facilities because of the company's dissatisfaction with Medicaid payment rates.[36] Although that company subsequently changed its plans, the problem of provider dissatisfaction may become even more serious in the future.

For individual practitioners, such as physicians and dentists, low rates of payment may discourage participation in the program and thereby create serious problems in access to care. According to the federal statute, state Medicaid plans must ensure that payment is "sufficient to enlist enough providers so that care and services are available under the plan at least to the extent that such care and services are available to the general population in the geographic area."[37] In practice, however, Medicaid payment rates are often too low to satisfy this federal mandate. For example, only 16 percent of dentists in North Carolina participate in the Medicaid program, which led beneficiaries to file suit against state officials on the grounds that they have been denied the equal access required by federal law.[38]

The SCHIP Program

In the BBA of 1997, Congress created the State Children's Health Insurance Program (SCHIP) as Title XXI of the Social Security Act.[39] The purpose of the new law was to provide federal funding to the states to provide health insurance coverage for targeted low-income children who do not have access to other forms of coverage. In essence, these children fall through the cracks in the system because their families have too much money to qualify for Medicaid and not enough money to purchase health insurance in the private market. Under Title XXI, states have the option of using the federal funds to expand their state Medicaid program, create a separate program, or do some combination of both.

SCHIP is similar to Medicaid in that each state operates its own program pursuant to a federally approved plan, with funding from both federal and state governments. However, important differences exist between SCHIP and Medicaid, as explained in a report by the U.S. General Accounting Office, which is now known as the Government Accountability Office.

> Medicaid is an open-ended entitlement, meaning the federal government will pay its share of state expenditures for people covered under a state's approved Medicaid plan, and enrollment for those eligible cannot be limited. . . .

In contrast to Medicaid, SCHIP is not an open-ended entitlement. The Congress in 1997 appropriated a fixed amount for
the program. . . . In certain circumstances states may restrict
enrollment if their allotment of federal funds has been expended,
but to date, SCHIP spending for most states has fallen well below
allotment levels for a variety of reasons.[40]

In fact, the federal SCHIP statute explicitly provides that, "[n]oth-
ing in this title shall be construed as providing an individual with an entitlement to child health assistance under a State child health plan."[41]
However, the statute does provide a state entitlement to the allotment of
federal funds and thereby obligates the federal government to pay those
amounts to the states.[42] As some commentators have explained, "The legislation entitles states, not children."[43]

Fraud and Abuse of the Medicare and Medicaid Programs

Fraud and abuse has been one of the top enforcement priorities of the federal Department of Justice and United States attorneys. In addition, many
states are devoting substantial resources to fighting Medicaid fraud. The
priority given to healthcare fraud and abuse should not be surprising in
light of the amount of money involved. Several healthcare companies have
had to pay more than $100 million each to resolve charges of fraud and
abuse. For example, in October 2001, a pharmaceutical manufacturer agreed
to pay $875 million in settlement of civil claims and criminal charges, includ-
ing more than $559 million as a result of filing false and fraudulent Medicare
and Medicaid claims.

In addition to fines and other monetary penalties, some types of
healthcare fraud and abuse are punishable by imprisonment in the federal
penitentiary. Moreover, one of the most severe penalties for a healthcare
provider is exclusion from the Medicare and Medicaid programs, because
that could effectively put the provider out of business.

Suits can also be brought by whistle-blowers, who claim that particular healthcare providers have cheated the federal government.[44] Under
the federal False Claims Act (FCA), the whistle-blower may receive a share
of any money that the provider is forced to pay to the government, and
that may amount to millions of dollars for the whistle-blower. Under these
circumstances, disgruntled employees or former employees, from executives
to billing clerks, have a tremendous incentive to turn in their employers.

As will be discussed, some healthcare providers and provider associations have argued that the government is inappropriately using fraud and
abuse laws to challenge honest mistakes and good-faith differences of

opinion. Government officials, however, repeatedly insist that there are no penalties for honest mistakes, other than returning the money that was erroneously claimed. Moreover, commentators have found providers' complaints to be somewhat exaggerated.[45]

Some cases of alleged fraud and abuse have involved differences of opinion over the proper interpretation of complex reimbursement rules. However, other cases have involved providers that were clearly dishonest, such as those that billed for services they never provided at all. Even if only a small percentage of Medicare and Medicaid claims are improper, that could represent millions or even billions of dollars in government funds.

As described in Figure 8.1, false or fraudulent claims are only one of three categories in the substantive law of healthcare fraud and abuse. In addition, laws prohibit kickbacks in exchange for referrals and certain types of self-referral arrangements. Each of these three categories is examined in detail in the sections that follow, together with a discussion of compliance programs and corporate integrity agreements.

False Claims

Healthcare facilities and practitioners provide services to individual Medicare and Medicaid beneficiaries and then rely on the government or its agents to pay the bills for services that have already been rendered. From the perspective of the government and its taxpayers, this situation presents an interesting practical problem. When the government purchases tangible goods, such as computer equipment or battleships, agents of the government can inspect the goods to ensure that they have been delivered and meet all applicable specifications. When the government purchases services, however, it may be more difficult to verify that the tasks were really performed and appropriately completed. Verifying the appropriate performance of services is even more difficult when the services are not provided at a government facility or are not provided to agents of the government.

That is precisely the problem presented by the Medicare and Medicaid programs. Specifically, these programs contend with the following issues:

1. The government is usually purchasing services rather than tangible goods.
2. The services are provided to beneficiaries of the programs rather than to agents of the government.
3. The services are usually provided at thousands of remote locations rather than at an office of a payment program.
4. The complexity of professional services makes it very difficult to question their quality and appropriateness.
5. The personal and confidential nature of medical care makes it impossible for agents of the government to observe the services at the time they are performed.

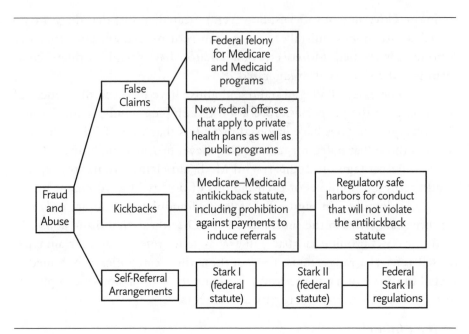

Under these circumstances, the government ordinarily has to rely on the word of the provider that is asking to be paid or on written documentation created by that provider.

Government payment programs have various mechanisms to audit claims, and most healthcare providers are both honest and careful. However, the payment system necessarily operates in large part on good faith and trust. When that trust is abused, the government can rely on the law of false or fraudulent claims.

In requesting payment from government programs, healthcare facilities and practitioners submit claims and make certain representations with regard to the nature and appropriateness of their services. If they knowingly and intentionally misrepresent the facts to obtain payments to which they are not entitled, that would constitute fraud on the Medicare and Medicaid programs. One type of fraud is submitting claims to be paid for services that were never rendered. Another type of fraud is knowingly and intentionally submitting a claim under an inappropriate diagnostic or procedural code to obtain a higher rate of reimbursement, which is referred to as "upcoding." Like a dishonest salesperson who knowingly lies in claiming that a cubic zirconium is really a valuable diamond, healthcare providers who knowingly and intentionally give false statements to government programs have made fraudulent claims.

As indicated by empirical research, some physicians think making false statements about a patient's condition to third-party payers, such as managed care organizations, may be justifiable as a way to obtain services that patients need and could not otherwise afford.[46] In addition to raising serious issues of personal and professional ethics, lying to the Medicare or Medicaid programs in that manner would subject a provider to civil and criminal liability under the law of fraud and abuse.

Aside from misrepresenting a patient's condition or the nature of the services rendered, some providers have billed Medicare or Medicaid for patients they never treated at all. As described in the following excerpt from a Special Fraud Alert by the HHS Office of Inspector General (OIG), some providers have even attempted to defraud the government by billing for services to patients who were already dead at the time of the alleged services.[47]

DEPARTMENT OF HEALTH AND HUMAN SERVICES

Office of Inspector General

PUBLICATION OF OIG SPECIAL FRAUD ALERT: FRAUD AND ABUSE IN THE PROVISION OF SERVICES IN NURSING FACILITIES

. . . Nursing facilities and their residents have become common targets for fraudulent schemes. Nursing facilities represent convenient resident "pools" and make it lucrative for unscrupulous persons to carry out fraudulent schemes. The OIG has become aware of a number of fraudulent arrangements by which health care providers, including medical professionals, inappropriately bill Medicare and Medicaid for the provision of unnecessary services and services which were not provided at all. Sometimes, nursing facility management and staff also are involved in these schemes . . .

Claims for Services Not Rendered or Not Provided as Claimed

Common schemes entail falsifying bills and medical records to misrepresent the services, or extent of services, provided at nursing facilities. Some examples follow:

- One physician improperly billed $350,000 over a 2-year period for comprehensive physical examinations of residents without ever seeing a single resident. The physician went so far as to falsify medical records to indicate that nonexistent services were rendered.
- A psychotherapist working in nursing facilities manipulated Medicare billing codes to charge for 3 hours of therapy for each resident when, in fact, he spent only a few minutes with each resident. In a nursing facility, 3 hours of psychotherapy is highly unusual and often clinically inappropriate.
- An investigation of a speech specialist uncovered documentation showing that he overstated the time spent on each session claimed. Claims analysis showed that the speech specialist actually claimed to spend 20 hours with residents every day, far more time than possible. Further investigation revealed that some residents had never met the specialist, and some

were dead at the time when the specialist claimed to have provided speech services to them.

- A company providing mobile X-ray services made visits to nursing facilities, and billed for taking two X-rays when only one was actually taken. The case also presented serious concerns about quality of care when the investigation revealed that company personnel were not certified to take X-rays.

Claims Falsified to Circumvent Coverage Limitations on Medical Specialties

Practitioners of medical specialties have been found to misrepresent the nature of services provided to Medicare and Medicaid beneficiaries because the Federally funded programs have stringent coverage limitations for some specialties, including podiatry, audiology, and optometry. For instance:

- The OIG has learned about podiatrists whose entire practices consisted of visits to nursing facilities. Non-covered routine care is provided, e.g., toenail clipping, but Medicare is billed for covered services which were not provided or needed. In one case, an investigator discovered suspicious billing for foot care when it was reported that a podiatrist was performing an excessive number of toenail removals, a service that is covered but not frequently or routinely needed. This podiatrist billed Medicare as much as $100,000 in one year for toenail removals. Investigators discovered one resident for whom bills were submitted claiming a total of 11 toenail removals.
- An optometrist claimed reimbursement for covered eye care consultations when he, in fact, performed routine exams and other non-covered services. His billing history indicated that he claimed to have performed as many as 25 consultations in one day at a nursing home. This is an unreasonably high number, given the nature of a Medicare-covered consultation.
- An audiologist made arrangements with a nursing facility and affiliated physicians to get orders for hearing exams that were not medically necessary. The audiologist used this access to residents exclusively to market hearing aids. In this case, the facility and physicians, in addition to the audiologist, could be held liable for false or fraudulent claims if they acted with knowledge of the claims for unnecessary service.

What to Look for in the Provision of Services to Nursing Facilities

The following situations may suggest fraudulent or abusive activities:

- "Gang visits" by one or more medical professionals where large numbers of residents are seen in a single day. The practitioner may be providing medically unnecessary services, or the level of service provided may not be of a sufficient duration or scope consistent with the service billed to Medicare or Medicaid.

- Frequent and recurring "routine visits" by the same medical professional. Seeing residents too often may indicate that the provider is billing for services that are not medically necessary.
- Unusually active presence in nursing facilities by health care practitioners who are given or request unlimited access to resident medical records. These individuals may be collecting information used in the submission of false claims.
- Questionable documentation for medical necessity of professional services. Practitioners who are billing inappropriately may also enter, or fail to enter, important information on medical charts . . .

To Report Suspected Fraud, Call or Write

1-800-HHS-TIPS, Department of Health and Human Services, Office of Inspector General, P.O. Box 23489, L'Enfant Plaza Station, Washington, D.C. 20026-3489. Dated: May 29, 1996.
June Gibbs Brown,
Inspector General.

As a legal matter, the consequences of submitting an incorrect claim depend in large part on the provider's knowledge and intent at the time it was submitted. For example, did the provider know the claim was improper, or was the claim so obviously improper that the provider should have known it was unlawful? Did the provider act with intent to defraud the government? Alternatively, was this just an honest mistake or carelessness on the part of the provider? In addition to affecting issues of liability and punishment, the answers to these questions will determine whether the case will be governed by civil or criminal law.

With regard to criminal law, federal statutes make it a crime to defraud any branch of the federal government, and a specific statute relates to fraud in federally supported healthcare programs. Federal law imposes criminal penalties on any person who "*knowingly and willfully* makes or causes to be made any false statement or representation of a material fact in any application for any benefit or payment under a Federal health care program . . . " [emphasis added].[48] Under that statute, fraudulent claims in connection with the Medicare or Medicaid programs are felonies and are punishable by fines and imprisonment for up to five years.[49]

In a criminal prosecution for Medicare or Medicaid fraud under that statute, the government bears the heavy burden of proving that the defendant made the false statement or representation "knowingly and willfully." In addition, because it is a criminal proceeding, the government must prove its case beyond a reasonable doubt. If the defendant's request for payment from the government was based on a reasonable interpretation of complex reimbursement rules, the government would not be able to meet its burden of proof in a criminal case. For example, in *U.S. v. Whiteside*, two hospital executives allegedly made a false statement on cost reports by claiming that all of the interest on a loan was capital related.[50] The government obtained criminal convictions against the two executives, but those convictions were reversed on appeal, because there was no clear regulation on how interest must be classified, and it was an issue on which reasonable people could differ. As the appellate court explained, "[i]n a case where the truth or falsity of a statement centers on an interpretive question of law, the government bears the burden of proving beyond a reasonable doubt that the defendant's statement is not true under a reasonable interpretation of the law."[51]

In contrast, it is easier for the government to meet its burden of proof in a civil case under the federal FCA.[52] The FCA provides in pertinent part as follows:

(a) Liability for certain acts. Any person who—

(1) knowingly presents, or causes to be presented, to an officer or employee of the United States Government or a member of the Armed Forces of the United States a false or fraudulent claim for payment or approval . . .

is liable to the United States Government for a civil penalty of not less than $5,000 and not more than $10,000, plus 3 times the amount of damages which the Government sustains because of the act of that person. . . .

(b) Knowing and knowingly defined. For purposes of this section, the terms "knowing" and "knowingly" mean that a person, with respect to information—

(1) has actual knowledge of the information;

(2) acts in deliberate ignorance of the truth or falsity of the information; or

(3) acts in reckless disregard of the truth or falsity of the information,

and no proof of specific intent to defraud is required.

Under the FCA, the government would not have to prove that the defendant made a false statement or representation knowingly and willfully, as required under the criminal statute. Rather, in a civil FCA case, the government is only required to prove that the defendant acted knowingly, and that term is defined broadly to include not only actual knowledge but also deliberate ignorance or reckless disregard of the truth. The FCA also explicitly provides that "no proof of specific intent to defraud is required." However, it is not enough for the government to merely prove that the claim was submitted by mistake, even if the mistake was caused by negligence or carelessness.[53]

To prevail in a civil FCA case, the government is *not* required to prove that the defendant healthcare provider had actual knowledge of the Medicare or Medicaid reimbursement regulations. For example, in *U.S. v. Mackby*, the Court of Appeals for the Ninth Circuit upheld the trial court's finding that the owner of a physical therapy clinic violated the FCA by knowingly causing false claims to be submitted, even though he claimed not to have known about the Medicare rules.[54] In that case, the owner of the clinic had told the office manager and a billing company to use the provider identification number of his father, a physician, on claims submitted to Medicare for physical therapy services, although his father had provided no services for the physical therapy clinic or its patients. As the appellate court explained,

> [t]he evidence established that Mackby was the managing director of the clinic. He was responsible for day-to-day operations, long-term planning, lease and build-out negotiations, personnel, and legal and accounting oversight. It was his obligation to be familiar with the legal requirements for obtaining reimbursement from Medicare for physical therapy services, and to ensure that the clinic was run in accordance with all laws. His claim that he did not know of the Medicare requirements does not shield him from liability. By failing to inform himself of those requirements, particularly when twenty percent of Asher Clinic's patients were Medicare beneficiaries, he acted in reckless disregard or in deliberate ignorance of those requirements, either of which was sufficient to charge him with knowledge of the falsity of the claims in question.[55]

Thus, the court affirmed the civil judgment against Mackby under the FCA. The court also noted that in a civil suit under the FCA, the government only has to prove its case by a preponderance of the evidence, rather than having to prove its case beyond a reasonable doubt.

Although the original civil penalty under the FCA was $5,000 to $10,000 for each improper claim, plus three times the amount of actual damage incurred by the government, the civil penalty is subject to adjustment for inflation. As of January 2007, the civil penalty was $5,500 to $11,000.[56] The amounts of those penalties can equal huge sums of money when they are multiplied by the number of individual claims that are determined to be improper. As others have pointed out, healthcare providers may file thousands of small claims, and the government often extrapolates from a sample of false claims to derive a much larger number of claims that it alleges to be false.[57] The amount of money sought by the government may be so high that agreeing to a settlement is the provider's only practical alternative.[58] In fact, if the amount of money sought by the government under the FCA were so large that it would bankrupt or severely damage a healthcare organization, the trustees or directors of that organization may be required by their fiduciary duty to reach a settlement. As stewards of the organization's resources, the trustees or directors simply cannot take the risk of losing the case at trial.

Although most of the laws on fraud and abuse relate to government-funded programs such as Medicare and Medicaid, it is important to note that defrauding private health plans is also against the law. In 1996, Congress established some new federal crimes that relate to private and public healthcare benefit plans.[59] Under those new criminal laws, any person who knowingly defrauds any public or private healthcare benefit program may be imprisoned for up to ten years.[60]

Kickbacks

Under the federal Medicare Anti-Kickback Act, it is unlawful to knowingly and willfully give or receive anything of value to induce someone to refer a Medicare or Medicaid patient or to induce someone to purchase something for which payment may be made under those programs.[61] The statute is broadly worded and applies to any remuneration, whether direct or indirect, overt or covert, in cash or in kind. In addition, it applies to both the party that offers or pays the illegal remuneration and the party that solicits or receives it, but it does not apply to payments to bona fide employees of the organization that is making the payment. Violating the act is a felony and punishable by a fine of $25,000 and up to five years in prison, as well as exclusion from government payment programs. In addition to criminal enforcement, the OIG may bring administrative proceedings for the purpose of imposing civil monetary penalties and exclusion from government programs.

As a matter of policy, the concern is that payment for referrals could increase the costs of the Medicare and Medicaid programs by giving physicians and other providers an incentive to provide unnecessary treatment. In addition, compensation for referrals could interfere with a provider's independent judgment as to when and where to refer a particular patient. Thus, it would be unlawful as well as unethical for a hospital to pay physicians for patient referrals or for a pharmaceutical manufacturer to pay physicians or pharmacists to prescribe or dispense a particular drug.[62] Similarly, it would be illegal and unethical for a skilled nursing facility or home health agency to give anything of value, in cash or in kind, to the discharge planners at a hospital for the purpose of inducing them to refer patients for postdischarge services. It is important for healthcare professionals and managers to develop the ability to recognize situations in which money or something else of value is flowing from someone who would benefit from referrals to someone in a position to refer.

As a legal matter, the primary issue under this federal statute is the intent of the parties. In other words, payment or other consideration is unlawful if it was made with the intent of inducing referrals or purchases. In some cases, ascertaining the intent of the parties is fairly easy. For example, if a hospital made a monthly payment to each physician on its medical staff and if the amount of each payment was based on the number of patients referred to the hospital by that physician during the previous month, the intent to induce referrals would be obvious. Similarly, if a clinical laboratory paid physicians for each sample they sent to that laboratory, it would be obvious that the intent of the parties was to pay for referrals and encourage more referrals in the future. However, many situations in the healthcare system are not that clear, and a business relationship with a potential source of referrals may be motivated by a combination of different factors.

In trying to develop a reasonable rule of law, one approach would be to consider the payment to be unlawful if the *sole* purpose of the payment was to induce referrals. However, from the perspective of prosecutors and enforcement agencies, a "sole purpose" test would be too difficult for them to meet and would allow dishonest people to evade the Anti-Kickback Act by merely pointing to *some* legitimate motivation for their payments. Another alternative would be to consider the payment to be unlawful if the *primary* purpose of the payment was to induce referrals, but that type of standard might be difficult to apply in particular cases.

Therefore, courts have developed a different legal standard for evaluating conduct under the Anti-Kickback Act, and that standard is very favorable to prosecutors and enforcement agencies. Under the prevailing legal standard, it is unlawful to give or receive a payment if any part of the motivation for that payment is to induce referrals. In other words, it is unlawful if *one purpose* of the payment is to induce referrals.[63] This standard has been referred to as the "lust in your heart test," because any subjective desire for referrals would make an arrangement unlawful, even if the primary motivation is completely appropriate. For example, if a hospital pays a physician at fair-market value for legitimate services that actually were rendered, the payment is nevertheless unlawful if a small part of the motivation was to encourage referrals of Medicare or Medicaid patients.

Despite the objections of some healthcare providers, federal courts have consistently upheld the one-purpose standard in applying the Medicare Anti-Kickback Act. As the Tenth Circuit held, "a person who offers or pays remuneration to another person violates the Act so long as one purpose of the offer or payment is to induce Medicare or Medicaid patient referrals."[64] In a related case, defendants argued that use of the one-purpose test would make almost every relationship between a physician and a hospital illegal, because the hospital executive would always be thinking about referrals to some extent.[65] However, the Tenth Circuit disagreed with the defendants in that case and explained that merely hoping for or expecting referrals as a result of payments that were made entirely for legitimate purposes is not against the law. Similarly, it is not unlawful for a physician to refer patients to a hospital that also pays the physician for services rendered, provided that the payment is made entirely for the performance of those services. In approving the jury instructions that were given by the district court in that case, the Tenth Circuit explained that:

> [t]his application of the Act by the district court clearly allows business relationships between a hospital and physician where the motivation to enter into the relationship is for legal reasons entirely distinct from the collateral hope for or decision to make referrals. Accordingly, contrary to defendants' assertion, the Act, as applied in this case, does not make all conduct illegal when a hospital executive or physician has referrals in mind.[66]

Despite such attempts at clarification, the prevailing interpretation of the law causes substantial uncertainty for healthcare providers, and it may be difficult to determine whether a particular arrangement is lawful. As always, the goal of the legal system is to develop a set of understandable rules that will prohibit undesirable conduct without interfering with desirable conduct. In other words, the task is to tailor the rules to stop the "bad guys" without making criminals out of the "good guys." However, with regard to the Anti-Kickback Act, it is not at all clear that our legal system has achieved that delicate balance. Moreover, the uncertainty about what conduct is lawful has resulted in widespread cynicism and disrespect for the law.

To give some additional guidance to providers, Congress required HHS to issue regulations that set forth "safe harbors" from the Anti-Kickback Act.[67] Those regulations are referred to as safe harbors because they provide a zone of safety from legal liability if all of the requirements in the regulations are satisfied. However, the mere fact that an arrangement does not fit within a safe harbor does not mean the arrangement is illegal. Rather, arrangements that do not satisfy all of the requirements of a safe harbor would have to be evaluated under the terms of the Anti-Kickback statute itself.

In 1991, the OIG issued final safe harbor regulations that describe payment practices that will not be subject to criminal prosecution and will not provide a basis for exclusion from the Medicare or Medicaid programs.[68] The OIG clarified and expanded those regulations in 1999.[69] Since then, the OIG has issued additional safe harbors from time to time on specific issues, such as arrangements to provide technology for electronic prescription information and electronic health records.[70]

Some people believe the safe harbor regulations are too restrictive and still leave uncertainty about what conduct the government is likely to challenge. Therefore, in the 1996 Health Insurance Portability and

Accountability Act, Congress required the OIG to issue advisory opinions with regard to proposed conduct under the Anti-Kickback Act.[71] Previously, the OIG had expressed concern that issuing advisory opinions would inhibit its law enforcement functions and argued that it would be impractical to issue advisory opinions about conduct under a statute that was based on subjective intent. However, Congress enacted the requirement, and the OIG has been issuing advisory opinions that are available to the public on OIG's web site at www.oig.hhs.gov.

Self-Referrals

Even if physicians do not receive kickbacks in exchange for referrals, they may have financial incentives to refer patients to facilities that they own in whole or in part. As with kickbacks, incentives for self-referral have a tendency to increase costs and interfere with the physician's independent medical judgment. In fact, several studies have documented that physicians with financial interests in healthcare facilities tend to make more referrals for tests and treatments than physicians without those financial interests.[72]

To address this problem of self-referral, Congress enacted the Ethics in Patient Referrals Act, which is § 1877 of the Social Security Act.[73] This statute is commonly referred to as the "Stark Law," because its primary sponsor was Congressman Pete Stark. As originally enacted in 1989, the Stark Law only applied to clinical laboratory services. However, in 1993, Congress expanded the prohibition to cover many types of "designated health services" under a revised statute that is commonly referred to as "Stark II,"[74] and Congress has made further statutory changes since that date.[75] On January 4, 2001, HCFA (now CMS) issued Phase I of its Stark regulations,[76] and it issued Phase II of those regulations on March 26, 2004.[77] On August 8, 2006, CMS issued a final rule to create a new exception for certain arrangements involving electronic prescriptions and electronic health records, which was designed to complement the OIG's new safe harbor under the Anti-Kickback statute.[78]

In addressing the problem of self-referral, Congress might have taken several possible approaches. One alternative was to permit self-referral, but require the physician to disclose her ownership interests and compensation arrangements to the patient. These financial arrangements can create incentives for physicians to make more referrals and can influence the decisions patients make about their treatment. Therefore, it is arguable that these financial incentives ought to be disclosed to the patient. However, in enacting the Stark Law, Congress did not choose to require disclosure as the means of dealing with physician self-referral, but instead prevented physicians from engaging in certain types of arrangements.

Under this federal law, physicians are not actually prohibited from owning an interest in a healthcare facility. However, the law makes it impractical to do so in many situations, by prohibiting certain referrals as well as reimbursement for services that were rendered as a result of a prohibited referral. Specifically, if a physician or immediate family member has an ownership interest or compensation arrangement with an entity, the physician may not refer a patient to the entity, and the entity may not bill the government program for services that were rendered as a result of the referral. Under these circumstances, many healthcare organizations do not want—or will not permit—referring physicians to have ownership interests or compensation arrangements, because they do not want to lose the opportunity to bill for their referrals.

In effect, the Stark self-referral law uses a transactional approach in which certain arrangements are lawful or unlawful depending on their structure, rather than focusing on the intent of the parties. In that respect, the Stark Law is different from the Anti-Kickback Act, which is based on the parties' intent in making a particular payment. However, the safe harbor regulations under the Anti-Kickback Act also use a transactional approach that is similar in some respects to the approach of the Stark self-referral law. Most importantly, healthcare providers must meet the requirements of *both* the Anti-Kickback Act *and* the Stark self-referral law.

The Stark Law applies to many types of designated health services, such as radiology, clinical laboratory, physical and occupational therapy, home health, outpatient drugs, certain types of supplies, and both inpatient and outpatient hospital services. However, the statute and regulations are extremely complex, and they contain numerous exceptions and definitions, each of which must be considered in evaluating whether a particular arrangement is lawful.

The complexity of the Stark Law demonstrates the difficulty of prohibiting undesirable conduct without inhibiting activities that are beneficial to society. We want to prohibit those self-referral arrangements that have a tendency to increase cost and interfere with the physician's independent medical judgment. Moreover, we want to make the prohibition sufficiently broad that physicians will not be able to circumvent the law by merely changing the outward structure of their business relationships. However, we do not want to prohibit the ordinary and necessary patterns of medical practice, such as referring a patient for ancillary services in the physician's office or referring a patient to another physician in the same group practice. Therefore, the Stark Law provides several exceptions for legitimate group practices, as defined in the statute and regulations.[79] In addition, there is an exception for those in-office ancillary services that meet all of the requirements set forth in the law.[80] There is even an exception that allows physicians to refer patients to a hospital if they have an ownership interest in the hospital as a whole or in the chain or network that owns the hospital.[81]

 Although the statute and regulations are complex, providers can obtain clarification by asking CMS to issue an advisory opinion with regard to a particular arrangement. In the BBA of 1997, Congress required CMS to issue advisory opinions with regard to most self-referral arrangements.[82] These advisory opinions are available online at the web site of CMS.[83]

Compliance Programs for Healthcare Providers

In recent years, many healthcare organizations have recognized the importance of instituting a comprehensive compliance program. A compliance program is an in-house system of policymaking, education, information gathering, reporting, and accountability. The purpose of this type of program is to prevent illegal and unethical conduct such as Medicare and Medicaid fraud.

An effective compliance program benefits an organization in several ways. First, a compliance program will help to prevent some problems from occurring. Second, when problems do occur, despite the organization's best efforts, an effective compliance program will help to limit the extent of the problem and reduce the amount of the penalties assessed by the government. An organization is likely to receive a much lighter penalty if it already had an effective compliance program in effect at the time the problem occurred. Moreover, as discussed in Chapter 4, the directors of a healthcare corporation might be held legally liable if they fail to ensure that the corporation has an effective compliance program.[84] Finally, a compliance program will help to ensure that the officers, directors, and employees meet all of the standards of ethical conduct that are established by the organization.

An effective compliance program requires a genuine commitment by the top management and board of the organization, and everyone in the organization needs to understand that the management and board take it very seriously. To communicate that message, compliance should be part of each individual's periodic salary and performance review.

The OIG has strongly encouraged healthcare organizations to establish compliance programs and has published compliance program guidance for various types of healthcare organizations. These guidance documents are not model compliance programs, but rather they are guidelines on how to develop an effective program in various segments of the healthcare industry.[85]

As indicated by the OIG, compliance programs should not be limited to merely ensuring compliance with the law, but they should also be designed to encourage ethical business behavior.[86] Thus, a compliance program is more than a system of risk management and damage control. Merely complying with legal requirements and avoiding fines or imprisonment should be viewed as the minimum acceptable effort and not something of which an organization should be particularly proud. Rather, in developing and implementing a compliance program, each organization should strive for a standard of ethical behavior that exceeds the requirements of law.

In the meantime, the federal government has been attempting to link compliance and quality of care and has increasingly focused its attention on quality of care as an aspect of fraud and abuse. The OIG has expressed its hope that voluntary compliance programs will not only prevent fraud and reduce healthcare costs, but will also enable organizations to improve the quality of care.[87] In some situations, the federal government has taken the position that providing poor quality of care may constitute fraud and abuse.[88]

In fraud and abuse cases, the OIG often enters into a settlement with the healthcare provider. If the OIG permits the organization to continue as a participant in federal programs, the OIG will ordinarily require the organization to operate under the terms of a Corporate Integrity Agreement. In addition to requiring organizations to make improvements in their financial controls, the OIG has used Corporate Integrity Agreements to require providers to establish mechanisms to promote quality of care. Under these circumstances, quality of care is now part of the law of fraud and abuse, and compliance is inextricably linked with efforts to reduce medical errors and promote the quality of care.

Notes

1. Medicare Prescription Drug, Improvement, and Modernization Act of 2003, Pub. L. No. 108-173, 117 Stat. 2066.
2. D.M. Harris, "Beyond Beneficiaries: Using the Medicare Program to Accomplish Broader Public Goals," *Washington & Lee Law Review*, 60(4) (2003): 1251–1314, at 1252, 1312.
3. *Id.*
4. *Fischer v. United States*, 529 U.S. 667, 680 (2000).
5. Balanced Budget Act of 1997, Pub. L. No. 105-33, 111 Stat. 251 (1997).
6. 42 U.S.C. § 1395a(a) (2006).
7. T.S. Jost, "The Most Important Health Care Legislation of the Millennium (So Far): The Medicare Modernization Act," *Yale Journal of Health Policy, Law & Ethics*, 5 (2005): 437–449, at 445 ("The MMA for the first time means-tests part of the Medicare program.").
8. *Id.* at 445–46.
9. See R.A. Berenson and D.M. Harris, "Using Managed Care Tools in Traditional Medicare: Should We? Could We?" *Law & Contemporary Problems*, 65 (2002): 139–167.
10. 42 U.S.C. § 1395 (2006).
11. See, e.g., *Home Health Care, Inc. v. Heckler*, 717 F.2d 587, 590–91 (D.C. Cir. 1983).

12. *Fischer v. United States*, 529 U.S. 667, 680 (2000).

13. See *United States v. Baylor University Medical Center*, 736 F.2d 1039, 1946 (5th Cir. 1984).

14. See *Modaber v. Culpepper Memorial Hospital, Inc.*, 674 F.2d 1023, 1025–26 (4th Cir. 1982).

15. Centers for Medicare & Medicaid Services, "Press Release: Medicare 'Pay For Performance (P4P)' Initiatives" (January 31, 2005). [Online document; retrieved 2/11/07.] www.cms.hhs.gov/apps/media/press/release.asp?Counter=1343.

16. See 42 U.S.C. § 1320a–7a(b) (2006).

17. See S. 1194, 105th Cong. (1997).

18. See H.R. 2784, 105th Cong. (1997).

19. See note 1, *supra*.

20. See Jost, *supra* note 7, at 446.

21. 42 U.S.C. § 1395w–111(i) (2006).

22. H.R. 4, 110th Cong., 1st Sess. (2007).

23. See Medicare Preservation Act of 1995, H.R. 2425, 104th Cong. (1995) (passed by the House of Representatives).

24. See, e.g., *Mandy R. v. Owens*, 464 F.3d 1139 (10th Cir. 2006); *Westside Mothers v. Olszewski*, 454 F.3d 532 (6th Cir. 2006).

25. Deficit Reduction Act of 2005, Pub. L. No. 109-171, § 6036 (effective July 1, 2006).

26. See 42 U.S.C. § 1396p(c) (2006).

27. See 42 C.F.R. §§ 440.210, 440. 220 (2006).

28. 42 U.S.C. § 1396d(a)(4)(B) (2006).

29. See generally *Westside Mothers v. Olszewski*, 454 F.3d 532, 543–44 (6th Cir. 2006).

30. See *Pinneke v. Priesser*, 623 F.2d 546, 549 (8th Cir. 1980).

31. See, e.g., *Pereira v. Kozlowski*, 996 F.2d 723 (4th Cir. 1993) (three-year-old child needing heart transplant).

32. See New and Pending Demonstration Project Proposals Submitted Pursuant to Section 1115(a) of the Social Security Act: November and December 1994, 60 Fed. Reg. 4,418, 4,420 (Jan. 23, 1995).

33. *Harris v. McRae*, 448 U.S. 297, 316 (1980).

34. See *id.* at 324–325.

35. See, e.g., *Committee to Defend Reproductive Rights v. Myers*, 625 P.2d 779 (Cal. 1981).

36. See M. Michael and C. Adams, "For Medicaid Patients, Doors Slam Closed: Citing Finances, Nursing Home Evicts the Needy," *Wall Street Journal*, April 7, 1998, B1.

37. 42 U.S.C. § 1396a(a)(30)(A) (2006).

38. *Antrican v. Buell*, 290 F.3d 178 (4th Cir. 2002).

39. Balanced Budget Act of 1997, Pub. L. No. 105-33, §§ 4901(a) *et seq.*, 111 Stat. 251, 552 (1997) (codified at 42 U.S.C. §§ 1397aa *et seq.*).

40. U.S. General Accounting Office, *Medicaid and SCHIP: Recent HHS Approvals of Demonstration Waiver Projects Raise Concerns*, GAO-02-817 (July 2002) (footnotes omitted).

41. 42 U.S.C. § 1397bb(b)(4) (2006).

42. 42 U.S.C. § 1397aa(c) (2006).

43. S. Rosenbaum, et al., "The Children's Hour: The State Children's Health Insurance Program," *Health Affairs*, 17 (1998): 75, 77.

44. See 31 U.S.C. §§ 3729 *et seq.* (2006).

45. See T.S. Jost and S.L. Davies, "The Empire Strikes Back: A Critique of the Backlash Against Fraud and Abuse Enforcement," *Alabama Law Review*, 51 (1999): 239–309.

46. V.G. Freeman, et al., "Lying for Patients: Physician Deception of Third-Party Payers," *Archives of Internal Medicine*, 159 (1999): 2263–2270.

47. Publication of OIG Special Fraud Alert: Fraud and Abuse in the Provision of Services in Nursing Facilities, 61 Fed. Reg. 30,623 (June 17, 1996).

48. 42 U.S.C. § 1320a–7b(a) (2006).

49. See *id.*

50. 285 F.3d 1345 (11th Cir. 2002).

51. *Id.* at 1351.

52. 31 U.S.C. § 3729 (2006).

53. *United States ex rel. Hochman v. Nackman*, 145 F.3d 1069, 1073 (9th Cir. 1998).

54. 261 F.3d 821 (9th Cir. 2001).

55. *Id.* at 828.

56. 28 CFR § 85.3(a)(9) (2006).

57. Jost and Davies, *supra* note 45, at 247–248, 305.

58. See generally T.H. Stanton, "Fraud-and-Abuse Enforcement in Medicare: Finding Middle Ground," *Health Affairs*, 20(4) (2001): 28–42, at 32.

59. See Health Insurance Portability and Accountability Act of 1996, Pub. L. No. 104-191, §§ 241–250, 110 Stat. 1936, 2016–2021 (codified in scattered sections of 18 U.S.C.).

60. *Id.* at § 242 (codified at 18 U.S.C. § 1347).

61. See 42 U.S.C. § 1320a–7b(b)(1)–(2) (2006).

62. See Publication of OIG Special Fraud Alerts, 59 Fed. Reg. 65,372 (Dec. 19, 1994).

63. See, e.g., *United States v. Greber*, 760 F.2d 68, 72 (3rd Cir. 1985).

64. *United States v. McClatchey*, 217 F.3d 823, 835 (10th Cir. 2000).

65. *United States v. LaHue*, 261 F.3d 993 (10th Cir. 2001).

66. *Id.* (citation omitted).
67. Medicare and Medicaid Patient and Program Protection Act of 1987, Pub. L. No. 100-93, § 14, 101 Stat. 680, 697 (1987) (codified at 42 U.S.C. § 1320a–7b).
68. See Medicare and State Health Care Programs: Fraud and Abuse; OIG Anti-Kickback Provisions, 56 Fed. Reg. 35,952, 35,984–87 (July 29, 1991) (codified at 42 C.F.R. pt. 1001).
69. Medicare and State Health Care Programs: Fraud and Abuse; Clarification of the Initial OIG Safe Harbor Provisions and Establishment of Additional Safe Harbor Provisions Under the Anti-Kickback Statute, 64 Fed. Reg. 63,518 (Nov. 19, 1999).
70. Medicare and State Health Care Programs: Fraud and Abuse; Safe Harbors for Certain Electronic Prescribing and Electronic Health Records Arrangements Under the Anti-Kickback Statute; Final Rule, 71 Fed. Reg. 45,110 (August 8, 2006).
71. Health Insurance Portability and Accountability Act of 1996, Pub. L. No. 104-191, § 205, 110 Stat. 1936, 2000 (codified at 42 U.S.C. § 1320a–7d).
72. See Medicare and Medicaid Programs; Physicians' Referrals to Health Care Entities with Which They Have Financial Relationships, 63 Fed. Reg. 1,659, 1,661 (Jan. 9, 1998) (explanatory information for proposed Stark II regulations).
73. Ethics in Patient Referrals Act, Pub. L. No. 101-239, § 6204, 103 Stat. 2106, 2236 (1989) (codified at 42 U.S.C. § 1395nn).
74. Omnibus Budget Reconciliation Act of 1993, Pub. L. No. 103-66, § 13,562, 107 Stat. 312, 596 (1993) (codified at 42 U.S.C. § 1395nn).
75. See, e.g., Social Security Act Amendments of 1994, Pub. L. No. 103-432, § 152, 108 Stat. 4398, 4436 (1994) (codified at 42 U.S.C. § 1395nn).
76. Medicare and Medicaid Programs; Physicians' Referrals to Health Care Entities with Which They Have Financial Relationships, 66 Fed. Reg. 856 (Jan. 4, 2001) (final rule).
77. Medicare Program; Physicians' Referrals to Health Care Entities with Which They Have Financial Relationships (Phase II), 69 Fed. Reg. 16,054 (March 26, 2004) (interim final rule).
78. 71 Fed. Reg. 45,140 (August 8, 2006) (final rule).
79. See, e.g., 42 U.S.C. § 1395nn(b)(1) (2006); 63 Fed. Reg. at 1,687–91, 1,721.
80. See 42 U.S.C. § 1395nn(b)(2) (2006); 63 Fed. Reg. at 1,684–85, 1723.
81. See 63 Fed. Reg. at 1,713 (introduction to proposed regulations).
82. Balanced Budget Act of 1997, Pub. L. No. 105-33, § 4314, 111 Stat. 251, 389 (1997) (codified at 42 U.S.C. §1395nn).

83. Centers for Medicare & Medicaid Services, Physician Self Referral. [Online information; retrieved 2/12/07.] www.cms.hhs.gov/ PhysicianSelfReferral/07_advisory_ opinions.asp#TopOfPage.

84. See *In re Caremark International, Inc.*, 698 A.2d 959, 970 (Del. Ch. 1996).

85. See, e.g., OIG Supplemental Compliance Program Guidance for Hospitals, 70 Fed. Reg. 4,858 (January 31, 2005).

86. See Publication of the OIG Compliance Program Guidance for Hospitals, 63 Fed. Reg. 8,987 (Feb. 23, 1998) at 8,988, 8,990, 8,998.

87. 63 Fed. Reg. at 8,998.

88. See K.A. Peterson, Note, "First Nursing Homes, Next Managed Care?: Limiting Liability in Quality of Care Cases Under the False Claims Act," *American Journal of Law & Medicine*, 26 (2000): 69–88, n. at 72; J.R. Munich and E.W. Lane, "When Neglect Becomes Fraud: Quality of Care and False Claims," *St. Louis University Law Journal*, 43 (1999): 27–52, at 36.

ANTITRUST LAW IN THE HEALTHCARE FIELD

The U.S. economic system is based on free enterprise and market competition. The competitive market promotes the welfare of consumers by reducing price, increasing quality, and providing freedom of choice. To protect the competitive market and the free-enterprise system, Congress enacted the antitrust laws more than a century ago. As the U.S. Supreme Court has explained, "[a]ntitrust laws in general, and the Sherman Act in particular, are the Magna Carta of free enterprise. They are as important to the preservation of economic freedom and our free-enterprise system as the Bill of Rights is to the protection of our fundamental personal freedoms."[1]

In applying antitrust laws to the healthcare industry, unique and fascinating problems of law and public policy are involved because of the peculiarities of healthcare economics and the pervasiveness of government regulation. First, a significant dispute is ongoing as to whether market competition in the healthcare industry promotes or inhibits the welfare of consumers. As discussed in Chapter 5 with regard to certificate-of-need (CON) regulation, there is a serious question as to whether competition among healthcare providers reduces the cost of services, as it does in other industries. In fact, the economic theory of the CON laws is that consumers are better served by less competition, greater cooperation, and more intensive government regulation.

In addition, healthcare providers and payers operate under a complex mixture of market competition and government regulation, which significantly affects the application of antitrust law in this context. As a practical matter, we know how to apply antitrust laws to ordinary competitive markets, by applying standard antitrust doctrines. We also know that we would not apply antitrust laws to sectors of the economy that are completely regulated, such as public utilities or other natural monopolies, in which market competition has been replaced by government regulation. What makes the application of antitrust law to healthcare so interesting is figuring out how to apply antitrust principles to a unique market that is neither fully competitive nor fully regulated, but rather somewhere in the middle of these two extremes.

Some people argue that the healthcare industry should be exempt from antitrust law or at least that antitrust laws should be applied differently in the healthcare context. Others argue that antitrust law should be strictly applied to healthcare providers to encourage competition on price and quality. Predictably, this debate has not been resolved at one extreme or the other, but rather on an issue-by-issue basis. Thus, the healthcare industry is subject to standard antitrust principles in some ways, and healthcare is treated somewhat differently from most other industries in other ways.

These are not just theoretical issues, but rather issues that provide real policy choices:

1. Should Congress grant statutory exemptions or immunities from antitrust liability for particular activities by healthcare providers, such as joint negotiation with third-party payers?
2. Should state legislatures enact statutes to replace competition with regulatory supervision of healthcare providers in their respective states and thereby displace the operation of federal antitrust laws?

The healthcare industry has a long history of resistance to competition by some providers and third-party payers. In an effort to preserve the status quo, some physicians have resisted competition from nonphysician practitioners and have opposed expanding new methods of healthcare financing and delivery, such as prepaid group practice and managed care. Healthcare professionals have often tried to justify their actions as necessary to ensure quality of care[2] and have tried to preserve the status quo by means of ethical rules that have the effect of restricting competition.

However, the U.S. Supreme Court has made it very clear that the goals of ensuring quality and maintaining ethical standards do not justify interference with free-market competition. It is no defense to argue that restraining competition is justified by the need to preserve quality or protect the public interest.

In an analogous situation involving professional engineering services, a professional organization's ethical code prohibited competitive bidding by members of the organization.[3] When the federal government challenged the ethical rule under the antitrust laws, the organization tried to justify its rule by arguing that price competition by professional engineers would reduce the quality of services and thereby endanger public health and safety. The Supreme Court flatly rejected the organization's defense and characterized it as "nothing less than a frontal assault on the basic policy of the Sherman Act."[4] In a subsequent case involving an organization of dentists, the Supreme Court reasoned that a professional organization "is not entitled to pre-empt the working of the market by deciding for itself that its customers do not need that which they demand."[5]

Even if they are trying to meet other important societal goals, health-care professionals and organizations may not take matters into their own hands in ways that violate the antitrust laws. Under the economic policy adopted by Congress, we rely on competition to ensure quality and to reduce prices.[6] If competition does not adequately protect the public interest in a particular industry, then the solution is to ask Congress to grant a legislative exemption from the antitrust laws or to ask state legislatures to regulate that industry in particular ways. However, healthcare professionals and organizations may not take matters into their own hands and interfere with competition on the grounds of quality, consumer protection, or even cost containment.

The Federal Antitrust Laws

Organizations and individuals face severe civil and criminal penalties for violating federal antitrust laws. In criminal cases for price fixing, individuals have been sent to prison and corporations have been required to pay significant fines. In addition, federal and state governments may enforce antitrust laws in civil cases.

Private parties who are injured by antitrust violations may file their own civil actions in federal district court. In that type of case, a successful plaintiff would recover an amount of money equal to three times its actual damages, which is referred to as "treble damages," as well as the attorney's fees the plaintiff incurred in bringing the case. Under these circumstances, antitrust cases usually involve large sums of money, and even a successful defense can be extremely time consuming and expensive. Moreover, federal antitrust laws are applicable to nonprofit and for-profit organizations.

Section 1 of the Sherman Act

Section 1 of the Sherman Act[7] prohibits every contract, combination, or conspiracy in restraint of interstate commerce. Thus, as indicated in Figure 9.1, the plaintiff or prosecutor must prove three elements under § 1.

First, there must be a contract, combination, or conspiracy, which requires at least two independent parties that can agree, combine, or conspire with each other. Ordinarily, officers and employees of the same corporation cannot conspire with each other or with their corporation. Similarly, two parts of the same organization cannot conspire with each other. Thus, some courts hold that a hospital's medical staff is part of the hospital organization or is an agent of the hospital for the purpose of credentialing. In those jurisdictions, a physician complaining about an adverse credentialing decision by the hospital and its medical staff could not establish that there are two parties capable of conspiring and would not be able to satisfy that element of a § 1 claim.[8]

FIGURE 9.1
Section 1 of
the Sherman
Act

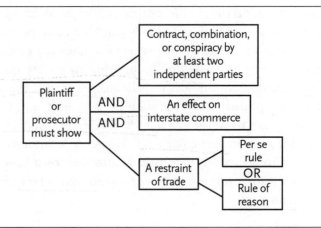

As indicated in Figure 9.1, the second element under § 1 is an effect on interstate commerce. Usually this is fairly easy to prove, because the concept of interstate commerce is interpreted broadly. For example, the Supreme Court held that an alleged conspiracy to block the construction of a local hospital, if proven, would demonstrate a sufficient effect on interstate commerce to invoke the federal antitrust laws.[9] In that case, the Supreme Court reasoned that preventing the construction of a hospital would reduce the flow of money and equipment across state lines. Subsequently, the Supreme Court held that even an individual physician whose clinical privileges had been revoked by a hospital had alleged a sufficient connection with interstate commerce to apply the federal antitrust laws.[10]

The final element of a § 1 claim is the need to demonstrate a restraint of trade. Taken literally, every contract or agreement is a restraint of trade. For example, if person A makes a contract with person B to paint A's house for $1,000, that contract literally restrains A from accepting a subsequent offer from person C to do the same job for less money. Therefore, the courts have held that, despite its unlimited language, § 1 of the Sherman Act really only prohibits "unreasonable" restraints of trade.

As indicated in Figure 9.1, whether a restraint is unreasonable for purposes of § 1 may generally be determined in two ways: the per se rule and the rule of reason. Some types of restraint, such as price-fixing among competing sellers, almost always have an adverse effect on competition. Therefore, rather than engage in a lengthy trial about the actual effect on competition in a particular case, courts will simply hold that the agreement is unlawful per se. Under those circumstances, the plaintiff will not need to prove that there is an adverse effect on competition, and the defendant will not be allowed to argue that its activities really promoted competition on the facts of that particular case. Traditionally, courts have used per se analysis in cases of price-fixing, boycott, and market allocation.

Price-Fixing

Price-fixing is one of the most serious types of antitrust violation. Under the antitrust laws, each seller of goods or services must decide on its own price and may not agree with other competing sellers on the prices that each of them will charge. In the healthcare field, it would be unlawful for competing hospitals or other providers to agree on their prices or agree not to grant discounts to third-party payers.[11] An agreement on price between competitors would be unlawful even if they agreed to reduce their prices or not increase their prices. Cost containment is not a defense to a claim of violating federal antitrust laws. Thus, the Supreme Court held that it was unlawful per se for a group of competing physicians to agree among themselves on the maximum fees they would charge to certain third-party payers.[12]

However, price-fixing is not limited to an explicit agreement on price, which is reached in the proverbial "smoke-filled back room." Rather, price-fixing may include other methods of collectively affecting prices. For example, using the same sales agent to handle each competitor's goods or services would have the same practical effect as an explicit agreement on price among the competing sellers. In some cases, even the exchange of price information among competitors may violate antitrust laws by making it easier to avoid competing on the basis of price.

Boycotts

Boycotts are joint, collective, or concerted refusals to deal with another party. Each person or firm may decide on its own not to do business with a particular person or corporation. However, it would be unlawful for competitors to agree among themselves that none of them will do business with that person or corporation. For example, physicians in the Michigan State Medical Society had unlawfully agreed among themselves that none of them would participate in the Medicaid program until the state increased the rates of payment for physician services.[13] Although an individual provider may decide not to participate in Medicaid or any other payment program, competing providers may not agree as a group to refuse to participate to pressure a payer to increase its rates.

Market Allocation

Finally, antitrust laws prohibit agreements among competitors to allocate particular products and services or particular territories to each of the competing sellers. Thus, it would be unlawful for two hospitals to agree that one would have the only magnetic resonance imaging scanner in the region and the other would have the only lithotripter in the region. Although that type of decision may be made by a state CON agency, competing providers cannot make that type of decision on their own.

If a restraint does not fit within the category of per se illegal conduct, it will be evaluated under the so-called rule of reason. The rule of reason is really a misnomer. It has nothing to do with whether a challenged practice is reasonable or whether it is reasonable to promote competition over other societal values in the circumstances of that case. As the Supreme Court has explained, "the Rule of Reason does not support a defense based on the assumption that competition itself is unreasonable."[14] Rather, the rule of reason is merely a balancing of the positive and negative effects on competition as a result of the challenged conduct. As a practical matter, most business practices will increase competition in some ways and reduce competition in other ways. Under the rule of reason, the court will balance the positive effects on competition against the negative effects. If the net effect is that the challenged conduct reduces the level of competition in the marketplace, the conduct will be unlawful under § 1 because it is an unreasonable restraint under the rule of reason.

In recent years, however, the Supreme Court has taken a more complicated approach to determining whether a restraint is unreasonable and has indicated an increasing reluctance to apply the traditional per se rule. Rather than categorizing all conduct as either per se unlawful or subject to the rule of reason, the court has recognized a new category called "quick look" analysis and has acknowledged that the different categories of analysis can be somewhat blurred.

> The truth is that our categories of analysis of anticompetitive effect are less fixed than terms like "*per se*," "quick look," and "rule of reason" tend to make them appear. We have recognized, for example, that "there is often no bright line separating *per se* from Rule of Reason analysis". . . . As the circumstances here demonstrate, there is generally no categorical line to be drawn between restraints that give rise to an intuitively obvious inference of anticompetitive effect and those that call for more detailed treatment.[15]

With regard to boycotts, the Supreme Court has limited its use of the per se rule to those classic situations in which firms try to prevent suppliers or customers from dealing with their competitors. Therefore, when a group of competing dentists agreed among themselves to not cooperate with utilization review procedures of dental insurers, the Supreme Court stated, "we decline to resolve this case by forcing the Federation's policy into the 'boycott' pigeonhole and invoking the *per se* rule."[16] In light of the Court's reluctance to apply the per se rule and its willingness to use intermediate methods of analysis, it is difficult to predict how far courts will go in allowing defendants an opportunity to prove that their challenged conduct was really procompetitive in the context of their particular industry.

Some healthcare providers have argued that price-fixing in the healthcare industry should be treated differently from other industries because of the unique characteristics of the healthcare marketplace. Specifically, they have argued that price-fixing in healthcare should be evaluated under the rule of reason rather than the per se rule. However, the Supreme Court has held that, despite the peculiarities of healthcare economics, federal courts should apply the same rules to price-fixing in the healthcare field as in any other industry.[17]

Nevertheless, the Supreme Court has indicated that *some* practices in the healthcare industry should be treated differently because they involve the services of professionals such as medical doctors.[18] In the 1975 case of *Goldfarb v. Virginia State Bar*, the Court held that members of "learned professions" are not exempt from federal antitrust laws, but some activities by professionals will be viewed differently from activities by nonprofessionals.[19] If healthcare professionals attempt to excuse their anticompetitive conduct on the grounds of "public service or ethical norms," their conduct will be evaluated under the rule of reason rather than the per se rule.[20] Thus, healthcare professionals are not immune from antitrust liability, but some conduct in the professional context might be viewed under more flexible standards.

In 1999, the Supreme Court reaffirmed the *Goldfarb* principle of special consideration for restraints that are imposed by professionals or professional organizations. In *California Dental Association v. FTC*,[21] the court reasoned that a professional association's ethical rules, which prohibited certain types of advertising, required a detailed analysis by the court to determine their actual effect on competition. In other industries, restrictions on advertising may be viewed as obviously anticompetitive, because they are agreements by competing sellers to refrain from competing with each other. In the context of professional services, however, advertising restrictions might be procompetitive by preventing deceptive or misleading advertising in a market with informational disparities between provider and patient.[22] For that reason, healthcare professionals and professional associations will have broader latitude to argue that their restrictions will really promote competition and should not be declared unlawful under federal antitrust laws.

Section 2 of the Sherman Act

Another important statute is § 2 of the Sherman Act, which prohibits monopolization.[23] Showing that two parties are involved who can agree, combine, or conspire is not necessary to prove monopolization under § 2 of the Sherman Act. A single entity acting alone may commit the offense of monopolization, and a § 2 claim for monopolization might be used as a fallback position by the plaintiff in an antitrust case.

It is important to note that monopolization is not the same as merely having a monopoly. Some monopolies are perfectly lawful. For example, it is lawful to have monopoly power because of a better product or greater skill in business or because of historical circumstances. Similarly, it is lawful to have a monopoly because of a government franchise, such as a patent or CON. As indicated in Figure 9.2, the plaintiff or prosecutor in a monopolization case under § 2 must demonstrate (1) the possession of monopoly power in a relevant market *and* (2) the willful acquisition or maintenance of that monopoly power. For the plaintiff in a § 2 case to prove a *willful* acquisition or maintenance of monopoly power, it is not sufficient to merely show that the defendant acted intentionally or voluntarily to make as much money as possible. Rather, the plaintiff must prove that the defendant did something coercive or inappropriate to obtain or keep its monopoly power, such as predatory pricing or other exclusionary tactics.

What if a hospital has a monopoly as a result of holding the only CON for a particular service and then opposes another hospital's application for a CON to establish a competing service? As stated earlier, the initial acquisition of the monopoly would not constitute monopolization under § 2, because it was lawfully acquired by means of a franchise from the government. Moreover, the CON-holder's opposition to another hospital's CON application would not constitute willful maintenance of monopoly power, because it is lawful to oppose a competitor through the legal processes of government. In fact, a specific defense from antitrust liability protects both public and private parties in requesting action from an agency of government. This defense is referred to as the Noerr-Pennington immunity because of the cases in which the doctrine was originally developed.[24]

Under that doctrine, which is based on the First Amendment to the U.S. Constitution, individuals and organizations have the right to petition any agency of government for a legislative, judicial, or administrative action, even if their goal in obtaining governmental action is to harm their competitors. For example, one category of licensed healthcare professionals may request state legislation to restrict the scope of practice by other types of practitioners, and thereby limit competition from those other practitioners. Similarly, healthcare facilities may request a state CON agency to deny applications filed by their competitors. However, the Noerr-Pennington immunity would be forfeit if the alleged petitioning conduct is merely a "sham."[25]

Section 7 of the Clayton Act

Finally, § 7 of the Clayton Act prohibits mergers and acquisitions that may reduce the level of competition in the marketplace. Specifically, § 7 prohibits acquisitions in any relevant geographic market and relevant product market if the effect of the acquisition "*may be* substantially to lessen competition, or to *tend* to create a monopoly."[26] The language Congress used enables enforcement agencies to prove a violation of § 7 more easily, because they do not need to prove that a merger or acquisition will definitely reduce competition

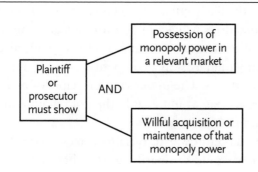

FIGURE 9.2
Section 2 of
the Sherman
Act (Mono-
polization)

or create a monopoly. However, the government's advantage under the language of § 7 is reduced somewhat by the fact that the government bears the burden of proof in seeking a preliminary and permanent injunction.

Specific Areas of Antitrust Concern in the Healthcare Industry

Mergers and Acquisitions

With the trend toward consolidation in the healthcare industry, mergers and acquisitions raise important concerns of public policy. Once they become parts of a single organization, former competitors will no longer compete with each other on price or quality. From the point of view of a large-scale buyer of healthcare services, such as a managed care organization (MCO), the merger or acquisition may prevent the buyer from making providers bargain against each other for preferred provider contracts at a discount. Moreover, from the point of view of an individual consumer of healthcare services, the merger may eliminate nonprice competition, by which the merging parties formerly competed for the consumer's business by offering the most attractive package of quality, service, convenience, amenities, and choices. Concerns have also been raised about the elimination of some women's reproductive health services when a secular hospital merges with a religious hospital that opposes performance of those services.[27]

In one sense, a merger poses more of a threat to competition than temporary price-fixing, because the merged entities will never again compete with each other on price or quality, whereas price-fixing may be temporary. However, a merger may have procompetitive effects, such as efficiencies and economies of scale, and it may create a more effective competitor, which has the ability to challenge other providers in the market. Therefore, under federal antitrust law, a merger is not unlawful per se, but rather it is evaluated on its specific facts to determine, or at least attempt to predict, the likely effect of that particular merger on competition.

In predicting the likely effect of a merger on competition, we assume that business organizations will act in an economically rational manner to maximize their profits. Thus, we assume that they will raise their prices above the levels that would exist in a competitive market, if they can obtain the market power to do so. The underlying principle of merger analysis is not to allow a merger that would enable the combined entity to raise its prices above the competitive level.

To have the market power to raise its prices above the competitive level, a merged entity would ordinarily need to have a large market share and few significant competitors. Therefore, we should not permit a merger that would give the combined entity a large market share in a concentrated market. This requires a determination of the product market and geographic market in which the merging parties do business. We cannot measure market shares in a vacuum, but only as parts of a specific product and geographic market. Once we define the relevant market, we can determine whether the merged entity would still face sufficient competition in that market to restrain its ability to raise prices, reduce quality, or limit output.

The U.S. Department of Justice (DOJ) and the Federal Trade Commission (FTC) have established an antitrust safety zone for small hospital mergers.[28] Specifically, the DOJ and FTC have stated that they will not challenge a merger of acute-care hospitals if one of the two hospitals had fewer than 100 beds and an average daily census of fewer than 40 patients per day during the previous three years. According to the federal agencies, a merger with such a small hospital would probably not reduce competition: First, it may be a rural hospital with no local competitors. Second, a small hospital has few economies of scale and is probably not an effective competitor. Therefore, eliminating that small hospital as an independent competitor would probably not have an adverse effect on competition.

If a merger does not fit within that limited safe harbor, the DOJ and FTC will analyze the merger under the five-step analysis of their Horizontal Merger Guidelines,[29] and federal courts will use a similar analysis. These guidelines apply to horizontal mergers in all industries and not merely to mergers of healthcare providers. A horizontal merger is a combination of entities at the same level of production or distribution, such as a merger of competing sellers of the same product or service. In contrast, a vertical merger is a combination of entities at different levels, such as a manufacturer and a retailer.

It is also important to note that certain large mergers require prior notice to the federal government under the Hart-Scott-Rodino Antitrust Improvements Act.[30] Regardless of whether a Hart-Scott-Rodino filing is required, the government will use the following five-step analysis for horizontal mergers.

Step 1: Definition, Measurement, and Concentration of the Relevant Market

Ordinarily, government agencies argue that the merging parties operate in a very small market, of which they would have a very large share after the merger. However, the merging parties respond that they really operate in a huge market, of which they would have only a very small share. For example, hospitals desiring to merge will often argue that they really compete with other hospitals outside of their immediate area, but government agencies may view hospital markets as being very local.

Therefore, in evaluating the likely competitive effect, the first step is to determine the relevant product or service market in which the proposed merger would take place. This is done by considering what would happen if someone had a hypothetical monopoly of a particular product or service. If one company had a monopoly of a particular product and then attempted to raise its prices, would buyers have to pay those higher prices, or could buyers defeat that attempted exercise of market power by shifting their purchases to other products? If the buyers could realistically switch to other products, those alternatives are part of the same product market.

The same analysis must be used to define the relevant geographic market. If one company had a monopoly of the product or service in a particular geographic area, could buyers realistically defeat an attempted price increase by going elsewhere to purchase that product or service? If the buyers could go elsewhere, those other locations are part of the same geographic market.

However, it is important to note that merging firms may sell more than one product or service and may have a different geographic market for each of their various products or services. For example, hospitals may have different geographic markets for their routine inpatient care, such as labor and delivery, as opposed to their tertiary care, such as open-heart surgery. Patients may be willing to travel farther for some services than for others. In each case, the inquiry is not where patients currently go, but rather where they realistically could go to purchase the product or service in the event of a significant price increase by the hypothetical monopolist. Moreover, it is not necessary to demonstrate that *all* patients would go elsewhere in the event of a price increase, but merely that there would be a "critical loss" of enough patients to make the price increase unprofitable.[31] It is also interesting to note that patients may now be willing to travel farther for certain services than they were in the past, because MCOs give financial incentives, such as lower cost sharing, to encourage patients to use particular providers. This phenomenon has had the effect of increasing the size of some geographic markets.

Once the market has been properly defined, the concentration of the market is measured by means of the Herfindahl-Hirschman Index

(HHI). As indicated in Figure 9.3, the HHI is calculated by squaring the market shares of each firm in the relevant market, which gives appropriately greater weight to the larger and more competitively significant firms.

Specifically, the enforcement agencies will look at the postmerger concentration of the market as well as the change in the HHI as a result of the merger. If the postmerger HHI is below 1,000, the market is considered to be unconcentrated and the merger will be unlikely to have an adverse effect on competition. However, if the postmerger HHI is above 1,800, the market will be highly concentrated and may raise competitive concerns, depending on the increase in the HHI as a result of the merger and the other factors described in the remaining steps of the analysis.

The example set forth in Figure 9.3 shows a three-hospital market that is dominated by Hospital A, which has a 60 percent market share. The two merging hospitals (B and C) each have only 20 percent of the market, and the premerger HHI is 4,400. In squaring the market share of the newly merged entity, you should not simply add the squares of their separate 20 percent market shares. Rather, you should square the 40 percent market share for the newly merged entity, which would yield 1,600 points for the combined entity after the merger.

With a postmerger HHI of 5,200 and an increase of 800 as a result of the merger, both the concentration of the market and the change would indicate a serious potential for anticompetitive effects. However, it is not merely a numbers game, and other factors can be significant. In fact, that merger might actually have procompetitive effects by turning two marginal providers, which have few economies of scale and limited services, into a single competitor. This new competitor could achieve significant economies of scale and offer a broader range of services. In that way, the merger might create a significant new competitor to challenge the dominant Hospital A and thereby increase the overall level of competition in the relevant market. For these reasons, it is crucial to consider the remaining steps of the five-step merger analysis.

Step 2: Consider the Potential Adverse Effects on Competition from the Merger

The primary concern in considering potential adverse effects on competition is protecting the ability of the buyers, such as MCOs and other third-party payers, to force healthcare providers to bargain against each other on quality and price. In fact, the federal enforcement agencies will probably ask large-scale buyers in the area for their views about a proposed merger.

Step 3: Would New Firms Entering the Market Be Likely to Prevent Those Anticompetitive Effects?

Even if a seller has market power, any attempt to exercise that power, such as raising prices, could be defeated by the entry of a new firm into the

FIGURE 9.3
Example of a
Merger of
Hospitals B
and C

Hospital	Market Share	Premerger HHI	Postmerger HHI
A	60%	3,600	3,600
B	20%	400	} 1,600
C	20%	400	
Total	100%	4,400	5,200

market. In fact, even the potential entry of a new firm into a market might deter an exercise of market power. Under those circumstances, a merger would pose little threat to competition, regardless of the market concentration determined by the HHI.

However, a new firm could not defeat or deter an exercise of market power if significant legal or practical barriers to entering the market exist. In the hospital industry, significant legal barriers to market entry exist in many states in the form of CON laws. In addition, there are practical barriers of time and cost for constructing a new hospital.[32]

In contrast to the merger of hospitals, in a case involving the merger of physician groups, the federal district court found that the merged groups would not have market power, regardless of their combined market share.[33] As the court reasoned, it would be relatively easy for new physicians to enter the local market by means of recruitment, establishment of new practices, or establishment of satellites of existing practices from outside the market. Moreover, the new physicians would not be required to obtain CON approval or incur the time and cost required for building a new hospital. Therefore, if the two physician groups merged and then raised their prices, that price increase could be defeated through the entry of new physicians into the market.

Step 4: Do Any Significant Net Efficiencies Result from the Merger?

As already discussed, a merger may promote competition by creating efficiencies, such as economies of scale. However, the federal enforcement agencies are skeptical of efficiency claims in proposed mergers. The efficiencies must be demonstrated and must not be merely speculative. In the antitrust analysis of a merger, efficiency is not an excuse for reducing the level of competition. Rather, the merging parties would need to prove that efficiencies from the merger would make the market more competitive.

In the hospital context, some efficiencies can be achieved without a merger, through a limited sharing of support services or joint purchasing with volume discounts. Those efficiencies would not be relevant to the merger analysis, because they could be achieved without a merger. The most significant efficiencies for merging hospitals could be achieved by consolidating departments, eliminating duplicative personnel, and closing facilities or converting facilities to other uses. Obviously, practical difficulties arise when making those types of major changes, because the changes might adversely affect employees and physicians at one or both of the merging facilities. In addition, the changes might cause inconvenience, economic harm, and negative publicity in the local community. Nevertheless, those are the types of efficiencies that are most likely to satisfy the federal antitrust authorities under this step of the merger analysis.

Step 5: Is Either Party to the Merger a "Failing Firm"?

If the acquired firm would go out of business and close its operations in the absence of the merger, the merger would not really have the effect of eliminating a competitor from the market. However, strict requirements must be met for this "failing firm" test. The allegedly failing firm must be unable to satisfy its financial obligations and unable to reorganize its operations under the bankruptcy law. In addition, the merging parties must be able to demonstrate that no alternative buyer could acquire the failing firm with less harm to competition than the proposed merger.

By using this five-step analysis, the DOJ and FTC will decide whether to challenge a particular merger, including a merger of hospitals. Initially, the government agencies were very successful in challenging hospital mergers, and won most of their cases.[34] However, between 1994 and 2000, federal and state agencies lost all of the seven cases they tried in federal courts.[35] In some of those cases, the government attempted to define the relevant product and geographic markets in an arbitrary and unrealistic manner, and the courts correctly rejected the government's challenge to those mergers.[36] However, the courts also seem to have been improperly influenced by their overt hostility to MCOs and by their desire to protect hospitals, especially nonprofit hospitals, from the cost-cutting process of managed care.[37] In light of those cases, many hospitals concluded that they had greater flexibility to engage in mergers and acquisitions, and that trend of consolidation may have contributed to an increase in the price of hospital services in the United States.

Nevertheless, the FTC has recently taken a new approach to hospital mergers by challenging a merger in Evanston, Illinois, more than four years after it was completed and attempting to require the hospitals to separate their operations.[38] A postmerger challenge provides some significant advantages to government agencies. Rather than attempting to predict the likely effect of a proposed merger, the government might be able to introduce evidence of an actual adverse effect on competition as a result of the consummated merger. In addition, the FTC can pursue the case through its own internal process of administrative review, rather than bearing the burden of proving its case in federal court. If the FTC's administrative decision is later appealed in federal court, the appellate court should give deference to the FTC's administrative decision.

However, a postmerger challenge presents a significant problem in fashioning an appropriate remedy. Requiring merged hospitals to separate, after operating as a single organization for several years, is somewhat like trying to unscramble eggs. In the Evanston case, in 2005, the FTC's chief administrative law judge ordered Evanston Hospital to fully divest Highland Park Hospital, with which it had merged in 2000. As of this writing, the case is still pending and is likely to be appealed to the federal court. This important case may lead to a new trend in antitrust enforcement action with regard to hospital mergers, and it may have a significant effect on future merger activity in the healthcare industry.

Defenses in Hospital Merger Cases

In addition to the five-step merger analysis described, the parties to a merger can raise certain defenses that may provide immunity from antitrust liability or damages. These defenses are described in Figure 9.4.

In the merger context, the most important defense is the doctrine of state action immunity. According to the U.S. Supreme Court, Congress did not intend the federal antitrust laws to apply to the acts of a state.[39] In light of the usual relationship between federal and state authority, this doctrine is somewhat counterintuitive. In effect, state action immunity is the opposite of federal preemption, because state governments have the authority to negate federal antitrust law by deciding that the state does not want free-market competition in a particular sector of its economy. If the state elects to displace competition and substitute state government regulation, the federal antitrust laws will *not* apply in that sector of the state's economy.

Moreover, under some circumstances, federal antitrust laws do not apply to private parties that are acting under the authority of a state. For private parties to be protected by state action immunity, they must show two things.[40] First, the state must have adopted a clearly articulated policy to replace competition with regulation. Second, the private conduct must be actively supervised by the government of the state.

In the context of medical staff membership and clinical privileges, some hospitals have tried to use the state action immunity as a defense to an antitrust claim by an excluded physician. However, the U.S. Supreme Court held that peer-review activities are not protected by state action immunity, because those activities are not really supervised by—or subject to reversal by—officials of the state government.[41]

FIGURE 9.4
Antitrust
Defenses

Defense	Who can raise it?	What does the defendant need to prove?	What is the effect of prevailing on that defense?
State Action Immunity	Any defendant	Clearly articulated state policy to displace competition and active state supervision (but municipalities do not need to prove active state supervision)	Immunity from antitrust liability
Local Government Antitrust Act	Only units of local government	That it is a unit of local government	Immunity from antitrust damages
Health Care Quality Improvement Act	Any defendant in the peer-review or credentialing process involving an individual physician's membership or privileges	Fairness standards in § 11112(a), with a rebuttable presumption in favor of the defendant. Also, must have reported the results to state authorities	Immunity from antitrust damages
Noerr–Pennington Immunity	Any defendant	A genuine attempt to secure governmental action (but the immunity may be lost if the petitioning activity was a sham)	Immunity from antitrust liability

In the context of mergers and acquisitions, healthcare providers in some states have obtained legislation in an attempt to extend state action immunity to certain cooperative activities. State legislatures in at least 18 states have enacted statutes, known as hospital cooperation acts, that establish a process for regulatory approval and supervision of particular activities by healthcare providers. The statutes express a clearly articulated state policy to replace competition with regulation and create a process for active state supervision of the private conduct. In those states, healthcare providers are not required to submit their activities to state government review. If the providers decide to do so, however, they may be immune from antitrust liability under the state action doctrine. Nevertheless, it is unclear whether a state regulatory scheme will be sufficient, in its statutory authority or its practical application, to provide the active state supervision required for immunity from federal antitrust law.[42]

In addition to questions about their legal effectiveness, state hospital cooperation acts raise important issues of public policy. As discussed earlier, a long-standing debate argues whether consumers of healthcare services are better served by government regulation or market competition.

Even if government regulation is preferable, there is a serious question as to whether all state governments have the resources and expertise to properly evaluate hospital mergers and supervise postmerger conduct on an ongoing basis. Furthermore, it is unclear whether state government decisions are sufficiently insulated from political influence by hospitals and members of their governing boards.

Finally, a problem exists in applying the state action doctrine to mergers or acquisitions by public hospitals.[43] If a public hospital is owned by a municipality, it would not need to demonstrate active state supervision to qualify for state action immunity. Therefore, a merger or acquisition by a public hospital would be immune from federal antitrust law merely by showing a clearly articulated state policy to displace competition, and that is very easy to show.

Even if the public hospital cannot obtain immunity from antitrust *liability* under the state action doctrine, it would still have immunity from antitrust *damages* under the Local Government Antitrust Act of 1984.[44] This federal statute provides that units of local government cannot be held liable for damages in antitrust cases. Therefore, in a suit under federal antitrust law, hospitals that are owned by units of local government are subject only to injunctive relief.

Medical Staff Membership and Clinical Privileges

As discussed in Chapter 7, medical peer review and credentialing are important parts of the system of quality control in healthcare organizations. However, peer review has an inherent danger of anticompetitive conduct, because individual physicians and other practitioners are being evaluated and possibly excluded by their direct competitors. Although the ultimate decisions on membership and privileges are made by the governing body, the competing providers on the medical staff wield substantial influence over those decisions. Therefore, it is not only important to preserve the system of medical peer review but also to ensure that a viable legal remedy is available to correct decisions that are biased or anticompetitive.

Most legal theories are ineffective in challenging an improper denial or termination of privileges, as explained in Chapter 7. In many cases, the record will contain evidence of both anticompetitive motives, on the part of the peer reviewers, and professional deficiencies, on the part of the applicant. When a decision is made to deny or revoke a practitioner's privileges, the written decision is usually prepared by the organization or its lawyer. Therefore, it would not be surprising for the decision to contain some self-serving evidence of the applicant's inadequate performance. If the aggrieved practitioner appeals to a state court, the court will use a limited standard of judicial review. Under those circumstances, the state court is likely to uphold the decision of the organization because there will be some evidence to support it.

In a federal antitrust case, the court should not be limited by that superficial standard of review. Instead, the federal court should permit the aggrieved practitioner to argue and produce evidence to show that the allegedly inadequate performance was merely a pretext to cover up the anti-competitive conduct.

Nevertheless, the effectiveness of the antitrust remedy has been severely curtailed, and it is extremely difficult for an excluded physician to prevail on an antitrust claim. First, some federal circuit courts have held that a hospital cannot conspire with its medical staff or with the individual peer reviewers, on the grounds that the courts consider the medical staff to be part of the hospital organization or agents of the hospital for purposes of peer review. As discussed previously, a physician whose privileges were improperly denied or revoked could not satisfy the conspiracy element of a § 1 claim in circuits that follow such reasoning. In addition, courts have held that excluding a single physician from a medical staff or managed care network ordinarily does not give rise to an antitrust claim, because it only harms an individual competitor and does not reduce the overall level of competition in the market. Finally, Congress has created a statutory defense for good-faith peer-review activities by enacting the Health Care Quality Improvement Act (HCQIA) of 1986.[45] The purpose of the HCQIA is to encourage peer review by providing immunity from damages in physician-credentialing cases that meet the requirements of the statute. Although the aggrieved physician may sue for an injunction to require the organization to grant or restore clinical privileges, the physician cannot obtain monetary damages.

To qualify for HCQIA immunity, the organization must have provided adequate notice and a hearing and must have reported the results to the state authorities. Moreover, the peer reviewers must meet the fairness standards set forth in the statute, such as acting with a reasonable belief that the action was in furtherance of quality care. However, the statute provides that a professional review action is presumed to have met those fairness standards, unless the plaintiff physician can rebut that presumption by a preponderance of the evidence. Moreover, courts have interpreted the HCQIA in a manner that is very favorable to hospitals and peer reviewers by focusing on what reasonable peer reviewers would have done and by ignoring evidence of actual bad faith on the part of the peer reviewers.[46] Under these circumstances, the HCQIA makes it much more difficult for a physician to prevail in a credentialing case, and it provides significant protection for participants in the peer-review process.

PROBLEM 9.1: NORTH FLORIDA WOMEN'S CENTER

The North Florida Women's Center (the "Center") is a nonprofit organization that provides counseling and assistance to women in Tallahassee, Florida, and nearby areas of Florida and Georgia. Last year, the Center's board of directors decided to expand its services by providing healthcare services to women, including obstetric and gynecological (OB/GYN) services, family planning, contraception, and abortion. The Center will provide these services on a sliding-fee scale, depending on the patient's income and health insurance.

The Center has entered into a written contract with Mary Ellen Stuart, M.D., who is licensed to practice medicine in the state of Florida and is board certified in OB/GYN. Dr. Stuart will care for a large number of patients, some of whom will have no health insurance and limited financial resources. Therefore, both the Center and Dr. Stuart intend to make extensive use of nonphysician providers, such as physician assistants, family nurse practitioners, and midwives. They also want their patients to have a choice in childbirth. Therefore, patients will be able to choose between home birth with only a midwife or hospital birth with Dr. Stuart. Dr. Stuart does not intend to use midwives at the hospital.

In October 1996, Dr. Stuart applied for medical staff membership and clinical privileges at Tallahassee General Hospital ("General"), which is owned and operated by the county and is one of seven hospitals in the county. Because General is close to the Georgia state line, General and its physicians treat a substantial number of patients from Georgia and Florida.

On November 15, 1996, while her application was pending, the 50 current members of General's OB/GYN staff held a meeting, which was called for the purpose of reviewing Dr. Stuart's application. At the meeting, several doctors expressed their concerns about Dr. Stuart, the Center's new healthcare program, the issue of home birth, and the use of midwives. They were worried about having to take care of the Center's home birth patients in an emergency. For example, if a home birth patient had a medical emergency during home delivery, the patient would be rushed to General, where she would be cared for by the OB/GYN physician on call, even though she was not the patient of that physician and that physician had never seen the patient before the emergency. The physicians indicated that the potential malpractice liability under those circumstances was problematic.

At the same meeting, a few doctors expressed their concern for the possible loss of business they would suffer with the opening of the Center's health services program. Although they did not want to care for indigent patients, they were concerned that they would lose some paying patients because the Center will offer more choices in childbirth and a sliding-fee scale. The administrator of General was present at the meeting and said that the hospital would lose obstetric business if the Center and Dr. Stuart gave women the option of delivering their babies at home.

Dr. Samuel Jackson, who is chief of the OB/GYN department at General, reported that he had reviewed a sample of medical records for patients treated by Dr. Stuart at another hospital, and it was his professional opinion that Dr. Stuart did not provide good-quality care. In addition, he said Dr. Stuart had been sued for medical malpractice two years ago, and her malpractice carrier had settled the case before trial by paying the plaintiff $500,000. After hearing this information at the meeting, the OB/GYN physicians voted to recommend denial of Dr. Stuart's application for medical staff membership and clinical privileges on the grounds that she had failed to demonstrate her professional competence.

The next day, the hospital administrator notified Dr. Stuart in writing of the action taken at the meeting to recommend denial of her application for medical staff membership and clinical privileges. The administrator advised her that she had the right to a hearing on her application before the credentials committee of the medical staff. Dr. Stuart exercised her right to that hearing, at which she testified and was represented by legal counsel.

At the hearing before the credentials committee, the chief of the OB/GYN department, Dr. Jackson, testified that on the basis of his review of medical records, Dr. Stuart did not provide good-quality care. He also told the credentials committee about Dr. Stuart's malpractice settlement. In response, Dr. Stuart testified that her care of patients was appropriate and told her side of the story with regard to the malpractice case. After hearing the evidence, the credentials committee recommended that her application for medical staff membership and clinical privileges be denied, and that recommendation was adopted by the board of trustees of General on December 28, 1996. The next day, the hospital administrator notified Dr. Stuart of the decision and also reported the decision to the Florida State Board of Medical Examiners as required by state law.

One month later, Dr. Jackson and another member of General's OB/GYN staff, Dr. George Alexander, met with a representative of Happy Family Health Plan. The administrator of General was also present at that meeting. The two physicians told the representative of Happy Family that they were concerned about the unsafe practices at the Center's new healthcare program. The two physicians also stated that they hoped Happy Family would not accept the Center and Dr. Stuart as participating providers with eligibility to receive payment from Happy Family. In fact, the doctors said that they were so concerned about the Center's unsafe practices that if Happy Family agreed to pay the Center and Dr. Stuart for services rendered to Happy Family patients, all of the other members of the OB/GYN staff at General would feel ethically bound to stop treating Happy Family patients.

The representative of Happy Family asked the two physicians whether all of the other OB/GYN physicians at General felt the same way. The doctors responded that all of the physicians at the meeting on November 15 had agreed that Dr. Jackson and Dr. Alexander should speak to Happy Family on their behalf. In addition, the administrator of General stated that General might have to reevaluate its contractual arrangement with Happy Family the next time that General's provider contract with Happy Family came up for renewal. One week later, Happy Family wrote to the Center and Dr. Stuart to state that Happy Family would not accept them as participating providers and therefore would not pay the Center or Dr. Stuart for services rendered to Happy Family patients.

Under the facts set forth above, what claims could Dr. Stuart assert *against the other physicians*, and what defenses could *the other physicians raise?* Be sure to discuss the elements of each potential claim and defense, as well as your evaluation of the likelihood of success on each claim or defense.

Note: Do not discuss any potential claims against the hospital; however, you may consider the hospital's participation as a possible conspirator.

Price Negotiations Between Healthcare Providers and Third-Party Payers

Competing healthcare providers must act independently in setting their respective prices and negotiating with third-party payers. As a general rule, healthcare providers may not join forces with their competitors in an effort to increase their bargaining power against the insurance companies, health maintenance organizations, and other third-party payers who purchase their services.

Some physicians and medical organizations have expressed frustration that antitrust laws permit a large-scale buyer to use its market power to force down the prices for physician services, but nevertheless prohibit physicians from combining forces to "level the playing field." The reason for this apparently disparate treatment is that the physicians and medical group practices are independent competitors, whereas a large-scale buyer such as an insurance company is a single entity acting alone. Of course, it would be unlawful for a group of payers to agree among themselves on the prices they would pay for physician services, but a single payer, acting alone, may use its market power to force down the price of physician services.[47]

Some physicians have argued that they should be allowed to negotiate jointly with third-party payers, and that their joint negotiation should be immune from antitrust scrutiny under the exemption for collective bargaining by labor unions. However, most physicians in private practice are not bona fide employees of the third-party payers, and therefore, those independent physicians would not be entitled to the protection of the labor union exemption from antitrust laws. Some physicians have even urged Congress to amend the law to treat independent, competing physicians in the same manner as employees who are members of labor unions, and bills to that effect have been introduced in Congress.[48] However, there is little or no justification for amending the law to treat competing physicians in private practice as if they were members of a bona fide labor union in collective bargaining with their employer.

In some situations, independent physicians and medical groups may lawfully work together, and in other situations such collective effort would be unlawful. Depending on the circumstances, it may be unlawful for a group of competing physicians to establish a single organization for the purpose of negotiating with payers on behalf of all of the physicians.[49] In fact, some physicians and other providers have established organizations, such as independent practice associations (IPAs), to negotiate on their behalf in selling the services of all of the competitors. Some IPAs are lawful and procompetitive, but other IPAs are merely vehicles for price fixing by independent competitors. The latter group has been described as "sham IPAs."

Although competitors are required to make their own decisions on the prices at which they will sell their goods or services, participants in a single economic entity may legally agree among themselves on the prices that will be charged by that entity. For example, if physicians A and B decide to form a medical group practice, they may decide together on the prices at which the combined firm will sell the services of each physician. However, if A and B remain independent from each other, they may not agree on price or use a joint sales agent to sell the services of both physicians.

Between these two extremes are many business arrangements in which people and organizations work together in some respects but retain their independence for all other purposes. As discussed in Chapter 4, these arrangements may be referred to as joint ventures. For example, providers could establish a physician–hospital organization (PHO), which is a type of integrated delivery system. As a practical matter, the providers in a PHO or integrated delivery system may have to reach an agreement on the prices at which the organization will sell the services of all of its members. From an antitrust perspective, the issue is whether to characterize the providers' agreement on price as (1) an unlawful price-fixing conspiracy among independent competitors or (2) the lawful operation of a single economic entity like a bona fide group practice.

If the new organization is not an integrated entity, its pricing agreement is merely "naked" price-fixing among independent competitors. It could be characterized as a "sham joint venture," and its conduct will be unlawful per se. However, if the new organization is really an integrated joint venture, such as a group of providers who share financial risk for services they provide through the organization, the providers' agreement on price will not be viewed as unlawful per se. Rather, the collective pricing of an integrated entity or joint venture will be evaluated under the more flexible rule of reason. Therefore, the threshold issue is determining whether the entity is sufficiently integrated to qualify for rule-of-reason treatment.

Qualifying for rule-of-reason treatment does not necessarily mean the arrangement will be lawful under the antitrust laws. Even if a network or joint venture is sufficiently integrated to be analyzed under the rule of reason, it would be lawful only if it has a positive net effect on competition. Therefore, a finding of integration is only the first step and must be followed by an analysis of the likely competitive effects in the relevant market. This second step is similar to the antitrust analysis of a merger because it requires consideration of the probable effect on competition in the relevant product and geographic markets.

For example, some PHOs have tried to include substantially all of the physicians in an area. Similarly, a joint venture might try to include most of the healthcare providers in a particular category, such as including most of the primary care physicians in the relevant geographic market. Under those circumstances, the collective pricing by the joint venture would probably prevent MCOs and other buyers from effectively having physicians bargain against each other for preferred provider contracts at a discount. In addition, other networks might have difficulty finding enough physicians to effectively compete with that joint venture. Therefore, the formation of that joint venture and its collective pricing would probably have an adverse effect on competition and would probably be unlawful, even under the more flexible rule of reason. In contrast, a joint venture that included a smaller percentage of providers in each category might aggressively compete with other networks and providers on quality and price and thereby increase the level of competition in the relevant market.

To develop a joint venture or network that is not too large, it might be necessary to exclude some providers that want to participate in the group. Although the excluded providers might complain, their exclusion should not create an antitrust problem, because excluding a few providers from a network would probably not have an adverse effect on competition. In fact, excluding individual providers might promote competition on price and quality and might encourage excluded providers to form a competing network. Therefore, exclusion of providers is usually analyzed under the rule of reason.[50]

It is also important to note that formatting a lawful joint venture only provides legal protection for those agreements among the participants that are necessary to accomplish the legitimate purposes of the joint venture. It does not allow the participants to enter into collateral agreements to fix prices or divide markets for unrelated services. In one case, two hospitals had entered into a lawful joint venture, under the supervision of the state, to jointly provide certain high-technology services. However, they later agreed not to compete with each other in regard to other types of healthcare services and fixed the prices for unrelated services by means of collective negotiation through a joint sales agent. In a challenge by the state attorney general, the federal district court held that joint negotiations with third-party payers and the market allocation agreement were unlawful per se, regardless of the legality of the original joint venture.[51]

Conclusion

In applying antitrust laws to the healthcare industry, the underlying question of law and policy is how to address healthcare concerns *other than* competition, such as quality, access, and care for the indigent. Although we usually rely on the competitive market to improve quality and make services available, most people recognize that, in the healthcare system, competition alone cannot meet all of our policy goals. In fact, as one commentator has pointed out, competition and antitrust law have disrupted the traditional system of financing care for the indigent, under which hospitals had earned supra competitive returns as a result of their market power and then used those supra competitive returns to cross-subsidize their care for the indigent.[52] In the context of mergers between religious hospitals and secular hospitals, concerns have been raised about whether antitrust law can adequately protect the availability of women's reproductive services when the merging parties agree to eliminate services to which the religious hospital objects.[53]

It may be possible to incorporate some of these policy concerns into the standard antitrust analysis. For example, antitrust laws encourage healthcare providers to compete on the basis of quality. One way to compete on the basis of quality is by limiting participation on a medical staff or network to doctors of the highest quality. However, definitions of quality are broader than medical skill or patient outcomes such as mortality rates. In this sense, competition on the basis of quality is broadly defined to include all types of nonprice competition, such as amenities, convenience, and choice.

Nevertheless, some healthcare policy concerns cannot be incorporated into standard antitrust doctrine. In those cases, other ways must be found to deal with those concerns, such as by means of government regulation. It would be better to acknowledge the need for other legal approaches in some situations, rather than allowing courts to ignore or distort the law in healthcare antitrust cases.

Notes

1. *United States v. Topco Assocs., Inc.*, 405 U.S. 596, 610 (1972).
2. U.S. Federal Trade Commission and U.S. Department of Justice, *Improving Health Care: A Dose of Competition* (July 2004), Chapter 1, page 28. [Online document; retrieved 2/14/07] www.ftc.gov/reports/healthcare/040723healthcarerpt.pdf.
3. *Nat'l Soc'y of Prof'l Eng'rs v. United States*, 435 U.S. 679 (1978).
4. *Id.* at 695.
5. *FTC v. Ind. Fed'n of Dentists*, 476 U.S. 447, 462 (1986).
6. *Nat'l Soc'y of Prof'l Eng'rs*, 435 U.S. at 695.

7.   15 U.S.C. § 1 (2007).

8.   See, e.g., *Oksanen v. Page Memorial Hosp.*, 945 F.2d 696, 703 (4th Cir. 1991).

9.   *Hosp. Bldg. Co. v. Trs. of Rex Hosp.*, 425 U.S. 738, 744 (1976).

10. *Summit Health Ltd. v. Pinhas*, 500 U.S. 322, 333 (1991).

11. See *United States v. N.D. Hosp. Assoc.*, 640 F. Supp. 1028, 1039 (D.N.D. 1986).

12. *Ariz. v. Maricopa County Med. Soc'y*, 457 U.S. 332, 348–51 (1982).

13. See *In re Michigan State Medical Society*, 101 F.T.C. 191, 312–14 (1983).

14. *Nat'l Soc'y of Prof'l Eng'rs*, 435 U.S. at 696.

15. *Cal. Dental Assoc. v. FTC*, 526 U.S. 756, 779–80 (1999).

16. *Ind. Fed'n of Dentists*, 476 U.S. at 458.

17. *Ariz. v. Maricopa County Med. Soc'y*, 457 U.S. at 348–51.

18. See *Goldfarb v. Va. State Bar*, 421 U.S. 773 (1975).

19. *Id.* at 788 n.17.

20. See *Maricopa*, 457 U.S. at 348–49.

21. 526 U.S. 756 (1999).

22. *Id.* at 771–73 and n.10.

23. 15 U.S.C. § 2 (2007).

24. See *United Mine Workers v. Pennington*, 381 U.S. 657 (1965); *Eastern Railroad Presidents Conference v. Noerr Motor Freight, Inc.*, 365 U.S. 127 (1961).

25. *Prof'l Real Estate Investors, Inc. v. Columbia Pictures Indus., Inc.*, 508 U.S. 49 (1993).

26. 15 U.S.C. § 18 (2007) (emphasis added).

27. See generally J.C. Appelbaum and J.C. Morrison, "Hospital Mergers and the Threat to Women's Reproductive Health Services: Applying the Antitrust Laws," *New York University Review of Law and Social Change* 1 (2001): 26.

28. See U.S. Department of Justice and Federal Trade Commission, *Statements of Antitrust Enforcement Policy in Health Care*, statement No. 1. [Online information; retrieved 2/13/07.] www.ftc.gov/reports/hlth3s.htm.

29. See U.S. Department of Justice and Federal Trade Commission, *1992 Horizontal Merger Guidelines* (with April 8, 1997, Revisions to Section 4 on Efficiencies). [Online information; retrieved 2/13/07.] www.ftc.gov/bc/docs/horizmer.htm.

30. 15 U.S.C. § 18a (2007).

31. See *FTC v. Tenet Health Care Corp.*, 186 F.3d 1045, 1050 (8th Cir. 1999).

32. See *In re Hosp. Corp. of Am.*, 106 F.T.C. 361 (1985), *aff'd*, 807 F.2d 1381 (7th Cir. 1986).

33. See *HTI Health Servs., Inc. v. Quorum Health Group, Inc.*, 960 F. Supp. 1104 (S.D. Miss. 1997).

34. T.L. Greaney, "Whither Antitrust? The Uncertain Future of Competition Law in Health Care," *Health Affairs* 21(2):185 (March/April 2002).

35. U.S. Federal Trade Commission and U.S. Department of Justice, *supra* note 2, Chapter 4, page 1 and note 7.

36. See, e.g., *Tenet Health Care Corp.*, 186 F.3d at 1053–54 ("The FTC's contention that the merged hospitals would have eighty-four percent of the market for inpatient primary and secondary services within a contrived market area that stops just short of including a regional hospital . . . that is closer to many patients than the Poplar Bluff hospitals, strikes us as absurd.").

37. See *id.* at 1055 ("Third-party payers have reaped the benefit of a price war . . . at the arguable cost of quality for their subscribers. Antitrust laws simply do not protect that benefit."); *FTC v. Butterworth Health Corp.*, 946 F. Supp. 1285, 1299 (W.D. Mich. 1996), *aff'd per curiam*, 121 F.3d 708 (6th Cir. 1997). See also Greaney, *supra* note 34.

38. *In re Evanston Northwestern Healthcare Corp. and ENH Med. Group, Inc.*, File No. 011 0234, Docket No. 9315. [Online information; retrieved 2/13/07.] www.ftc.gov/os/adjpro/d9315/index.htm.

39. *Parker v. Brown*, 317 U.S. 341, 350–51 (1943).

40. *Cal. Retail Liquor Dealers Ass'n v. Midcal Aluminum, Inc.*, 445 U.S. 97 (1980).

41. *Patrick v. Burget*, 486 U.S. 94 (1988).

42. See *FTC v. Ticor Title Ins. Co.*, 504 U.S. 621 (1992).

43. See D.M. Harris, "State Action Immunity from Antitrust Law for Public Hospitals: The Hidden Time Bomb for Health Care Reform," *University of Kansas Law Review*, 44 (1996): 459–516.

44. 15 U.S.C. §§ 34–36 (2007).

45. See 42 U.S.C. §§ 11101–11152 (2007).

46. See, e.g., *Austin v. McNamara*, 979 F.2d 728, 733–34 (9th Cir. 1992).

47. See *Kartell v. Blue Shield of Mass., Inc.*, 749 F.2d 922 (1st Cir. 1984).

48. See, e.g., *The Quality Health-Care Coalition Act of 2000*, H.R. 1304, 106th Cong. (2000).

49. See *In re Preferred Physicians, Inc.*, 110 F.T.C. 157 (1988) (consent order).

50. See U.S. Department of Justice and U.S. Federal Trade Commission, *supra* note 28, Statement No. 9.

51. *N.Y. ex rel. Spitzer v. Saint Francis Hosp.*, 94 F. Supp. 2d 399 (S.D.N.Y. 2000).
52. J.F. Blumstein, "The Application of Antitrust Doctrine to the Healthcare Industry: The Interweaving of Empirical and Normative Issues," *Indiana Law Review*, 31 (1998): 91, 93–94.
53. See generally Appelbaum and Morrison, *supra* note 27.

PATIENT CARE ISSUES

THE LAW OF TORT LIABILITY

One of the unfortunate realities of life is that some patients are going to have bad outcomes. Despite the tremendous advances in medical science, some patients are not going to get better, but are going to get worse or even die. As a legal matter, how should our society deal with the problem of adverse medical outcomes and medical injuries?

One theoretical alternative would be to prosecute healthcare providers under criminal law in the event of an adverse outcome. When patients die, we could call the police to arrest the physicians and prosecute them for homicide. Certainly, imposing a criminal penalty would create a strong incentive for physicians to exercise their utmost skill and care. However, imposing criminal penalties would be inappropriate because adverse outcomes can occur without any error on the part of the physician. Moreover, criminal prosecution would quickly deplete the nation's supply of practicing physicians, because some physicians would be sent to jail and others would drop out of the profession. Although a trend appears to be emerging toward increased use of criminal law in the patient care context, as discussed in Chapter 2, criminal penalties have been imposed on healthcare providers only in extreme cases.

Another theoretical alternative for dealing with a bad result is to allow patients to sue physicians or other providers for breach of contract. However, most healthcare professionals do not guarantee specific results for their patients, but merely promise that they will do their best and use the appropriate level of skill and care in treating their patients. Therefore, rather than encouraging patients to sue healthcare professionals for breach of contract, our legal system deals with adverse outcomes under the tort liability system of medical malpractice.

A *tort* is a wrongful act that one person commits against another. In contrast to a breach of contract, a tort is not based on a voluntary contractual obligation. Nor is a tort necessarily a violation of the criminal law, which applies to wrongs against society as a whole. Rather, a tort is a wrongful act performed against another person, such as punching someone in the nose or injuring someone in an automobile accident. In our legal system, the injured person may recover monetary damages from the person who caused the injury to compensate the injured party for medical expenses, lost wages, and intangible losses such as pain and suffering. The law of torts is primarily a matter of state law rather than federal law.

There are different kinds of torts. Some torts, such as battery or defamation, are referred to as intentional torts because they require an intentional act, as opposed to mere carelessness. However, unlike intentional torts, the tort of negligence does not require proof of intent. Rather, negligence is based on a failure to exercise reasonable care under the circumstances. Thus, if Mr. Jones intentionally ran down Mrs. Smith with his automobile in an attempt to kill or injure her, that would constitute the intentional tort of battery. However, if Mr. Jones did not intend to hurt Mrs. Smith, but merely ran over her as a result of not exercising proper care, that would constitute the tort of negligence. Because healthcare providers do not intend to injure their patients, medical malpractice is considered to be a type of negligence rather than an intentional tort.

In the context of medical injuries, the law of tort liability raises important issues of health policy. As discussed later, one of the goals of malpractice law is to improve the quality of care by driving out bad providers and causing other providers to be very careful. However, the "deterrent effect" of malpractice law is unclear. The current system of legal liability also appears to cause other serious problems of cost, quality, and efficiency. Therefore, in addition to understanding the current law of medical malpractice, it is important to consider the need for a change and to evaluate the various proposals for reform.

The Tort of Negligence

Under the law of negligence, the plaintiff must prove four elements of the tort to recover damages from the defendant. These four elements are duty, breach of duty, causation, and damages.

1. *Duty.* The element of duty is the legal obligation to exercise reasonable care under the circumstances, whether you are driving a car, building a bridge, or performing surgery. In the healthcare field, physicians owe a duty to their patients to exercise the level of skill and care that is provided by similar professionals under similar circumstances. Ordinarily, members of a jury would not know what a physician must do to meet the standard of care in particular circumstances. Therefore, that standard of care usually must be established by the testimony of an expert witness who is familiar with the routine practice in the same or similar communities.

2. *Breach of duty.* The plaintiff must also establish that the healthcare professional breached the duty by failing to meet the applicable standard of care. In most cases, it is necessary to introduce expert

testimony on this issue. The result is often a battle of experts from each side.

3. *Causation*. The plaintiff must prove that the healthcare professional's breach of duty was the *cause* of the plaintiff's injuries. Even if the plaintiff can establish a duty and a breach of duty, he may not recover damages if the injuries or death would have occurred anyway, regardless of what the healthcare professional had done.

4. *Damages*. The plaintiff must prove that she suffered damages.

If the plaintiff can prove all four of these elements, monetary damages may be awarded to compensate the plaintiff for tangible losses, such as medical expenses and lost wages, and for intangible losses, such as pain and suffering.

Imposing Negligence Liability on the Institution or Organization

If the plaintiff can prove all four elements of negligence with regard to the individual healthcare professional, that professional may be held personally liable for damages. Aside from the liability of the individual healthcare professional, one of the most important and interesting issues in the law of medical malpractice is the extent to which a healthcare organization, such as a hospital or health maintenance organization (HMO), may be held liable to an injured patient.

As a general rule, our legal system only imposes liability on a person or organization when that person or organization was at fault, not merely because an injury has occurred. However, under a legal doctrine known as *respondeat superior*, organizations may be held vicariously liable for the negligent acts of their employees or agents who are acting within the scope of their employment, even if the organization was not at fault in any way. In other words, the organization is held liable for the negligent act of its employee or agent, rather than for any negligence or fault of its own.

For example, if a truck driver negligently injures another person while driving for a trucking company, the company that employs the driver will be held vicariously liable for its employee's negligence. In fact, the trucking company will be held vicariously liable under those circumstances even if the company was extremely careful in selecting, training, and supervising its drivers. Although holding the company liable when it did nothing wrong may seem unfair, it would be even more unfair to place all of the loss on the person who was injured in the crash. If the injured person could only sue the truck driver, he may be unable to obtain sufficient compensation, because the truck driver may have few assets and little insurance coverage. Therefore, to ensure fair compensation to injured persons, the law will hold the trucking company vicariously liable. Then the company can spread the cost of compensation to society at large by increasing the cost of the goods and services it provides to its customers. In addition, the company can protect itself for the future by purchasing liability insurance. Rather than making the injured person bear the risk of an underinsured truck driver with insufficient assets, we use the employer as a mechanism to compensate the injured party and spread the costs to society as a whole. In this way, our legal system imposes vicarious liability for reasons of public policy, even though the organization was not at fault.

In the healthcare context, the issue of vicarious liability arises when patients attempt to impose liability on a hospital or other organization as a result of the negligence of a physician or other individual practitioner. In those cases, it is necessary to consider whether the physicians or other practitioners are employees or agents of the organization. That raises the recurring issue of the legal relationship between physicians and healthcare organizations.

As discussed in Chapter 7, only a minority of physicians are actually hospital employees. In addition, some physicians have contractual relationships with a hospital to provide services in a particular department of the hospital, such as radiology, anesthesiology, pathology, or the emergency department. Generally, those hospital-based physicians are not employees of the hospital but are generally considered to be independent contractors. Finally, many physicians in private practice are neither employees of the hospital nor hospital-based physicians, but are merely members of the hospital's medical staff and have clinical privileges to admit and treat patients at the hospital.

Thus, the first step in determining whether to impose vicarious liability in a particular case is to determine the nature of the relationship between the organization and the allegedly negligent physician. If the physician was acting as an employee or agent of the hospital, the court is more likely to hold that the hospital is vicariously liable for the physician's negligent act. Therefore, it is easier for a court to impose vicarious liability on a hospital for the negligent act of an employed physician than for the negligent act of a physician in private practice who is merely a member of the medical staff. In the past, hospitals were usually not held liable for the negligent acts of physicians on the grounds that hospitals could not control the manner in which the physicians practiced medicine. However, the trend in recent years has been to impose greater liability on hospitals and other organizations for the acts of physicians under the legal doctrine of respondeat superior.

Even if the physician is not actually an employee or agent of the organization, the court may hold the organization vicariously liable under the doctrine of ostensible agency, which is also referred to as apparent authority. If the hospital made it appear to the public that the doctor was an agent of the hospital, and if the patient reasonably assumed that the doctor was an agent of the hospital, the doctor will be treated as an agent of the hospital for purposes of imposing vicarious liability on the hospital. For example, courts are likely to hold that emergency department physicians are ostensible agents of the hospital, because patients go to the hospital for emergency care and the hospital provides a doctor who reasonably appears to be an agent or employee of the hospital. Moreover, in holding the hospital vicariously liable on the ground of ostensible agency, the court will not be bound by the actual terms of the physician's written contract with the hospital nor by a sign in the emergency department that disclaims any agency relationship between the physician and the hospital.

Under these circumstances, there are two separate grounds on which a hospital might be held vicariously liable for the negligence of an individual physician. Depending on the facts, a hospital might be held vicariously liable on the basis of an actual employment or agency relationship. Alternatively, a hospital might be held vicariously liable on the basis of ostensible agency.

Aside from being held vicariously liable for the physician's negligence under the doctrines of actual agency or ostensible agency, hospitals are now held liable for their *own* negligence under a legal theory that is referred to as corporate negligence. The legal doctrine of corporate negligence is based on the hospital's breach of its own duty to the patient, such as the duty to exercise reasonable care in permitting physicians to treat patients at the hospital.

In *Bost v. Riley*,[1] the appellate court reviewed the development of the doctrine of corporate negligence. The following paragraphs describe the circumstances surrounding the case, and a portion of the judicial decision in that case is also provided.

The name of the patient was Wade Lee Bost. Because Mr. Bost died as a result of his injuries, the lawsuit against the healthcare providers was filed by the administratrix (a female administrator) of his estate. Therefore, the administratrix is the plaintiff.

Mr. Bost died without having made a will, which is referred to as dying intestate. Therefore, the court occasionally referred to Mr. Bost as "the intestate" or "plaintiff's intestate." These facts are not relevant to the outcome of the case or the legal principles of malpractice liability, but they are helpful in reading and understanding the court's decision.

At trial, the plaintiff (the administratrix) introduced her evidence to prove that the healthcare providers were liable for negligence with regard to Mr. Bost. Because the plaintiff had the burden of proof, she was required to present her case first.

At the conclusion of the plaintiff's case, defendant Catawba Memorial Hospital asked the trial judge to throw out the plaintiff's case against it by making a motion for a directed verdict in favor of the hospital. The trial judge granted the hospital's motion, which ended the plaintiff's case against the hospital. In other words, the hospital convinced the trial judge that, as a legal matter, it could not be held liable for negligence and should be dismissed as a defendant in the case. Thus, defendant Catawba Memorial Hospital did not even have to introduce any evidence on its behalf, and the jury was not allowed to consider the case against the hospital.

Obviously, the plaintiff was unhappy about that decision by the trial judge and appealed the issue to the state court of appeals. The issue on appeal was whether a hospital could be held liable for negligence under such circumstances as were presented by the plaintiff. In terms of the technicalities of legal procedure, the plaintiff was appealing the trial judge's decision to grant Catawba Memorial Hospital's motion for a directed verdict at the close of the plaintiff's case. Following is the judicial opinion of the appellate court with regard to that appeal.

Bost v. Riley, 44 N.C. App. 638, 262 S.E. 2d 391 (Citations Omitted), *Cert. Denied*, 300 N.C. 194, 269 S.E. 2d 621 (1980) (Including the Syllabus by the Reporter of Decisions)

Plaintiff's intestate, Wade Lee Bost (Lee), was involved in a bicycle accident on 23 July 1974 in which he injured the left side of his body. On 25 July 1974 Lee was seen in the emergency room of defendant Catawba Memorial Hospital, Inc. (Catawba) and was admitted to Catawba under the supervision of defendant Dr. William J. Riley. Riley conducted tests and diagnosed Lee's injury as a delayed rupture of the spleen. Riley, a surgeon, performed a splenectomy on Lee and replaced blood lost as a result of the rupture. Following the operation, Lee was placed in the intensive care unit, fed intravenously and given various medications. Defendant Riley went on vacation from 29 July 1974 through 11 August 1974, leaving Lee in the care of his two partners, defendant Drs. Bernard L. Rabold and Louis Hamman.

Lee's progress improved from the time of the operation until the late evening of 29 July 1974, when he began experiencing abdominal pain, increased intraperitoneal fluid, perspiration, decreased blood pressure, rapid breathing and vomiting. Defendants Rabold and Hamman diagnosed Lee's condition as peritonitis, an infection of the peritoneal cavity. The doctors placed Lee on the antibiotic Geopen. Between 3 August 1974 and 4 August 1974 Lee's vital signs improved somewhat and the doctors, sensing an improved condition, removed Lee from the intensive care unit.

On 5 August 1974, Lee's condition took a sudden turn for the worse. His temperature shot up to 104 degrees, his blood pressure dropped substantially, his skin became pale and his abdomen showed a marked increase in distention and tenderness. Defendants Rabold and Hamman operated on Lee on 6 August 1974 and found a volvulus, a twisting of the intestine which blocked the passage of its contents and the blood supply. The doctors resected approximately three feet of gangrenous bowel. Post-operatively, Lee recovered poorly, developing a fecal fistula, malnutrition and septicemia, and was treated with antibiotics, steroids, hyperalimentation and transfusions.

On 23 August 1974 Lee was transferred to Baptist Hospital in Winston-Salem, his condition critical, under the care of Dr. Richard T. Myers. Three additional operations were performed on Lee, but his condition continued to deteriorate. On 27 January 1975 Lee died of liver failure induced by sepsis.

Plaintiff administratrix of Lee's estate sued defendants Riley, Rabold, Hamman and Catawba for malpractice. In the complaint it was alleged the defendant surgeons were negligent, inter alia, in failing to take adequate preoperative blood studies prior to the operation of 25 July 1974, damaging organs in the area of this operation, failing to diagnose and adequately treat Lee's intestinal infection, failing to adequately monitor Lee's progress, failing to provide Baptist Hospital with adequate information of Lee's condition, failing to keep plaintiff informed about Lee's true condition, removing an excess quantity of Lee's bowel, and failing to adequately treat Lee's condition both prior and subsequent to the operation performed on 6 August 1974. Plaintiff charged Catawba with negligence in the selection of the defendant surgeons to practice surgery in that hospital and allowing the surgeons to perform such surgery, in failing to adequately supervise and monitor the activities of the defendants, and in failing to adequately monitor the condition of Lee or require the defendant surgeons to keep better progress notes on Lee's condition.

At trial, plaintiff called as adverse witnesses the defendant surgeons and other personnel of Catawba, as well as two radiologists and Dr. Richard T. Myers, the surgeon who treated Lee at Baptist Hospital. Plaintiff also called Dr. Stanley R. Mandel, a surgeon practicing at North Carolina Memorial Hospital at Chapel Hill, who had reviewed Lee's medical records. At the close of plaintiff's evidence, all of the defendants moved for a directed verdict. The trial court granted only the motion of defendant Catawba . . .

WELLS, Judge.

Plaintiff alleges error by the trial court in the admission and exclusion of evidence, the making of prejudicial remarks before the jury, granting defendant Catawba's motion for a directed verdict, charging the jury, and failing to grant plaintiff's motion for a new trial . . .

Plaintiff also assigns as error the trial court's granting of defendant Catawba's motion for a directed verdict at the close of plaintiff's evidence. Generally, a directed verdict under G.S. 1A-1, Rule 50(a) may be granted only if the evidence is insufficient to justify a verdict for the nonmovant as a matter of law.

Plaintiff argues that the evidence it presented at trial was sufficient to withstand defendant Catawba's motion under both the theory of respondeat superior and the doctrine of corporate negligence. Catawba could be found vicariously liable under respondeat superior if the negligence of any of its employees, agents, or servants, acting within the scope of their authority, contributed to Lee's death. However, because plaintiff's evidence failed to show that the physicians treating Lee were acting as employees, agents, or servants of Catawba, the principle of respondeat superior is inapplicable to this case.

In contrast to the vicarious nature of respondeat superior, the doctrine of "corporate negligence" involves the violation of a duty owed directly by the hospital to the patient. Prior to modern times, a hospital undertook, "only to furnish room, food, facilities for operation, and attendants, and [was held] not liable for damages resulting from the negligence of a physician in the absence of evidence of agency, or other facts upon which the principle of respondeat superior [could have been] supplied." In contrast, today's hospitals regulate their medical staffs to a much greater degree and play a much more active role in furnishing patients medical treatment. In abolishing the doctrine of charitable immunity, formerly available to charitable hospitals as a defense to negligence actions in North Carolina, Justice (later Chief Justice) Sharp acknowledged the changed structure of the modern hospital, quoting from *Bing v. Thunig*, 2 N.Y. 2d 656, 666, 143 N.E. 2d 3, 8, 163 N.Y.S. 2d 3, 11 (1957):

> The conception that the hospital does not undertake to treat the patient, does not undertake to act through its doctors and nurses, but undertakes instead simply to procure them to act upon their own responsibility, no longer reflects the fact. Present-day hospitals, as their manner of operation plainly demonstrates, do far more than furnish facilities for treatment. They regularly employ on a salary basis a large staff of physicians, nurses and interns, as well as administrative and manual workers, and they charge patients for medical care and treatment, collecting for such services, if necessary, by legal action. Certainly, the person who avails himself of "hospital facilities" expects that the hospital will attempt to cure him, not that its nurses or other employees will act on their own responsibility.

There has recently been a great deal of discussion about the liability of a hospital for its corporate negligence.

The proposition that a hospital may be found liable to a patient under the doctrine of corporate negligence appears to have its genesis in the leading case of *Darling v. Hospital*, 33 Ill. 2d 326, 211 N.E. 2d 253 (1965), *cert. denied*, 383 U.S. 946, 16 L.Ed. 2d 209, 86 S.Ct. 1204 (1966). In *Darling*, the plaintiff broke his leg while playing in a college football game and was seen at the defendant hospital's emergency room by the physician on call. With the assistance of hospital personnel the physician put a plaster cast on the plaintiff's leg. The cast was put on in such a manner as to restrict the blood flow in plaintiff's leg. Plaintiff was in great pain and his toes become swollen and dark in color, and later cold. When the doctor removed the cast two days later much of plaintiff's leg tissue had died and the leg had to be amputated below the knee.

The Supreme Court of Illinois affirmed the jury's finding of negligence on the part of the hospital. The Court held that the jury could have found the hospital was negligent, inter alia, in failing to have a sufficient number of trained nurses attending the plaintiff, failing to require a consultation with or examination by members of the hospital staff, and failing to review the treatment rendered to the plaintiff. Since *Darling*, the courts of other states have found that a hospital's corporate negligence extends to permitting a physician known to be incompetent to practice at the hospital.

While the doctrine of corporate negligence has never previously been either expressly adopted or rejected by the courts of our State, it has been implicitly accepted and applied in a number of decisions. The Supreme Court has intimated that a hospital may have the duty to make a reasonable inspection of equipment it uses in the treatment of patients and remedy any defects discoverable by such inspection. The institution must provide equipment reasonably suited for the use intended. The hospital has the duty not to obey instructions of a physician which are obviously negligent or dangerous. We have suggested that a hospital could be found negligent for its failure to promulgate adequate safety rules relating to the handling, storage and administering of medications, or for its failure to adequately investigate the credentials of a physician selected to practice at the facility.

Since all of the above duties which have been required of hospitals in North Carolina are duties which flow directly from the hospital to the patient, we acknowledge that a breach of any such duty may correctly be termed corporate negligence, and that our State recognizes this as a basis for liability apart and distinct from respondeat superior. If, as our Supreme Court has stated, a patient at a modern-day hospital has the reasonable expectation that the hospital will attempt to cure him, it seems axiomatic that the hospital have the duty assigned by the *Darling* Court to make a reasonable effort to monitor and oversee the treatment which is prescribed and administered by physicians practicing at the facility.

The plaintiff in the present case has introduced evidence tending to show that the defendant surgeons failed to keep progress notes on Lee's condition for a number of days in succession following the operation of 6 August 1974, in violation of a rule promulgated by Catawba. Catawba took no action against the surgeons for their violation. While this evidence is sufficient to show that Catawba may have violated the duty it owed to Lee to adequately monitor and oversee his treatment, plaintiff has offered no evidence to show that this omission contributed to Lee's death. Where a hospital's breach of duty is not a contributing factor to the patient's injuries, the hospital may not be held liable.

Neither may the previously discussed impeachment testimony of Mr. Bost, which was hearsay, alleging that Dr. Myers called Catawba an "inferior hospital" and that Catawba unreasonably delayed its referral of Lee to Baptist Hospital, be considered substantive evidence of the quality of care administered by Catawba. There was also no evidence at trial that Catawba failed to use reasonable care in selecting the defendant surgeons to practice at the hospital. Accordingly, the trial court correctly granted defendant Catawba's motion for a directed verdict. However, as discussed previously, there must be a new trial with respect to the defendant surgeons for the trial court's failure to admit the above testimony as impeachment evidence.

Since plaintiff's other assignments of error are not likely to occur on retrial, we decline to address them here.

As to defendant hospital, affirmed; as to individual defendants, new trial.

Malpractice in the Context of Cost Containment and Managed Care

The legal principles discussed thus far, which were developed in the health-care facility context, have been extended to apply to new types of health-care organizations in the system of managed care, such as HMOs. As in the hospital context, the outcome of each case is likely to depend on the nature of the relationship between the organization and the participating physicians in its network.

If the physician is actually an employee or agent of the HMO, the HMO may be held vicariously liable for the negligence of the individual physician, even if the HMO was careful in selecting and supervising its physicians. Ordinarily, a court would be more likely to impose vicarious liability in the context of a staff-model HMO with full-time employed physicians, as opposed to an individual practice association model, which is a looser network of independent physicians in private practice. Even if the physician is not really an employee or agent of the HMO, courts may hold the HMO liable on the grounds of ostensible agency. In that type of case, the court may find that the HMO held the physician out to the public as "its physician" and led the patient to reasonably believe the physician was an agent of the HMO.[2] Finally, HMOs and other organizations may be held liable under the doctrine of corporate negligence for their own failure to exercise reasonable care in screening and monitoring physicians in their networks.

In addition, several aspects of cost containment and managed care have significant implications in applying the law of medical malpractice. The first aspect that may affect malpractice litigation is the use of financial incentives for physicians to reduce the use of expensive tests and treatments. To reduce the cost of providing healthcare services, some managed care organizations (MCOs) give financial incentives to physicians, such as capitation arrangements and withholds, which shift a portion of the financial risk from the payer to the provider. If the physician is sued for providing inadequate care to the patient, however, the existence of a financial incentive to provide less care will certainly not be a defense for the physician. In fact, the existence of a financial incentive to provide less care may encourage the jury to make a finding of liability and to award a higher amount of damages

Second, health plans and MCOs may require or at least encourage their patients to use physicians on the health plan's or MCO's list of preferred providers. For that reason, courts are more likely to hold MCOs vicariously liable on the ground that participating physicians are ostensible agents of the MCO. As in the case of physicians in hospital emergency departments, courts are likely to disregard the MCO's disclaimer of an agency relationship in its contract with the physician or in materials that are provided to enrollees.

The third aspect of cost containment and managed care that may affect malpractice litigation is the effort by health plans and MCOs to control the use of expensive tests and treatments through restrictive payment policies and aggressive utilization review. By imposing stricter guidelines for coverage, many MCOs and other payers may be refusing to pay for services that had previously been covered and that had become the standard of medical practice in the community. As discussed, the legal standard of care is established by the routine practice of similar professionals in the same or similar communities, rather than by the payment policies of third-party payers. Eventually, widespread changes in payment guidelines may cause changes in the routine practice of physicians in the community and may result in a "dumbing down" of the standard of care. In the meantime, however, physicians may be held liable for failure to meet the *current* standard of care, even though some of the payers have begun to refuse to pay for that care. In short, the goal of healthcare cost containment is not a legally recognized defense to a provider's failure to comply with the prevailing standard of care.

In the meantime, a great deal of publicity, as well as a great deal of misunderstanding, has arisen with regard to a patient's right to sue HMOs and other healthcare benefit plans. Under the federal Employee Retirement Income Security Act (ERISA), which is discussed in Chapter 16, some health benefit plans are immune from claims under state law for improper denial of benefits. That immunity has been the subject of extensive debate in Congress and discussion in the media. It is important to note, however, that the immunity applies only to claims for improper denial of benefits or improper handling of claims. In cases of medical malpractice, healthcare professionals and facilities are still subject to the traditional rules, and ERISA does *not* preempt those medical malpractice claims. Even with regard to health plans such as HMOs, some legal theories might provide exceptions to ERISA immunity and might allow HMOs to be held legally liable under some circumstances.

Informed Consent

The legal doctrine of informed consent is based on the principle that people have a right to make the decisions about their own medical treatment. The classic statement of that principle was set forth in 1914 by Justice Benjamin Cardozo, who served on the New York Court of Appeals and the U.S. Supreme Court. As Justice Cardozo explained, "[e]very human being of adult years and sound mind has a right to determine what shall be done with his own body; and a surgeon who performs an operation without his patient's consent, commits an assault, for which he is liable in damages."[3] Moreover, for consent to be valid, it must be fully informed. Therefore, the patient must be advised of the risks and benefits of the particular treatment, as well as possible alternatives, before the treatment takes place.

The American Medical Association acknowledges the patient's right to obtain information from the doctor and explains that, "[f]rom ancient times, physicians have recognized that the health and well-being of patients depends upon a collaborative effort between physician and patient."[4] However, as one author has pointed out, in ancient times it was considered ethical to conceal the patient's true condition, and even the American Medical Association's first Code of Ethics, in 1847, urged patients to obey their physicians and ignore their own "crude opinions."[5] Despite those historical attitudes, informed consent is now an accepted part of medical culture and patient expectations.

Of course, practical problems occur in explaining complex medical choices to patients with varying levels of education, especially under the time pressures of cost containment and managed care. In addition, some patients may be worried about their condition and unable to make decisions about treatment, and some patients do not even want to make those decisions for themselves. Even if patients want to make their own decisions, those decisions are susceptible to subtle influence by their physicians. In spite of all these practical problems, informed consent is a worthwhile goal for providers and consumers in the healthcare system, and it is an important expression of the ethical principle of autonomy.

Like medical malpractice, informed consent is primarily a matter of state law. Although state laws differ in some respects, most state courts agree on some general principles. As a general rule, consent may be given expressly, or it may be implied from the circumstances. In an emergency, when a patient cannot communicate and there is no time to contact a surrogate decision maker, consent may be implied and the patient may be deemed to consent to the necessary emergency treatment. However, if a patient who is about to undergo treatment explicitly refuses to consent to a particular type of procedure, then, even if an emergency arises during the treatment, the patient might not be deemed to consent to the performance of that procedure.[6]

Theoretically, one could argue that performing a medical procedure without informed consent constitutes the intentional tort of battery, on the grounds that it is a harmful or offensive touching that is committed with intent and without a valid consent. However, most courts are extremely reluctant to categorize the lack of informed consent as the intentional tort of battery, because of the harsh standards under the law of battery and the possibility that the patient could recover punitive damages from the physician. Therefore, the vast majority of courts consider a lack of informed consent to be a type of negligence, rather than an intentional tort. Even in those jurisdictions that rely on a negligence theory, however, a battery action may be permitted in those rare cases in which the physician obtained no consent whatsoever or performed a different type of operation.[7] In contrast, the usual informed consent case involves an issue as to the adequacy of the information that was provided, and almost all courts evaluate that issue under the law of negligence.

As in any negligence case, the plaintiff must prove the four elements of duty, breach of duty, causation, and damages. Specifically, the plaintiff must prove that the healthcare professional breached the duty to reasonably disclose the risks to the patient and thereby caused the patient to suffer damages. In a claim for lack of informed consent, however, the plaintiff is *not* required to prove that the treatment was performed in a negligent manner, as is required in other negligence cases.

Whenever a medical procedure is performed, there is a chance that something will go wrong, even without any fault on the part of the healthcare provider. If a plaintiff is unable to prove that the treatment was performed in a negligent manner, the plaintiff may still argue that she would not have undergone the procedure if the risks had been adequately disclosed. In other words, the injured patient may argue that she suffered damages as a result of agreeing to the procedure without adequate disclosure of the risks. Thus, a suit for lack of informed consent can be maintained *even if* the medical procedure was performed in a careful and appropriate manner. Under these circumstances, a claim for lack of informed consent is often a second count or a fallback position in a suit, which begins by alleging negligence in diagnosis or treatment and then alleges a lack of informed consent.

As stated already, the element of duty in this type of case is the duty to reasonably disclose the risks. To determine whether the physician satisfied that duty, the court must determine *which* risks the physician was required to disclose. Obviously, some risks are so significant that they might affect the patient's decision on whether to undergo the procedure, and those risks could be described as "material." However, other risks are so theoretical and statistically insignificant that it would only waste time and create confusion to require their disclosure by the physician. In many states, a physician's duty to disclose the risks of treatment is measured by the standard of practice of similar physicians in similar circumstances. In those states, it would be necessary to introduce expert testimony on the standard of practice for disclosure to patients under circumstances similar to those in the particular case. However, some states measure the duty to disclose the risks by what a reasonable patient would want to know in deciding whether to have the procedure. Under that test, the focus is on a reasonable patient in what the physician knows or ought to know to be the circumstances of the particular patient.

At the present time, most courts view informed consent as requiring only disclosure of the risks, benefits, and alternatives to the treatment recommended by the physician. However, on the cutting edge of the law, a few courts and commentators have suggested that a physician might be required to disclose other types of information to the patient as a prerequisite to obtaining the patient's informed consent. In fact, from the patient's point of view, there may be other types of information that would be material to the decision about whether to undergo the recommended procedure.

For example, some patients may want their physician to disclose his level of experience in performing the particular procedure, as well as his mortality rate compared with that of other physicians who perform the same procedure.[8] Similarly, patients may want to know if their physician has a disability, such as alcoholism or drug addiction, that might affect her performance.[9] In addition, patients may want to know if the surgeon is HIV-positive or has AIDS. A few courts have considered whether HIV-positive physicians have a duty to disclose their HIV status to their patients to obtain informed consent for invasive medical procedures, but that issue is still unresolved.[10] In considering the advice of their physicians, some patients may want to know if their physicians have financial or other interests that might affect their independent medical judgment.

In one famous case, *Moore v. Regents of the University of California*,[11] the physician successfully treated the patient for leukemia by removing his spleen. However, the patient was not informed that the physician and others were using the patient's discarded spleen to develop a lucrative cell line, which they patented and sold to biotechnology and pharmaceutical companies. Under these circumstances, the patient could not argue that the procedure had been performed in a negligent manner. However, according to the patient, the physician had failed to obtain his informed consent because the physician did not disclose the personal interests that might affect his medical judgment. In that case, the Supreme Court of California agreed with the patient and held that, "a physician who is seeking a patient's consent for a medical procedure must, in order to satisfy his fiduciary duty and to obtain the patient's informed consent, disclose personal interests unrelated to the patient's health, whether research or economic, that may affect his medical judgment."[12]

However, it is unclear whether the court really appreciated the implications of its decision for the law of informed consent. In the modern healthcare system, physicians have numerous economic interests, such as investments in healthcare facilities and equipment, that could affect their medical judgment in referring a patient for additional tests and treatments. Moreover, under the system of managed care, some physicians have financial incentives to reduce the level of care provided to their patients. If the holding of the California Supreme Court in *Moore* really means what it says, physicians—at least in California—who fail to disclose their financial incentives may be held liable for failing to obtain their patients' informed consent. However, it is unclear whether the holding in *Moore* will be interpreted literally or whether it will be applied outside its original factual context, either in California or elsewhere.

In fact, despite some cases to the contrary, most courts still interpret the element of duty as merely requiring disclosure of the risks, benefits, and alternatives to the treatment that is recommended by the physician. Therefore, most courts would hold that information about the physician does not need to be disclosed as a prerequisite to obtaining the patient's informed consent. Even if the patient specifically asks the physician about his experience in performing a particular procedure, courts differ as to whether a misrepresentation on that issue by the physician would constitute a lack of informed consent.[13] As stated by the Supreme Court of Pennsylvania, "we hold that information personal to the physician, whether solicited by the patient or not, is irrelevant to the doctrine of informed consent."[14]

Aside from the issue of determining what a physician is required to disclose to satisfy the element of duty is a separate issue of how to evaluate the element of causation in a claim for lack of informed consent. In other words, how should the court determine whether the alleged failure to disclose was actually the cause of the patient's injuries? If the patient would have agreed to the procedure, even if the risks had been disclosed, any failure to disclose the risks was not the cause of the patient's injuries.

One alternative is to rely on the testimony of the injured patient, in hindsight, that she would not have undergone the medical procedure if the risks had been fully disclosed. This is referred to as the subjective test because the patient is testifying about what is, or was, in his own mind. Obviously, relying on self-serving testimony by the patient in hindsight on the issue of the patient's subjective belief is subject to a great deal of abuse. Therefore, courts in most states use an objective test of whether a reasonable person, in the circumstances of the patient, would have consented to the medical procedure if the risks had been disclosed. In a jury trial, it is the role of the jury to determine what a reasonable person would have done under the circumstances.

In these ways, the law tries to accommodate the right of the patient to self-determination and the legitimate interest of the provider in avoiding unreasonable claims. It is also important to note that the doctrine of informed consent is more than just a type of claim by an injured patient against a healthcare provider. Rather, informed consent is the theoretical basis for the patient's right to refuse treatment, including the right to a natural death, as discussed in Chapter 12. In addition, informed consent is an important part of the federal regulations on experimentation with human subjects.[15]

PROBLEM 10.1: MEDICAL MALPRACTICE AND INFORMED CONSENT

John Parker, age 35, is a self-employed consultant. When he moved to Littleville in 1999, he purchased health coverage for himself and his family from an MCO known as the Littleville Family Health Plan (the "Plan").

The Plan provides physician services to its enrollees through a network of independent physicians in private practice. Each of those participating physicians has entered into a written agreement with the Plan. The standard participating physician agreement between the Plan and each physician explicitly provides that the physicians are not employees or agents of the Plan. The Plan does not provide copies of its participating physician agreements to the patients who are enrolled in the Plan.

However, at the time that he enrolled, the Plan did send Mr. Parker an 87-page brochure. On page 54, the brochure from the Plan contained the following language:

> We are very happy that you have chosen the Plan to meet all of your health care needs. To obtain services under the Plan, you will need to select a primary care physician (PCP) from the enclosed list of the Plan's participating physicians. Please note that these participating physicians are not employees or agents of the Plan.

Mr. Parker did not know any doctors in the area, but he selected Dr. Susan Green as his PCP because she was on the list provided to him by the Plan. Dr. Green is a solo practitioner in private practice, and she leases office space for her practice in a shopping center in the suburbs of Littleville.

On July 14, 2001, Mr. Parker began experiencing dizzy spells. He called Dr. Green's office and made an appointment to see her the next day. On July 15,

2001, Dr. Green examined Mr. Parker in her office and made a diagnosis of Swinehausen's syndrome. The standard treatment for that medical condition is to prescribe one tablet of pentamite (10 milligrams) once a day for three weeks. In her discussion with Mr. Parker, Dr. Green explained the risks and benefits of pentamite as well as the alternative forms of treatment, and Mr. Parker consented to take the pentamite as recommended by Dr. Green.

Dr. Green had a large supply of pentamite in her office, because a sales representative for a pharmaceutical company had given her several boxes as free samples. Rather than waste time and money by sending Mr. Parker to a pharmacy, Dr. Green simply gave Mr. Parker one of the sample boxes of pentamite.

The dosage information from the manufacturer stated that the appropriate dose of pentamite was one tablet (10 milligrams), once a day for three weeks. However, Dr. Green misread the dosage information and instructed Mr. Parker, both orally and in writing, to take ten tablets of pentamite (10 milligrams each) once a day for three weeks. Mr. Parker did precisely as he was instructed by Dr. Green. At the end of the second week of taking the pentamite as instructed, Mr. Parker had a sudden heart attack and died.

As the administratrix of his estate, Mr. Parker's wife filed a lawsuit in state court against Dr. Green and the Plan. According to the allegations set forth in the complaint, Dr. Green was negligent in her treatment of Mr. Parker by prescribing the wrong dosage of pentamite. In addition, the complaint alleged that Dr. Green had failed to obtain Mr. Parker's informed consent to the pentamite treatment. Although Dr. Green had informed Mr. Parker about some of the risks of taking pentamite, she failed to inform Mr. Parker of the risk that she might prescribe the incorrect dosage and thereby cause his death. According to the complaint, if Dr. Green had properly advised Mr. Parker of the risk of prescribing an incorrect dosage of pentamite, Mr. Parker would not have consented to take that medication, and he would still be alive today.

With regard to the Plan, the plaintiff alleged that it should be held liable for Dr. Green's negligence. In addition, the plaintiff claims that the Plan should be held liable for its own negligence in this case.

Please analyze each of the claims made by the plaintiff against Dr. Green and the Plan. Be sure to discuss all of the elements of each claim as well as your estimate of the likelihood of success on each claim. If you think you need any additional facts, state the facts that you think are needed, and explain how those facts would affect your analysis. In your answer to this problem, do not discuss the federal ERISA law.

Proposals for Medical Malpractice Reform

The two purposes of the legal liability system for medical injuries are compensation and deterrence. As a society, we want to provide fair compensation to injured persons. In addition, by imposing liability on those healthcare providers that act in a negligent manner, we hope to deter negligent conduct in the future. There is a general consensus that the current liability system does not work and does not accomplish those two policy goals. However, there are wide disagreements as to the reasons for the failure as well as the direction in which the system should be changed.

The Need for Reform in the Current System

Many healthcare providers and insurance companies complain that patients recover excessive amounts of money, including large awards for pain and suffering, because juries sympathize with injured people and assume that the damages will be covered by liability insurance. In some states and for some specialties, malpractice insurance rates have increased dramatically, and providers periodically encounter what they describe as a "crisis" in the availability of insurance. In a 2002 report, the U.S. Department of Health and Human Services (HHS) wrote that a "litigation crisis" has increased the cost and reduced the availability of malpractice insurance for many physicians, thereby threatening access to care.[16]

In addition, responding to malpractice litigation can be time consuming and expensive for healthcare providers. Even an unjustified claim can have an adverse effect on a physician's professional reputation. Some critics argue that the tort liability system increases healthcare costs by encouraging the practice of defensive medicine. Under that theory, physicians order unnecessary tests and treatments to protect themselves against subsequent claims of medical malpractice. Once those unnecessary tests and treatments become the routine practice in the community, they are part of the standard of care from which physicians depart at their peril. According to the 2002 HHS report, eliminating defensive medicine would save the federal government and taxpayers between $25.3 billion and $44.3 billion per year.[17]

Not surprisingly, plaintiffs' lawyers dispute those arguments and insist that tort liability is necessary to compensate patients who are severely injured as a result of medical negligence. Moreover, they argue that neither medical licensing boards nor peer-review committees have done a good job of policing the medical profession, and, therefore, private malpractice litigation is the only viable way to drive out the bad physicians and deter negligent conduct in the future. They dispute the claims of defensive medicine and argue that the malpractice system actually contributes very little to the overall problem of healthcare costs. There are also some indications that the malpractice insurance "crisis" was caused, at least in part, by the failure of insurance companies to charge sufficient premiums in previous years and by the reduction in their investment income from the stock and bond markets.[18]

The empirical evidence on many of these issues is inconclusive, and there are contradictory studies and reports that use different methodologies and assumptions. In 2003, the U.S. General Accounting Office concluded that premiums for medical malpractice insurance had increased "dramatically" in some areas and for some specialties and that those increases had resulted from a variety of factors.[19] However, other researchers found that data contradict the perception of a crisis in malpractice insurance premiums.[20] Similarly, the evidence is inconclusive on the issue of whether the increase in premiums has an adverse effect on access to care.[21] With regard to the issue of defensive medicine, the U.S. Congressional Budget Office concluded that limiting liability for medical malpractice would only lead to very small savings in overall healthcare costs.[22]

There is also dispute about whether there are too many lawsuits for medical malpractice, and, particularly, whether there are too many frivolous suits. One highly respected study in the *New England Journal of Medicine* concluded that the vast majority of patients who are injured as a result of negligence never even file a medical malpractice claim.[23] In that 1991 study, the researchers looked at 30,775 patient records from the state of New York. They determined that 1,133 of those patients had suffered an adverse event, which was defined as an injury resulting from medical management, regardless of whether that event was caused by negligence. Of those 1,133 adverse events, the researchers determined that 280 were actually caused by negligence, but only eight of those patients filed a medical malpractice claim.

On the basis of that empirical evidence, the authors of the study concluded that the medical malpractice system was *not* accomplishing its goals of compensating injured persons and deterring negligent conduct in the future. As the authors reasoned, the tort liability system does not really compensate patients who are injured as a result of negligence, because approximately 97 percent of those patients never even file a medical malpractice claim. Moreover, because 97 percent of the cases of negligence did not result in a claim, the vast majority of negligent providers were neither identified nor held responsible for their actions. In a more recent article, experts identified some of the reasons that malpractice litigation may fail to deter negligent conduct, including the availability of liability insurance, the "poor fit" between negligence and the filing of claims, and the ability of hospitals to externalize—or force others to pay—the costs of the hospital's negligence.[24]

Empirical research also contradicts the perception that a large percentage of malpractice claims are frivolous or baseless. In one recent analysis, about two-thirds of the claims were meritorious in that the patient's injury was caused by an error.[25] The authors of that study also concluded that the litigation process was usually successful in distinguishing valid claims from invalid claims.[26] Therefore, underclaiming is a more serious problem than overclaiming, and "portraits of a malpractice system that is stricken with frivolous litigation are overblown."[27]

From the evidence of this empirical research, one could argue that the current malpractice liability system should be strengthened to make it easier for patients to recover damages and hold providers accountable for their negligence. However, in the debates on comprehensive healthcare reform, most of the proposals for malpractice reform have focused on ways to make it harder for patients to recover damages and hold providers liable as a means of reducing overall healthcare costs. Obviously, those proposals raise serious questions of ethics and public policy. First, it is not clear that limiting the ability of patients to recover damages would actually reduce healthcare costs for society as a whole. Moreover, even if healthcare costs could be reduced in that way, it may be inappropriate to solve the cost problem of society at the expense of patients who were injured as a result of negligence. Instead of reforming the tort liability system as a means of reducing healthcare costs, we should reform the system to better accomplish its original goals of compensation and deterrence. Alternatively, it is arguable that the current system should be replaced by a new type of system that could accomplish all of these goals in a more efficient and equitable manner.

Advantages and Disadvantages of Various Proposals for Reform

Because medical malpractice is primarily a matter of state law, most of the proposals for reform are at the state government level. However, some of the federal proposals for healthcare reform have included changes to the tort liability system for medical injuries, and Congress has considered several specific proposals to limit recovery for medical malpractice. For example, the Clinton administration's proposed Health Security Act would have limited attorneys' contingency fees, required a certificate of merit from a medical specialist before filing a complaint, and made other changes to the malpractice litigation system.[28] In 1995, the Republican majority in the House of Representatives proposed to limit damages for pain and suffering in malpractice cases and proposed other changes that would have made it more difficult for patients to recover damages for medical malpractice.[29] Although the 1995 House bill was not enacted into law, the debate on that bill led to an ironic situation. Ordinarily, the House Republican majority advocated a reduced role for the federal government and expanded authority for the states, but they argued in this case for a federal preemption of many aspects of state liability laws. At the same time, the Democratic administration, which often supported an active role for the federal government, argued that medical malpractice should be left under the traditional control of the individual states.

In recent years, Congress has continued to consider proposals for malpractice reform at the federal level. For example, in 2002, Representative James Greenwood (R-PA) introduced a bill with 107 cosponsors for federal legislation that would preempt state liability laws, unless those state laws were more favorable to healthcare providers.[30] In 2005, the House of Representatives passed a bill that would have preempted certain types of state laws, but that bill was not passed by the Senate and did not become a law.[31] Although Congress provided some confidentiality for information that is voluntarily provided to certain safety organizations,[32] no federal legislation for malpractice reform has been enacted as of this writing.

In the absence of significant federal legislation on medical malpractice, many states have enacted or considered their own proposals for reform. State legislatures have enacted laws that limit the amount of recoverable damages in various ways, as well as laws that limit attorney's fees and impose additional procedural requirements in malpractice cases. In addition to changing the system of liability, several states have taken steps to promote the quality of care, such as requirements to report medical errors. For example, in 2002 the Pennsylvania legislature enacted a statute that requires medical facilities to implement a patient safety plan, including a system for reporting incidents and a legal obligation to notify patients about a "serious event."[33]

One approach is to provide by statute that no plaintiff in a medical malpractice case may recover more than a specified amount, which is referred to as a "damage cap." Depending on the terms of the statute, the limit may apply to all damages or only to noneconomic damages, such as pain and suffering. For example, California's Medical Injury Compensation Reform Act limits noneconomic damages to $250,000, whereas Indiana's statute imposes a limit on *all* damages in medical malpractice cases. The argument in favor of damage caps is that they appear to be the most effective way to limit the size of malpractice awards. However, the counterargument is that damage caps are unfair to the most severely injured patients.[34] Moreover, if plaintiffs are limited in their recovery for pain and suffering, their attorney's fees may have to be paid out of the damages they receive for their actual economic loss.

Aside from damage caps, many states have enacted or considered other reforms to reduce the amount of the plaintiff's recovery. For example, under the collateral source rule, healthcare providers may be held liable for all of the damages incurred by the patient, including medical expenses and lost wages, even if the patient has already received compensation for those losses through health or disability insurance. The theory behind the collateral source rule is that the negligent provider should not reap the benefit of the insurance premiums that were paid over many years by the patient. However, the rule may allow double recovery by the patient from both the healthcare provider and the collateral source. Therefore, several states have changed the rule to require the court to reduce the damages by the amount of other benefits or to require the court to notify the jury about the patient's other benefits. In addition, several states have enacted limits on legal fees, imposed strict qualifications for medical expert witnesses, or made legislative changes to the standard of care in cases of medical malpractice and informed consent.

Another widely discussed proposal relates to the procedure for handling medical liability cases and is referred to as alternative dispute resolution. For example, the parties to a case may be required to participate in a process of mediation in an effort to reach a negotiated settlement. Moreover, some states have encouraged or required malpractice cases to be screened by a panel before the case may be heard in court, in which instance the panel's decision may be admissible in any subsequent court proceeding. Some people believe this type of informal alternative dispute resolution may avoid the time and expense of full-blown civil litigation, but others argue that the requirement for pretrial screening will merely add another step to a lengthy and expensive process. Aside from mediation and screening panels, another proposal is to substitute binding arbitration by a panel of arbitrators as an alternative to a trial in court before a judge and jury. Arguably, binding arbitration would be faster and more economical than a trial by jury and is less likely to be influenced by bias or sympathy. However, because it would deprive the parties of their right to trial by jury, it could only be used when both of the parties agree to do so. Therefore, binding arbitration is purely voluntary.

To encourage the fair and efficient resolution of disputes, some states have enacted reforms to promote disclosure and facilitate apologies for medical errors. For example, the Illinois legislature established a pilot program called "Sorry Works!"

> Under the program, participating hospitals and physicians shall promptly acknowledge and apologize for mistakes in patient care and promptly offer fair settlements. Participating hospitals shall encourage patients and families to retain their own legal counsel to ensure that their rights are protected and to help facilitate negotiations for fair settlements.[35]

Finally, some people believe we should abandon our current fault-based system of tort liability and substitute a no-fault system of guaranteed compensation for medical injuries. In advocating a no-fault system, people use the analogy of the current system of workers' compensation for employment-related injuries. In the past, workers who were injured on the job had to sue their employers in a fault-based system, and it was difficult for employees to prevail. Therefore, only a small percentage of injured workers would recover any damages, but those who won their cases might recover a large amount of damages. Because of the obvious inequities of that traditional system, state governments adopted workers' compensation programs. Under those new programs, employees could receive compensation in limited amounts from an administrative agency of the state without the need to prove that their employer was at fault. However, the employees would no longer have the right to sue their employer in court for unlimited damages. Thus, the workers traded the amount of recovery for the certainty of recovery.

By analogy, some people believe medical injuries should be compensated through an administrative agency process without the need for the patient to prove that the healthcare provider was at fault. Like workers' compensation, injured patients would be limited in their amount of recovery, but would have the assurance of some compensation for their injuries.

Proponents of a no-fault system argue that it would be faster and fairer than the current tort liability system. In addition, a no-fault system would provide compensation for claims that are too small to pursue through the traditional litigation process. However, critics of the no-fault system respond that it would not adequately compensate those patients who suffer severe injuries and require the greatest degree of compensation. In addition, a no-fault system may increase the overall cost of medical claims. Moreover, even without the need to prove fault, it would still be necessary to go through the process of proving causation, because only injuries resulting from medical treatment would be compensated under the no-fault system. Finally, critics argue that a no-fault system would eliminate the deterrent effect of the current fault-based system by removing some of the incentive for physicians to exercise care in treating their patients.

Despite all of these criticisms, a no-fault system for compensating medical injuries may have substantial merit. Creating a partial no-fault system may also be possible, which would be limited to those avoidable adverse events that result from defects in the system or process of care.[36]

Clearly, malpractice reform is an important part of the ongoing effort to reduce medical errors, improve patient safety, and increase the overall quality of care. At the same time, it is necessary to develop a system of compensation that would be more efficient and less costly for the parties and the healthcare system as a whole. The challenge for the future is to make progress toward the goal of a more effective, efficient, and equitable system of compensation and deterrence. It is unlikely that imposing caps on damages would significantly reduce overall healthcare costs. Nevertheless, some people claim that reducing malpractice liability would make it possible for doctors to disclose their medical errors, and thereby promote systems-based improvements in quality of care. At the present time, however, available data do not support the claim that reducing liability would increase disclosure of medical errors.[37]

Notes

1. 44 N.C. App. 638, 262 S.E. 2d 391, *cert. denied*, 300 N.C. 194, 269 S.E. 2d 621 (1980).

2. See, e.g., *Petrovich v. Share Health Plan of Illinois, Inc.*, 696 N.E.2d 356, 362 (Ill. App. Ct. 1998) (genuine issue of material fact as to whether IPA-model HMO was vicariously liable on a theory of apparent agency), *aff'd*, 719 N.E.2d 756 (Ill. 1999); *Boyd v. Albert Einstein Medical Center*, 547 A.2d 1229, 1235 (Pa. Super. Ct. 1998) (genuine issue of fact as to whether doctors were ostensible agents of the HMO).

3. *Schloendorff v. Society of New York Hospital*, 105 N.E. 92, 93 (N.Y. 1914).

4. American Medical Association, *Fundamental Elements of the Patient-Physician Relationship*. [Online document; retrieved 2/14/07.] www.ama-assn.org/ama/pub/category/8313.html.

5. J. Katz, "Informed Consent—Must it Remain a Fairy Tale?" *Journal of Contemporary Health Law & Policy*, 10 (1994): 69–91, 73.

6. *Curtis v. Jaskey*, 759 N.E.2d 962 (Ill. App. Ct. 2001).

7. *Howard v. University of Medicine and Dentistry of New Jersey*, 800 A.2d 73 (N.J. 2002).

8. *Johnson v. Kokemoor*, 545 N.W.2d 495, 506–507 (Wisc. 1996) (trial court properly admitted evidence of defendant physician's lack of experience as comparative mortality and morbidity statistics).

9. Compare *Hidding v. Williams*, 578 So.2d 1192, 1198 (La. Ct. App. 1991) (physician breached the informed consent doctrine by failing to disclose prolonged alcohol abuse), with *Ornelas v. Fry*, 727 P.2d 819, 823–24 (Ariz. Ct. App. 1986) (trial court correctly refused to admit evidence of physician's alcoholism, because of a lack of foundation to establish the relevance of that evidence).

10. See, e.g., *Doe v. Noe*, 707 N.E.2d 588, 589 (Ill. App. Ct. 1998) ("While we acknowledge and follow the holding in *Majca* requiring actual exposure to state a cause of action under these circumstances, we believe that the duty issue now remains unresolved.").

11. 793 P.2d 479 (Cal. 1990).

12. *Id*. at 485.

13. Compare *Howard v. University of Medicine and Dentistry of New Jersey*, 800 A.2d 73, 83 (N.J. 2002) (allowing plaintiff to attempt to prove that physician's misrepresentations constitute a lack of informed consent, subject to strict criteria), with *Duttry v. Patterson*, 771 A.2d 1255 (Pa. 2001) (evidence of doctor's experience and personal information is not relevant in an informed consent claim, even if the patient asks, but patient may have a claim for misrepresentation).

14. *Duttry*, 771 A.2d at 1259 (footnote omitted).

15. See 45 C.F.R. §§ 46.116–46.117 (2006).

16. U.S. Department of Health and Human Services, *Confronting the New Health Care Crisis: Improving Health Care Quality and Lowering Costs by Fixing Our Medical Liability System* (July 24, 2002): 1–2.

17. *Id.* at 7 and n.31.

18. R.A. Zimmerman and C. Oster, "Assigning Liability: Insurers' Missteps Helped Provoke Malpractice "Crisis,'" *Wall Street Journal*, June 24, 2002, A1.

19. U.S. General Accounting Office, *Medical Malpractice Insurance: Multiple Factors Have Contributed to Increased Premium Rates*, GAO-03-702 (2003): 3–4.

20. M.A. Rodwin, et. al., "Malpractice Premiums and Physicians' Income: Perceptions of a Crisis Conflict with Empirical Evidence," *Health Affairs*, 25(3) (2006): 750–758.

21. See U.S. General Accounting Office, *Medical Malpractice: Implications of Rising Premiums on Access to Health Care*, GAO-03-836 (2003) (confirming some reports of localized service reduction, while finding that some anecdotal reports could not be confirmed); D. Dranove and A. Gron, "Effects of the Malpractice Crisis on Access to and Incidence of High-Risk Procedures: Evidence from Florida," *Health Affairs*, 24(3) (2005): 802–810, 808 ("As might be expected in an area of such debate, our findings provide potential support for both sides of the debate.").

22. U.S. Congressional Budget Office, *Limiting Tort Liability for Medical Malpractice* (January 8, 2004).

23. H.H. Hiatt, et al., "A Study of Medical Injury and Medical Malpractice: An Overview," *New England Journal of Medicine*, 321(7) (1989): 480–484; R.A. Localio, et al., "Relation Between Malpractice Claims and Adverse Events Due to Negligence," *New England Journal of Medicine*, 325(4) (1991): 245–321.

24. M.M. Mello and T.A. Brennan, "Symposium: What We Know and Do Not Know About the Impact of Civil Justice in the American Economy and Policy. Deterrence of Medical Errors: Theory and Evidence for Malpractice Reform," *Texas Law Review* 80(7) (2002): 1595–1637.

25. D.M. Studdert, et al., "Claims, Errors, and Compensation Payments in Medical Malpractice Litigation," *New England Journal of Medicine*, 354(19) (2006): 2024–2033, 2029.

26. *Id.* at 2029, 2031. See also T. Baker, "Reconsidering the Harvard Medical Practice Study Conclusions About the Validity of Medical Malpractice Claims," *Journal of Law, Medicine & Ethics*, 33(3) (2005): 501–514, 511 (2005)("Negligence matters a great deal to the outcome of a medical malpractice claim, and the litigation process weeds out most of the weaker claims.").

27. Studdert, et al., *supra* note 25, at 2031.

28. See Health Security Act, H.R. 3600, 103rd Cong. §§ 5301–5312 (1993).

29. See Medicare Preservation Act of 1995, H.R. 2425, 104th Cong. §§ 15301–15315 (1995).

30. Help Efficient Accessible Low Cost Timely Health Care (HEALTH) Act, H.R. 4600, 107th Cong. (introduced April 25, 2002).

31. H.R. 5, 109th Cong. (2005).

32. Patient Safety and Quality Improvement Act of 2005, Pub. L. No. 109-41, 119 Stat. 424 (2005).

33. 40 Pa. Cons. Stat. §§ 1303.307, 1303.308 (2006).

34. See, e.g., F. Cornelius, "Crushed By My Own Reform," *New York Times*, October 7, 1994, A2. See also D.M. Studdert, et al., "Are Damage Caps Regressive? A Study of Malpractice Jury Verdicts in California," *Health Affairs*, 23(4) (2004): 54–67.

35. 710 Ill. Comp. Stat. 45/405 (2005).

36. Mello and Brennan, *supra* note 24, at 1621–28.

37. See D.A. Hyman and C. Silver, "The Poor State of Health Care Quality in the U.S.: Is Malpractice Liability Part of the Problem or Part of the Solution?" *Cornell Law Review*, 90(4): 893–993, 893(2005) ("[T]here is no foundation for the widely held belief that fear of malpractice liability impedes efforts to improve the reliability of health care delivery systems."); T.H. Gallagher, et al., "U.S. and Canadian Physicians' Attitudes and Experiences Regarding Disclosing Errors to Patients," *Archives of Internal Medicine*, 166: 1605–1611 (2006).

11

LEGAL AND ETHICAL OBLIGATIONS TO PROVIDE CARE

If you are ever arrested and charged with a crime, you will have the right to a lawyer. In fact, if you cannot afford a lawyer, one will be appointed for you at society's expense.

What if, instead of a lawyer, you need a doctor? Do you have the right to a doctor? If you cannot afford a doctor, will one be appointed for you at society's expense?

These questions raise the broader issue of whether citizens of the United States have a legal right to healthcare. Unlike the right to appointed counsel in criminal cases and unlike the right to a free public education through the 12th grade, the U.S. system of government generally does not provide a comparable right to healthcare services.

Under the U.S. Constitution, the government cannot take away your life, liberty, or property without due process of law. In other words, the government cannot do bad things *to* you. However, the government generally has no legal obligation to do things *for* you. According to the U.S. Supreme Court, the government has no legal obligation to provide necessary services, even if you would die without those services.[1]

This limited role of government may reflect the eighteenth-century views of the nation's founders, who essentially wanted the king of England and other government authorities to leave them alone. In contrast, in the modern social welfare state, government plays a much more active role in protecting and helping individual members of society. Many people believe that government should do things *for* people, rather than merely leaving them alone. However, the U.S. system has not yet developed a legal right to healthcare services, and the Constitution does not require the government to provide or pay for care.

Although not required to do so by the Constitution, Congress, by creating the Medicare and Medicaid programs, chose to pay for specific services for people who are elderly, disabled, or indigent. Under those programs, the government has flexibility to decide which groups of people will be eligible for benefits, such as persons with end-stage renal disease, who are eligible for Medicare regardless of their age. In addition, as discussed in Chapter 8, the government may provide Medicaid coverage for some services, such as labor and delivery, but not for other services, such as elective abortion. In fact, Congress could terminate the entire Medicare and Medicaid programs by simply repealing the statutes, because, again, there is no underlying constitutional obligation to provide or pay for care.

Similarly, the traditional common-law rules provided that doctors and hospitals had no legal obligation to treat people who needed their services, even in an emergency. Although there are now some limited exceptions to those traditional rules, the old rules still apply whenever the situation does not fit within one of the limited exceptions. Therefore, the first step toward analyzing the legal obligation to provide care is to understand the common-law rules, and the second step is to determine the scope of the exceptions to those rules.

Traditional Common-Law Rules for Doctors and Hospitals

The physician–patient relationship is based on a contract, which is a voluntary agreement between the parties. After that voluntary relationship is established, a physician who fails to meet the applicable standard of care may be subject to a negligence claim for breach of duty under the law of torts. However, the physician would not have any duty to that patient until a relationship is voluntarily established in accordance with the law of contracts. In other words, once the relationship is voluntarily formed, a suit for breach of duty is governed by the tort law principles of negligence, but the formation of the relationship is governed by the law of contracts.

The contract between physician and patient may be in writing, but a written agreement is not required. Rather, the contract may be created by the conduct of the parties. If a person requests medical examination or treatment, and if the doctor begins to examine or treat that person, a contract has been created in the eyes of the law. Under some circumstances, physicians might also take on the obligation to provide services to additional patients by voluntarily entering into a contract with a hospital to be "on call" or by agreeing to accept patients who have coverage through a particular plan.

Ordinarily, physicians have no legal obligation to accept a patient, even in an emergency. As a general rule, U.S. law does not impose any legal obligation to help a stranger in distress. If a person sees a drowning swimmer who could be rescued easily and safely, and if the person has no special relationship with that swimmer, such as being a caretaker or lifeguard, the person is not legally required to do anything to save the swimmer and cannot be held legally liable for allowing the swimmer to drown.[2] Similarly, if a person with a gunshot wound crawls to the office of a physician, and if the wounded person has no prior relationship with that physician, the physician has no legal obligation to treat the patient. Although many states have enacted so-called "Good Samaritan statutes," those statutes do not require physicians or other healthcare professionals to treat strangers in distress, but merely provide immunity from liability if they voluntarily choose to do so.

On the other hand, the physician would have a *moral* and *ethical* obligation to treat the person under those circumstances. According to the Principles of Medical Ethics of the American Medical Association, the physician ordinarily has the right to refuse to treat any particular patient, but that right does not apply in the case of a medical emergency.[3] As a legal matter, however, a physician is ordinarily not obligated to treat a person, even in an emergency, if she does not have a preexisting physician–patient relationship with the person.

Once a physician has entered into a contractual relationship with a patient, the physician will have certain duties to the patient, as discussed previously. The physician may not simply stop treating the patient, even if the patient is uncooperative or fails to pay the physician's bill. If the physician prematurely stops treating the patient, he could be held liable for abandonment. Therefore, a physician who wishes to terminate the relationship must ordinarily finish treating the patient for the current medical problem, make alternative arrangements for the patient's treatment, or provide the patient with notice and a reasonable opportunity to make other arrangements for medical coverage.

Similarly, hospitals generally have no legal obligation to accept and treat any particular patient, even in an emergency.[4] However, there are some exceptions to that general rule. First, as part of the Consolidated Omnibus Budget Reconciliation Act of 1985 (COBRA), Congress enacted the Emergency Medical Treatment and Active Labor Act (EMTALA),[5] and thereby provided a limited obligation to treat patients in the event of a medical emergency. EMTALA is also referred to as the "COBRA antidumping law" because it prohibits hospitals from improperly transferring or "dumping" emergency patients from one hospital to another as a result of a patient's inability to pay. As described in detail later, EMTALA requires the hospital to provide an appropriate medical screening examination to determine whether a patient has an emergency medical condition. If so, EMTALA requires the hospital to provide further treatment to stabilize the condition or a proper transfer in accordance with the requirements of the statute.

As a second exception to the general rule of no duty to treat, many public and nonprofit hospitals accepted obligations to provide a certain volume of free care and make their services available to the community as a condition of grants or loans under the federal Hill-Burton program.[6] However, many hospitals that were obligated to provide free care have already fulfilled those obligations, and the remaining obligations under the Hill-Burton program are extremely vague.

Finally, a specific hospital may have legal obligations to provide care as a result of the law or document that established that particular hospital. For example, in enacting a statute to create a public hospital for its citizens, a state legislature might have specified in the statute that the public hospital will provide services to all persons in need, or at least all residents of the state, regardless of their ability to pay. Similarly, a board of county commissioners might have provided by resolution or ordinance that its local public hospital shall provide care without regard to a patient's ability to pay. Even if the hospital is owned and operated by a private, non-profit corporation, the charter or other documents that created the corporation, as well as the deed or lease by which the corporation acquired the hospital property, may stipulate obligations to provide care. However, those obligations, if any, would only apply to that particular hospital. Therefore, the most important exception to the general rule of no duty to treat is the COBRA antidumping law (EMTALA).

The COBRA Antidumping Law

Historically, people without money or health insurance had serious problems obtaining emergency medical care. In addition to being denied access to some hospitals, indigent patients were often transferred to or "dumped on" public hospitals, despite the risks of delay in receiving emergency treatment. Many indigent women in active labor were transferred or told to go to a different hospital, which caused serious risks to the women and their unborn children. Under state law, those patients often had no legal remedy for harm caused by the denial of care. As already discussed, physicians were not required to enter into a relationship with patients, and hospitals were not required to accept and treat patients, even in an emergency. In addition, patient dumping was a financial burden on public hospitals and teaching hospitals that provided a disproportionate share of uncompensated emergency care and maternity care for the indigent. Eventually, enough people came to believe "there ought to be a law," and Congress responded by enacting the COBRA antidumping law, also known as EMTALA.[7]

In enacting that law, Congress addressed an important goal of public policy, but it did so by an indirect method that failed to acknowledge the obligation of society as a whole. Rather than compensating local hospitals with federal funds for providing all necessary emergency care, Congress simply declared that hospitals must provide emergency care to all individuals without regard to their ability to pay. Although hospitals may charge patients *after* emergency services are rendered, the practical reality is that many of those bills will be uncollectible, and hospitals will end up providing a large volume of emergency services for free. Of course, that is good for patients who would otherwise go without care, but ultimately the cost of that care will be borne by the healthcare system and all of those who use it.

In 2003, Congress appropriated funds to compensate hospitals for their un-reimbursed costs of providing emergency services to undocumented immigrants under EMTALA.[8] However, it is unclear whether that funding will be renewed, and it does not compensate hospitals for all of their costs of providing services that are mandated by EMTALA. To a large extent, EMTALA is still an unfunded mandate or a tax on the hospital industry, which passes on the cost of care for the indigent to other patients and payers through the process of "cost shifting."

Nevertheless, Congress did accomplish the important policy goal of ensuring that all people will receive necessary emergency treatment, regardless of their ability to pay. To do so, Congress had to find a constitutionally permissible way to require public and private hospitals to give away a portion of their services for free, or at least to provide emergency care regardless of the patient's ability to pay. Even if the government is trying to accomplish an important public purpose, as it was in this case, the government cannot deprive individuals or organizations of their property, including their goods and services, without just compensation. Congress avoided that potential constitutional problem by relying on its power as a large-scale buyer of healthcare services through the federal Medicare program: As a condition of participation in the Medicare program, the government requires hospitals to provide emergency care without regard to the patient's ability to pay. EMTALA applies, therefore, to every hospital that has an emergency department and chooses to participate in the Medicare program.

The requirements of EMTALA apply to *all* patients, not merely to senior citizens who are eligible for Medicare. In fact, EMTALA contains specific provisions for women in active labor, very few of whom are eligible for benefits under the Medicare program. EMTALA even applies to patients who have health insurance and those who are covered by managed care plans, as discussed later.

As indicated in Figure 11.1, when a person comes to the emergency department and requests examination or treatment, the hospital must provide an appropriate medical screening exam to determine whether an emergency medical condition exists. If the person has no emergency medical condition, the hospital has no further obligation under EMTALA. However, if the patient does have an emergency medical condition, the hospital has two options, as set forth in Figure 11.1. The hospital may provide the further medical examination and treatment that is required to stabilize the patient's condition. Alternatively, the hospital could transfer the patient to another medical facility, but that transfer would have to meet all of the strict requirements provided by the federal law.

FIGURE 11.1
The COBRA
Antidumping
Law
(EMTALA)

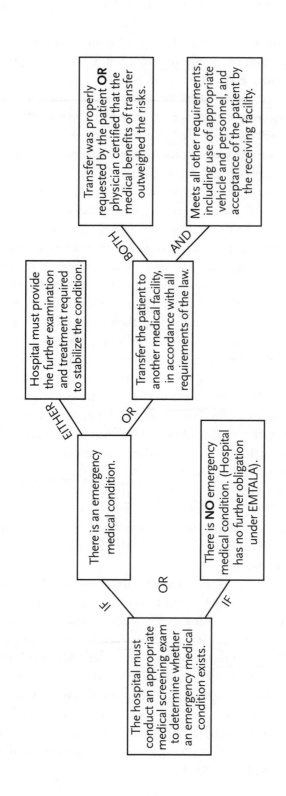

Note: These requirements apply to all patients and to every hospital that has an emergency department and participates in the Medicare program.

Under a 1989 amendment to the law, a hospital may not delay the medical screening exam or the additional examination and treatment to inquire about the patient's method of payment or insurance status. For patients covered by managed care plans, the U.S. Department of Health and Human Services (HHS) has repeatedly stated that hospitals must comply with all of their obligations under EMTALA regardless of any requirement of the managed care plan to obtain prior authorization for treatment.[9] In addition, federal law requires each hospital to post a sign in the emergency department that specifies the rights of patients under EMTALA. HHS has developed the model sign in Figure 11.2, which it considers sufficient to meet the hospital's notice requirement.

If a hospital fails to meet its obligations under EMTALA, the government may take enforcement action against the hospital, including civil monetary fines and possible termination of the hospital's Medicare provider agreement.[10] In addition, EMTALA may be enforced in a private civil action in federal court by any individual who suffers personal harm as a direct result of a hospital's violation of the law. In a private civil action against a hospital under EMTALA, the plaintiff would need to prove the element of causation by demonstrating that the harm to the patient was a result of the violation.

Coming to the Emergency Department

The requirements of EMTALA are triggered when a person "comes to the emergency department."[11] As a policy matter, it is important to ensure that people receive appropriate emergency services even if they happen to walk in the wrong door or the wrong building on the hospital campus. Moreover, as seen in the tragic case of Christopher Sercye that was discussed in Chapter 1, no one should lie bleeding outside the door of an emergency department in the driveway or parking lot of a hospital. Clearly, EMTALA obligations should extend beyond the physical walls of the emergency department. However, the federal government has found it difficult to delineate precisely where a hospital's EMTALA obligations apply, especially with regard to separate buildings on the hospital campus or near the hospital, hospital-owned ambulances, and remote outpatient departments that are not equipped to provide any emergency services.

Under the original regulations issued by HHS in 1994, a person was considered to have come to the emergency department if she was "on the hospital property."[12] Later, HHS amended its regulations to explicitly provide that the hospital property includes "the entire main hospital campus . . . including the parking lot, sidewalk, and driveway."[13] In addition, HHS defined the term "campus" to include areas and structures within 250 yards of the main hospital buildings.[14] However, HHS explained that this would not include separate entities such as restaurants or independent physicians' offices, even if they are located within 250 yards of the main hospital

FIGURE 11.2
HHS's Model
Sign Entitled
"It's the
Law!"

IT'S THE LAW!

IF YOU HAVE A MEDICAL EMERGENCY OR ARE IN LABOR

YOU HAVE THE RIGHT TO RECEIVE, within the capabilities
of this hospital's staff and facilities:

- An appropriate medical **SCREENING EXAMINATION**
- Necessary **STABILIZING TREATMENT (including treatment
  for an unborn child)**

and if necessary

- An appropriate **TRANSFER** to another facility

even if

YOU CANNOT PAY or DO NOT HAVE MEDICAL INSURANCE

or

YOU ARE NOT ENTITLED TO MEDICARE OR MEDICAID

This hospital (does/does not) participate in the Medicaid program

building.[15] Other HHS regulations had applied EMTALA obligations to off-campus facilities of the hospital, such as remote outpatient departments that are classified and paid as hospital based.[16]

Not surprisingly, these regulations resulted in confusion on the part of providers as well as objections to specific requirements. On September 9, 2003, HHS issued final regulations to address some of those concerns and clarify the legal obligations of hospitals under EMTALA.[17] The new regulations limit the types of off-campus facilities that are required to comply with EMTALA.[18]

In the meantime, another important issue in determining the applicability of EMTALA is whether the federal requirements apply to persons who have already been admitted as inpatients of the hospital. If the statute is read literally, it could be interpreted to apply to patients who are admitted as inpatients of the hospital, stabilized, and then have an emergency episode before they are discharged from the hospital. In fact, the statute might even be read to apply to elective, nonemergency patients whose condition deteriorates during the inpatient admission. In 1999, a representative of the HHS Office of Inspector General (OIG) indicated that the OIG considered EMTALA to apply to inpatients,[19] and at least one appellate court had indicated that EMTALA might apply even after several days of hospitalization.[20] However, other appellate courts had rejected attempts to apply EMTALA to inpatients in various situations to reflect their analysis of Congressional intent.[21] As one court had explained,

> EMTALA is a limited "anti-dumping" statute, not a federal malpractice statute. Its core purpose is to get patients into the system who might otherwise go untreated and be left without a remedy because traditional medical malpractice law affords no claim for failure to treat. Numerous cases and the Act's legislative history confirm that Congress's sole purpose in enacting EMTALA was to deal with the problem of patients being turned away from emergency rooms for non-medical reasons. Once EMTALA has met that purpose of ensuring that a hospital undertakes stabilizing treatment for a patient who arrives with an emergency condition, the patient's care becomes the legal responsibility of the hospital and the treating physicians. And, the legal adequacy of that care is then governed not by EMTALA but by the state malpractice law that everyone agrees EMTALA was not intended to preempt.[22]

Aside from the availability of a state law remedy, applying EMTALA to inpatients could raise issues of federalism by subjecting an area of traditional state regulation to the rulemaking, investigation, and enforcement authority of federal agencies. As a matter of legislative intent, Congress did not likely intend federal agencies to regulate the practice of medicine and the delivery of hospital care for every inpatient in a "code blue" situation such as cardiac arrest.

As part of its final regulations in 2003, HHS considered the applicability of EMTALA to inpatients. The final regulations provide that a hospital's EMTALA obligations end when a patient is admitted as an inpatient in good faith.[23] Moreover, EMTALA obligations do not apply to an inpatient who was admitted to the hospital on a nonemergency basis for elective diagnosis or treatment.[24] The final regulations also clarify that outpatients who are already receiving nonemergency services at the hospital are not covered by EMTALA, even if they have an emergency during the course of the outpatient encounter.[25] Thus, if an outpatient is receiving a nonemergency stress test at the hospital and has a heart attack during the test, the patient would not have the legal protection of EMTALA. However, if the hospital failed to meet the applicable standard of care in treating that patient, the patient would have other legal remedies under the state law of medical malpractice.

The Appropriate Medical Screening Examination

When required by the statute, hospitals must provide an "appropriate medical screening examination." However, the statute does not define that term, nor does it explain what type of screening exam will be considered "appropriate." Although no statutory definition exists, the statute does provide some helpful information. First, it explains that the purpose of the exam is to determine whether the patient has an emergency medical condition. Second, the statute provides that the exam must be "within the capability of the hospital's emergency department, including ancillary services routinely available to the emergency department."[26] Thus, the hospital may not refuse to provide radiological or laboratory services that are located outside the emergency department if those services are ordinarily available to patients in the emergency department.

In considering whether a medical screening exam was appropriate, the federal courts have also provided some useful standards. To comply with EMTALA, a hospital is required to uniformly apply its standard screening procedure for all patients with the same medical condition. Thus, the EMTALA standard is not the same as the medical malpractice standard of care, which is based on the practice of similar providers in similar communities. Rather, the EMTALA standard for an appropriate medical screening exam is the particular hospital's own practice. In EMTALA cases, plaintiffs must demonstrate that they received disparate treatment from the hospital's emergency department.[27] In other words, patients must demonstrate that they did not receive the same treatment the hospital ordinarily provides to its paying patients.

However, federal courts have differing opinions as to whether disparate treatment is sufficient to prove a violation of EMTALA or whether the plaintiff must also show a bad motive for the disparate treatment.[28] In some cases, the hospital may provide disparate treatment because of the patient's race or financial status or because the patient has a particular medical condition such as AIDS. Each of those reasons would constitute a bad motive for the disparate treatment. However, in other cases, the hospital may provide disparate treatment without intending to do so, and that may simply constitute negligence in the emergency department.

In addressing that issue, some federal courts have concluded that Congress intended EMTALA to provide a legal remedy for *all* cases of disparate treatment. As those courts have reasoned, the language of the statute applies to all patients and is not explicitly limited to patients who are denied access or transferred for an improper reason. In those jurisdictions, the patient is only required to demonstrate that he received disparate treatment and does not have to prove that the disparate treatment was based on an improper motive.

However, other federal courts have reasoned that the intent of Congress in enacting EMTALA was only to protect patients from those denials of access and transfers that were based on their financial status or some other improper motive. According to those courts, Congress never intended to make a federal case out of every instance of negligence in a hospital emergency department, and those cases of ordinary negligence should continue to be governed by the state law of medical malpractice.

In those jurisdictions, a patient who received disparate treatment without any improper motive on the part of the hospital could not prevail in a private civil action under EMTALA, but still might be able to prevail in a civil action for medical malpractice under the law of the particular state.

The U.S. Supreme Court has not resolved this conflict among the circuits, but it did address the issue of improper motive under a different subsection of EMTALA. With regard to the requirement of stabilization under subsection (b), the Supreme Court held that the plaintiff is not required to demonstrate an improper motive.[29] The Supreme Court did not express any opinion on whether a failure to provide an appropriate medical screening exam under subsection (a) requires a showing of improper motive. However, it did note that most of the circuit courts do not require a showing of improper motive with regard to the appropriate medical screening exam under subsection (a). Of course, Congress could resolve this issue by passing an amendment to the statute to explicitly set forth the requirements for recovery in a private civil action under EMTALA.

If the hospital provides an appropriate medical screening exam but fails to discover the patient's emergency condition, the hospital will not be held liable under EMTALA. As the Ninth Circuit has explained,

> [t]hus, Plaintiffs argue, in effect, that a hospital should be liable under EMTALA if its staff negligently fails to detect an emergency medical condition. EMTALA, however, was not enacted to establish a federal medical malpractice cause of action nor to establish a national standard of care. Thus, we have held that a hospital has a duty to stabilize only those emergency medical conditions that its staff detects. Every circuit to address this issue is in accord. To restate our ruling in *Jackson*, we hold that a hospital does not violate EMTALA if it fails to detect or if it misdiagnoses an emergency condition. An individual who receives substandard medical care may pursue medical malpractice remedies under state law.[30]

Requirements for a Proper Transfer

For a transfer to meet the requirements of the statute, it would have to be requested by the patient, or a physician would have to certify in writing that the benefits of the transfer outweigh the risks to the patient and any unborn child of the patient. Moreover, the sending facility must provide treatment to minimize the risk, the receiving facility must have space and agree to accept the patient, the records and documents must be sent with the patient, and the transfer must be accomplished with an appropriate vehicle and personnel. Thus, it is not enough that a physician merely states that the patient would be better off at a different facility.

As demonstrated by *Owens v. Nacogdoches County Hospital District*,[31] the court will not simply defer to the medical judgment of the treating physician with regard to the appropriateness of the transfer. In that case, Rebecca Owens of Nacogdoches County, Texas, was 16 years old, pregnant, and poor. On the afternoon of August 3, 1987, she began to experience labor pains and went to the emergency department of Memorial Hospital. She asked to be admitted to the hospital to deliver her baby.

Ms. Owens was examined at the hospital by Dr. Bruce Thompson. After about 30 minutes, Dr. Thompson discharged her and told her to go to a different hospital in Galveston, which was about four hours away. Instead of driving directly to Galveston, Ms. Owens went to the office of East Texas Legal Services to get the help of a lawyer. Her lawyer tried to negotiate with Memorial Hospital and then obtained a temporary restraining order from the federal court to require Memorial to admit her. Eventually, she was admitted to Memorial and delivered her baby on August 7, 1987.

Ms. Owens sued Memorial Hospital for damages as a result of mental anguish and fear. After hearing the evidence from Ms. Owens and the hospital, the court awarded her $25,000 in damages and another $25,000 in attorneys' fees. In addition, the court granted a permanent injunction requiring Memorial Hospital to admit Ms. Owens for delivery in any future pregnancy as required by law.

At the trial, the hospital argued that the transfer had been medically justified, but the court did not believe the testimony offered by the hospital. Rather, it determined that the only reason for sending her to Galveston was that she could not afford to pay for her care. Moreover, the court noted that Ms. Owens and her baby might have died if he had been born on the side of the road.

As a legal matter, the issue in the case was whether Ms. Owens had been properly transferred in accordance with the requirements of the statute. Because a proper transfer requires the use of an appropriate vehicle, the court concluded that it was not a proper transfer. As the court explained, "a 1976 Ford Pinto with no medical equipment, whose only other occupant besides the patient is her boyfriend, is not the equivalent of an ambulance for the purposes of the Antidumping Act."[32] Therefore, the transfer was improper, even though the physician claimed that the transfer was medically justified.

Moreover, the court criticized the hospital for its staffing arrangements that, according to the court, would inevitably lead to a pattern of patient dumping. As the court explained, "Memorial Hospital has callously and negligently allowed a situation to develop in which all emergency obstetric and gynecological services to indigent patients—an enormous and ever-increasing load—have been left to on-call private physicians like Dr. Thompson, and the dumping of pregnant women has been the inevitable result."[33] However, the court did not suggest how the hospital ought to arrange for physician staffing to meet the hospital's obligations under

EMTALA or who should bear the cost of those arrangements. Should hospitals require physicians in private practice to provide indigent care for free as a condition of medical staff membership? Alternatively, should hospitals compensate physicians for providing indigent care, as an expense to be passed on to all paying patients of the hospital? The *Owens* court did not even suggest any answers to those questions.

PROBLEM 11.1: MS. JOAN GRANT

Ms. Joan Grant was a 45-year-old attorney in private practice. She was enrolled in the GoodHealth health maintenance organization (HMO) through her law firm's self-insured employee benefit plan. Generally, she had been in good health, got plenty of exercise, and ate oat bran for breakfast every morning.

On the evening of April 15, 1996, while she was rushing to finish her tax return, she developed a splitting headache. She decided that she would have to obtain an extension to file her tax return. Because her doctor's office was closed for the night, she asked a friend to drive her to the emergency department of Community General Hospital (Community). She arrived at Community at approximately 9:30 p.m.

Community is an acute-care general hospital licensed by the state; it participates in the Medicare program. It is owned and operated by General Hospital Corporation, which is a for-profit business corporation.

Community has arranged for 24-hour medical coverage of its emergency department by means of a contract with Village Emergency Physicians, P.A. (VEPPA), which employs Dr. Ellen Jones and three other physicians. The contract between Community and VEPPA states that Dr. Jones and the other physician employees of VEPPA are not employees or agents of the hospital and further states that the hospital will not be liable for any negligence by VEPPA or its physician employees. In that regard, the hospital has placed the following sign on the wall in the emergency department:

> Community General Hospital wants you to know
> that the physicians working in the emergency
> department are employees of VEPPA and are
> *not* employees or agents of the hospital.
> Have a nice day!

On her arrival at Community's emergency department, Ms. Grant told the nurse on duty that she had a splitting headache, and she was briefly examined by nurse Rebecca Smith. Then she was examined by the doctor on duty, Dr. Jones. Ms. Grant had no prior relationship with Dr. Jones.

According to the hospital's written protocols for the emergency department, if an adult patient complains of a splitting headache and if that patient does not appear to be intoxicated, the patient should be given a computed tomography (CT) scan of the head as soon as possible. In addition to being

Community's protocol, that method of diagnosis is the ordinary practice at all of the hospitals in the area. However, some of the third-party payers have begun to refuse to pay for CT scans under these circumstances.

Nurse Smith asked Ms. Grant about her health insurance. Ms. Grant said that she was covered by the GoodHealth HMO and gave Nurse Smith an HMO membership card that contained her policy number and a phone number for the HMO. Nurse Smith called the office of the HMO to verify Ms. Grant's coverage and to request authorization for the CT scan. However, the clerk on duty at the HMO informed Nurse Smith that GoodHealth HMO no longer pays for CT scans of the head under these circumstances. Instead, the HMO clerk said that the hospital should instruct Ms. Grant to call her primary care physician at the HMO when the office opened at 9 a.m. the next day.

Nurse Smith informed Dr. Jones of the HMO's decision, and Dr. Jones discharged Ms. Grant at 10:30 p.m. with instructions to call her primary care physician at the HMO the next morning. Dr. Jones did not tell Ms. Grant that the usual diagnostic test for her condition was a CT scan, which Ms. Grant could have paid for with the credit card that she carried in her wallet.

Ms. Grant's friend took her home, where she died of an aneurysm at approximately 11:45 p.m. that night. At the request of the next of kin, an autopsy was performed on the body of Ms. Grant. According to the autopsy report, Ms. Grant died of a rare type of aneurysm that does not show up on a CT scan.

What claims could be asserted against Community by Ms. Grant's estate? In discussing each potential claim against Community, be sure to discuss the elements of each claim and the likelihood of success on each claim.

Note: In responding to these questions, do not discuss any potential claims against individual healthcare professionals, VEPPA, the GoodHealth HMO, or the law firm's health plan.

Prohibitions Against Discrimination

Ordinarily, providers may refuse to accept new patients without the need for any reason at all. However, they may *not* refuse to accept new patients for an improper reason, such as racial bias. Providers may refuse to accept new patients because they are already operating at full capacity, because they want to go on vacation, or because they want to spend more time with their families. However, providers may not lawfully refuse to accept new patients because of the prospective patient's race, gender, national origin, or disability.

It is important to remember that, as recently as the 1960s, some healthcare facilities practiced overt racial discrimination, including exclusionary admission practices and segregated areas within the facilities. In fact, Congress had allowed recipients of federal Hill-Burton funds to maintain "separate but equal" facilities until that practice was prohibited by the federal courts.[34]

Title VI of the Civil Rights Act of 1964 prohibits discrimination on the basis of race, color, or national origin by any program or activity that receives federal financial assistance (FFA).[35] Most healthcare facilities are subject to the requirements of Title VI because they accept Medicare and Medicaid funds, which are considered to be FFA.[36] Even if a healthcare facility is not a recipient of FFA, racial discrimination is prohibited by other laws.

As stated previously, Title VI also prohibits discrimination on the basis of national origin. That has been interpreted to prohibit discrimination on the basis of a person's inability to speak English.[37] According to a revised Policy Guidance issued by HHS on August 8, 2003, recipients of FFA, such as healthcare facilities, "are required to take reasonable steps to ensure meaningful access to their programs and activities by LEP [limited English proficient] persons."[38] The extent of a healthcare facility's obligation to provide services such as interpreters depends on facts and circumstances such as the number and percentage of LEP patients and the resources available to the healthcare facility.

At the present time, some of the most complex issues of discrimination involve persons with disabilities. In addition to facing architectural barriers, persons with disabilities may need auxiliary aids and services, such as sign-language interpreters or electronic devices. Moreover, some persons with disabilities have been unable to obtain healthcare services because of the unwillingness of providers to treat them. In particular, some healthcare providers have been unwilling to provide services to patients with AIDS or HIV-positive patients, who are considered to be persons with a disability.

In § 504 of the Rehabilitation Act of 1973, Congress prohibited discrimination against persons with handicaps in any program that receives FFA.[39] As already stated, hospitals and other healthcare facilities that receive Medicare and Medicaid funds are considered to be recipients of FFA. However, individual physicians and other practitioners in private practice were not considered to be subject to that law. In addition, other limitations existed and issues remained unresolved with regard to the scope of the 1973 legislation. Therefore, the Rehabilitation Act of 1973 did not solve the problems of access for persons with disabilities.

Eventually, Congress addressed these problems by enacting Title III of the Americans with Disabilities Act (ADA) of 1990.[40] The ADA made a major change in the law of disability discrimination by extending the reach of federal law beyond federally funded programs and into the private offices of physicians, dentists, and other individual practitioners. However, most courts hold that the ADA does not prevent health insurance companies from discriminating on the basis of disability in structuring their benefits for particular diseases, such as AIDS.[41]

According to § 12182 of the ADA, "[n]o individual shall be discriminated against on the basis of disability in the full and equal enjoyment of the . . . services . . . of any place of public accommodation."[42] Each word in that statute is carefully defined and loaded with meaning. For example, the term "public accommodation" is defined to include a hospital and the "professional office of a healthcare provider."[43]

With regard to a healthcare facility or practitioner's office, the prohibition against discrimination is broader than merely allowing persons with disabilities in the door. Healthcare providers cannot deny participation, allow participation in an unequal manner, or provide for a different or separate participation on the basis of a person's disability, subject to certain exceptions that are set forth in the statute or regulations.[44] In addition to removing architectural barriers, healthcare facilities may be required to provide auxiliary aids, including special equipment and personnel. For example, in 1998, 32 hospitals in Connecticut agreed with the U.S. Department of Justice (DOJ) and the state government to settle a class-action lawsuit under the ADA by offering to provide auxiliary services, such as telecommunication devices and interpreters for hearing-impaired patients.

Perhaps the most difficult definitional question under the ADA is determining whether a particular person has a "disability." According to the federal regulations, disability is "a physical or mental impairment that substantially limits one or more of the major life activities of such individual; a record of such an impairment; or being regarded as having such an impairment."[45] Of course, that linguistic formulation raises more questions than it answers. According to the DOJ, the term "physical or mental impairment" includes "HIV disease (whether symptomatic or asymptomatic)."[46] Moreover, the U.S. Supreme Court held that, on the facts established in the case then before the court, asymptomatic HIV infection caused the plaintiff to have a disability for purposes of the ADA.[47]

Under these circumstances, physicians, dentists, and other individual practitioners cannot refuse to treat HIV-positive patients on the grounds of their diagnosis, even in their private professional offices. According to the Centers for Disease Control and Prevention, healthcare professionals can protect themselves from the spread of HIV by using universal precautions. In other words, rather than singling out HIV-positive patients for special treatment, providers should treat all patients as if they might be HIV-positive. In the federal government's view, there is no scientific justification for refusing to perform surgery or other invasive procedures on HIV-positive patients, nor is there any justification for segregating them within healthcare facilities or medical offices. As indicated by the following statement from the DOJ, the government may take action against healthcare providers in cases of alleged refusal to treat HIV-positive patients.

FOR IMMEDIATE RELEASE CR

TUESDAY, MARCH 10, 1998

WASHINGTON, D.C., AREA HOSPITAL AGREES TO NEW POLICY FOR TREATING PATIENTS WITH HIV, UNDER AGREEMENT WITH JUSTICE DEPARTMENT

WASHINGTON, D.C.—After allegedly denying surgical treatment to a patient who is HIV-positive, George Washington University Hospital agreed today to take steps to ensure people with HIV and other infectious diseases are not turned away because of their disabilities, the Justice Department announced.

The agreement stems from a complaint filed with the Justice Department under the Americans with Disabilities Act (ADA) by Ron Flowers, a 32-year-old Washington resident. The complaint alleged that Flowers, who is HIV-positive, was denied surgical treatment at George Washington University Hospital in March 1996.

"People with infectious diseases such as HIV must be able to enter the nation's hospitals and clinics confident that they will receive appropriate medical treatment," said Bill Lann Lee, Acting Assistant Attorney General for Civil Rights. "George Washington University's renewed commitment to serving all members of its community is a model for other hospitals."

Under the terms of the settlement, George Washington University and the Hospital will:

- implement a policy prohibiting its medical staff from making treatment decisions based on a patient's infectious disease status unless medically appropriate;
- provide information regarding this and other non-discrimination policies to patients through pamphlets and other materials posted throughout the hospital;
- provide annual training for its staff regarding this policy and their responsibilities to treat patients with infectious diseases under the Americans with Disabilities Act and the Rehabilitation Act;
- sponsor a symposium for cardiothoracic surgeons across the region on cardiothoracic surgery and HIV;
- pay the complainant significant compensatory damages.

The ADA prohibits discrimination against persons with disabilities. Title III of the ADA prohibits discrimination in public accommodations and commercial facilities like hospitals and other medical care facilities.

According to the complaint, Flowers was admitted to George Washington University Hospital after suffering two strokes. Tests revealed that a growth on

Flowers' aortic valve was the likely cause. According to the complainant, although the medically appropriate treatment for his condition was open-heart surgery, the cardiothoracic surgeons at the Hospital refused to perform the operation because he is HIV-positive.

Flowers subsequently received the surgery at another local hospital and has fully recovered. As the ADA permits, Flowers filed a private lawsuit, which is being resolved separately.

"Access to medical care should be available to all people, and as advances in medicine extend the lives of people with HIV, compliance with the ADA is even more critical," added Lee . . .

98–106

In addition to securing adequate treatment for persons with disabilities, issues of access and discrimination may arise in connection with the allocation of scarce organs for human transplantation. At the present time, there simply are not enough donated organs to meet the need for them, and thousands of people die each year while waiting for an organ. To prevent the development of a commercial organ market, with organs going to the highest bidder, Congress has prohibited the purchase or sale of organs for use in human transplantation.[48] Instead, organs are allocated by the United Network for Organ Sharing, which operates the system under contract with HHS.

Theoretically, this system is designed to ensure the most equitable allocation of scarce human organs. However, problems may arise with regard to the fairness of the system. For example, in 1991, the OIG of HHS reported that African Americans had to wait almost twice as long as European Americans for their first kidney transplant.[49]

Moreover, in allocating organs on the basis of a patient's medical condition, it is important to avoid making decisions that discriminate on the basis of a potential recipient's disability. For many years, there have been disputes over the priorities that should be given to various categories of patients in allocating scarce human organs. For example, some people have argued that patients with acute liver failure should receive priority over patients with chronic disease, but other people strongly disagree. Similarly, there have been disagreements over whether priority should be given to potential recipients who reside in the city or region in which the organ was donated or, alternatively, whether organs should be distributed on a national basis. Finally, there has been a debate over whether organs should be made available to persons who are not residents of the United States. Obviously, these decisions pose complex issues of policy, ethics, and medical technology and will continue to be the subject of future debate.

One possible solution to these complex allocation issues is to make more organs available for transplantation. According to some people, the best way to make more organs available is to permit people to sell their organs in a free, competitive market. Some people believe competent adults should be permitted to sell one of their two kidneys, and they point out that relatives and friends of a patient are currently permitted to donate one of their kidneys to a particular recipient. However, many people oppose the concept of an organ market because it would allow organs to go to the highest bidder and would discourage people from donating their organs to the existing transplantation system.

Under these circumstances, many people are focusing their efforts on encouraging voluntary donation of organs after the death of the donor. If individuals never expressed their desires about donating their organs, the law does not presume their consent to donation. Rather, individuals must affirmatively state their intention to donate their organs, which can be accomplished by signing an organ donor card or other document of gift under their state's version of the Uniform Anatomical Gift Act. Even then, as a practical matter, organ procurement organizations will not accept the organs without consent of the donor's family. Therefore, people who want to donate their organs should make their wishes very clear to members of their family.

In an effort to increase the supply of available organs, Congress has required all hospitals that participate in the Medicare program to have protocols for asking the families of potential donors about their willingness to donate the patient's organs.[50] In addition, HHS adopted a final rule in 1998 that requires hospitals in the Medicare program to report all hospital deaths and imminent deaths to their regional organ procurement organization.[51]

Hopefully, by encouraging voluntary donation, we will be able to promote access to this form of lifesaving medical treatment. Until there are enough organs to go around, however, we must be careful to avoid discrimination on the grounds of race, disability, or any other unlawful basis. Patients needing transplants have no legal right to care, except in the limited circumstances discussed in this chapter, but they do have the right to be free from unlawful discrimination.

Notes

1. See *DeShaney v. Winnebago County Department of Social Services*, 489 U.S. 189, 195–96 (1989).
2. See W.P. Keeton, et al., *Prosser and Keeton on the Law of Torts*, 5th ed., § 56 (1984): 375.
3. See American Medical Association, *Code of Medical Ethics, Principles of Medical Ethics*, point VI (2001). [Online document; retrieved 1/18/07.] www.ama-assn.org/apps/pf_new/pf_online?f_n= browse&doc=policyfiles/E-0.00.HTM&&s_t=&st_p=&nth=

1&prev_pol=policyfiles/HnE/H-525.998.HTM&nxt_pol=policy-files/E-1.00.HTM&.

4. See *Brooks v. Maryland General Hospital, Inc.*, 996 F.2d 708, 710 (4th Cir. 1993) (noting that hospitals have no legal duty under state tort law to provide emergency care to everyone).

5. 42 U.S.C. § 1395dd (2006).

6. Hospital Survey and Construction Amendments of 1949, 42 U.S.C. §§ 291 *et seq.* (2006); 42 C.F.R. § 124.4 (2005).

7. See Emergency Medical Treatment and Active Labor Act (EMTALA), 42 U.S.C. § 1395dd (2006).

8. Medicare Prescription Drug, Improvement, and Modernization Act of 2003, 108 Pub. L. No. 173 § 1011 (2003).

9. Solicitation of Comments on the OIG/HCFA Special Advisory Bulletin on the Patient Anti-Dumping Statute, 63 Fed. Reg. 67,486 (Dec. 7, 1998) (proposed Special Advisory Bulletin); OIG/HCFA Special Advisory Bulletin on the Patient Anti-Dumping Statute, 64 Fed. Reg. 61,353, 61,356 (Nov. 10, 1999) (Special Advisory Bulletin); Medicare Program; Changes to the Hospital Inpatient Prospective Payment System and Fiscal Year 2003 Rates, 67 Fed. Reg. 31,404, 31,471, 31,507 (May 9, 2002) (proposed rule).

10. See U.S. General Accounting Office, *Emergency Care: EMTALA Implementation and Enforcement Issues*, GAO-01–747 (June 22, 2001).

11. 42 U.S.C. § 1395dd(a) (2006).

12. Medicare Program; Participation in CHAMPUS and CHAMPVA, Hospital Admissions for Veterans, Discharge Rights Notice, and Hospital Responsibility for Emergency Care, 59 Fed. Reg. 32,086, 32,121 (June 22, 1994), codified at 42 C.F.R. § 489.24 (2006).

13. Office of Inspector General, Medicare Program; Prospective Payment System for Hospital Outpatient Services, 65 Fed. Reg. 18,434, 18,548 (April 7, 2000).

14. *Id.* at 18,538 (adding a new 42 C.F.R. § 413.65).

15. 67 Fed. Reg. 31,506 (May 9, 2002). [Online information; retrieved 4/23/07.] www.cms.hhs.gov/QuarterlyProviderUpdates/Downloads/cms1203p2.pdf.

16. See U.S. General Accounting Office, *supra* note 10, at 6, 14.

17. 68 Fed. Reg. 53,222–53,264 (Sept. 9, 2003).

18. 42 C.F.R. § 413.65(g)(1) (2005).

19. BNA's Health Care Daily Report, "Emergency Care: HHS Broadly Interprets EMTALA to Include Inpatients of Hospital Grounds," Executive Briefing (June 30, 1999).

20. *Thornton v. Southwest Detroit Hosp.*, 895 F.2d 1131, 1135 (6th Cir. 1990).

21. See, e.g., *Bryant v. Adventist Health System/West*, 289 F.3d 1162, 1167 (9th Cir. 2002) ("the stabilization requirement normally ends when the patient is admitted for inpatient care").

22. *Bryan v. Rectors and Visitors of the University of Virginia*, 95 F.3d 349, 351 (4th Cir. 1996) (citations omitted).

23. 42 C.F.R. § 489.24(d)(2) (2006). See also 68 Fed. Reg. at 53,244–53,245 (Sept. 9, 2003).

24. 42 C.F.R. § 489.24(d)(2).

25. See 68 Fed. Reg. at 53,239.

26. 42 U.S.C. § 1395dd(a) (2006).

27. See *Baber v. Hospital Corporation of America*, 977 F.2d 872 (4th Cir. 1992).

28. See *id.* at 880 n.8.

29. *Roberts v. Galen of Virginia, Inc.*, 525 U.S. 249, 253 (1999).

30. *Bryant v. Adventist Health System/West*, 289 F.3d 1162, 1166 (9th Cir. 2002) (citations and footnote omitted).

31. 741 F. Supp. 1269 (E.D. Tex. 1990).

32. *Id.* at 1276.

33. *Id.* at 1280.

34. See *Simkins v. Moses H. Cone Memorial Hospital*, 323 F.2d 959, 967–70 (4th Cir. 1963), *cert. denied*, 376 U.S. 938 (1964).

35. 42 U.S.C. § 2000d (2006).

36. See *United States v. Baylor University Medical Center*, 736 F.2d 1039, 1045–1046 (5th Cir. 1984).

37. T.S. Jost, "Racial and Ethnic Disparities in Medicare: What the Department of Health and Human Services and the Centers for Medicare and Medicaid Services Can, and Should Do," *DePaul Journal of Health Care Law* 9 (2006): 667–718, 700–702.

38. Department of Health and Human Services, *Guidance to Federal Financial Assistance Recipients Regarding Title VI Prohibition Against National Origin Discrimination Affecting Limited English Proficient Persons*, 68 Fed. Reg. 47,311, 47,314 (Aug. 8, 2003).

39. 29 U.S.C. § 794 (2006).

40. See 42 U.S.C. §§ 12181 *et seq.* (2006).

41. C. Olender, "Capping AIDS Benefits: Does Title III of the ADA Regulate the Content of Insurance Policies?" *American Journal of Law & Medicine*, 28 (2002): 107–125 at 108–109.

42. 42 U.S.C. § 12182(a) (2006). See also 28 C.F.R. § 36.201(a) (2006) (Department of Justice regulations).

43. 42 U.S.C. § 12181(7)(F) (2006). See also 28 C.F.R. § 36.104 (2006) (defining "place of public accommodation").

44. See 28 C.F.R. § 36.202 (2006).

45. 28 C.F.R. § 36.104 (2006).

46. *Id.*

47. *Bragdon v. Abbott*, 524 U.S. 624, 641 (1998).

48. See National Organ Transplant Act, 42 U.S.C. § 274e (2006).

49. See Office of Inspector General, Department of Health and Human Services, *The Distribution of Organs for Transplantation: Expectations and Practices*, No. OEI-01–89-00550 (1991): ii.

50. 42 U.S.C. § 1320b–8 (2006).

51. 42 C.F.R. § 482.45 (2006).

LEGAL AND ETHICAL ISSUES IN TERMINATION OR REFUSAL OF CARE AND PHYSICIAN-ASSISTED SUICIDE

In Chapter 11, we considered the extent of the legal right to *obtain* health-care services. Now we are shifting our focus to the right to *refuse* services, including the right to refuse life-sustaining treatment and the right to die. Obviously, decisions to accept or refuse medical treatment are intensely personal and may involve religious and ethical beliefs. Therefore, reasonable people may disagree about the "right" thing to do in a particular case, and it is wise to begin the discussion by acknowledging a healthy respect for the diversity of opinion on these sensitive issues.

This area of law provides a fascinating example of the interaction between state and federal authority in the regulation of healthcare services. As a general rule, issues of termination or refusal of care will be governed by the laws of the individual states. However, federal law plays a role in these issues in at least three important ways.

First, the U.S. Supreme Court has recognized, albeit somewhat tentatively, that there *may* be a right to refuse medical treatment under the federal constitution. As the Supreme Court explained, "[w]e have also assumed, and strongly suggested, that the Due Process Clause protects the traditional right to refuse unwanted lifesaving medical treatment."[1] Such a constitutional right, however, would not necessarily override a state's law that imposes conditions on the refusal of treatment. As discussed in Chapter 2, in *Cruzan* the U.S. Supreme Court held that Missouri's requirement to show clear and convincing evidence of the patient's desires did not violate any right of the patient under the U.S. Constitution.[2]

In addition to the possibility of a federal constitutional right, a second area of federal involvement is a statute enacted by Congress as part of the Medicare law.[3] That statute, entitled the Patient Self-Determination Act, requires healthcare facilities participating in the Medicare program to inform patients of their rights to refuse treatment and make advance directives, even though the rights are provided by the laws of the particular state.[4] Pursuant to that federal statute, facilities must have written policies for advising patients of their rights. Although the original federal legislation from 1990 had already required facilities to document in the medical record whether the patient had made an advance directive, Congress added a requirement in 1997 that the documentation be placed "in a prominent part of the individual's current medical record."[5]

As a third area of federal involvement, the U.S. government has attempted to prevent or discourage physician-assisted suicide (PAS), even if a state government decides to permit it. For example, Congress has prohibited the use of federal funds in connection with assisted suicide, mercy killing, or euthanasia, even in states where assisted suicide is lawful.[6] Therefore, in a state such as Oregon, which provides a limited right to PAS, the Medicare program will not pay for the lethal drug or the physician's service in writing the prescription. In addition, as discussed in detail later, the federal government grants physicians the authority to write prescriptions for controlled substances, and threatened to revoke that authority for any physician who uses federally controlled substances for the purpose of PAS. Aside from these limited assertions of federal authority, however, most issues of termination or refusal of care will be governed by the laws of the particular state.

There has been a great deal of publicity with regard to living wills and other advance directives, especially in cases of patients who were terminally ill or in a persistent vegetative state. However, those cases are merely a subset of a broader category of cases that involve the right to refuse any type of unwanted medical care. Therefore, the starting point in analyzing these issues is to understand the legal principles of the right to refuse ordinary medical or surgical care. Those principles can then be applied to the specific problem of withholding or withdrawing artificial means of life support. Finally, we can consider whether those legal principles of the right to refuse treatment can be extended to create a right to have the assistance of a physician in committing suicide.

The Right to Refuse Treatment

Some patients refuse to accept blood transfusions on the grounds of religious beliefs. In other situations, patients refuse to undergo surgery that is recommended by their physicians because they do not want to take the risk of surgery or because they believe they are likely to get better without undergoing the surgical procedure. In light of the practice of defensive medicine, as discussed in Chapter 10, it may be reasonable for patients to be skeptical of some tests and treatments that are recommended by their physicians. Therefore, patients may choose to decline those tests and treatments that pose a significant risk of injury or complications. In each of those cases, the patient is simply exercising her right to say no.

From a legal perspective, the right to refuse treatment is based on the doctrine of informed consent or at least on the same policy goals that led to the development of that doctrine. As discussed in Chapter 10, the focus of informed consent in medical malpractice cases is the patient's right to know the risks, benefits, and alternatives to the course of treatment suggested by the physician. However, the right to know would be meaningless without the other aspect of informed consent, which is the right to say no. In other words, the right of informed consent is more than just the right to be fully informed. Rather, it is the right to consent or, more important, the right to refuse to give one's consent.

In 1914, Benjamin Cardozo, who was then a New York Court of Appeals judge, wrote that "every human being of adult years and sound mind has a right to determine what shall be done with his own body."[7] In the abstract, that is a noble proposition and one with which almost everyone would agree. However, many situations are encountered in which our society will *not* allow people to decide what will be done with their own bodies. For example, most states outlaw prostitution. In addition, the government prohibits adults from using controlled substances without a prescription, even in the privacy of their homes. In the healthcare context, the government has the authority to force people to be vaccinated against communicable diseases, even if they are being treated against their will.[8] Also, although most people have two kidneys and need only one, federal law prohibits people from selling one of their kidneys if the sale affects interstate commerce.[9]

Thus, despite the general principle enunciated by Justice Cardozo, individuals of adult years and sound minds will not be allowed to decide what will be done with their own bodies and will not be allowed to refuse medical treatment in some situations. In those cases, the interests of the individual will be outweighed by the interests of society as a whole.

In addition, it is important to resist the temptation to characterize the refusing person as incompetent or not of sound mind merely because he is rejecting a treatment that almost everyone else would accept. In the past, some courts and some medical professionals have tended to declare that patients refusing lifesaving medical care were mentally incapable of making their own decisions or that they did not understand the facts. Some severely ill or injured patients may lack the mental capacity to understand the situation and make a rational decision. However, judges and medical professionals need to be cognizant of their bias in favor of medical intervention, particularly if they believe treatment is necessary to save the patient's life. In some cases, the patient may believe she is more likely to be cured by prayer, meditation, diet, herbal remedies, or alternative medicine rather than the drugs or surgery recommended by the physician. In those circumstances, our society should respect the right of the individual to refuse medical treatment for personal, cultural, or religious reasons and should not violate that right by declaring that the person "must be crazy."

Nevertheless, cases will arise in which the patient is mentally incapable of making a rational decision. In those cases, two separate inquiries will be relevant. First, is this a situation in which our society will allow an individual to refuse treatment? If the answer to that question is no, it is unnecessary to address the second question. However, if society would allow a person to refuse treatment in that situation, but the person is unable to make or communicate a decision, medical personnel, family members, or judges need to determine what the individual would have wanted or else find some way to make a decision on behalf of the patient.

The following excerpt is from the classic case of *Application of the President and Directors of Georgetown College*. In reading this case, try to determine which of the two inquiries the court was attempting to answer.

APPLICATION OF THE PRESIDENT AND DIRECTORS OF GEORGETOWN COLLEGE, INC., 331 F.2D 1000 (D.C. CIR.) (CITATIONS AND FOOTNOTES OMITTED), CERT. DENIED, 377 U.S. 978 (1964)

Attorneys for Georgetown Hospital applied for an emergency writ at 4:00 P.M., September 17, 1963, seeking relief from the action of the United States District Court for the District of Columbia denying the hospital's application for permission to administer blood transfusions to an emergency patient. The application recited that "Mrs. Jesse E. Jones is presently a patient at Georgetown University Hospital," "she is in extremis," according to the attending physician "blood transfusions are necessary immediately in order to save her life," and "consent to the administration thereof can be obtained neither from the patient nor her husband." The patient and her husband based their refusal on their religious beliefs as Jehovah's Witnesses. The order sought provided that the attending physicians "may" administer such transfusions to Mrs. Jones as might be "necessary to save her life." After the proceedings detailed in Part IV of this opinion, I signed the order at 5:20 P.M. . . .

The temporary order issued was more limited than the order proposed in the original application, in that the phrase "to save her life" was added, thus limiting the transfusions in both time and number. Such a temporary order to preserve the life of the patient was necessary if the cause were not to be mooted by the death of the patient . . .

Let us now reconstruct the narrative of events through the medium of the contemporaneous Memorandum of Facts filed in this cause, the substance of which is as follows: Mrs. Jones was brought to the hospital by her husband for emergency care, having lost two thirds of her body's blood supply from a ruptured ulcer. She had no personal physician, and relied solely on the hospital staff. She was a total hospital responsibility. It appeared that the patient, age 25, mother of a seven-month-old child, and her husband were both Jehovah's Witnesses, the teachings of which sect, according to their interpretation, prohibited the injection of blood into the body. When death without blood became imminent, the hospital sought the advice of counsel, who applied to the District Court in the name of the hospital for permission to administer blood. Judge Tamm of the District Court denied the application, and counsel immediately applied to me, as a member of the Court of Appeals, for an appropriate writ.

I called the hospital by telephone and spoke with Dr. Westura, Chief Medical Resident, who confirmed the representations made by counsel. I thereupon proceeded with counsel to the hospital, where I spoke to Mr. Jones, the husband of the patient. He advised me that, on religious grounds, he would not approve a blood transfusion for his wife. He said, however, that if the court ordered the transfusion, the responsibility was not his. I advised Mr. Jones to obtain counsel immediately. He thereupon went to the telephone and returned in 10 or 15 minutes to advise that he had taken the matter up with his church and that he had decided that he did not want counsel.

I asked permission of Mr. Jones to see his wife. This he readily granted. Prior to going into the patient's room, I again conferred with Dr. Westura and several other doctors assigned to the case. All confirmed that the patient would die without blood and that there was a better than 50 per cent chance of saving her life with it. Unanimously they strongly recommended it. I then went inside the patient's room. Her appearance confirmed the urgency which had been represented to me. I tried to communicate with her, advising her again as to what the doctors had said. The only audible reply I could hear was "Against my will." It was obvious that the woman was not in a mental condition to make a decision. I was reluctant to press her because of the seriousness of her condition and because I felt that to suggest repeatedly the imminence of death without blood might place a strain on her religious convictions. I asked her whether she would oppose the blood transfusion if the court allowed it. She indicated, as best I could make out, that it would not then be her responsibility.

I returned to the doctors' room where some 10 to 12 doctors were congregated, along with the husband and counsel for the hospital. The President of Georgetown University, Father Bunn, appeared and pleaded with Mr. Jones to authorize the hospital to save his wife's life with a blood transfusion. Mr. Jones replied that the Scriptures say that we should not drink blood, and consequently his religion prohibited transfusions. The doctors explained to Mr. Jones that a blood transfusion is totally different from drinking blood in that the blood physically goes into a different part and through a different process in the body. Mr. Jones was unmoved. I thereupon signed the order allowing the hospital to administer such transfusions as the doctors should determine were necessary to save her life . . .

Before proceeding with this inquiry, it may be useful to state what this case does not involve. This case does not involve a person who, for religious or other reasons, has refused to seek medical attention. It does not involve a disputed medical judgment or a dangerous or crippling operation. Nor does it involve the delicate question of saving the newborn in preference to the mother. Mrs. Jones sought medical attention and placed on the hospital the legal responsibility for her proper care. In its dilemma, not of its own making, the hospital sought judicial direction.

It has been firmly established that the courts can order compulsory medical treatment of children for any serious illness or injury, and that adults, sick or well, can be required to submit to compulsory treatment or prophylaxis, at least for contagious diseases. And there are no religious exemptions from these orders . . .

Of course, there is here no sick child or contagious disease. However, the sick child cases may provide persuasive analogies because Mrs. Jones was in extremis and hardly compos mentis at the time in question; she was as little able competently to decide for herself as any child would be. Under the circumstances, it may well be the duty of a court of general jurisdiction, such as the United States District Court for the District of Columbia, to assume the responsibility of guardianship for her, as for a child, at least to the extent of authorizing treatment to save her life. And if, as shown above, a parent has no power to forbid the saving of his child's life, a fortiori the husband of the patient here had no right to order the doctors to treat his wife in a way so that she would die.

The child cases point up another consideration. The patient, 25 years old, was the mother of a seven-month-old child. The state, as parens patriae, will not allow a parent to abandon a child, and so it should not allow this most ultimate of voluntary abandonments. The patient had a responsibility to the community to care for her infant. Thus the people had an interest in preserving the life of this mother . . .

The Gordian knot of this suicide question may be cut by the simple fact that Mrs. Jones did not want to die. Her voluntary presence in the hospital as a patient seeking medical help testified to this. Death, to Mrs. Jones, was not a religiously-commanded goal, but an unwanted side effect of a religious scruple. There is no question here of interfering with one whose religious convictions counsel his death, like the Buddhist monks who set themselves afire. Nor are we faced with the question of whether the state should intervene to reweigh the relative values of life and death, after the individual has weighed them for himself and found life wanting. Mrs. Jones wanted to live.

A third set of considerations involved the position of the doctors and the hospital. Mrs. Jones was their responsibility to treat. The hospital doctors had the choice of administering the proper treatment or letting Mrs. Jones die in the hospital bed, thus exposing themselves, and the hospital, to the risk of civil and criminal liability in either case. It is not certain that Mrs. Jones had any authority to put the hospital and its doctors to this impossible choice. The normal principle that an adult patient directs her doctors is based on notions of commercial contract which may have less relevance to life-or-death emergencies. It is not clear just where a patient would derive her authority to command her doctor to treat her under limitations which would produce death. The patient's counsel suggests that this authority is part of constitutionally protected liberty. But neither the principle that life and liberty are inalienable rights, nor the principle of liberty of religion, provides an easy answer to the question of whether the state can prevent martyrdom. Moreover, Mrs. Jones had no wish to be a martyr. And her religion merely prevented her consent to a transfusion. If the law undertook the responsibility of authorizing the transfusion without her consent, no problem would be raised with respect to her religious practice. Thus, the effect of the order was to preserve for Mrs. Jones the life she wanted without sacrifice of her religious beliefs.

The final, and compelling, reason for granting the emergency writ was that a life hung in the balance. There was no time for research and reflection. Death could have mooted the cause in a matter of minutes, if action were not taken to preserve the status quo. To refuse to act, only to find later that the law required action, was a risk I was unwilling to accept. I determined to act on the side of life.

In *Georgetown College*, the court apparently believed that a person in those circumstances should not be allowed to refuse treatment, which relates to the first inquiry discussed earlier. Moreover, even if a person would be allowed to refuse treatment under those circumstances, the court believed this particular patient really wanted to receive the lifesaving blood transfusion. Therefore, the court addressed both inquiries to some extent.[10]

However, the court's analysis may be questioned on several grounds. As a factual matter, was the patient really incapable of making her own decision? Even if she was mentally incompetent, should the court have allowed her husband to make a decision on her behalf because he was her next of kin and certainly knew what she wanted? Finally, did the religious beliefs of the patient and her husband really permit a blood transfusion, as long as it was performed over their objection, or was that merely a convenient rationalization for the decision that the court was determined to make?

Georgetown College is a classic case, and it has long been required reading for students of healthcare law and ethics. It is important to note, however, that attitudes and values in American society have changed somewhat since that case was decided in 1964. Since that time, people have come to expect more freedom to make their own individual decisions, regardless of the interests of society as a whole. In fact, many modern courts would not follow the precedent of *Georgetown College*, but rather would allow an individual patient to refuse a blood transfusion on the grounds of religious belief.[11] Nevertheless, modern courts are still likely to order blood transfusions for children over the religious objections of their parents.[12]

Perhaps the most interesting aspect of the *Georgetown College* decision is the court's reliance on society's interest in keeping the patient alive because she had a child who was only seven months old.[13]

However, if we accept the proposition that a parent has a duty to society to accept unwanted medical treatment, it leads to an even more difficult question. Does a female patient who is pregnant with a viable fetus have a duty to society to accept unwanted medical and surgical treatment to preserve the *potential* life of her unborn child? That issue will be addressed in Chapter 13, in connection with the problem of maternal–fetal conflict. First, however, it is necessary to apply the legal principles of the right to refuse treatment to cases involving termination of artificial means of life support.

The Right to a Natural Death

As a subset of the right to refuse treatment, the right to a natural death applies the legal principles of informed consent in the context of decisions at the end of life. In many of those cases, however, the patient is unable to expressly give or withhold consent because of his mental or physical condition. For example, if the patient is in a persistent vegetative state and made no living will or other advance directive, it may be difficult or impossible to determine what the patient would have wanted with regard to the continuation or termination of artificial life support.

In some circumstances, the law allows consent to be given by someone other than the patient. For example, a parent has the right to consent to surgery on behalf of a minor child. By analogy, it is reasonable that the decision to continue or discontinue life support for an incompetent patient should be made by a surrogate, such as a close relative, legal guardian, or judge. In some jurisdictions, courts make a substituted judgment for the patient by trying to determine what the patient would have wanted. However, other courts take a different approach and try to determine what would be in the best interest of the patient. Regardless of their approach, most courts insist that they will never consider the patient's reduced quality of life in determining whether the patient should be treated or allowed to die. However, those courts probably do consider the patient's quality of life as a practical matter. Finally, some states have statutes that permit the termination of treatment under specified conditions, even without any evidence of the patient's intent.[14]

As a practical matter, it can be very difficult to terminate artificial means of life support if there is a disagreement among members of the patient's family. That was the situation in the case of Terri Schiavo, who was in a persistent vegetative state. Her husband obtained an order from the Florida court for termination of treatment, but her parents objected and wanted the treatment to be continued. After numerous proceedings in state courts, federal courts, the Florida legislature, and the U.S. Congress, her feeding tube was removed and Ms. Schiavo died.

Despite the media attention and political maneuvering, that case was not a significant development in the law on termination of treatment. As one commentator has noted, "[t]he case of Terri Schiavo resulted in no changes in the law, nor were any good arguments made that legal changes were necessary."[15] Although the Florida legislature purported to author- ize the governor to take action to prevent withholding of nutrition and hydration,[16] the state statute only applied to that one patient as a practical matter.[17] Moreover, the Florida Supreme Court held that the statute was unconstitutional under the legal doctrine of separation of powers.[18] As the Court explained, "it is without question an invasion of the authority of the judicial branch for the Legislature to pass a law that allows the executive branch to interfere with the final judicial determination in a case."[19] Similarly, the special act that was passed by the U.S. Congress and signed by President George W. Bush had limited significance as precedent for future cases, because it was expressly limited to that one patient and did not even affect the outcome of that particular case.[20]

In contrast to the case of Terri Schiavo, courts in other cases have tried to develop legal precedents for handling similar situations in the future. Many courts have tried to articulate a legal standard or formula by which all of these cases could be decided, such as the subjective test, the limited objective test, and the pure objective test.[21] However, those standards are often illogical and impractical and may be little more than attempts to jus- tify common sense in terms of legal doctrine. For example, the Supreme Judicial Court of Massachusetts applied the substituted judgment doctrine, which attempts to determine the preferences of the incompetent person. In that case, the court was considering whether to order or withhold chemotherapy for a profoundly retarded adult with leukemia. As the Massachusetts court explained,

> [w]e believe that both the guardian *ad litem* in his recommenda-
> tion and the judge in his decision should have attempted (as they
> did) to ascertain the incompetent person's actual interests and
> preferences. In short, the decision in cases such as this should be
> that which would be made by the incompetent person, if that per-
> son were competent, but taking into account the present and
> future incompetency of the individual as one of the factors which
> would necessarily enter into the decision-making process of the
> competent person.[22]

However, in a similar case, the New York Court of Appeals rejected the Massachusetts substituted judgment approach in considering whether to order blood transfusions for a profoundly retarded adult with bladder cancer. According to the New York court,

> John Storar was never competent at any time in his life. He was always totally incapable of understanding or making a reasoned decision about medical treatment. Thus it is unrealistic to attempt to determine whether he would want to continue potentially life prolonging treatment if he were competent. As one of the experts testified at the hearing, that would be similar to asking whether "if it snowed all summer would it then be winter?" Mentally, John Storar was an infant and that is the only realistic way to assess his rights in this litigation.[23]

In light of these different legal standards, it may be more effective to focus on the specific facts of each case and not merely on the legal formula. In most cases, it appears that the court makes a reasonable decision in light of the facts. Specifically, at least four factual variables have a significant effect on the outcome of a particular case. These four variables are (1) the patient's mental competence, (2) any formal or informal expression of the patient's desires, (3) the physical condition of the patient, and (4) the type of treatment that might be withheld or withdrawn.

First, as a conceptual matter, it is useful to distinguish between those patients who are competent and those who are incompetent.[24] In addition, for those patients who are currently incompetent, a further distinction can be made between those who were formerly competent and those who were never competent.[25] If a patient is competent, the patient is asked what she wants at the present time, and there is no need to consider whether the patient had previously executed a living will or other advance directive. However, if the patient is currently incompetent, the relevant questions are whether the patient ever made an advance directive and, if not, whether the patient gave any informal indication of desires with regard to artificial life support. If the patient was never competent, because the patient is an infant or a person with mental retardation, it is useless to evaluate the patient's expressions of intent because the patient was never legally capable of forming any intent.

Therefore, for those patients who are not currently competent but were formerly competent, the next factual variable is whether the patient made a formal or informal declaration of desires with regard to extraordinary means of life support.[26] Obviously, the best evidence of the patient's desires is a formal advance directive, such as a living will. Under the laws of each state, people may execute these formal documents to specify whether they would wish to continue or discontinue various types of treatment in the event that they are ever in a specified medical condition. In addition, almost all states allow a person to execute a durable power of attorney or a healthcare power of attorney to designate another person as an agent to make those types of treatment decisions for the patient. If the patient did not execute a living will or designate a healthcare agent, it makes sense to consider whether the patient had given any informal indications of intent, such as in conversations with relatives or friends.

The third factual variable in these cases is the physical condition of the patient. Although all of the patients in these cases are seriously ill, there are significant distinctions among the individual patients. For example, some of the patients are terminally ill, but others could continue to live for many years in a persistent vegetative state. Although some of the patients are unconscious and oblivious to their surroundings, others are conscious and in continual pain. Finally, some of the patients are capable of breathing on their own, but others are dependent on mechanical respirators.

The fourth variable is the type of treatment that might be withheld or withdrawn from the patient. In fact, the various types of treatment can be arranged along a spectrum from the most passive to the most active interventions. At the most passive extreme, a decision might be made not to resuscitate the patient in the event that he stops breathing or has a heart attack. This is referred to as a "no code order" or a "do not resuscitate order." Rather than taking active steps to end the life of the patient, this alternative merely lets nature take its course in bringing about the patient's death.

At the other extreme is active euthanasia, including PAS, which is discussed in detail in a later section. Some people have argued that PAS is no different from the withdrawal of life-support equipment, because both actions result in the patient's death. However, the U.S. Supreme Court has recognized a "distinction between letting a patient die and making that patient die."[27]

Between the extremes of passive inaction and active euthanasia are various types of treatment that might be withheld or withdrawn. Decisions could be made to perform or withhold blood transfusions, antibiotics, chemotherapy, surgery, or kidney dialysis for a patient in a particular case. Each of those potential interventions would be intrusive to a greater or lesser degree. In addition, the withholding of each intervention would have a different immediate effect on the patient. For example, removing a patient from a respirator would likely result in the death of the patient within a short and predictable period of time, whereas withholding chemotherapy may not result in death for several months.

Finally, some people believe there is a distinction between withholding medical treatment and withholding artificial nutrition and hydration. In many cases, the action under consideration is the termination of the patient's food and water through the removal of a nasogastric (NG) tube or other mechanical device. Therefore, it is important to focus on the specific facts about each individual patient in evaluating these cases and in answering Problem 12.1.

CHART 12.1
Termination of
Treatment
Cases

Name of Patient	Mental Condition (Competence)	Physical Condition	Type of Treatment at Issue	Patient's Instructions	Court's Decision

PROBLEM 12.1: CASES ON TERMINATION OF TREATMENT

The facts about several individual patients are set forth here. Each of these patients was the subject of a judicial decision by the court of a particular state. In some cases, the court permitted the withholding or withdrawal of treatment, which presumably resulted in the patient's death. However, in three of these cases, the court held that treatment should be continued, and therefore, the patient was not allowed to die.

For each case, the decision of the court is also provided. The goal of this problem is to determine whether the court's decision in each case was reasonable in light of the specific facts of the case.

Read the description of each case and record the details in Chart 12.1. With regard to the patients for whom treatment was continued, explain in writing any ways in which those cases were factually distinguishable from the cases in which treatment was terminated.

CASE 1: CRUZAN V. DIRECTOR, MISSOURI DEPARTMENT OF HEALTH[28]

After Nancy Beth Cruzan was injured in a car accident, she was in a persistent vegetative state and had virtually no chance of regaining her cognitive function. However, she was not terminally ill and was breathing on her own. Her parents asked hospital employees to terminate the artificial nutrition and hydration, but they refused to do so without a court order. Ms. Cruzan had never executed an advance directive, and the only evidence of her desires was a somewhat casual statement to a friend. Specifically, Ms. Cruzan had indicated that she would not want to continue living if she were ever in a severely impaired condition.

Ms. Cruzan's parents sought an order from a Missouri state court to terminate the artificial nutrition and hydration. The Missouri court refused to order the termination of treatment on the ground that there was no clear and convincing evidence of the patient's desire to terminate artificial nutrition and hydration. As discussed in Chapter 2, this case became the subject of a famous decision by the U.S. Supreme Court. However, because of the limited role of the federal courts, the U.S. Supreme Court did not consider the broad question of whether Ms. Cruzan should be allowed to die. Rather, the U.S. Supreme Court merely determined that the state law of Missouri, which required clear and convincing evidence of the patient's intent, did not violate the U.S. Constitution. Therefore, the Missouri court was entitled to apply its requirement of clear and convincing evidence.

CASE 2: BOUVIA V. SUPERIOR COURT OF LOS ANGELES COUNTY[29]

Elizabeth Bouvia was a 28-year-old quadriplegic with cerebral palsy. She was almost completely immobile and in continual pain. Her condition was irreversible and although she needed medication for pain, she was mentally competent.

Ms. Bouvia had to be spoon-fed, and eating sometimes caused nausea and vomiting. If she were fed through an NG tube, she could be kept alive for another 15 to 20 years. However, Ms. Bouvia dictated instructions to her lawyers that she did not want an NG tube and signed the document with a pen that she held in her mouth. Nevertheless, the hospital's medical staff inserted an NG tube against her will to prevent her from starving herself to death.

Ms. Bouvia asked the California state court to order the hospital and physicians to remove the NG tube. In response, the hospital and physicians argued that the state has legitimate interests in preserving life, preventing suicide, and maintaining the ethical standards of the medical profession. Eventually, the California Court of Appeals held that the hospital and physicians must remove the NG tube, which was inserted against her will. As the court of appeals explained, "[i]t is incongruous, if not monstrous, for medical practitioners to assert their right to preserve a life that someone else must live, or, more accurately, endure, for '15 to 20 years.'"[30] Moreover, the court held that the physicians had a duty to relieve her pain and suffering while she starved herself to death.

CASE 3: SATZ V. PERLMUTTER[31]

Abe Perlmutter was a 73-year-old man who was paralyzed by Lou Gehrig's disease. He was terminally ill and needed a respirator to breathe. However, he was competent and could communicate with the judge. He had previously pulled out his respirator, but hospital employees reconnected it. Now he wanted to stop the hospital employees from interfering with the removal of his respirator, which would result in his death within an hour. Mr. Perlmutter told the judge, "It can't be worse than what I'm going through now."[32] In that case, the Florida court ordered the hospital not to interfere with removal of the respirator.

CASE 4: BROPHY V. NEW ENGLAND SINAI HOSPITAL[33]

Paul Brophy was permanently comatose as a result of a ruptured aneurysm. Although he was unable to swallow, he could survive for several more years with a tube for nutrition and hydration. Previously, he had made some oral statements that he would not want artificial life support and that under those circumstances he might as well be dead. At the request of the patient's family, the Massachusetts court allowed the withdrawal of the tube.

CASE 5: IN RE EICHNER[34]

Brother Joseph Fox was a member of a Catholic religious order. He was in a vegetative state, was on a respirator, and had no reasonable chance of recovery. His superior, Father Eichner, wanted the hospital staff to remove the respirator from Brother Fox.

In formal philosophical and religious discussions, Brother Fox had expressed his desire that he not receive any extraordinary means of life support, and he reiterated that view shortly before his final hospitalization. Therefore, the New

York Court allowed the removal of the respirator on the grounds that there was clear and convincing evidence of the patient's desires.

CASE 6: IN RE MARY O'CONNOR[35]

Mary O'Connor, aged 77 years old, had suffered several strokes but was not in pain. Although she was incompetent as a result of the strokes, she was not in a coma or persistent vegetative state. Rather, she was conscious and might become more alert in the future.

The hospital wanted to insert an NG tube for nutrition and hydration to avoid a potentially painful death by starvation and thirst. However, the patient's two adult daughters objected to the use of the NG tube. The only evidence of the patient's desires was in conversations with her daughters and coworkers to the effect that she would not want artificial life support. However, she had never discussed the specific issue of nutrition and hydration and had not discussed the possibility of a painful death. In this case, the New York court refused to stop the insertion of the NG tube on the grounds that there was no clear and convincing evidence of the patient's desires.

Some people have compared this case to the decision in *Eichner*, in which the New York court allowed termination of treatment for Brother Joseph Fox. Specifically, critics have charged that the New York court is unfair to ordinary people like Mary O'Connor who express their desires in conversations with family and friends and do not have the opportunity to participate in formal philosophical discussions like Brother Fox.

CASE 7: SUPERINTENDENT OF BELCHERTOWN STATE SCHOOL V. SAIKEWICZ[36]

Joseph Saikewicz was profoundly retarded, but he was conscious. Although he was 67 years old, he had a mental age of two years and eight months and had never learned to speak. He had leukemia, and the issue was whether he should be given chemotherapy. Most competent patients with leukemia choose to undergo chemotherapy, which can be successful. However, Mr. Saikewicz would not have cooperated with the chemotherapy and would not have understood the reason for the treatment. In this case, the Massachusetts court ruled that chemotherapy should be withheld.

CASE 8: IN RE STORAR[37]

John Storar was profoundly retarded and conscious. Although he was 52 years old, he had a mental age of only 18 months. He was terminally ill with bladder cancer and on drugs for the pain. Regardless of any treatment, Mr. Storar would die within three to six months. However, he was losing blood in his urine and would die within weeks if he did not receive blood transfusions. The facility wanted to give blood transfusions to Mr. Storar, but his mother objected. Although the patient disliked the transfusions, he could be sedated. In this case, the New York court held that the facility should be allowed to give blood transfusions to the patient over the objections of his mother.

Physician-Assisted Suicide

Even if a patient has the right to refuse life-sustaining treatment, that right does not necessarily include the right to have another person, such as a physician, assist in ending the patient's life. Some people think access to PAS should be a right, whereas others strongly disagree. The ethical arguments in favor of PAS are based on the principle of autonomy or self-determination in making important personal decisions, as well as the principle of beneficence or mercy in helping to relieve the suffering of terminally ill patients.[38] However, others argue that it is simply immoral to kill an innocent person, even if it is done to relieve suffering; that legalized PAS would be difficult to control; and that killing a patient is an inappropriate role for a physician.[39]

The American Medical Association (AMA) takes the position that for a physician to participate in assisted suicide would be unethical. According to the AMA's Council on Ethical and Judicial Affairs, "[p]hysician-assisted suicide is fundamentally incompatible with the physician's role as healer, would be difficult or impossible to control, and would pose serious societal risks."[40] However, the AMA is merely a private professional organization, and its ethical opinions do not have the force of law. In fact, some physicians believe assisted suicide should be lawful and also believe it would be ethical in appropriate cases. Moreover, evidence exists that PAS is now performed quietly on an underground basis where it cannot be supervised or regulated by law.[41]

At the present time, assisted suicide is a crime in almost every state. Therefore, the state government could send physicians and other healthcare professionals to prison or take away their license if they participate in PAS. To challenge those state laws, some physicians, patients, and advocacy groups had argued that the state laws violate their rights under the U.S. Constitution. They asked the federal courts to rule that the state laws are unconstitutional and unenforceable. Although some lower federal courts agreed with the plaintiffs, the U.S. Supreme Court held that the state laws are constitutional and indicated that PAS may be allowed or prohibited at the option of the state.

In *Washington v. Glucksberg,*[42] the Supreme Court explained that the right to refuse unwanted medical treatment, as discussed in *Cruzan,* is not the same as a right to assisted suicide. Therefore, the Supreme Court rejected the notion that patients have a constitutionally protected liberty interest in committing PAS. Moreover, the court concluded that the state has important interests to protect, and the prohibition of assisted suicide is reasonably related to those interests. Therefore, the state law that prohibits assisted suicide does not offend the Fourteenth Amendment to the U.S. Constitution.

On the same day, the U.S. Supreme Court reached a similar conclusion in *Vacco v. Quill*.[43] That case dealt with the New York law that allows patients to refuse lifesaving medical treatment but makes helping someone commit suicide a crime. Therefore, under New York law, patients on life-support equipment can choose to die quickly by having the equipment removed, but patients who need no artificial life support cannot choose to die quickly because they are not allowed to obtain any lethal drugs. According to the federal Court of Appeals for the Second Circuit, the withdrawal of life support is the same as assisted suicide; therefore, the distinction made by the New York law violates the Equal Protection Clause of the Fourteenth Amendment. However, the U.S. Supreme Court disagreed and concluded that there is a "distinction between letting a patient die and making that patient die."[44] Therefore, the Supreme Court held that the New York law prohibiting assisted suicide is consistent with the U.S. Constitution.

In light of these decisions, individuals do not have a constitutional right to PAS, and states may prohibit the practice if they so desire. However, states also have the option of permitting assisted suicide, as the state of Oregon has done to a limited extent. As former Chief Justice William Rehnquist wrote in *Washington v. Glucksberg*, "[t]hroughout the Nation, Americans are engaged in an earnest and profound debate about the morality, legality, and practicality of physician-assisted suicide. Our holding permits this debate to continue, as it should in a democratic society."[45]

In 1994, the citizens of Oregon voted to approve the state's Death with Dignity Act, which is the first law in the United States to permit a type of PAS.[46] After some legal challenges, the Oregon statute finally became effective on October 27, 1997. In a referendum in November 1997, Oregon citizens reaffirmed their support for the assisted suicide law. In Oregon, physicians may now prescribe lethal drugs under specified conditions. However, physicians may not administer the lethal drugs to the patient. In the first eight years since the Oregon law became effective, 246 patients took lethal drugs for the purpose of PAS.[47] In addition, seriously ill residents of Oregon may take comfort in the availability of the procedure to obtain lethal drugs or the opportunity to request lethal drugs that they might never need to use.

Some federal officials tried to prevent Oregon physicians from participating in PAS in accordance with the Oregon statute. This dispute highlights the effect of policy and politics on the law, as well as the interaction of state and federal law in regulating the U.S. healthcare system. As discussed in Chapter 5, the regulation of medical practice is a traditional state function. However, the federal government regulates the distribution of controlled substances, such as the lethal drugs that are used in PAS.

At the urging of Senator Orrin Hatch (R-UT) and Congressman Henry Hyde (R-IL), in November 1997 the federal Drug Enforcement Administration (DEA) indicated that Oregon physicians might be sanctioned by federal authorities if they prescribe drugs for assisted suicide in accordance with the Oregon statute. However, U.S. Attorney General Janet Reno subsequently overruled the DEA and stated that Oregon physicians will not be penalized by the federal government for actions taken pursuant to the state's assisted suicide law. In the meantime, some members of Congress attempted to enact a statute that would have prohibited physicians from performing assisted suicide with federally controlled drugs.[48]

Later, the U.S. Attorney General who replaced Reno in the George W. Bush administration, John Ashcroft, reversed Reno's position and reinstated the original DEA position. In a memorandum issued on November 9, 2001, Attorney General Ashcroft wrote that the DEA has the authority to suspend or revoke the registration to dispense controlled substances of any physician who uses those substances for PAS.[49] The state of Oregon sued the U.S. attorney general in federal court for an injunction against enforcing Ashcroft's memorandum. On April 17, 2002, the federal district court ruled in favor of the state of Oregon and issued a permanent injunction to prohibit the attorney general from suspending or revoking the DEA registration of Oregon physicians who participate in PAS in accordance with the terms of the Oregon statute. The U.S. Court of Appeals for the Ninth Circuit essentially agreed with the district court and continued the injunction in effect. Finally, on January 17, 2006, the U.S. Supreme Court affirmed the judgment of the Court of Appeals, and rejected Attorney General Ashcroft's position.[50]

The issue in that case, which is known as *Gonzales v. Oregon*, was not whether patients have a constitutional right to PAS. As discussed previously, the Supreme Court had already resolved that issue by holding that there is no such constitutional right. Instead, *Gonzales v. Oregon* dealt with an issue of statutory interpretation with regard to the authority of federal officials under the federal Controlled Substances Act (CSA).[51] The issues were whether the U.S. attorney general and the DEA have authority under the federal statute to revoke the registration to use controlled substances of a physician who uses those substances to assist in a suicide in accordance with Oregon law, and whether an Oregon physician is subject to federal criminal prosecution under those circumstances. In resolving those issues of statutory interpretation, the Supreme Court concluded that Congress had never intended to give federal officials that type of control over the practice of medicine, which has been regulated traditionally by the government of each state. The following reading is an excerpt from the opinion of the U.S. Supreme Court in that case.

Gonzales v. Oregon, 546 U.S. 243 (2006) (Citations and Footnotes Omitted)

The question before us is whether the Controlled Substances Act allows the United States Attorney General to prohibit doctors from prescribing regulated drugs for use in physician-assisted suicide, notwithstanding a state law permitting the procedure. As the Court has observed, "Americans are engaged in an earnest and profound debate about the morality, legality, and practicality of physician-assisted suicide." The dispute before us is in part a product of this political and moral debate, but its resolution requires an inquiry familiar to the courts: interpreting a federal statute to determine whether Executive action is authorized by, or otherwise consistent with, the enactment.

In 1994, Oregon became the first State to legalize assisted suicide when voters approved a ballot measure enacting the Oregon Death With Dignity Act (ODWDA). ODWDA, which survived a 1997 ballot measure seeking its repeal, exempts from civil or criminal liability state-licensed physicians who, in compliance with the specific safeguards in ODWDA, dispense or prescribe a lethal dose of drugs upon the request of a terminally ill patient.

The drugs Oregon physicians prescribe under ODWDA are regulated under a federal statute, the Controlled Substances Act (CSA or Act). The CSA allows these particular drugs to be available only by a written prescription from a registered physician. In the ordinary course the same drugs are prescribed in smaller doses for pain alleviation.

A November 9, 2001 Interpretive Rule issued by the Attorney General addresses the implementation and enforcement of the CSA with respect to ODWDA. It determines that using controlled substances to assist suicide is not a legitimate medical practice and that dispensing or prescribing them for this purpose is unlawful under the CSA. The Interpretive Rule's validity under the CSA is the issue before us.

We turn first to the text and structure of the CSA. Enacted in 1970 with the main objectives of combating drug abuse and controlling the legitimate and illegitimate traffic in controlled substances, the CSA creates a comprehensive, closed regulatory regime criminalizing the unauthorized manufacture, distribution, dispensing, and possession of substances classified in any of the Act's five schedules. The Act places substances in one of five schedules based on their potential for abuse or dependence, their accepted medical use, and their accepted safety for use under medical supervision. Schedule I contains the most severe restrictions on access and use, and Schedule V the least. Congress classified a host of substances when it enacted the CSA, but the statute permits the Attorney General to add, remove, or reschedule substances. He may do so, however, only after making particular findings, and on scientific and medical matters he is required to accept the findings of the Secretary of Health and Human Services (Secretary). These proceedings must be on the record after an opportunity for comment.

The present dispute involves controlled substances listed in Schedule II, substances generally available only pursuant to a written, nonrefillable prescription by a physician. A 1971 regulation promulgated by the Attorney General requires that every prescription for a controlled substance "be issued for a legitimate medical purpose by an individual practitioner acting in the usual course of his professional practice."

To prevent diversion of controlled substances with medical uses, the CSA regulates the activity of physicians. To issue lawful prescriptions of Schedule II drugs, physicians must "obtain from the Attorney General a registration issued in accordance with the rules and regulations promulgated by him." The Attorney General may deny, suspend, or revoke this registration if, as relevant here, the physician's registration would be "inconsistent with the public interest." When deciding whether a practitioner's registration is in the public interest, the Attorney General "shall" consider:

"(1) The recommendation of the appropriate State licensing board or professional disciplinary authority."
"(2) The applicant's experience in dispensing, or conducting research with respect to controlled substances."
"(3) The applicant's conviction record under Federal or State laws relating to the manufacture, distribution, or dispensing of controlled substances."
"(4) Compliance with applicable State, Federal, or local laws relating to controlled substances."
"(5) Such other conduct which may threaten the public health and safety."

The CSA explicitly contemplates a role for the States in regulating controlled substances, as evidenced by its pre-emption provision.

"No provision of this subchapter shall be construed as indicating an intent on the part of the Congress to occupy the field in which that provision operates . . . to the exclusion of any State law on the same subject matter which would otherwise be within the authority of the State, unless there is a positive conflict between that provision . . . and that State law so that the two cannot consistently stand together."

Oregon voters enacted ODWDA in 1994. For Oregon residents to be eligible to request a prescription under ODWDA, they must receive a diagnosis from their attending physician that they have an incurable and irreversible disease that, within reasonable medical judgment, will cause death within six months. Attending physicians must also determine whether a patient has made a voluntary request, ensure a patient's choice is informed, and refer patients to counseling if they might be suffering from a psychological disorder or depression causing impaired judgment. A second "consulting" physician must examine the patient and the medical record and confirm the attending physician's conclusions. Oregon physicians may dispense or issue a prescription for the requested drug, but may not administer it.

The reviewing physicians must keep detailed medical records of the process leading to the final prescription, records that Oregon's Department of Human Services reviews. Physicians who dispense medication pursuant to ODWDA must also be registered with both the State's Board of Medical Examiners and the federal Drug Enforcement Administration (DEA). In 2004, 37 patients ended their lives by ingesting a lethal dose of medication prescribed under ODWDA.

In 1997, Members of Congress concerned about ODWDA invited the DEA to prosecute or revoke the CSA registration of Oregon physicians who assist suicide. They contended that hastening a patient's death is not legitimate medical practice, so prescribing controlled substances for that purpose violates the CSA. The letter received an initial, favorable response from the director of the DEA, but Attorney General Reno considered the matter and concluded that the DEA could not take the proposed action because the CSA did not authorize it to "displace the states as the primary regulators of the medical profession, or to override a state's determination as to what constitutes legitimate medical practice." Legislation was then introduced to grant the explicit authority Attorney General Reno found lacking; but it failed to pass.

In 2001, John Ashcroft was appointed Attorney General. Perhaps because Mr. Ashcroft had supported efforts to curtail assisted suicide while serving as a Senator, Oregon Attorney General Hardy Myers wrote him to request a meeting with Department of Justice officials should the Department decide to revisit the application of the CSA to assisted suicide. Attorney General Myers received a reply letter from one of Attorney General Ashcroft's advisers writing on his behalf, which stated

"I am aware of no pending legislation in Congress that would prompt a review of the Department's interpretation of the CSA as it relates to physician-assisted suicide. Should such a review be commenced in the future, we would be happy to include your views in that review."

On November 9, 2001, without consulting Oregon or apparently anyone outside his Department, the Attorney General issued an Interpretive Rule announcing his intent to restrict the use of controlled substances for physician-assisted suicide. Incorporating the legal analysis of a memorandum he had solicited from his Office of Legal Counsel, the Attorney General ruled:

> "assisting suicide is not a 'legitimate medical purpose' within the meaning of 21 CFR 1306.04 (2001), and that prescribing, dispensing, or administering federally controlled substances to assist suicide violates the Controlled Substances Act. Such conduct by a physician registered to dispense controlled substances may 'render his registration . . . inconsistent with the public interest' and therefore subject to possible suspension or revocation under 21 U.S.C. 824(a)(4). The Attorney General's conclusion applies regardless of whether state law authorizes or permits such conduct by practitioners or others and regardless of the condition of the person whose suicide is assisted."

There is little dispute that the Interpretive Rule would substantially disrupt the ODWDA regime. Respondents contend, and petitioners do not dispute, that every prescription filled under ODWDA has specified drugs classified under Schedule II. A physician cannot prescribe the substances without DEA registration, and revocation or suspension of the registration would be a severe restriction on medical practice. Dispensing controlled substances without a valid prescription, furthermore, is a federal crime.

In response, the State of Oregon, joined by a physician, a pharmacist, and some terminally ill patients, all from Oregon, challenged the Interpretive Rule in federal court. The United States District Court for the District of Oregon entered a permanent injunction against the Interpretive Rule's enforcement.

A divided panel of the Court of Appeals for the Ninth Circuit granted the petitions for review and held the Interpretive Rule invalid. It reasoned that, by making a medical procedure authorized under Oregon law a federal offense, the Interpretive Rule altered the "'usual constitutional balance between the States and the Federal Government'" without the requisite clear statement that the CSA authorized such action. The Court of Appeals held in the alternative that the Interpretive Rule could not be squared with the plain language of the CSA, which targets only conventional drug abuse and excludes the Attorney General from decisions on medical policy.

We granted the Government's petition for certiorari . . .

Executive actors often must interpret the enactments Congress has charged them with enforcing and implementing. The parties before us are in sharp disagreement both as to the degree of deference we must accord the Interpretive Rule's substantive conclusions and whether the Rule is authorized by the statutory text at all . . .

The Attorney General has rulemaking power to fulfill his duties under the CSA. The specific respects in which he is authorized to make rules, however, instruct us that he is not authorized to make a rule declaring illegitimate a medical standard for care and treatment of patients that is specifically authorized under state law.

The starting point for this inquiry is, of course, the language of the delegation provision itself. . . . The CSA does not grant the Attorney General this broad authority to promulgate rules . . .

The Interpretive Rule thus purports to declare that using controlled substances for physician-assisted suicide is a crime, an authority that goes well beyond the Attorney General's statutory power to register or deregister . . .

The authority desired by the Government is inconsistent with the design of the statute in other fundamental respects. The Attorney General does not have the sole delegated authority under the CSA. He must instead share it with, and in some respects defer to, the Secretary [of HHS], whose functions are likewise delineated and confined by the statute. The CSA allocates decisionmaking powers among statutory actors so that medical judgments, if they are to be decided at the federal level and for the limited objects of the statute, are placed in the hands of the Secretary. In the scheduling context, for example, the Secretary's recommendations on scientific and medical matters bind the Attorney General. The Attorney General cannot control a substance if the Secretary disagrees.

In a similar vein the 1970 Act's regulation of medical practice with respect to drug rehabilitation gives the Attorney General a limited role; for it is the Secretary who, after consultation with the Attorney General and national medical groups, "determine[s] the appropriate methods of professional practice in the medical treatment of . . . narcotic addiction." . . .

The structure of the CSA, then, conveys unwillingness to cede medical judgments to an Executive official who lacks medical expertise. . . .

The Government contends the Attorney General's decision here is a legal, not a medical, one. This generality, however, does not suffice. The Attorney General's Interpretive Rule, and the Office of Legal Counsel memo it incorporates, place extensive reliance on medical judgments and the views of the medical community in concluding that assisted suicide is not a "legitimate medical purpose." This confirms that the authority claimed by the Attorney General is both beyond his expertise and incongruous with the statutory purposes and design.

The idea that Congress gave the Attorney General such broad and unusual authority through an implicit delegation in the CSA's registration provision is not sustainable. "Congress, we have held, does not alter the fundamental details of a regulatory scheme in vague terms or ancillary provisions—it does not, one might say, hide elephants in mouseholes."

The importance of the issue of physician-assisted suicide, which has been the subject of an "earnest and profound debate" across the country, makes the oblique form of the claimed delegation all the more suspect. Under the Government's theory, moreover, the medical judgments the Attorney General could make are not limited to physician-assisted suicide. Were this argument accepted, he could decide whether any particular drug may be used for any particular purpose, or indeed whether a physician who administers any controversial treatment could be deregistered. This would occur, under the Government's view, despite the statute's express limitation of the Attorney General's authority to registration and control, with attendant restrictions on each of those functions, and despite the statutory purposes to combat drug abuse and prevent illicit drug trafficking.

We need not decide whether . . . deference would be warranted for an interpretation issued by the Attorney General concerning matters closer to his role under the CSA, namely preventing doctors from engaging in illicit drug trafficking. In light of the foregoing, however, the CSA does not give the Attorney General authority to issue the Interpretive Rule as a statement with the force of law.

. . . In any event, . . . we follow an agency's rule only to the extent it is persuasive, and for the reasons given and for further reasons set out below, we do not find the Attorney General's opinion persuasive . . .

In deciding whether the CSA can be read as prohibiting physician-assisted suicide, we look to the statute's text and design. The statute and our case law amply support the conclusion that Congress regulates medical practice inso-far as it bars doctors from using their prescription-writing powers as a means to engage in illicit drug dealing and trafficking as conventionally understood. Beyond this, however, the statute manifests no intent to regulate the practice of medicine generally. The silence is understandable given the structure and limitations of federalism, which allow the States "'great latitude under their police powers to legislate as to the protection of the lives, limbs, health, com-fort, and quiet of all persons.'"

The structure and operation of the CSA presume and rely upon a function-ing medical profession regulated under the States' police powers. The Attorney General can register a physician to dispense controlled substances "if the appli-cant is authorized to dispense . . . controlled substances under the laws of the State in which he practices." When considering whether to revoke a physician's registration, the Attorney General looks not just to violations of federal drug laws; but he "shall" also consider "[t]he recommendation of the appropriate state licensing board or professional disciplinary authority" and the registrant's compliance with state and local drug laws. The very definition of a "practi-tioner" eligible to prescribe includes physicians "licensed, registered, or oth-erwise permitted, by the United States or the jurisdiction in which he practices" to dispense controlled substances. Further cautioning against the conclusion that the CSA effectively displaces the States' general regulation of medical practice is the Act's pre-emption provision, which indicates that, absent a pos-itive conflict, none of the Act's provisions should be "construed as indicating an intent on the part of the Congress to occupy the field in which that provi-sion operates . . . to the exclusion of any State law on the same subject mat-ter which would otherwise be within the authority of the State."

Oregon's regime is an example of the state regulation of medical practice that the CSA presupposes. Rather than simply decriminalizing assisted suicide, ODWDA limits its exercise to the attending physicians of terminally ill patients, physicians who must be licensed by Oregon's Board of Medical Examiners. The statute gives attending physicians a central role, requiring them to provide prog-noses and prescriptions, give information about palliative alternatives and coun-seling, and ensure patients are competent and acting voluntarily. Any eligible patient must also get a second opinion from another registered physician, and the statute's safeguards require physicians to keep and submit to inspection detailed records of their actions.

Even though regulation of health and safety is "primarily, and historically, a matter of local concern," there is no question that the Federal Government can set uniform national standards in these areas. In connection to the CSA, however, we find only one area in which Congress set general, uniform stan-dards of medical practice. Title I of the Comprehensive Drug Abuse Prevention and Control Act of 1970, of which the CSA was Title II, provides that:

[The Secretary], after consultation with the Attorney General and with national organizations representative of persons with knowledge and experience in the treatment of narcotic addicts, shall determine the appropriate methods of professional practice in the medical treatment of the narcotic addiction of various classes of narcotic addicts, and shall report thereon from time to time to the Congress.

This provision strengthens the understanding of the CSA as a statute combating recreational drug abuse, and also indicates that when Congress wants to regulate medical practice in the given scheme, it does so by explicit language in the statute.

In the face of the CSA's silence on the practice of medicine generally and its recognition of state regulation of the medical profession it is difficult to defend the Attorney General's declaration that the statute impliedly criminalizes physician-assisted suicide. This difficulty is compounded by the CSA's consistent delegation of medical judgments to the Secretary and its otherwise careful allocation of powers for enforcing the limited objects of the CSA. The Government's attempt to meet this challenge rests, for the most part, on the CSA's requirement that every Schedule II drug be dispensed pursuant to a "written prescription of a practitioner." A prescription, the Government argues, necessarily implies that the substance is being made available to a patient for a legitimate medical purpose. The statute, in this view, requires an anterior judgment about the term "medical" or "medicine." The Government contends ordinary usage of these words ineluctably refers to a healing or curative art, which by these terms cannot embrace the intentional hastening of a patient's death. It also points to the teachings of Hippocrates, the positions of prominent medical organizations, the Federal Government, and the judgment of the 49 States that have not legalized physician-assisted suicide as further support for the proposition that the practice is not legitimate medicine.

On its own, this understanding of medicine's boundaries is at least reasonable. The primary problem with the Government's argument, however, is its assumption that the CSA impliedly authorizes an Executive officer to bar a use simply because it may be inconsistent with one reasonable understanding of medical practice. Viewed alone, the prescription requirement may support such an understanding, but statutes "should not be read as a series of unrelated and isolated provisions." The CSA's substantive provisions and their arrangement undermine this assertion of an expansive federal authority to regulate medicine . . .

The Government's interpretation of the prescription requirement also fails under the objection that the Attorney General is an unlikely recipient of such broad authority, given the Secretary's primacy in shaping medical policy under the CSA, and the statute's otherwise careful allocation of decisionmaking powers. Just as the conventions of expression indicate that Congress is unlikely to alter a statute's obvious scope and division of authority through muffled hints, the background principles of our federal system also belie the notion that Congress would use such an obscure grant of authority to regulate areas traditionally supervised by the States' police power. . . . For all these reasons, we conclude the CSA's prescription requirement does not authorize the Attorney General to bar dispensing controlled substances for assisted suicide in the face of a state medical regime permitting such conduct.

The Government, in the end, maintains that the prescription requirement delegates to a single Executive officer the power to effect a radical shift of authority from the States to the Federal Government to define general standards of medical practice in every locality. The text and structure of the CSA show that Congress did not have this far-reaching intent to alter the federal-state balance and the congressional role in maintaining it.

The judgment of the Court of Appeals is affirmed.

Notes

1. *Washington v. Glucksberg*, 521 U.S. 702, 719 (1997) (citations omitted).
2. *Cruzan v. Director, Missouri Department of Health*, 497 U.S. 261 (1990).
3. See generally, D.M. Harris, "Beyond Beneficiaries: Using the Medicare Program to Accomplish Broader Public Goals," *Washington and Lee Law Review*, 60(4) (2003): 1251–1314 at 1280–84.
4. See Patient Self-Determination Act, Omnibus Budget Reconciliation Act of 1990, § 4206, 42 U.S.C. § 1395cc(f) (2006).
5. Balanced Budget Act of 1997, Pub. L. No. 105-33, § 4641, 111 Stat. 251, 487 (1997) codified as amended at 42 U.S.C. § 1395cc(f)(1)(B).
6. See Assisted Suicide Funding Restriction Act of 1997, Pub. L. No. 105-12, 111 Stat. 23 (1997) (codified as amended at 42 U.S.C. §§ 14401 *et seq.*).
7. *Schloendorff v. Society of New York Hospital*, 211 N.Y. 125, 129–30 (1914).
8. *Jacobson v. Massachusetts*, 197 U.S. 11, 25 (1905) (upholding Massachusetts statute on compulsory vaccination).
9. See 42 U.S.C. § 274e (2006).
10. *Application of the President and Directors of Georgetown College, Inc.*, 331 F.2d 1000, 1008–1009 (D.C. Cir.), *cert. denied*, 377 U.S. 978 (1964).
11. See, e.g., *Public Health Trust of Dade County, Florida v. Wons*, 541 So.2d 96 (Fla. 1989) (a competent adult patient may refuse a blood transfusion, even if the patient is a parent of minor children).
12. See, e.g., *In re Guardianship of L.S. and H.S.*, 87 P.3d 521, 526 (Nevada 2004) ("Other jurisdictions have uniformly held that when medical treatment is available and necessary to save a minor's life, the state may intervene.").

13. *Application of the President and Directors of Georgetown College, Inc.*, 331 F.2d at 1008.

14. See, e.g., N.C. Gen. Stat. § 90-322 (2005).

15. G.J. Annas, "'Culture of Life' Politics at the Bedside—The Case of Terri Schiavo," *New England Journal of Medicine*, 352(16) (2005): 1710–1715 at 1714.

16. See 2003 Fla. Laws, Ch. 418.

17. Annas, *supra* note 15 at 1712. See also *Bush v. Schiavo*, 885 So.2d 321, 336 (Fla. 2004) ("In theory, the Act could have applied during its fifteen-day window to more than one person, but it is undeniable that in fact the criteria fit only Theresa Schiavo.").

18. *Bush v. Schiavo*, 885 So.2d at 337.

19. *Id.* at 332.

20. See Annas, *supra* note 15, at 1713–14. See also An Act for the Relief of the Parents of Theresa Marie Schiavo, Pub. L. No. 109-3, 119 Stat. 15 (2005); *Schiavo ex rel. Schindler v. Schiavo*, 403 F.3d 1289 (11th Cir. 2005).

21. See, e.g., *In re Conroy*, 486 A.2d 1209 (N.J. 1985).

22. *Superintendent of Belchertown State School v. Saikewicz*, 370 N.E.2d 417, 431 (Mass. 1977).

23. *In re Storar*, 420 N.E.2d 64, 72–73 (N.Y. 1981).

24. See B.R. Furrow, et al., *Health Law*, (Second Edition), Hornbook Series (St. Paul, MN: West Group, 2000): at 838–840.

25. See *id.* at 842, 858.

26. See *id.* at 842–853.

27. *Vacco v. Quill*, 521 U.S. 793, 807 (1997).

28. 497 U.S. 261 (1990).

29. 225 Cal. Rptr. 297 (Cal. Ct. App. 1986).

30. *Id.* at 305.

31. 362 So.2d 160 (Fla. Dist. Ct. App.), *aff'd*, 379 So.2d 359 (Fla. 1980).

32. *Id.* at 161.

33. 497 N.E.2d 626 (Mass. 1986).

34. 420 N.E.2d 64 (N.Y. 1981).

35. 531 N.E.2d 607 (N.Y. 1988).

36. 370 N.E.2d 417 (Mass. 1977).

37. 420 N.E.2d 64 (N.Y. 1981).

38. See J.D. Arras, "Physician-Assisted Suicide: A Tragic View," *Journal of Contemporary Health Law & Policy*, 13 (1997): 361–389.

39. *Id.*

40. American Medical Association, Council on Ethical and Judicial Affairs, *Code of Medical Ethics of the American Medical Association: Current Opinions with Annotations* (2006–2007 Edition) (Chicago: American Medical Association, 2006): § 2.211.

41. See A.D. Lowe, "Facing the Final Exit," *ABA Journal*, 83 (September 1997): 48–52.
42. 521 U.S. 702 (1997).
43. 521 U.S. 793 (1997).
44. *Id.* at 807.
45. *Washington*, 521 U.S. at 735.
46. See Or. Rev. Stat. §§ 127.800–127.897 (1997).
47. Oregon Department of Human Services, "Eighth Annual Report on Oregon's Death with Dignity Act," (March 9, 2006) at 5. [Online document; retrieved 2/1/07.] egov.oregon.gov/DHS/ph/pas/docs/year8.pdf.
48. See, e.g., proposed Pain Relief Promotion Act of 1999, H.R. 2260, 106th Cong. (introduced June 17, 1999).
49. Dispensing of Controlled Substances to Assist Suicide, 66 Fed. Reg. 56607, 56607–56608 (Nov. 9, 2001).
50. *Gonzales v. Oregon*, 546 U.S. 243 (2006).
51. 21 U.S.C. §§ 801 *et seq.* (2006).

HUMAN REPRODUCTION

The U.S. Constitution explicitly protects many important rights, such as freedom of speech and freedom of religion. Although the Constitution explicitly protects the right to bear arms, it is silent on the right to bear children, as well as the right *not* to bear children. Although these rights are not explicitly mentioned in the Constitution, the U.S. Supreme Court has stated that the right to bear children is "one of the basic civil rights of man."[1]

This type of implicit individual right is often referred to as the right of privacy. It includes the right to make personal decisions about important issues of individual and family life. As the Supreme Court has explained, "[i]f the right of privacy means anything, it is the right of the *individual*, married or single, to be free from unwarranted governmental intrusion into matters so fundamentally affecting a person as the decision whether to bear or beget a child."[2]

Any attempt by the state to regulate human reproduction raises important constitutional issues. As in cases involving the right to refuse treatment, individuals may allege that their state government is violating their rights under the federal constitution. Under these circumstances, individuals may ask a federal court to declare that the state law violates the U.S. Constitution and may ask the court to issue an injunction against the state's enforcement of its law.

In a number of cases involving the right to refuse treatment, the U.S. Supreme Court has upheld state laws and rejected constitutional challenges. For example, in *Cruzan*, the Supreme Court held that Missouri's state law requirement of clear and convincing evidence for termination of treatment does not violate the U.S. Constitution.[3] Similarly, the Supreme Court held that states may prohibit physician-assisted suicide, as Washington and New York have done.[4]

In the area of reproductive rights, however, the outcome of constitutional litigation has been very different. Rather than leaving reproductive issues to the states, the Supreme Court has struck down state laws and set constitutional limits on the authority of state governments to regulate with regard to reproduction. Within those limits, states have some discretion to enact and enforce their own laws. In the following materials, the issue of what states may and may not regulate is addressed with regard to sterilization, contraception, and abortion. In later sections, the chapter addresses some of the complex issues of emergency contraception and maternal–fetal conflict.

Sterilization

Sterilization generally refers to the surgical procedures of vasectomy for men and tubal ligation for women. Although sterilization prevents reproduction, the procedure may be reversible in some cases.

The legal and ethical issues of sterilization may arise in at least three different contexts. First, sterilization may be the unavoidable result of a procedure that is performed for therapeutic reasons. Under those circumstances, the patient was not seeking to be sterilized as a means of preventing reproduction. Therefore, the primary legal issue is that of informed consent. Before agreeing to the therapeutic procedure, the patient has the right to know the consequences of the procedure, including the effect on future ability to procreate.

In another context, a person may wish to be sterilized as a voluntary decision to avoid having any additional children. In that situation, the state has an interest in ensuring that the person is mentally and legally competent, is fully aware of the consequences of the procedure, and has made a considered decision in requesting to be sterilized. The state has an even stronger interest in protecting a minor from an inappropriate sterilization, especially when the procedure is requested by a parent or guardian of the minor. For all of these reasons, states may choose to regulate voluntary sterilization for adults and may require court approval for sterilization of a minor.

The context that surrounds the most difficult legal and ethical issues is involuntary sterilization of persons who are developmentally disabled or mentally retarded. In many of those cases, people have argued that sterilization was in the best interest of the disabled person. The reality, however, is that many persons with disabilities have been sterilized for the convenience of their families or the institutions in which they resided.

Apart from determining whether sterilization is in the best interest of the disabled person, some people have argued that society has a legitimate interest in preventing persons with disabilities from having any children. In the 1927 case of *Buck v. Bell*,[5] the U.S. Supreme Court upheld a Virginia statute that authorized the involuntary sterilization of so-called "mental defectives" such as Ms. Carrie Buck.[6] See the following excerpt.

Buck v. Bell, Superintendent of State Colony for Epileptics and Feeble Minded, 274 U.S. 200 (1927) (Citations Omitted)

MR. JUSTICE HOLMES delivered the opinion of the Court.

This is a writ of error to review a judgment of the Supreme Court of Appeals of the State of Virginia, affirming a judgment of the Circuit Court of Amherst County, by which the defendant in error, the superintendent of the State Colony for Epileptics and Feeble Minded, was ordered to perform the operation of salpingectomy upon Carrie Buck, the plaintiff in error, for the purpose of making her sterile. The case comes here upon the contention that the statute authorizing the judgment is void under the Fourteenth Amendment as denying to the plaintiff in error due process of law and the equal protection of the laws.

Carrie Buck is a feeble minded white woman who was committed to the State Colony above mentioned in due form. She is the daughter of a feeble minded mother in the same institution, and the mother of an illegitimate feeble minded child. She was eighteen years old at the time of the trial of her case in the Circuit Court, in the latter part of 1924. An Act of Virginia, approved March 20, 1924, recites that the health of the patient and the welfare of society may be promoted in certain cases by the sterilization of mental defectives, under careful safeguard, etc.; that the sterilization may be effected in males by vasectomy and in females by salpingectomy, without serious pain or substantial danger to life; that the Commonwealth is supporting in various institutions many defective persons who if now discharged would become a menace but if incapable of procreating might be discharged with safety and become self-supporting with benefit to themselves and to society; and that experience has shown that heredity plays an important part in the transmission of insanity, imbecility, etc. The statute then enacts that whenever the superintendent of certain institutions including the above named State Colony shall be of opinion that it is for the best interests of the patients and of society that an inmate under his care should be sexually sterilized, he may have the operation performed upon any patient afflicted with hereditary forms of insanity, imbecility, etc., on complying with the very careful provisions by which the act protects the patients from possible abuse . . .

There can be no doubt that so far as procedure is concerned the rights of the patient are most carefully considered, and as every step in this case was taken in scrupulous compliance with the statute and after months of observation, there is no doubt that in that respect the plaintiff in error has had due process of law.

The attack is not upon the procedure but upon the substantive law. It seems to be contended that in no circumstances could such an order be justified. It certainly is contended that the order cannot be justified upon the existing grounds. The judgment finds the facts that have been recited and that Carrie Buck "is the probable potential parent of socially inadequate offspring, likewise afflicted, that she may be sexually sterilized without detriment to her general health and that her welfare and that of society will be promoted by her sterilization," and thereupon makes the order. In view of the general declarations of the legislature and the specific findings of the Court, obviously we cannot say as matter of law that the grounds do not exist, and if they exist they justify the result. We have seen more than once that the public welfare may call upon the best citizens for their lives. It would be strange if it could not call upon those who already sap the strength of the State for these lesser sacrifices, often not felt to be such by those concerned, in order to prevent our being swamped with incompetence. It is better for all the world, if instead of waiting to execute degenerate offspring for crime, or to let them starve for their imbecility, society can prevent those who are manifestly unfit from continuing their kind. The principle that sustains compulsory vaccination is broad enough to cover cutting the Fallopian tubes. Three generations of imbeciles are enough.

But, it is said, however it might be if this reasoning were applied generally, it fails when it is confined to the small number who are in the institutions named and is not applied to the multitudes outside. It is the usual last resort of constitutional arguments to point out shortcomings of this sort. But the answer is that the law does all that is needed when it does all that it can, indicates a policy, applies it to all within the lines, and seeks to bring within the lines all similarly situated so far and so fast as its means allow. Of course so far as the operations enable those who otherwise must be kept confined to be returned to the world, and thus open the asylum to others, the equality aimed at will be more nearly reached.

Judgment affirmed.

Today, courts and legislatures have a more enlightened view about sterilization of persons with developmental disabilities, and they would not follow the holding or the analysis of *Buck v. Bell.* In fact, most Americans would strongly object to the suggestion made by Justice Holmes that we should "prevent those who are manifestly unfit from continuing their kind."[7] Modern courts would promote the best interests of the individual by means of detailed procedural requirements and would not sterilize individuals or groups for the supposed "good of society."

Contraception and Abortion

As recently as the 1960s, using any drug or device for the purpose of preventing conception was a crime in some states. In the state of Connecticut, for example, a physician could be fined or imprisoned for counseling or assisting anyone in using a contraceptive device.

For ten days in 1961, the Planned Parenthood League of Connecticut operated a center in New Haven. Its executive director and medical director were arrested for providing advice on contraception to married persons. After they were found guilty, however, the U.S. Supreme Court reversed their convictions on the grounds that the Connecticut statute violated the U.S. Constitution.[8] Although the justices disagreed about the basis for the constitutional right, Justice William Douglas relied on the right of privacy as applied to the intimate relationship of married couples. As Justice Douglas explained, the Connecticut law "operates directly on an intimate relation of husband and wife and their physician's role in one aspect of that relation."[9]

In 1972, the Supreme Court took the next step by extending that right to unmarried people as a matter of equal protection of the laws.[10] As the Supreme Court explained in that case, unmarried people have the same right of access to contraceptives as married people.[11] The Supreme Court reasoned that all people have the right of privacy "to be free from unwarranted governmental intrusion into matters so fundamentally affecting a person as the decision whether to bear or beget a child."[12] Thus, by 1972, the stage had been set for the most contentious issue of reproductive rights for both married and unmarried persons—the issue of abortion.

One year later, in 1973, the U.S. Supreme Court decided the landmark case of *Roe v. Wade*.[13] In that case, the court considered the constitutionality of a Texas statute that made it a crime to obtain an abortion except when necessary to save the life of the mother. Jane Roe was the fictitious name of a woman who wanted to obtain an abortion in Texas. However, her situation did not fit within the sole exception for an abortion—that which is necessary to save the life of the mother. Therefore, she sued a state official in federal court and asked the federal court to prevent the state from enforcing its law. Ultimately, the U.S. Supreme Court held that the Texas abortion statute violated Ms. Roe's constitutional right of personal privacy and established a framework for analyzing individual rights and state authority in this area of the law.

In addition to focusing on the issue of individual rights, the Supreme Court in *Roe v. Wade* emphasized the physician's right to practice medicine without interference by the state. Until a certain point in the pregnancy, "the attending physician, in consultation with his patient, is free to determine, without regulation by the State, that, in his medical judgment, the patient's pregnancy should be terminated."[14] Moreover,

> [t]he decision vindicates the right of the physician to administer medical treatment according to his professional judgment up to the points where important state interests provide compelling justifications for intervention. Up to those points, the abortion decision in all its aspects is inherently, and primarily, a medical

decision, and basic responsibility for it must rest with the physician. If an individual practitioner abuses the privilege of exercising proper medical judgment, the usual remedies, judicial and intra-professional are available.[15]

However, the court also recognized that the state has legitimate interests in protecting maternal health and potential life. According to the court, those state interests become compelling at different points in the pregnancy. The court based its analysis of individual rights and state interests on the concept of trimesters of pregnancy. "For the stage prior to approximately the end of the first trimester, the abortion decision and its effectuation must be left to the medical judgment of the pregnant woman's attending physician."[16] After that point, the state may regulate abortion in ways that protect the health of the mother. Furthermore, after the point of viability, the state may protect potential life by prohibiting abortion except when necessary to preserve the life or health of the mother.

For many years, people speculated that the Supreme Court might overrule its 1973 decision in *Roe v. Wade*. However, in 1992, the Supreme Court issued its decision in *Planned Parenthood of Southeastern Pennsylvania v. Casey*.[17] In that case, the court reaffirmed the right of a woman to terminate her pregnancy before the point of viability, which it described as "the most central principle of *Roe v. Wade*."[18] However, as explained in the following excerpt from *Casey*, the Supreme Court rejected the trimester framework of *Roe*. Rather, in *Casey* the court emphasized viability as the point at which the state's interest in protecting potential life may override the individual rights of the pregnant woman.

Planned Parenthood of Southeastern Pennsylvania v. Casey, 505 U.S. 833 (1992) (Citations Omitted)

Liberty finds no refuge in a jurisprudence of doubt. Yet 19 years after our holding that the Constitution protects a woman's right to terminate her pregnancy in its early stages, that definition of liberty is still questioned. Joining the respondents as amicus curiae, the United States, as it has done in five other cases in the last decade, again asks us to overrule *Roe*.

At issue in these cases are five provisions of the Pennsylvania Abortion Control Act of 1982, as amended in 1988 and 1989 . . . The Act requires that a woman seeking an abortion give her informed consent prior to the abortion procedure, and specifies that she be provided with certain information at least 24 hours before the abortion is performed . . . Another provision of the Act requires that, unless certain exceptions apply, a married woman seeking an abortion must sign a statement indicating that she has notified her husband of her intended abortion. The Act exempts compliance with these three requirements in the event of a "medical emergency," which is defined in § 3203 of the Act . . .

Before any of these provisions took effect, the petitioners, who are five abortion clinics and one physician representing himself as well as a class of physicians who provide abortion services, brought this suit seeking declaratory and injunctive relief. Each provision was challenged as unconstitutional on its face . . .

It must be stated at the outset and with clarity that *Roe*'s essential holding, the holding we reaffirm, has three parts. First is recognition of the right of the woman to choose to have an abortion before viability and to obtain it without undue interference from the State. Before viability, the State's interests are not strong enough to support a prohibition of abortion or the imposition of a substantial obstacle to the woman's effective right to elect the procedure. Second is a confirmation of the State's power to restrict abortions after fetal viability, if the law contains exceptions for pregnancies which endanger the woman's life or health. And third is the principle that the State has legitimate interests from the outset of the pregnancy in protecting the health of the woman and the life of the fetus that may become a child. These principles do not contradict one another; and we adhere to each.

Constitutional protection of the woman's decision to terminate her pregnancy derives from the Due Process Clause of the Fourteenth Amendment. It declares that no State shall "deprive any person of life, liberty, or property, without due process of law." The controlling word in the cases before us is "liberty." . . .

The inescapable fact is that adjudication of substantive due process claims may call upon the Court in interpreting the Constitution to exercise that same capacity which by tradition courts always have exercised: reasoned judgment. Its boundaries are not susceptible of expression as a simple rule. That does not mean we are free to invalidate state policy choices with which we disagree; yet neither does it permit us to shrink from the duties of our office . . .

Men and women of good conscience can disagree, and we suppose some always shall disagree, about the profound moral and spiritual implications of terminating a pregnancy, even in its earliest stage. Some of us as individuals find abortion offensive to our most basic principles of morality, but that cannot control our decision. Our obligation is to define the liberty of all, not to mandate our own moral code. The underlying constitutional issue is whether the State can resolve these philosophic questions in such a definitive way that a woman lacks all choice in the matter, except perhaps in those rare circumstances in which the pregnancy is itself a danger to her own life or health, or is the result of rape or incest . . .

The sum of the precedent enquiry to this point shows *Roe*'s underpinnings unweakened in any way affecting its central holding. While it has engendered disapproval, it has not been unworkable. An entire generation has come of age free to assume *Roe*'s concept of liberty in defining the capacity of women to act in society, and to make reproductive decisions; no erosion of principle going to liberty or personal autonomy has left *Roe*'s central holding a doctrinal remnant; *Roe* portends no developments at odds with other precedent for the analysis of personal liberty; and no changes of fact have rendered viability more or less appropriate as the point at which the balance of interests tips . . .

From what we have said so far it follows that it is a constitutional liberty of the woman to have some freedom to terminate her pregnancy. We conclude that the basic decision in *Roe* was based on a constitutional analysis which we cannot now repudiate. The woman's liberty is not so unlimited, however, that from the outset the State cannot show its concern for the life of the unborn, and at a later point in fetal development the State's interest in life has sufficient force so that the right of the woman to terminate the pregnancy can be restricted . . .

We conclude the line should be drawn at viability, so that before that time the woman has a right to choose to terminate her pregnancy . . .

We must justify the lines we draw. And there is no line other than viability which is more workable. To be sure, as we have said, there may be some medical developments that affect the precise point of viability, but this is an imprecision within tolerable limits given that the medical community and all those who must apply its discoveries will continue to explore the matter. The viability line also has, as a practical matter, an element of fairness. In some broad sense it might be said that a woman who fails to act before viability has consented to the State's intervention on behalf of the developing child.

The woman's right to terminate her pregnancy before viability is the most central principle of *Roe v. Wade*. It is a rule of law and a component of liberty we cannot renounce.

On the other side of the equation is the interest of the State in the protection of potential life. The *Roe* Court recognized the State's "important and legitimate interest in protecting the potentiality of human life." The weight to be given this state interest, not the strength of the woman's interest, was the difficult question faced in *Roe*. We do not need to say whether each of us, had we been Members of the Court when the valuation of the state interest came before it as an original matter, would have concluded, as the *Roe* Court did, that its weight is insufficient to justify a ban on abortions prior to viability even when it is subject to certain exceptions. The matter is not before us in the first instance, and coming as it does after nearly 20 years of litigation in *Roe*'s wake we are satisfied that the immediate question is not the soundness of *Roe*'s resolution of the issue, but the precedential force that must be accorded to its holding. And we have concluded that the essential holding of *Roe* should be reaffirmed . . .

Roe established a trimester framework to govern abortion regulations. Under this elaborate but rigid construct, almost no regulation at all is permitted during the first trimester of pregnancy; regulations designed to protect the woman's health, but not to further the State's interest in potential life, are permitted during the second trimester; and during the third trimester, when the fetus is viable, prohibitions are permitted provided the life or health of the mother is not at stake. Most of our cases since *Roe* have involved the application of rules derived from the trimester framework . . .

We reject the trimester framework, which we do not consider to be part of the essential holding of *Roe*. Measures aimed at ensuring that a woman's choice contemplates the consequences for the fetus do not necessarily interfere with the right recognized in *Roe*, although those measures have been found to be inconsistent with the rigid trimester framework announced in that case. A logical reading of the central holding in *Roe* itself, and a necessary reconciliation of the liberty of the woman and the interest of the State in promoting prenatal life, require, in our view, that we abandon the trimester framework as a rigid prohibition on all previability regulation aimed at the protection of fetal life. The trimester framework suffers from these basic flaws: in its formulation it misconceives the nature of the pregnant woman's interest; and in practice it undervalues the State's interest in potential life, as recognized in *Roe* . . .

The very notion that the State has a substantial interest in potential life leads to the conclusion that not all regulations must be deemed unwarranted. Not all burdens on the right to decide whether to terminate a pregnancy will be undue. In our view, the undue burden standard is the appropriate means of reconciling the State's interest with the woman's constitutionally protected liberty . . .

A finding of an undue burden is a shorthand for the conclusion that a state regulation has the purpose or effect of placing a substantial obstacle in the path of a woman seeking an abortion of a nonviable fetus. A statute with this purpose is invalid because the means chosen by the State to further the interest in potential life must be calculated to inform the woman's free choice, not hinder it. And a statute which, while furthering the interest in potential life or some other valid state interest, has the effect of placing a substantial obstacle in the path of a woman's choice cannot be considered a permissible means of serving its legitimate ends . . .

Some guiding principles should emerge. What is at stake is the woman's right to make the ultimate decision, not a right to be insulated from all others in doing so. Regulations which do no more than create a structural mechanism by which the State, or the parent or guardian of a minor, may express profound respect for the life of the unborn are permitted, if they are not a substantial obstacle to the woman's exercise of the right to choose. Unless it has that effect on her right of choice, a state measure designed to persuade her to choose childbirth over abortion will be upheld if reasonably related to that goal. Regulations designed to foster the health of a woman seeking an abortion are valid if they do not constitute an undue burden.

Even when jurists reason from shared premises, some disagreement is inevitable. That is to be expected in the application of any legal standard which must accommodate life's complexity. We do not expect it to be otherwise with respect to the undue burden standard. We give this summary:

(a) To protect the central right recognized by *Roe v. Wade* while at the same time accommodating the State's profound interest in potential life, we will employ the undue burden analysis as explained in this opinion. An undue burden exists, and therefore a provision of law is invalid, if its purpose or effect is to place a substantial obstacle in the path of a woman seeking an abortion before the fetus attains viability.

(b) We reject the rigid trimester framework of *Roe v. Wade*. To promote the State's profound interest in potential life, throughout pregnancy the State may take measures to ensure that the woman's choice is informed, and measures designed to advance this interest will not be invalidated as long as their purpose is to persuade the woman to choose childbirth over abortion. These measures must not be an undue burden on the right.

(c) As with any medical procedure, the State may enact regulations to further the health or safety of a woman seeking an abortion. Unnecessary health regulations that have the purpose or effect of presenting a substantial obstacle to a woman seeking an abortion impose an undue burden on the right.

(d) Our adoption of the undue burden analysis does not disturb the central holding of *Roe v. Wade*, and we reaffirm that holding. Regardless of whether exceptions are made for particular circumstances, a State may not prohibit any woman from making the ultimate decision to terminate her pregnancy before viability.

(e) We also reaffirm *Roe*'s holding that "subsequent to viability, the State in promoting its interest in the potentiality of human life may, if it chooses, regulate, and even proscribe, abortion except where it is necessary, in appropriate medical judgment, for the preservation of the life or health of the mother."

These principles control our assessment of the Pennsylvania statute, and we now turn to the issue of the validity of its challenged provisions . . .

Our Constitution is a covenant running from the first generation of Americans to us and then to future generations. It is a coherent succession. Each generation must learn anew that the Constitution's written terms embody ideas and aspirations that must survive more ages than one. We accept our responsibility not to retreat from interpreting the full meaning of the covenant in light of all of our precedents. We invoke it once again to define the freedom guaranteed by the Constitution's own promise, the promise of liberty . . .

It is so ordered.

In *Casey*, the Supreme Court upheld Pennsylvania's requirement for a 24-hour waiting period to obtain an abortion except in cases of medical emergency. According to the Court, the state's requirement of a 24-hour waiting period might cause a woman to choose childbirth over abortion. However, the state's requirement did not impose a substantial obstacle or an undue burden on the legal right to obtain an abortion. Many of the abortion cases in federal court have involved the issue of whether a particular state law constitutes a substantial obstacle or an undue burden.

Under the court's analysis in *Casey*, the state has legitimate interests in protecting maternal health and potential life. At any time during the pregnancy, the state may regulate abortion for the purpose of protecting maternal health. In addition, the state may promote its interest in potential life by trying to discourage abortion even before the point of viability. However, before viability, the state may not prohibit abortion and may not place "a substantial obstacle in the path of a woman seeking an abortion of a nonviable fetus."[19]

After the point of viability, the state may prohibit abortion, except when it is necessary to preserve the life or health of the mother. Thus, the state could prohibit abortion after the point of viability even if it is clear that the baby will be born with serious deformities, or even if the pregnancy was the result of rape or incest. However, under *Casey*, a state law that prohibits abortion after viability must contain exceptions that would permit abortion to preserve the *health* of the mother and not merely to save the *life* of the mother.

The requirement for an exception to preserve the health of the mother has been central to the dispute over so-called "partial-birth abortions." A partial-birth abortion is a late-term procedure "in which the person performing the abortion partially vaginally delivers a living fetus before killing the fetus and completing the delivery."[20] Technically, these procedures are referred to as intact dilation and evacuation or dilation and extraction. During the Clinton administration, Congress voted twice to ban the procedure in some situations, but President Clinton vetoed both of the proposed laws.[21] As passed by Congress, those bills had contained an exception to permit procedures that are necessary to save the life of the mother. However, President Clinton took the position that there should be another exception to permit procedures that are necessary to prevent serious harm to the health of the mother.[22]

In 2003, Congress again passed a bill to restrict partial birth abortions. However, that time the bill was signed into law by President George W. Bush as the Partial-Birth Abortion Ban Act of 2003.[23] In a legal challenge to that federal statute, the United States Court of Appeals for the Eighth Circuit held that the act was unconstitutional, because it does not contain an exception for the health of the mother.[24] However, in 2007, the U.S. Supreme Court reversed the decision of the Eighth Circuit.[25]

In its 2007 decision, the Supreme Court upheld the federal statute prohibiting certain partial-birth abortions, even though the statute did not contain an exception for abortions necessary to preserve the health of the mother. The Supreme Court did not reconsider its holdings in *Roe* and *Casey*, but neither did the majority of justices reaffirm the holdings of *Roe* and *Casey*. Instead, the majority merely assumed that the principles of *Roe* and *Casey* were controlling.

At the time of this writing, the full implications of this decision remain to be seen.

Emergency Contraception

In recent years, new issues of law and ethics have arisen in regard to emergency contraception (EC), which is a pharmaceutical method of preventing pregnancy after unprotected sex or after failure of another method of contraception. EC is not the same as medical abortion, which is a pharmaceutical method of terminating a pregnancy. In September 2000, the U.S. Food and Drug Administration (FDA) approved the use of mifepristone, commonly known as RU-486, for medical abortion up to 49 days of pregnancy.[26] In contrast to RU-486, which clearly is a method of abortion, EC operates before implantation and does not terminate a pregnancy.[27] With regard to EC, there are at least three important legal and ethical issues.[28] First, should EC be available "over the counter" (OTC) without a prescription to adults and to minors? Second, may pharmacists refuse to fill a prescription for EC or sell EC on the ground of their personal beliefs? Finally, should hospital emergency departments, including those operated by religious organizations, be required to provide EC or advice about the availability of EC to survivors of sexual assault?

The proposal to make EC available without a prescription was a very contentious issue. In May 2004, the FDA refused to switch the status of an EC drug known as Plan B to OTC status, despite the recommendations of FDA's staff and advisory committee.[29] Subsequently, in December 2006, the FDA announced its approval of Plan B on an OTC basis for women over the age of 18 years, but still requires the use of a prescription for women under age 18.[30] Even for women over the age of 18 years, Plan B will only be available in a pharmacy or store that is staffed by a pharmacist, and it will be kept behind the counter. As the FDA explained, "[t]his means Plan B will not be sold at gas stations or convenience stores, where other OTC products are routinely available."[31]

As a practical matter, access to Plan B may depend on the willingness of a pharmacist to dispense the drug to an adult or fill the prescription for a minor. Some pharmacists have refused to fill prescriptions for Plan B on the grounds of their personal or religious beliefs. Many states have enacted so-called "conscience clauses" that protect the right of healthcare professionals to refuse to participate in procedures to which they object, such as abortion. Depending on their precise wording, some of the existing and proposed state laws may be broad enough to allow pharmacists to refuse to fill prescriptions for Plan B or sell Plan B without a prescription.[32]

Should hospitals that provide treatment to survivors of sexual assault be required by law to provide access to EC, even if the hospital is owned by a religious organization that is opposed to EC? In 2005, Congress considered—but did not enact—a bill that would have prohibited giving any federal funds to a hospital that refuses to provide EC to a victim of sexual assault.[33] However, several states have enacted statutes on this issue. For example, a New Mexico statute requires that "[a] hospital that provides emergency care for sexual assault survivors shall . . . provide emergency contraception at the hospital to each sexual assault survivor who requests it."[34]

Maternal–Fetal Conflict

One of the recurring themes in healthcare law and ethics is determining when the interests of society will outweigh the interests of the individual. The state may force people to be vaccinated against their will and, in some circumstances, force people to accept unwanted blood transfusions. In the *Georgetown College* case that was discussed in Chapter 12, the court reasoned that the individual had a duty to society to care for her seven-month-old child and that the state had an interest in protecting the life of the mother. Therefore, the mother had a duty to society to accept unwanted medical treatment.

That reasoning raises some serious questions. What is the extent of a parent's duty to society to accept unwanted medical treatment? Moreover, if a parent has a duty to society to care for a child, does a woman who is pregnant with a viable fetus have a similar duty to society to protect the potential life of that viable fetus?

In *Planned Parenthood of Southeastern Pennsylvania v. Casey*, the Supreme Court held that the state has a legitimate interest in protecting the potential life of a viable fetus. Therefore, with few exceptions, the state may prohibit abortion after the point of viability. Should the state also have the power to prohibit a pregnant woman from taking other actions that might injure the viable fetus, such as abusing drugs and alcohol, smoking, and skydiving? Should the state have the power to require a pregnant woman to accept unwanted treatment to protect the potential life of the viable fetus? Many people believe such assertions of governmental power would violate the individual rights of the pregnant woman and constitute unwarranted interference in private decisions.

Another aspect of this issue is whether a pregnant woman's fetally toxic behavior provides a basis for civil commitment, termination of parental rights, or criminal prosecution for child abuse or delivering drugs to a minor.[35] For example, a state statute in South Dakota provides that a pregnant woman who is intoxicated and abusing drugs or alcohol "may be committed to an approved treatment facility for emergency treatment."[36]

Moreover, the Supreme Court of South Carolina held that a pregnant woman's drug abuse constituted criminal child neglect, because the defendant's viable fetus was a "person" within a meaning of the applicable statute.[37] However, many state courts have held that prenatal conduct does not provide a basis for criminal prosecution under the terms of the laws in those states.[38]

In another case that arose in South Carolina, the U.S. Supreme Court considered a state hospital's policy of testing some pregnant women for use of cocaine and providing police with the names of those women who tested positive and failed to cooperate in obtaining treatment.[39] The Supreme Court held that the hospital's system of diagnostic testing and reporting constituted an unreasonable search in violation of the Fourth Amendment, because the testing was performed by government employees without a warrant and without probable cause. In addition, the court assumed that the searches were performed without the consent of the patients. Finally, the court held that these searches did not fit within a narrow exception to the warrant requirement for "special needs" searches that are not conducted primarily for the purpose of law enforcement. "In this case, however, the central and indispensable feature of the policy from its inception was the use of law enforcement to coerce the patients into substance abuse treatment."[40]

In that case, the Supreme Court resolved a specific issue with regard to the use of warrantless searches without consent by employees of state government hospitals. However, that was a narrow ruling that left many questions unanswered. The court did not address the issue of searches performed with the consent of the patient or searches by employees of non-governmental hospitals. Moreover, the court acknowledged that hospital employees and healthcare professionals may have duties to report certain information to authorities about their patients, such as gunshot wounds and child abuse. Finally, the court did not resolve the underlying issues of maternal–fetal conflict, such as the possibility of criminal sanctions for drug abuse or other fetally toxic behavior.

In the meantime, other courts have addressed a different aspect of maternal–fetal conflict by considering whether a pregnant woman should be required to deliver by caesarean section when the attending physician believes the surgery is necessary to protect the life or health of the fetus. For example, the case of *In re A.C.*[41] dealt with whether a forced caesarean should have been performed on a terminally ill cancer patient who was pregnant with a viable fetus. In that case, the mother's wishes were somewhat unclear, but she apparently objected to the procedure. According to the appellate court, the issue should not be resolved by trying to balance the interests of the pregnant woman against the interests of the fetus and the state. Rather, the decision on whether to undergo the surgery should be left up to the pregnant woman, if she is competent. If she is not competent, the court should make a substituted judgment on the basis of what the court believes the patient would have wanted.

In that case, the appellate court relied in part on the legal principle that we do not force one person to undergo an operation for the benefit of another. The court in *A.C.* cited *McFall v. Shimp*,[42] which held that a person could not be forced to donate bone marrow to his relative, even if his relative would probably die without it. As the court in *McFall v. Shimp* explained,

> [t]he common law has consistently held to a rule which provides that one human being is under no legal compulsion to give aid or to take action to save another human being or to rescue . . . Morally, this decision rests with defendant, and, in the view of the court, the refusal of defendant is morally indefensible. For our law to *compel* defendant to submit to an intrusion of his body would change every concept and principle upon which our society is founded. To do so would defeat the sanctity of the individual, and would impose a rule which would know no limits, and one could not imagine where the line would be drawn.
>
> . . . For a society which respects the rights of *one* individual, to sink its teeth into the jugular vein or neck of one of its members and suck from it sustenance for *another* member, is revolting to our hard-wrought concepts of jurisprudence.[43]

In *A.C.*, the court relied in part on that principle and concluded that courts should not force a pregnant woman to undergo surgery for the benefit of her fetus, even if the fetus is viable and may no longer be aborted.

In addition, courts should refrain from ordering forced caesareans for other reasons. Physicians may be incorrect in concluding and testifying that a caesarean is necessary to preserve the life or health of the fetus.[44] Moreover, judicial hearings on this issue may be fundamentally unfair, because women in labor are likely to have difficulty obtaining immediate legal representation and an independent medical opinion. Finally, the possibility of being forced to have a caesarean may discourage some women from seeking medical care, especially if they are aware that they have a high risk of complications. For all of these reasons, most courts would not order a caesarean over the objections of the pregnant woman.

Notes

1. *Skinner v. Oklahoma*, 316 U.S. 535, 541 (1942) (Douglas, J.).
2. *Eisenstadt v. Baird*, 405 U.S. 438, 453 (1972) (citations omitted).
3. *Cruzan v. Director, Missouri Department of Health*, 497 U.S. 261, 280–84 (1990).

4. *Washington v. Glucksberg*, 521 U.S. 702, 735 (1997); *Vacco v. Quill*, 521 U.S. 793, 807–808 (1997).

5. 274 U.S. 200 (1927) (Holmes, J.).

6. But see P.A. Lombardo, "Three Generations, No Imbeciles: New Light on *Buck v. Bell*," *New York University Law Review*, 60 (1985): 30–62.

7. *Buck v. Bell*, 274 U.S. at 207.

8. See *Griswold v. Connecticut*, 381 U.S. 479, 485–86 (1965).

9. *Id*. at 482.

10. See *Eisenstadt*, 405 U.S. at 447.

11. See *id*. at 453 (citations omitted).

12. *Id*.

13. 410 U.S. 113 (1973).

14. *Id*. at 163.

15. *Id*. at 165–66.

16. *Id*. at 164.

17. 505 U.S. 833 (1992).

18. *Id*. at 871.

19. *Id*. at 877.

20. See Partial Birth Abortion Ban Act of 1995, H.R. 1833, 104th Cong. § 2 (1995) (vetoed on April 10, 1996).

21. See H.R. 1122, 105th Cong. (1997) (vetoed on Oct. 10, 1997); H.R. 1833, 104th Cong. (1995) (vetoed on April 10, 1996).

22. Partial-Birth Abortion Ban Act—Veto Message from the President of the United States (H. Doc. No. 104–198) (House of Representatives, April 15, 1996).

23. Pub. L. No. 108-105, 117 Stat. 1201 (codified at 18 U.S.C. § 1531).

24. *Carhart v. Gonzales*, 413 F.3d 791, 803 (8th Cir. 2005), *rev'd*., 127 S. Ct. 1610 (2007).

25. *Gonzales v. Carhart*, 127 S. Ct. 1610 (2007).

26. See generally C.E. Borgmann and B.S. Jones, "Legal Issues in the Provision of Medical Abortion," *American Journal of Obstetrics and Gynecology*, 183(2 suppl.) (2000): S84–S94.

27. D.A. Grimes, "Switching Emergency Contraception to Over the Counter Status," *New England Journal of Medicine*, 347(11) (2002): 846–849.

28. See *id*.

29. U.S. Government Accountability Office, "Decision Process to Deny Initial Application for Over-the-Counter Marketing of the Emergency Contraceptive Drug Plan B Was Unusual," GAO-06-109 (November 2005). [Online document; retrieved 2/1/07.] www.gao.gov/new.items/d06109.pdf.

30. U.S. Food and Drug Administration, Center for Drug Evaluation and Research, "Plan B: Questions and Answers," August 24, 2006, updated December 14, 2006. [Online information; retrieved 2/1/07.] www.fda.gov/cder/drug/infopage/planB/planBQandA 20060824.htm.

31. *Id.*

32. See M.J. Seamon, "Plan B for the FDA: A Need for a Third Class of Drug Regulation in the United States Involving a 'Pharmacist-Only' Class of Drugs," *William and Mary Journal of Women & the Law*, 12 (2006): 521–562, at 557–58.

33. Compassionate Assistance for Rape Emergencies Act, S.3945, 109th Cong. (2d Sess. 2006).

34. N. M. Stat. Ann. § 24-10D-3 (2006).

35. See generally "Development and Trends in the Law: Synopsis of State Case and Statutory Law," *Yale Journal of Health Policy, Law & Ethics*, 1 (2001): 237–296.

36. S.D. Codified Laws § 34-20A-63 (2006). See also *id.* at § 34-20A-70(3) (commitment of pregnant alcoholics or drug abusers who habitually lack self-control).

37. *Whitner v. South Carolina*, 492 S.E.2d 777 (S.C. 1997), *cert. denied*, 523 U.S. 1145 (1998).

38. See *id.* at 782.

39. *Ferguson v. City of Charleston*, 532 U.S. 67 (2001).

40. *Id.* at 80.

41. 573 A.2d 1235 (D.C. 1990).

42. 10 Pa.D. and C.3d 90 (Pa. Commw. Ct. 1978).

43. *Id.* at 91–92 (1978).

44. See, e.g., D.B. Kennedy, "A Public Guardian Represents Fetus: Courts Refuse Request for a C-Section and Boy Is Born Apparently Healthy," *ABA Journal*, 80 (March 1994): at 27.

LEGAL AND ETHICAL ISSUES IN HEALTH INSURANCE AND MANAGED CARE

14

SELECTIVE CONTRACTING WITH PROVIDERS

Throughout this book, we address the effect of cost containment and managed care on various aspects of the law and ethics of health. For example, Chapter 10 deals with the ways in which managed care affects the law of medical malpractice, and Chapter 11 discusses the applicability of the Emergency Medical Treatment and Active Labor Act to patients covered by managed care plans. In Part IV, the legal principles discussed in previous chapters are applied to the system of health insurance and managed care.

In an effort to reduce healthcare costs, many third-party payers have adopted various techniques that are collectively referred to as managed care. These techniques are not limited to health maintenance organizations (HMOs), but rather they are used by many insurance companies, health plans, and even the government payment programs described in Chapter 8. No uniform model of managed care exists, but a few common techniques are shared by health insurance companies, HMOs, and other managed care organizations (MCOs).

One technique of managed care is to use financial incentives that encourage physicians to reduce the cost of treatment. As discussed in Chapter 15, these incentives have the effect of aligning the financial interest of the physician with that of the payer rather than the patient. As a matter of law, ethics, and public policy, we may want to prohibit financial incentives to provide less care or at least require disclosure of those incentives to the patient.

In addition, most third-party payers control the cost of care by means of utilization review. When payers deny authorization for particular treatments, they insist they are not denying care or telling physicians how to practice medicine. According to the payers, they are merely interpreting the terms of coverage under the contract, and the physicians should provide, without coverage, whatever treatment they consider to be appropriate. However, as discussed in Chapter 16, that supposed distinction between coverage decisions and treatment decisions is specious, and a denial of payment is likely to result in a denial of treatment. As a practical matter, the system of managed care reduces healthcare costs by imposing limits on treatment and thereby raises the complex legal and ethical issues of rationing.

Another common technique of cost containment and managed care is referred to as selective contracting. Many third-party payers enter into contracts with "preferred" providers that are willing to cut their prices to obtain a greater volume of patients. The process of bidding for preferred provider contracts has increased the level of competition in the healthcare industry, but it raises significant legal and practical issues for providers that are excluded from a payer's network.

Many providers and patients objected to the use of these cost-containment techniques by third-party payers. In fact, there was a significant "backlash" against managed care.[1] Many states enacted laws to regulate specific aspects of managed care,[2] and market pressures forced MCOs to be somewhat more flexible in their use of utilization review and their limitations on provider networks. Nevertheless, the recent flexibility on the part of MCOs is merely a matter of degree, and third-party payers continue to use the techniques of managed care in an effort to contain the cost of care.

Limitations on Patients' Free Choice of Provider

Before the development of managed care, insured patients could choose to receive their treatment at almost any doctor's office or hospital. That system was referred to as "free choice of provider." People became so used to being able to choose their own doctor or hospital that many considered the free choice of provider to be their legal or constitutional right. As a legal matter, however, freedom of choice in private insurance plans was not a constitutional or statutory requirement but merely a term of a contract that was subject to negotiation and change.

Under the traditional system, patients could choose to go to the most expensive providers in the area, a practice that tended to increase overall healthcare costs. Although insurance companies were required to pay the bills for those expensive providers, they could pass on the costs to policyholders by raising premiums at the next opportunity. In an attempt to control their costs, many insurance companies tried to use charge screens for physicians, a mechanism through which the insurance company refused to pay more than the standard fees in each geographic area. In the long run, however, those mechanisms proved to be largely ineffective in keeping down healthcare costs. Therefore, people and organizations that were responsible for paying the bills looked for other means to control healthcare expenditures, including selective contracting with particular providers.

In selective contracting, payers enter into contracts with providers that are willing to grant discounts and agree to the payer's utilization review procedures. By reducing their prices and becoming the preferred providers for specific third-party payers, those physicians and healthcare facilities can increase their market share, or at least avoid a significant loss of market share. In economic terms, sellers of goods or services may be able to maximize their profits by selling a larger volume at a lower unit price, rather than selling fewer goods or services at a higher price. The financial arrangements between the MCO and the physician may take the form of a monthly capitation or a discounted fee-for-service payment.

Before they would be willing to reduce their prices, however, providers need to have some assurance that the payers can actually deliver additional patients who are covered by their plans. To direct those additional patients to preferred providers, third-party payers use various mechanisms to influence their enrollees' choice of provider.

For example, in some HMOs, patients were essentially required to go to a provider that participated in the plan, because the HMO would make no payment whatsoever for services that were rendered by nonplan providers. That restrictive form of managed care has met with a great deal of resistance in the competitive marketplace. Therefore, some HMOs now allow their enrollees to be treated by providers outside of the plan if the enrollees pay an additional fee for a "point-of-service" option.

Even without that type of strict limitation, payers can influence their enrollees' choice of provider by manipulating the patients' out-of-pocket costs for copayments and deductibles. For example, a plan could provide that the patient would have to pay a 20 percent copayment for services rendered by a provider who is not participating in the network, but little or no copayment would be required for the services of a participating or preferred provider. In some cases, the patient may be willing to pay the additional money to see a particular physician who is not a part of the network, especially if the patient had a preexisting relationship with that physician. That could become very costly, however, in the event of a serious illness or injury. Therefore, in the long run, these types of financial incentives will be effective in causing most patients to switch to participating providers to minimize their own out-of-pocket costs.

Limitations on Providers' Participation in Health Plans

As discussed, MCOs and other payers have the power to direct a substantial number of patients to those providers that are willing to give them a discount, and providers have a strong interest in being selected as a participating or preferred provider. By definition, all of the providers in the area cannot be preferred providers for a single payer. Therefore, payers have bargaining power to exact substantial discounts from providers as a condition of being selected as preferred providers for those payers.

This situation has led to the development of a bargaining process in which payers can force providers to bid against each other for the patients who are covered by each particular payer. If a provider is unwilling to meet or exceed the discount offered by another provider, the first provider will probably not obtain the patients who are covered by that payer. Moreover, if a large number of a provider's existing patients are covered through that payer, the provider may even lose a substantial portion of its existing patient base if it is not selected as one of the payer's preferred providers.

As a general rule, MCOs and other payers do not have a legal obligation to accept every physician who applies for membership in their provider network. Moreover, payers have a strong incentive to carefully review the applications of physicians for membership in the network.

As discussed in Chapter 10 on medical malpractice, an MCO may be held liable in tort on the same legal theories as a hospital. For example, the MCO might be held vicariously liable for the negligence of a participating physician on a theory of actual agency or ostensible agency. In addition, the MCO might be held liable under the doctrine of corporate negligence for its own failure to exercise reasonable care in screening and monitoring physicians in its network.

In addition to screening new applicants for network membership, an MCO might decide to terminate its existing relationship with a current member of its network. In some cases, the MCO may want to terminate a physician because of questions about that physician's professional performance. In other cases, however, the termination may be based entirely on business reasons, such as having an excess of physicians in that particular specialty. Regardless of the reason for termination, the practical effects are that the physician will no longer be able to treat the MCO's enrollees and the physician may suffer significant economic loss.

Contract-Law Issues

The relationship between a payer and a participating physician is set forth in a contract, which is referred to as a provider agreement. However, the use of contract-law principles does not necessarily mean the MCO will have the right to remove a physician from its network. Even if there is a written provider agreement that permits termination by either party without cause, a court may or may not allow the MCO to strictly enforce the terms of that contract.

A contract is a voluntary agreement between the parties. Ordinarily, the rights and obligations of the parties will be governed by the terms of the contract, including specific provisions on how the contract may be terminated. In some circumstances, however, considerations of public policy may override the written terms of the contract and may provide additional rights or obligations for the parties.

The written contract between an MCO and a physician will usually specify that the contract may be terminated by either party, with or without cause. In a termination "for cause," one party may terminate the contract as a result of the other party's failure to perform its obligations as set forth in the contract. In contrast, a provision for termination "without cause" allows either party to terminate the contract, without any reason, by merely giving sufficient notice in advance to the other party. Thus, in a termination "without cause," an MCO would have the right to terminate a physician from participation in its network without the need to demonstrate incompetence or unethical behavior on the part of the physician.

In *Harper v. Healthsource New Hampshire, Inc.*,[3] the written contract provided that either party could terminate the agreement without cause by giving six months' notice of intent to terminate. Healthsource terminated its agreement with Dr. Harper without cause, but Dr. Harper sued Healthsource in New Hampshire state court to challenge his termination by the plan. According to Dr. Harper, the provision allowing for termination of the contract without cause was void on the grounds that it violated the public policy of the state. In 1996, the Supreme Court of New Hampshire agreed with Dr. Harper, as explained in the following excerpt from the court's decision.

HARPER V. HEALTHSOURCE NEW HAMPSHIRE, INC., 674 A.2D 962 (N.H. 1996) (CITATIONS OMITTED)

We have applied public policy concerns to the healthcare arena before. In *Bricker*, we observed that "the public has a substantial interest in the operation of private hospitals and that of necessity in the public interest some measure of control by the courts is called for."

The public has a substantial interest in the relationship between health maintenance organizations and their preferred provider physicians as well. This relationship is perhaps the most important factor in linking a particular physician with a particular patient. As Harper correctly notes, the termination of his relationship with Healthsource affects more than just his own interest . . .

In RSA 420-C:1 (1991), the legislature stated the general policy behind the chapter, that is, that preferred provider agreements must be "fair and in the public interest." We conclude that the public interest and fundamental fairness demand that a health maintenance organization's decision to terminate its relationship with a particular physician provider must comport with the covenant of good faith and fair dealing and may not be made for a reason that is contrary to public policy.

A terminated physician is entitled to review of the termination decision under this standard, whether the termination was for cause, or without cause. This rule does not eliminate a health maintenance organization's contractual right to terminate its relationship with a physician without cause. If a physician's relationship, however, is terminated without cause and the physician believes that the decision to terminate was, in truth, made in bad faith or based upon some factor that would render the decision contrary to public policy, then the physician is entitled to review of the decision.

Harper is entitled to proceed upon the merits of his claim that Healthsource's decision to terminate its relationship with him was made in bad faith or violated public policy. In his petition, he asserted that his efforts to correct errors made in patient records played a role in Healthsource's decision, and he argues on appeal that public policy should condemn "an insurance company which, upon receipt of a letter from a medical provider asking for assistance in correcting . . . records of patient treatments, terminates the doctor's services."

Under the court's analysis in *Harper*, an MCO may terminate a participating physician for no reason at all, but the physician may not be terminated for an improper reason that violates the public policy of the state. This concept is similar to the public policy exception to the legal doctrine of employment at will, although the physicians in this type of MCO network are not really employees of the MCO. In the employment context, workers may be characterized as employees at will. This means that they may be terminated at any time without cause, and they may leave at any time without penalty. Although employees at will may be terminated for no reason at all, some courts have held that they may not be terminated for an improper reason that would be contrary to public policy. For example, a healthcare facility may have the right to terminate an employee at will without cause, but it may not terminate the employee in retaliation for the employee's refusal to give false testimony in a medical malpractice case.[4] By analogy, a participating physician whose contract was terminated without cause by an MCO should have an opportunity to demonstrate that the contract was terminated for an improper reason that violates the public policy of the state.

Subsequently, the Supreme Court of California cited the *Harper* decision in concluding that a contract provision for termination without cause was unenforceable.[5] An excerpt from that decision follows.

Potvin v. Metropolitan Life Insurance Company, 997 P.2d 1153 (Cal. 2000) (Citations and Footnotes Omitted)

After removal from defendant insurance company's "preferred provider" lists, plaintiff physician brought this action. Citing the common law right to fair procedure, which forbids arbitrary expulsions from private organizations under certain circumstances, plaintiff alleged he should have been given reasonable notice and an opportunity to be heard before his removal. . . .

On September 10, 1990, Metropolitan Life Insurance Company (MetLife) entered into an agreement with Dr. Louis E. Potvin, an obstetrician and gynecologist, to include him as one of 16,000 participants on two of its preferred provider lists. Potvin had practiced medicine for more than 35 years; he was a past president of the Orange County Medical Association; and he held full staff privileges at Mission Regional Hospital, where he had served as Chairman of the Obstetrics and Gynecology Department for nine years. Under the contract, Potvin was to provide medical services to MetLife's insureds in return for agreed-upon payment by MetLife. The agreement created no employment or agency relationship, and it allowed Potvin to also "contract with other preferred provider organizations, health maintenance organizations or other participating provider arrangements." It provided for termination by either party "at any time, with or without cause, by giving thirty (30) days prior written notice to the other party."

On July 22, 1992, MetLife notified Potvin in writing that effective August 31, 1992, it was terminating his preferred provider status. Potvin asked for clarification; MetLife replied that the termination, which the parties here also refer to as "delistment," was consistent with the contract, which allowed termination "without cause." When Potvin insisted on a further explanation, MetLife reiterated its right to terminate without cause. MetLife then stated that even though it did not have to give a reason, Potvin's "delistment from the provider network was related to the fact that [he] did not meet [MetLife's] current selection and retention standard for malpractice history." At the time, MetLife would not include or retain on its preferred provider lists any physician who had more than two malpractice lawsuits, or who had paid an aggregate sum of $50,000 in judgment or settlement of such actions. Potvin's patients had sued him for malpractice on four separate occasions, all predating his 1990 agreement with MetLife. In three of these actions, the plaintiffs had abandoned their claims, while the fourth case had settled for $713,000.

After MetLife failed to respond to Potvin's request for a hearing, Potvin filed this lawsuit. His complaint set forth two causes of action, one entitled "Violation of Business and Professions Code section 805 et seq. and for Violation of Fair Procedure," the other claiming breach of the preferred provider contract. Potvin alleged that MetLife's termination of his preferred provider status devastated his practice, reducing it to "a small fraction" of his former patients. He asserted that he was required to reveal his termination to other insurers and managed care entities, which then removed him from their preferred provider lists, and that he suffered rejection by "physician groups . . . dependent upon credentialling by MetLife" and by current MetLife preferred provider physicians, who ceased referring patients to him. . . .

The purpose of the common law right to fair procedure is to protect, in certain situations, against arbitrary decisions by private organizations. As this court has held, this means that, when the right to fair procedure applies, the decision-making "must be both substantively rational and procedurally fair." . . .

The private organizations in our [previous] cases (respectively, a labor union; local, regional, and national associations of orthodontists; and a hospital offering a surgical residency program) all shared an attribute of significance in our determination that they were subject to the common law right to fair procedure. Each one was a private entity affecting the public interest. . . .

Plaintiff here points out that when an insurance company with fiduciary obligations to its insureds maintains a list of preferred provider physicians to render medical services to the insureds, a significant public interest is affected. One practical effect of the health care revolution, which has made quality care more widely available and affordable through health maintenance organizations and other managed care entities, is that patients are less free to choose their own doctors for they must obtain medical services from providers approved by their health plan. The Managed Health Care Improvement Task Force stressed in its 1997 report to the California Legislature that the provision of health care "has a special moral status and therefore a particular public interest." But an even greater public interest is at stake when those medical services are provided through the unique tripartite relationship among an insurance company, its insureds, and the physicians who participate in the preferred provider network. As the New Hampshire Supreme Court noted recently in Harper v. Healthsource New Hampshire, the removal of a physician from a preferred provider list "affects more than just [the doctor's] own interest," adding that "[t]he public has a substantial interest in the relationship between health maintenance organizations and their preferred provider physicians."

Our conclusion that the relationship between insurers and their preferred provider physicians significantly affects the public interest does not necessarily mean that every insurer wishing to remove a doctor from one of its preferred provider lists must comply with the common law right to fair procedure. The obligation to do so arises only when the insurer possesses power so substantial that the removal significantly impairs the ability of an ordinary, competent physician to practice medicine or a medical specialty in a particular geographic area, thereby affecting an important, substantial economic interest. . . .

If participation in managed care arrangements is a practical necessity for physicians generally and if only a handful of health care entities have a virtual monopoly on managed care, removing individual physicians from preferred provider networks controlled by these entities could significantly impair those physicians' practice of medicine.

Here, Potvin alleged that among the adverse effects of removal from MetLife's preferred provider lists were rejection by "physician groups which were dependent upon credentialling by MetLife" and devastation of his practice, which was reduced to "a small fraction" of his former patients. Proof of these allegations might establish that, in terminating a physician's preferred provider status, MetLife wields power so substantial as to significantly impair an ordinary, competent physician's ability to practice medicine or a medical specialty in a particular geographic area, thereby affecting an important, substantial economic interest. . . .

Our holding . . . does not prevent an insurer subject to obligations of common law fair procedure from exercising its sound business judgment when establishing standards for removal of physicians from its preferred provider lists. We simply hold that, under principles recognized by the common law of this state for over a century, such removal must be "both substantively rational and procedurally fair.". . .

As we have explained, the common law right to fair procedure does not apply to an insurer's removal of a physician from its preferred provider list unless the insurer possesses power so substantial that the removal significantly impairs the ability of an ordinary, competent physician to practice medicine or a medical specialty in a particular geographic area, thereby affecting an important, substantial economic interest. Even when this common law right does apply, an insurer may remove a physician from its preferred provider list without regard to the financial effect on the physician, so long as the insurer's decision is "substantively rational and procedurally fair."

MetLife contends that even if removal of a physician from its preferred provider lists is subject to the common law right to fair procedure, here Potvin waived that right by agreeing that MetLife could terminate the provider arrangement without cause. Potvin responds that the public policy considerations supporting the common law right to fair procedure render the "without cause" clause in the MetLife preferred provider agreement unenforceable. Faced with similar arguments, the New Hampshire Supreme Court declined to enforce a "without cause" provision in a contract between a health maintenance organization and one of its preferred provider physicians, allowing the case to go to trial on the physician's claim that the summary termination of his provider status violated the contractual obligations of good faith and fair dealing. (*Harper v. Healthsource New Hampshire, supra*, 674 A.2d at pp. 964–966.) California courts, too, are loathe to enforce contract provisions offensive to public policy. We therefore agree with Potvin that the "without cause" termination clause is unenforceable to the extent it purports to limit an otherwise existing right to fair procedure under the common law.

Despite the forceful opinion of the California Supreme Court in *Potvin*, it is important to keep that decision in perspective. First, it was a hotly disputed decision, as four justices were in favor of the decision and three justices dissented. Moreover, courts in other states may decide not to follow the analysis in *Potvin* and *Harper*. For example, an intermediate appellate court in Colorado rejected a similar challenge by a physician to the termination of his contract without cause, because the Colorado legislature had adopted statutes that explicitly authorized the termination of provider agreements without cause.[6] As the Colorado court explained in that case, "[i]t is not for the courts to enunciate the public policy of the state if, as here, the General Assembly has spoken on the issue."[7]

Antitrust Law Issues

As discussed in Chapter 9, the bargaining process of selective contracting has increased the level of competition in the U.S. healthcare industry. However, some healthcare providers do not want to compete with one another, because competition may reduce their revenues and may appear to be unprofessional. Some providers have attempted to stop the bargaining process of managed care in various ways. Some of those ways of preventing competition are lawful, but others are clearly unlawful.

Federal antitrust laws prohibit collective action by providers in restraint of trade and provide payers with a basis to challenge providers that try to prevent competition. In responding to a payer's demand for a discount, providers may be tempted to agree among themselves that none of them will give any discount or do any business with that payer. However, as discussed in Chapter 9, those actions would constitute a price-fixing conspiracy or boycott and would clearly violate the federal antitrust laws.

Although antitrust laws provide a basis for payers to challenge collective action by providers, those laws do not provide a strong basis for physicians to challenge their termination or exclusion from payer networks. Physicians have not had much success in challenging the termination of provider agreements on federal antitrust grounds. For example, some physicians have argued that the payer's termination of the contract was an unreasonable restraint of trade. However, federal courts usually hold that contract termination does not give rise to an antitrust claim, because excluding an individual practitioner from a network does not necessarily reduce the level of competition in the marketplace.[8] Although an individual practitioner would be adversely affected by the termination, the purpose of the antitrust laws is to protect competition and not individual competitors.

Moreover, excluding certain providers from a network might promote competition by upholding standards of quality and preventing the network from becoming too large. If a network includes a large percentage of the healthcare providers in the area, it would be difficult for buyers to get providers to bargain against one another on price and quality, and it would be difficult to develop competing networks. Allowing a managed care network to become too large would pose a more serious threat to competition than excluding an individual practitioner from a network. Therefore, excluding providers from a network might promote competition and is usually evaluated under the rule of reason.

From a healthcare provider's point of view, the antitrust laws may seem to be extremely unfair. On the one hand, payers have the right to exclude providers from participating in their networks without running afoul of the antitrust laws. On the other hand, the antitrust laws prohibit healthcare providers from combining forces to deal with the demands of the payers. Although this may seem unfair to healthcare providers, the short answer is that the antitrust laws are designed to protect the ability of a single buyer, such as an MCO, to bargain for the lowest possible price in the marketplace, as long as the buyer is acting on its own and not in collusion with other buyers. Moreover, each healthcare provider retains the right to decide on its own not to give a discount or not to do business with an MCO or other payer. Antitrust law prohibits providers from combining forces to increase their bargaining power against payers by agreeing on prices or by agreeing not to do business with a particular payer.

Any Willing Provider Laws

There is one way in which providers may lawfully work together in an attempt to counteract the bargaining process of managed care. Under the Noerr-Pennington doctrine of antitrust law, as discussed in Chapter 9, providers have the First Amendment right to petition the government for legislative action in their favor. Individuals and organizations have the constitutional right to request legislation that will advance their own economic interests, even if that legislation would reduce the level of competition in the marketplace. Therefore, healthcare providers have the right to ask their state legislatures to pass laws that would effectively prevent the bargaining process for contracts in regard to specific services in their state.

Many providers and provider groups have obtained laws of that nature, which are referred to as "any willing provider" or AWP laws. In general, AWP laws are state statutes that require a payer to accept any provider who is willing to give the same discount the preferred provider offers for a specific type of service. For example, a Nebraska statute provides that, "[p]roviders willing and qualified to meet the terms and conditions of a preferred provider contract offered by an insurer or participant may agree to provide health services pursuant to such contract."[9]

In lobbying for the passage of AWP laws, provider organizations have argued that those laws will protect the patient's freedom of choice; therefore, AWP laws are in the best interest of the patients. However, if a state enacts an AWP law for a particular type of service, there would no longer be any significant advantage to being a preferred provider of that service. Under those circumstances, a provider would not be able to obtain a larger share of the market by cutting its price and would have little incentive to give a discount to be a preferred provider. Despite the supposed concern for the interests of patients, the actual results of AWP laws are to forestall the bargaining process of selective contracting and give greater power to providers in negotiating with payers.

Although some people are opposed to selective contracting, others argue that it is a necessary component of healthcare cost containment. Payers and others have argued that states should not enact AWP laws and that Congress should preempt those state laws by means of federal legislation. In fact, the Clinton administration's comprehensive healthcare reform proposal had generally provided for the federal preemption of state AWP laws.[10]

Legislative Responses to Selective Contracting

State legislatures have enacted a variety of laws with regard to the termination or nonrenewal of healthcare provider contracts.[11] Some of the common provisions in these state laws include mandatory procedural requirements such as notice and an opportunity for a hearing or appeal, as well as disclosure of the payer's criteria for participation in its network.[12] One of the primary goals of these state laws is to prevent payers from terminating physicians in retaliation for advocating for the needs of their patients.[13]

At the federal level, Congress has considered several proposals to modify the system of selective contracting. As of spring 2007, however, none of those proposals has been enacted.

Among the bills considered by Congress, some would prohibit MCOs from discriminating against providers on the basis of their type of state license.[14] Other proposals would require health plans to develop reasonable procedures for participation by providers, including notice of the rules and an opportunity to appeal adverse participation decisions.[15] In addition, several proposals include protections for healthcare professionals who advocate on behalf of their patients. Specifically, those proposals would prevent a health insurance company or health plan from terminating a provider in retaliation for the provider's participation in a benefit appeal or grievance procedure or in retaliation for disclosing information to a government agency, accreditation body, or the management of the insurance company or plan.[16] Competing proposals from both political parties have contained almost identical language on this issue,[17] which indicates that protection of healthcare providers for patient advocacy is not a controversial topic.

Congress has also considered giving additional protection to those patients whose providers are terminated by an MCO at a critical stage in the patient's course of treatment. For example, some proposals would require a health plan to permit a patient to continue treatment with a terminated provider during a transitional period, subject to certain limitations.[18]

These federal proposals for reform would modify the system of selective contracting to some extent. However, the major proposals from both political parties would continue to permit MCOs to use selective contracting in developing their provider networks.[19]

Regardless of whether any particular bill is enacted at the federal level, it is significant that none of the major proposals call for abolishing selective contracting. Moreover, there is little or no serious discussion of enacting an AWP law at the federal level. Despite all of the public discussion of the need to regulate MCOs and other payers, the policy debate is taking place within fairly limited parameters, and most people seem to be operating on the assumption that free choice of provider is essentially a thing of the past.

Notes

1. See, e.g., R.J. Blendon, et al., "Understanding the Managed Care Backlash," *Health Affairs* 17(4) (1998): 80–94.
2. F.A. Sloan and M.A. Hall, "Market Failures and the Evolution of State Regulation of Managed Care," *Law and Contemporary Problems* 65(4) (2002): 169–206.
3. *Harper v. Healthsource New Hampshire, Inc.*, 674 A.2d 962 (N.H. 1996).
4. See, e.g., *Sides v. Duke University*, 328 S.E.2d 818, 826 (N.C. Ct. App. 1985).
5. *Potvin v. Metropolitan Life Insurance Company*, 997 P.2d 1153 (Cal. 2000).
6. *Grossman v. Columbine Medical Group, Inc.*, 12 P.3d 269 (Colo. Ct. App. 2000).
7. *Id.* at 271.
8. See *Hassan v. Independent Practice Associates*, 698 F. Supp. 679, 695–696 (E.D. Mich. 1988).
9. Neb. Rev. Stat. § 44-4111(1).
10. See Health Security Act, H.R. 3600, 103rd Cong. – 1407 (1993).
11. L.C. Fentiman, "Patient Advocacy and Termination from Managed Care Organizations: Do State Laws Protecting Health Care Professional Advocacy Make Any Difference?" *Nebraska Law Review*, 82(2) (2003): 508–574.
12. *Id.* at 535–38.
13. See *id.*
14. See, e.g., H.R. 2563, 107th Cong. § 132(a) (2001).
15. See, e.g., H.R. 358, 106th Cong. § 143 (1999).
16. H.R. 2563, 107th Cong. § 135 (2001); S. 1052, 107th Cong. § 135 (2001).
17. See *id.*
18. See, e.g., S. 1052, 107th Cong. § 117 (2001); H.R. 358, 106th Cong. § 105 (1999).
19. See, e.g., H.R. 358, 106th Cong. § 143 (1999); H.R. 1415, 105th Cong. § 2770(c) (1997).

15

FINANCIAL INCENTIVES TO PROVIDE LESS CARE

In the traditional system of fee-for-service medicine, the financial interest of the physician was aligned with the interest of the patient. In most cases, the patient wanted to receive all potentially beneficial services, and the physician was usually happy to provide those services and receive payment for doing so. The physician decided what services were needed, and the patient's health insurance company would pay all or most of the bill. The patient relied on the physician and was not particularly concerned about the cost.

From the perspective of the insurance company, however, that traditional system suffered from a fundamental conflict of interest. Physicians were paid on a fee-for-service basis; therefore, they received more money by performing more services. The physicians who wanted to be paid for providing more services were also determining that the services should be provided. Under these circumstances, the financial interest of the physician was adverse to the interest of the third-party payer and instead was aligned with the interest of the patient.

Many people believe this traditional alignment of interests was desirable and appropriate. However, the fee-for-service system was inherently inflationary, and it contributed to rapid increases in healthcare costs. When insurance companies had to pay more money for healthcare services, they passed the increased cost to employers, individuals, and groups in the form of higher premiums. Eventually, in an effort to control those costs, third-party payers adopted various techniques of managed care. One of the most common techniques is the use of financial incentives for physicians to provide more cost-effective care.

Managed care organizations (MCOs) and other payers use financial arrangements such as capitation to control the cost of treating the patients enrolled in the plan. In addition, payers use financial incentives such as withholds and bonuses to encourage physicians to make fewer referrals to specialists and fewer admissions to hospitals. As a practical matter, these incentives have the effect of realigning the financial interest of the physician to be consistent with the interest of the payer rather than the interest of the patient.

Although these incentives may reduce healthcare costs for the payer and ultimately for society as a whole, they raise serious legal and ethical concerns for physicians and their patients. As a matter of public policy, we might decide to prohibit financial incentives that encourage physicians to provide less care, or at least prohibit the most extreme types of incentives. Even if we do not want to prohibit the use of incentives, we may want to require those incentives to be disclosed to the patient. If we decide that particular incentives ought to be disclosed, we need to address the further issue of whether disclosure should be made by the physician at the time of treatment or by the MCO at the time of enrollment. It is also important to consider whether disclosure of financial incentives would be practical, whether it really would be useful to patients, and whether it would reduce the level of trust in the therapeutic relationship.[1]

Another important issue in the system of managed care is the effect of financial incentives on the physician's role as advocate for the patient.[2] Because of the complexity of medical issues, the patient has to rely on the physician to explain to the payer why the proposed treatment is medically necessary. Traditionally, the physician acted as the patient's advocate in negotiating with the payer regarding utilization review and authorization for care. Now that the physician's financial interest is more aligned with that of the payer, however, it remains to be seen whether the physician can continue to be an effective advocate for the patient.[3]

The ethical aspects of these issues were addressed by the Council on Ethical and Judicial Affairs of the American Medical Association (AMA) in its report entitled "Ethical Issues in Managed Care."[4] According to that report, physicians have an ethical duty to act as advocates on behalf of their patients. "No other party in the health care system has the kind of responsibility that physicians have to advocate for patients, and no other party is in a position to assume that kind of responsibility."[5] Therefore, if the MCO denies care that would materially benefit the patient, "the physician's duty as patient advocate requires that the physician challenge the denial and argue for the provision of treatment in the specific case."[6] In addition, the AMA Council concluded that, in some cases, physicians even have a duty to initiate appeals for their patients.[7]

In light of these issues, it is important to examine how financial incentives operate in the systems of health insurance and managed care. It is also important to understand how those incentives are regulated by law at the present time. With that knowledge, we will be able to consider whether certain incentives should be prohibited by law and what types of disclosure should be required.

Types of Financial Incentives to Provide Less Care

When most people think about the financial incentives of managed care, they think about the system of capitation used by health maintenance organizations (HMOs). Under capitation, the physician would not be paid on a fee-for-service basis for each patient visit. Rather, the HMO would pay the physician a monthly amount for each person under her professional care. The physician would have to provide all of the agreed-upon services in exchange for the capitation payment and would bear the risk of excessive utilization. As the U.S. Supreme Court has stated, "In an HMO system, a physician's financial interest lies in providing less care, not more."[8]

In the following reading, the risks and incentives of HMOs are discussed from an economic perspective. The reading is an excerpt from an appellate decision in an antitrust case and was written by Chief Judge Richard Posner of the U.S. Court of Appeals for the Seventh Circuit.[9]

BLUE CROSS & BLUE SHIELD UNITED OF WISCONSIN V. MARSHFIELD CLINIC, 65 F.3D 1406, 1409–1410 (7TH CIR. 1995) (AS AMENDED ON DENIAL OF REHEARING)

An HMO is basically a method of pricing medical services. Instead of having the patient pay separately for each medical procedure, the patient pays a fixed annual fee for all the services he needs and the HMO undertakes to provide those services with the physicians with whom it has contracts. The different method of pricing used by the HMO has, of course, consequences both for the practice of medicine and for the allocation of the risk of medical expenses. The method of pricing gives the HMO an incentive to minimize the procedures that it performs, since the marginal revenue it derives from each procedure is zero. Hence HMOs are thought to reduce "waste" and to encourage preventive care, although those hostile to the HMO concept believe that the principal effect is merely to reduce the amount of medical care that patients receive. The risk-shifting feature of the concept lies in the fact that if a subscriber incurs above-average medical expenses, the excess cost is borne by the HMO rather than by the subscriber (or by his insurer, or more likely by both because of copayment and deductible provisions in the insurance policy), while if he incurs below-average medical expense the difference enures to the benefit of the HMO rather than to him or his insurer (or, again, both). To control the upside risk that it incurs, the HMO provides medical services through physicians with whom it has contracts specifying their compensation, rather than merely reimbursing some percentage of whatever fee they might happen to charge for their services. This means that the HMO must be able to line up enough physicians with whom to contract to provide its subscribers with a more or less complete menu of medical services.

HMOs, though they have made great strides in recent years because of the widespread concern with skyrocketing medical costs, remain relative upstarts in the market for physician services. Many people don't like them because of the restriction on the patient's choice of doctors or because they fear that HMOs skimp on service since, as we said, the marginal revenue of a medical procedure to an HMO is zero. From a short-term financial standpoint—which we do not suggest is the only standpoint that an HMO is likely to have—the HMO's incentive is to keep you healthy if it can but if you get very sick, and are unlikely to recover to a healthy state involving few medical expenses, to let you die as quickly and cheaply as possible. HMOs compensate for these perceived drawbacks by charging a lower price than fee-for-service plans.

We do not wish to associate ourselves with the critics of HMOs. All that is important to our consideration of this appeal is that many people believe—whether rightly or wrongly is of no moment—that HMOs are not an unalloyed blessing; and this means that the price that an HMO can charge is constrained not only by competition from other HMOs but also by competition from forms of medical-services contracting that are free from the perceived perverse incentive effects of the HMO form. As far as we know or the record shows, even in areas where there is only one HMO most of the people in its service area do not subscribe to it even if its prices are lower than those of fee-for-service providers.

As indicated by the foregoing reading, much of the criticism of financial incentives in managed care has been directed at HMOs in general and at capitation arrangements in particular. However, it is important to recognize that financial incentives to provide less care or make fewer referrals are not limited to capitation arrangements or even to HMOs. Those types of incentives can even be incorporated into a fee-for-service arrangement between an MCO and its participating physicians. For example, an MCO could pay its primary care physicians (PCPs) on a fee-for-service basis but could withhold a specified portion of each payment. Then, the MCO could put the withheld portion into a "pool" that would be used to pay for specialist and hospital care. If any money was left in the pool at the end of the year, the PCPs would receive at least part of whatever is left. In that way, the PCPs would have a financial incentive to avoid hospitalizing their patients or referring them to specialists to avoid depleting the money left in the pool.

In addition, other financial incentives to provide less care are much more subtle but just as effective. By ratcheting down the level of payment to providers, providers will likely be forced to reduce the time and resources they put into providing each service. Ideally, this might force providers to become more efficient, but it could also contribute to a gradual "dumbing down" of the standard of care. For example, if physicians have to see more patients every day to maintain their previous levels of income, they probably will not be able to spend as much time as they did in the past with each of their individual patients.

Finally, the system of selective contracting, as discussed in Chapter 14, contains an inherent incentive for physicians to provide fewer tests and treatments. In developing their networks, MCOs might select physicians whose computer profiles indicate a lower usage of diagnostic tests or a lower rate of hospital admission. After physicians have been selected as preferred providers, the MCO may have the right to terminate their contracts without cause if they fail to practice in a manner the MCO considers to be cost effective. If physicians provide "too many" tests or treatments, if they admit "too many" patients to the hospital, or if they make "too many" referrals to specialists, those physicians could quickly lose a large percentage of their patients and a large percentage of their income. Either consciously or subconsciously, the potential loss of patients and income might influence their treatment decisions, as well as their willingness to advocate on behalf of their patients in the process of utilization review.

As a matter of public policy, some types of financial incentives to reduce care are more problematic than others.[10] If a physician would actually gain or lose money as a result of a decision about treating or referring an individual patient, that incentive would be extremely effective and extremely dangerous. At the other extreme, there is less concern about incentives that are based on all of the costs incurred and all of the referrals made by all physicians on the MCO's panel in the aggregate. As stated by the AMA's Council on Ethical and Judicial Affairs, "[t]he strength of a financial incentive to limit care can be judged by various factors, including the percentage of the physician's income placed at risk, the frequency with which incentive payments are calculated, and the size of the group of physicians on which the economic performance is judged."[11] From the AMA's perspective, conflicts of interest could be reduced by limiting the size of financial incentives and by calculating the incentives on the basis of a large group of physicians.[12] In fact, this analysis suggests that some types of incentives to provide less care should be prohibited altogether, and those that are allowed should be limited by specific requirements of law.

Legal Implications of Financial Incentives to Provide Less Care

In the traditional healthcare system, providers had financial incentives to provide more tests and treatments. As discussed previously, physicians were paid on a fee-for-service basis. In addition, physicians had incentives to refer their patients to facilities in which they had some type of ownership interest, and there were opportunities to receive kickbacks in exchange for referrals. As a policy matter, those types of incentives were problematic because they tended to increase healthcare costs and posed a risk of interfering with the physician's independent judgment. Therefore, as discussed in Chapter 8 with regard to Medicare and Medicaid, the government responded to those concerns by developing a complex set of statutes and regulations that were designed to prevent fraud and abuse.

At least with regard to government healthcare programs, financial incentives to provide more tests, treatments, admissions, and referrals have been extensively regulated. However, there has been less regulation of the newer financial incentives that encourage physicians to provide less care or make fewer referrals. The newer financial incentives pose a similar risk of interfering with the physician's independent judgment, but these new incentives have a tendency to reduce healthcare costs.

Nevertheless, a few attempts have been made to regulate some of those new financial incentives in connection with government payment programs. Under the Medicare prospective payment system, the government pays hospitals a fixed amount for treating patients with a particular diagnosis. The government thereby gives hospitals a financial incentive to provide treatment in the most cost-effective manner and perhaps to discharge patients "quicker and sicker." However, decisions on treating and discharging patients are made by physicians on the medical staff, and hospitals may be tempted to provide incentives for physicians to make those decisions in ways that will benefit the hospital. To protect the interests of Medicare and Medicaid patients, the federal government has prohibited hospitals from giving financial incentives to physicians to encourage them to discharge patients more quickly or order fewer tests and treatments. Specifically, as discussed in Chapter 8, Congress enacted a federal statute that prohibits hospitals from paying physicians to reduce the level of services for Medicare and Medicaid patients.[13]

In 1999, the U.S. Department of Health and Human Services (HHS) Office of Inspector General (OIG) expressed particular concern about so-called "gainsharing arrangements," in which hospitals attempt to share their savings from cost reductions with physicians.[14] In a Special Advisory Bulletin, the OIG explained that federal law prohibits gainsharing arrangements that provide incentives to encourage physicians to limit services to Medicare and Medicaid beneficiaries. In 2005, however, the OIG issued a series of Advisory Opinions in which it approved the use of certain gainsharing arrangements under limited circumstances and subject to very specific safeguards.[15] This does not mean all gainsharing arrangements are now allowed by law. Rather, it means some gainsharing arrangements are likely to be permissible, and healthcare providers need to carefully structure their arrangements and consult with their lawyers.[16]

The managed care plans authorized by Medicare provide another example of regulating financial incentives to provide less care in the context of government payment programs. In addition to the traditional fee-for-service Medicare program, beneficiaries have the option to choose from a variety of managed care plans that meet specific requirements of federal law. As the options for Medicare managed care have evolved over the years, HHS has adopted a series of regulations to deal with physician incentives.[17] For example, in its rules for managed care plans known as Medicare+Choice organizations,[18] HHS addressed three important questions:

1. Which types of incentives are so violative of public policy that they should be prohibited altogether?
2. For those types of incentives that will be allowed, what regulatory limits should be placed on their use to protect the public interest?
3. What types of disclosures should be made to the government and to beneficiaries with regard to financial incentives to provide less care?

In adopting those rules, HHS essentially prohibited Medicare+Choice organizations from using incentives that relate to the treatment of any individual patient.[19] In addition, Congress imposed a similar requirement by statute for Medicare+Choice organizations.[20] Aside from limiting the types of financial incentives that may be used, HHS also imposed some requirements for disclosure of incentives to the government and the beneficiary.[21] However, those legal requirements with regard to the types of incentives and disclosure of incentives are applicable only to health plans in the Medicare managed care program.

Legal Theories for Requiring Disclosure of Incentives

Several legal theories might support a requirement for disclosing financial incentives. Those legal theories have the potential to expand the requirement of disclosure beyond Medicare MCOs to health plans that operate in the private sector.

First, it is arguable that a physician must disclose his financial incentives as a prerequisite to obtaining the informed consent of the patient. Traditionally, the doctrine of informed consent has only required the disclosure of the risks, benefits, and alternatives to the treatment recommended by the physician. However, as discussed in Chapter 10, some courts have held that the physician must disclose other types of material information before the patient can give informed consent. In *Moore v. Regents of the University of California*, the Supreme Court of California stated that, "a physician who is seeking a patient's consent for a medical procedure must, in order to . . . obtain the patient's informed consent, disclose personal interests unrelated to the patient's health, whether research or economic, that may affect his medical judgment."[22] Logically, those personal economic interests would include financial incentives to provide fewer tests and treatments or make fewer referrals. At this time, it is unclear whether the reasoning in *Moore* will be applied to the financial incentives of managed care, and it is also unclear whether that reasoning will be adopted by courts in other states. For example, the Supreme Court of Illinois concluded that, "a physician's failure to disclose HMO incentive plans is significantly unlike the egregious nature of the alleged behavior at issue in *Moore*."[23] Nevertheless, if the law of informed consent expands to require disclosure of managed care incentives, a physician's failure to disclose those incentives could provide a basis for tort liability in a civil action by the patient.

In addition to the legal doctrine of informed consent, disclosure of financial incentives may be required as a matter of professional ethics. According to the AMA's ethical guidelines, "[a]ny incentives to limit care must be disclosed fully to patients by plan administrators on enrollment and at least annually thereafter."[24] The AMA's guidelines appear to place the duty to disclose incentives on the MCO rather than on the physician. However, in a previous report, the AMA's Council on Ethical and Judicial Affairs had stated that physicians have an ethical duty to disclose conflicts of interest, financial incentives, and contractual provisions that restrict referral.[25]

In a different approach, some people have argued that MCOs have engaged in fraud or misrepresentation by failing to disclose their physician incentives to potential enrollees. Under that theory, MCOs have wrongfully induced people to enroll in their plans by failing to disclose material information about the negative aspects of their plans, such as their use of financial incentives to provide less care. Some of those suits were filed as class actions on behalf of all similarly situated enrollees, and the plaintiffs sought treble damages and attorneys' fees for alleged violation of the federal Racketeer Influenced and Corrupt Organizations Act, 18 U.S.C. § 1964(c).[26] In those class actions, the plaintiffs were not seeking damages for injuries caused by an MCO's refusal to authorize care, nor were they seeking damages for a specific denial of benefits. If the plaintiffs were to file claims for denial of benefits or refusal to authorize care, those claims might be preempted by the federal Employee Retirement Income Security Act (ERISA), as discussed in Chapter 16. Therefore, in those class-action suits, the claims were based instead on a different legal theory of fraud or misrepresentation by MCOs in failing to disclose their financial incentives and other negative aspects of their plans.[27]

Other claims for failure to disclose incentives have been based on the fiduciary duties that the federal ERISA statute imposes on employer-sponsored health plans. As one court has explained, "[w]hen an HMO's financial incentives discourage a treating doctor from providing essential healthcare referrals for conditions covered under the plan benefit structure, the incentives must be disclosed and the failure to do so is a breach of ERISA's fiduciary duties."[28] However, other courts have reached the opposite conclusion and held that there is no fiduciary duty under ERISA to disclose the financial incentives that are given to physicians.[29] The U.S. Supreme Court has considered some issues of fiduciary duty under ERISA, but has not decided the particular issue of the duty to disclose HMO financial incentives.

In *Pegram v. Herdrich*,[30] the Supreme Court unanimously held that an HMO and its physicians are not acting as fiduciaries under ERISA when they make decisions that involve both eligibility and medical treatment, such as determining medical necessity. However, the court left open the possibility that at other times an HMO might be acting as a fiduciary when it performs administrative functions for the employer-sponsored health plan. In *Pegram*, the plaintiff challenged the HMO's *use* of physician incentives, rather than its failure to *disclose* them.[31] The Supreme Court held that the HMO and its physicians did not violate ERISA's fiduciary duties by using financial incentives, but it recognized the possibility that a failure to disclose those incentives might violate the fiduciary duties of ERISA:[32]

> Although we are not presented with the issue here, it could be argued that Carle [the HMO] is a fiduciary insofar as it has discretionary authority to administer the plan, and so it is obligated to disclose characteristics of the plan and of those who provide services to the plan, if that information affects beneficiaries' material interests.[33]

Under these circumstances, the fiduciary duties of ERISA might provide a basis for requiring disclosure of financial incentives in the system of managed care.[34]

Gag Clauses in Provider Agreements

In considering whether to require the disclosure of financial incentives, it is important to distinguish that issue from the separate issue of prohibiting so-called "gag clauses." Those clauses are terms in provider agreements that prohibit a physician from disclosing certain information to the patient. Although gag clauses might prohibit the disclosure of financial incentives, they would be more likely to prohibit the physician from telling the patient about treatment alternatives that are not covered by the plan. For obvious reasons, the gag clause has been almost universally condemned as an inappropriate interference with the physician–patient relationship.

However, it appears that gag clauses are no longer a serious problem for several reasons. First, physicians are unlikely to comply with contract provisions they consider to be grossly unethical. In addition, the public reaction to gag clauses was so negative that they have been largely eliminated from the competitive market for managed care. In fact, as indicated in the following excerpt from a report by the U.S. General Accounting Office (GAO), which is now known as the Government Accountability Office, few if any HMO contracts prohibit physicians from discussing treatment options with their patients.

MANAGED CARE: EXPLICIT GAG CLAUSES NOT FOUND IN HMO CONTRACTS, BUT PHYSICIAN CONCERNS REMAIN (COVER LETTER TO REPORT, 8/29/97, GAO/HEHS-97-175)

Pursuant to a congressional request, GAO reviewed contractual limitations, known as gag clauses, imposed by health maintenance organizations (HMO), that interfere with the physician-patient relationship by impeding discussions of treatment options, focusing on: (1) the types of contract clauses that could impede a physician's ability to advise patients of all medically appropriate treatment options; (2) the extent to which these different types of clauses exist in current HMO contracts with physicians; and (3) the likely implications of HMO contract language on physician practice.

GAO noted that: (1) the managed care industry, physicians, and health care attorneys have different views regarding contract language that could limit a physician's ability to advise patients of all medically appropriate treatment options; (2) there is general agreement that a clause that prohibits discussion of procedures or providers not covered by the plan, and, to a lesser extent, one that requires physicians to consult with the plan before discussing treatment options with enrollees, is a gag clause; (3) however, some physicians and health-care lawyers believe that other clauses could restrict the information and advice that physicians provide about a patient's medical options; (4) other physician groups, lawyers, and the HMO industry disagree that such clauses limit medical communication and contend that these are standard contract clauses designed and used only to protect HMOs' business interests; (5) of the 529 HMOs in GAO's study, none used contract clauses that specifically restricted physicians from discussing all appropriate medical options with their patients; (6) two-thirds of responding plans and 60 percent of the contracts submitted had a nondisparagement, nonsolicitation, or confidentiality clause that could be interpreted by physicians as limiting communication about all treatment options; (7) contracts with such business clauses often contained anti-gag language stating that the contract or a specific provision should not be construed as restricting physician medical advice to patients or generally encouraging open communication; (8) of those contracts with one or more of these business clauses, anti-gag language was found in 67 percent of them; (9) this combination could mitigate the potential for business clauses to be read by physicians as limiting discussion of a patient's treatment options; (10) it appears that HMO contract provisions that may be interpreted as limiting the medical

information that physicians may provide patients are not likely to have a significant impact on physician practice; (11) physicians GAO interviewed maintained that they freely communicate with their patients regarding all medically
appropriate care because habitual practice, professional ethics, and fear of
medical liability are stronger influences on their behavior than contract requirements; and (12) physicians also pointed out that the increasing power of HMOs
in the health care marketplace and their ability to terminate physician contracts can bring significant pressure to bear on physicians to modify their practice patterns or discussions with patients, without relying on the clauses discussed above.

For Medicare MCOs, gag clauses have been prohibited by the
Balanced Budget Act of 1997 and by the rules of HHS.[35] In addition, a
series of legislative proposals to ban the use of gag clauses by all MCOs
and health plans has been initiated.[36] However, the sponsors of those bills
may be fighting a battle that has already been won in the competitive marketplace and in the reality of medical practice. Moreover, a legislative ban
on gag clauses might be futile, as long as MCOs have the contractual right
to terminate physician contracts without cause. In some situations, the
potential for terminating the provider agreement without cause may seal a
physician's lips more effectively than a gag clause would have done.

Notes

1. See generally T.E. Miller and C.R. Horowitz, "Disclosing Doctors'
   Incentives: Will Consumers Understand and Value the
   Information?" *Health Affairs*, 19(4) (2000): 149–155.
2. See generally E.H. Morreim, "Economic Disclosure and Economic
   Advocacy: New Duties in the Medical Standard of Care," *Journal of
   Legal Medicine*, 12 (1991): 275.
3. But see W.A. Sage, "Physicians as Advocates," *Houston Law Review*,
   35(5): 1529–1630 at 1534–1535 ("Physician advocacy should neither be taken for granted nor saddled with expectations which
   potentially are inconsistent with one another or with normative
   goals for the health care system.").
4. See Council on Ethical and Judicial Affairs of the American Medical
   Association, "Ethical Issues in Managed Care," *Journal of the
   American Medical Association*, 273 (1995): 330 [hereinafter
   Council on Ethical and Judicial Affairs].
5. *Id.* at 331.
6. *Id.* at 334.
7. See *id.* at 333.
8. *Pegram v. Herdrich*, 530 U.S. 211, 219 (2000).

9. *Blue Cross and Blue Shield United of Wisconsin v. Marshfield Clinic*, 65 F.3d 1406, 1409–1410 (7th Cir. 1995) (as amended on denial of rehearing).

10. E.B. Hirshfeld, "Should Third Party Payors of Health Care Services Disclose Cost Control Mechanisms to Potential Beneficiaries?" *Seton Hall Legislative Journal*, 14 (1990): 127.

11. Council on Ethical and Judicial Affairs, *supra* note 4.

12. See *id.* at 333, 335.

13. 42 U.S.C. § 1320a–7a(b) (2000).

14. Publication of the OIG, Special Advisory Bulletin on Gainsharing Arrangements and CMPs for Hospital Payments to Physicians to Reduce or Limit Services to Beneficiaries, 64 Fed. Reg. 37,985 (July 14, 1999).

15. See U.S. Department of Health and Human Services, Office of Inspector General, Advisory Opinions Nos. 05-01–06 (2005). [Online document; retrieved 2/6/07.] oig.hhs.gov/fraud/advisoryopinions/opinions.html.

16. See C. Logarta, "Introduction: Fifth Annual Health Law & Policy Colloquium: Provider Response to Cost Containment: Fraud & Abuse Issues," *Annals of Health Law* 15 (2006): 373–378, at 376 ("[T]he legal climate surrounding gainsharing remains unclear.").

17. See, e.g. 42 C.F.R. §§ 417.479, 422.208, 422.210, 422.111 (2006).

18. See, e.g., 42 C.F.R. §§ 422.208, 422.210, 422.111 (2006).

19. 42 C.F.R. § 422.208(c)(1) (2006).

20. 42 U.S.C. § 1395w-22j(4)(A)(i) (2006) ("No specific payment is made directly or indirectly under the plan to a physician or physician group as an inducement to reduce or limit medically necessary services provided with respect to a specific individual enrolled with the organization.").

21. 42 C.F.R. §§ 422.210(b), 422.111(c) (2006).

22. *Moore v. Regents of the University of California*, 793 P.2d 479, 485 (Cal. 1990).

23. *Neade v. Portes*, 739 N.E.2d 496, 505 (Ill. 2000) (holding that a physician's failure-to-disclose incentives do not give rise to a claim for breach of fiduciary duty, because that would merely duplicate the existing claim for medical malpractice).

24. Council on Ethical and Judicial Affairs, *supra* note 4 at 335.

25. *Id.* at 334.

26. C.C. Havighurst, "Consumers Versus Managed Care: The New Class Actions," *Health Affairs*, 20(4) (2001): 8–27 at 12–13 ("Lawyers invoke RICO because it provides both a good context in which to demonize HMOs and a statutory basis for demanding triple damages and attorneys' fees.").

27. See K.L. Cerminara, "Taking a Closer Look at the Managed Care Class Actions: Impact Litigation as an Assist to the Market," *Annals of Health Law*, 11 (2002): 1–24 at n.52 and accompanying text.

28. *Shea v. Esensten*, 107 F.3d 625, 629 (8th Cir.), *cert. denied*, 522 U.S. 914 (1997).

29. See, e.g., *Ehlmann v. Kaiser Foundation Health Plan of Texas*, 198 F.3d 552, 554–555 (5th Cir. 2000) ("ERISA imposes no such duty.").

30. 530 U.S. 211 (2000).

31. 530 U.S. at 228 n.8 ("her amended complaint alleges an obligation to avoid such incentives . . . failure to disclose is no longer the allegation of the amended complaint.").

32. See Havighurst, *supra* note 26 at 13–14.

33. *Pegram*, 530 U.S. at 228 n.8.

34. See A.J. Rosoff, "Breach of Fiduciary Duty Lawsuits Against MCOs: What's Left After *Pegram v. Herdrich?" Journal of Legal Medicine*, 22 (2001): 55–75 at 73 ("the *Pegram* decision seems to have opened the way to further exploration of fiduciary lawsuits under ERISA based on nondisclosure.").

35. See Balanced Budget Act of 1997, Pub. L. No. 105-33, § 1852(j)(3)(A), 111 Stat. 251, 295 (1997); 42 C.F.R. § 422.206(a) (2001).

36. See, e.g., H.R. 2563, 107th Cong. § 131 (2001).

CONTROLLING UTILIZATION OF HEALTHCARE SERVICES

Chapters 14 and 15 addressed the cost-control techniques of selective contracting and provider incentives in the systems of health insurance and managed care. In addition to those techniques, managed care organizations (MCOs) and other payers control the cost of care by limiting consumption of services through the process of utilization review (UR).

The Process and Consequences of Prospective Utilization Review

In the past, UR primarily involved the retrospective review of services that had already been rendered. Therefore, UR was for the most part a vehicle that addressed the issue of money, rather than access to care. However, MCOs and other payers now use prospective UR to authorize or refuse to authorize proposed treatments, referrals, and hospital admissions. If the patient fails to obtain prior approval or preadmission certification before entering the hospital, the payer might refuse to pay any of the cost or might pay only a reduced percentage of the cost. As a practical matter, if prior approval is denied, the patient may be unable to obtain the proposed course of treatment.

The process of prior approval begins with the patient's primary care physician (PCP), who acts as the gatekeeper for access to other healthcare services and facilities. The gatekeeper system provides some benefits to the patient, including continuity and coordination of care, but this system may reduce access to specialized facilities and services. For a patient to see a specialist, the PCP must make a referral in accordance with the procedures of the plan. Moreover, payers might encourage their PCPs to handle patients themselves as long as possible, rather than making immediate referrals to expensive specialists. As discussed in Chapter 15, some PCPs have financial incentives to refrain from referring their patients to specialists.

Even if the PCP thinks a referral, hospital admission, or course of treatment is appropriate, the payer may conduct its own review under the guidelines set forth in the plan. The payer's reviewers will determine whether, in their opinion, the proposed treatment is medically necessary. Obviously, many physicians view this process as an interference with their professional judgment. In addition, if a physician is paid on a fee-for-service basis, prospective UR may have the effect of reducing the physician's income. Payers argue, however, that they need to use prospective UR to prevent unnecessary treatment and reduce the cost of services for all participants in the plan.

Payers also insist they are not telling physicians how they should treat their patients but are merely making decisions about payment or coverage under the terms of the contract. In reality, the supposed distinction between coverage decisions and treatment decisions is specious, because most patients cannot afford to pay for their own medical care without third-party coverage. As one court explained, a denial of authorization or payment in prospective UR is tantamount to a denial of treatment.

> The stakes, the risks at issue, are much higher when a prospective cost-containment review process is utilized than when a retrospective review process is used.
>
> A mistake [sic] conclusion about medical necessity following retrospective review will result in the wrongful withholding of payment. An erroneous decision in a prospective review process, on the other hand, in practical consequences, results in the withholding of necessary care, potentially leading to a patient's permanent disability or death.[1]

If a payer's denial of authorization or payment causes the death of a patient, the patient's estate might try to sue the payer and seek damages to compensate the survivors for their loss and deter the payer from similar conduct in the future. However, depending on the circumstances, that type of case might be decided under legal rules that predate the modern systems of cost containment and managed care. Those old legal rules may lead to extremely unfair results when applied in this new context of managed healthcare services. Therefore, we may decide it is necessary to change the legal rules with regard to the liability of MCOs and other third-party payers for injuries caused by improper denial of benefits.

Another interesting issue in prospective UR is whether the employees or agents of a payer are practicing medicine when they determine that a requested treatment is medically unnecessary. If a payer's medical director may be disciplined for a decision to deny authorization for care on the ground that it is an erroneous medical decision, MCO medical directors might be more inclined to approve the treatment proposed by the patient's own physician. However, courts and officials in different states have reached different conclusions on this issue.

For example, in Arizona, the state Board of Medical Examiners took disciplinary action against a physician who made UR decisions as medical director of an MCO. In that case, the board's investigation of the medical director was prompted by a complaint from a treating physician whose proposed course of treatment was rejected by the medical director. On appeal, the intermediate appellate court in Arizona held that the board did have jurisdiction to investigate and discipline physicians who make decisions in the process of UR, and the Arizona Supreme Court subsequently refused to hear the case.[2] According to the intermediate appellate court, when a medical director substitutes her judgment for that of the attending physician and determines that a proposed treatment is not medically necessary, the medical director is making a medical decision. Therefore, the court held that a medical director is subject to the disciplinary authority of the state medical licensing board. Courts in some states have agreed with the reasoning of the Arizona court,[3] but the attorneys general of other states have taken contrary positions, at least with regard to the statutes in their respective states.[4]

Legal Liability for Improper Denial of Claims

In the past, insurance companies were tempted to deny and delay the payment of claims, because the only penalty for the company was the possibility of being forced to pay all those claims at some time in the future. For example, a life insurance company might use some excuse to refuse to pay claims for death benefits and force the widows, widowers, and orphans to try to sue the insurance company. Even if the survivors eventually win in court, the insurance company would only be required to pay the death benefits under the policies, which it should have paid in the first place.

To encourage insurance companies to pay claims in a prompt and reasonable manner, the law has developed a way to penalize insurers for improper handling and payment of claims. At the state level, courts and legislatures developed a variety of legal remedies against insurance companies, such as state-law tort claims for bad-faith denial of benefits. Regardless of how these state-law remedies are labeled or characterized, the significant fact about these remedies is that they allow the plaintiff to recover an amount of damages that far exceeds the value of the benefits under the policy of insurance. If the insurance company fails to handle the claim in a prompt and reasonable manner, the insurance company could be held liable for much more than the amount of the policy. Therefore, these state-law remedies provide strong incentives to encourage insurers to pay claims in a fair and expeditious manner.

As a general rule, these state-law remedies are applicable to all types of insurance companies, including life, casualty, and health insurance.

However, for participants in benefit plans that are sponsored by employers in the private sector, those state-law remedies may be negated by federal legislation. Specifically, the federal Employee Retirement Income Security Act (ERISA) of 1974[5] severely limits the remedies available to many patients when they are harmed by an improper denial of benefits.

As discussed in the sections that follow, the federal ERISA law regulates private, employer-sponsored healthcare benefit plans through which many employees and their dependents obtain their coverage. According to that federal law, private, employer-sponsored ERISA plans cannot be sued under the laws of the state for wrongful denial of benefits. Instead, the only legal remedy for the employee or dependent is to sue the health plan under the federal ERISA statute, in which case the plaintiff's recovery is essentially limited to the value of the benefits that should have been paid in the first place. Thus, the practical effect of ERISA is to return employees and their dependents to the situation existing *before* the development of state-law claims for bad-faith denial of benefits.

The Purpose and Effect of the Federal ERISA Law

Congress did not enact ERISA for the purpose of limiting the rights of patients in dealing with health maintenance organizations (HMOs) and other third-party payers. However, that has been the inadvertent and ironic result of a federal statute that was intended to protect the interests of employees and their dependents. ERISA was enacted before the growth of managed care, and it can lead to extremely unfair results when applied to a system in which care is "managed."

Congress enacted ERISA in 1974 to protect the rights of employees with regard to pensions and other employment-related benefits, including employee group health insurance. The federal law also helps employers who have employees in multiple states by facilitating uniformity throughout the country in the structure, administration, and regulation of their employee benefit plans. ERISA provides that, by complying with a single set of federal requirements, the employer will be exempt from all state-law requirements in structuring and operating its benefit plans.

Many states require all health plans that operate in the state to provide coverage for particular procedures and conditions, such as mammograms and prostate cancer screening. These state requirements are referred to as mandated-benefit laws, and significant differences in benefits are mandated by each individual state. If a large company has employees in all 50 states, for example, it would have to operate 50 different health benefit plans, with a different benefit package for the employees residing in each particular state. By enacting ERISA, Congress preempted—or displaced—state laws with regard to employee benefit plans and thereby allowed employers to operate nationwide benefit plans without regard to state-mandated benefit laws.

In addition, ERISA provides a uniform federal remedy for employees to challenge denial of their pensions, health insurance, or other benefits. Participants in an ERISA plan have the legal right to sue the plan in federal court to recover the benefits to which they are entitled under the plan. However, the participant's claim under the federal ERISA statute is the exclusive remedy against the ERISA plan. Any other remedy, such as a state-law claim for bad-faith denial of benefits, is preempted by federal law. Thus, a participant in an ERISA plan is entitled to recover the full amount of healthcare benefits that are payable under the plan, but may *not* recover damages in excess of that amount. A participant in an ERISA plan will *not* be able to recover punitive damages or compensation for pain and suffering as a result of an improper denial of healthcare benefits.

In creating new rights for employees, Congress also created a remedy to enforce those rights by suing in federal court for all of the benefits due under the plan. In some circumstances, that limited federal remedy may be effective and sufficient for the employee. For example, if pension benefits are wrongfully withheld, retirees can obtain reasonably effective relief by suing to recover the amount of benefits to which they are properly entitled under the plan. Similarly, in the traditional healthcare system that relied on retrospective UR, the employee could use the ERISA remedy to recover the money to pay for healthcare services that already had been provided. However, in a system of managed care that relies on prospective UR, the physical injury and emotional harm caused by the patient's inability to obtain necessary medical care cannot be adequately remedied by a subsequent award for the amount of benefits that were wrongfully denied. ERISA may have made sense back in 1974, under the healthcare system in effect at that time, but it is doubtful Congress ever intended to apply that law with regard to healthcare benefits in a system of prospective UR and actively managed care.

As applied to healthcare benefits in the system of managed care, the federal ERISA law creates two serious problems of public policy. First, ERISA plans have little or no financial incentive to authorize or pay for care. Many patients will not challenge their denials, and some of the patients who challenge the plan will ultimately lose. Even if patients or their estates were to sue the plan and win, the most severe penalty for a wrongful denial of care would be having to pay the original amount at some time in the future and possibly some attorney's fees. As a result of the federal ERISA law, employer-sponsored health plans have much to gain and little to lose by finding reasons to deny as many claims and requests as possible. Moreover, patients and their families will not be adequately compensated for their losses as a result of improper denials of care.

The second problem of public policy is that ERISA has created a disparity in cases of denial of care. In a rational legal system, similar cases should be decided in a similar manner, and the legal rights of individuals should not depend on fortuitous circumstances. However, because of ERISA, similar cases of treatment denial will lead to vastly different results, depending on where the patients obtained their health insurance coverage.

ERISA applies to employer-sponsored health plans in the private sector. It does not apply to health plans for state and local government employees or insurance coverage in the individual market. If a patient is covered under an individual policy or a state or local government plan, the MCO may be liable for huge compensatory and punitive damages under the law of the particular state. For example, in *Fox v. Health Net*,[6] the jury awarded $89 million against an HMO in a non-ERISA plan for improperly denying coverage of a bone marrow transplant for a patient with metastatic breast cancer. However, in a similar case involving a patient who was covered by an ERISA plan, *Spain v. Aetna Life Insurance Company*,[7] the patient's survivors could not recover compensatory or punitive damages for delay in authorizing a bone marrow transplant (see the excerpt from *Spain v. Aetna*.) As indicated by these cases, the legal rights of patients and their survivors will depend on the fortuitous circumstance of where the patient happened to obtain health insurance coverage. Moreover, only some types of health plans will be subject to the deterrent effect of potential damage awards.

Spain v. Aetna Life Insurance Company, 11 F.3d 129 (9th Cir. 1993) (Per Curiam), *Cert. Denied*, 511 U.S. 1052 (1994) (Citations Omitted)

Overview

A mother and daughter appeal the district court's dismissal of their wrongful death suit against Aetna Life Insurance Company ("Aetna"), the administrator of their husband's/father's employee benefit plan. They contend the district court erred by deciding that a state common law wrongful death action is preempted by the Employee Retirement Income Security Act ("ERISA") § 514(a), 29 U.S.C. § 1144(a). We do not agree and affirm the judgment.

Factual and Procedural Background

This suit is brought by Janelle and Margaret Spain (the "Spains"), Steven Spain's wife and daughter, respectively. Steven Spain was a plan participant and beneficiary in a self-funded employee benefit plan within the meaning of ERISA. His plan was administered by Aetna. Steven Spain was diagnosed as having testicular cancer. His doctors decided that an autologous bone marrow transplant ("ABMT") was necessary to attempt to save his life. Aetna pre-approved the first two parts of this three-part procedure. Initially, Aetna also authorized the last part of the procedure. However, Aetna later withdrew its authorization on the grounds that Steven Spain's diagnosed condition did not make him eligible for this procedure. Because Spain could not afford the final part of the procedure on his own, he brought suit against his employee benefit plan and its administrator, Aetna, to compel authorization of treatment. Two days after notification of the suit, the plan and Aetna authorized the last part of the procedure.

Appellants contend that "ABMT procedures can be performed successfully only during a very narrow window of time and by the time Aetna acknowledged its error and approved the procedure, Steven's window had closed." Thus, although the procedure was eventually completed, Appellants argue that Steven Spain's death was negligently caused by Aetna's initial denial in authorizing the procedure. At trial, the district court dismissed the case on the grounds that ERISA preempts Appellants' state law claim for wrongful death. This court has jurisdiction under 28 U.S.C. § 1291.

ANALYSIS

"The interpretation of ERISA, a federal statute, is a question of law subject to de novo review." Specifically, "ERISA preemption is a conclusion of law reviewed de novo."

The sole issue on review is whether ERISA preempts the state common law wrongful death action. ERISA's preemption clause is "deliberately expansive," and "contains one of the broadest preemption clauses ever enacted by Congress." The preemption clause states that the provisions provided by ERISA "shall supersede any and all State laws insofar as they may now or hereafter relate to any employee benefit plan . . ." 29 U.S.C. § 1144(a). Interpreting ERISA's preemption clause, the Supreme Court has instructed that "relates to" is to be "given its broad common-sense meaning." Therefore, a state cause of action relates to an ERISA benefit plan if operation of the law impinges on the functioning of an ERISA plan.

Appellants assert that Aetna's improper withdrawal of authorization for Steven Spain's ABMT procedure caused Steven Spain's death. Although Appellants do not seek benefits under the plan, their state common law cause of action seeks damages for the negligent administration of benefit claims. This circuit, following the lead of the Supreme Court in *Pilot Life Ins. Co. v. Dedeaux*, has held that "state common law causes of action arising from the improper processing of a claim are preempted by federal law." Hence, ERISA preempts Appellants' wrongful death action because the state law in its application directly "relates to" the administration and disbursement of ERISA plan benefits. Both the Fifth Circuit and Tenth Circuit, the only two circuits that have confronted the issue of whether ERISA preempts a state wrongful death action, have reached the same conclusion.

Further, a state wrongful death action is not "saved" by the sole exception to ERISA's preemption rule. Although the ERISA preemption clause is broad, Congress created an exception for "any law of any State which regulates insurance, banking, or securities." 29 U.S.C. § 1144(b)(2)(A). Under this exception, a law must not just have an impact on an insurance company, "but must be specifically directed toward that industry." The cause of action for wrongful death at issue in this appeal is a general tort and clearly was not specifically tailored by the state to regulate insurance, banking, or securities.

Congress carefully constructed the civil enforcement provisions allowed under ERISA. As the Court instructed, "the policy choices reflected in the inclusion of certain remedies and the exclusion of others under the federal scheme would be completely undermined if ERISA-plan participants and beneficiaries were free to obtain remedies under state law that Congress rejected in ERISA." As the Fifth Circuit stated:

> While we are not unmindful of the fact that our interpretation of the pre-emption clause leaves a gap in remedies within a statute intended to protect participants in employee benefit plans, the lack of an ERISA remedy does not affect a pre-emption analysis.

CONCLUSION

Because ERISA preempts the state common law wrongful death action and is not "saved" under the exception to ERISA's broad preemption, we affirm the judgment.

AFFIRMED.

The Statutory Language of ERISA

As enacted by Congress, the language of ERISA is incredibly confusing. One federal court described the preemption provision as "a veritable Sargasso Sea of obfuscation."[8] As the Supreme Court put it, the statutory provisions "perhaps are not a model of legislative drafting."[9]

In ERISA, Congress addressed the issue of federal preemption by means of three statutory clauses: the preemption clause, the saving clause, and the deemer clause.[10] Under the preemption clause, ERISA preempts state laws insofar as they relate to employee benefit plans that are regulated by ERISA. Thus, state law claims for wrongful denial of benefits are preempted by ERISA, and participants are limited to the exclusive remedy under the federal ERISA statute.

Under the saving clause, a few particular types of state laws are "saved" from preemption and therefore are not preempted. Specifically, state laws that regulate insurance are "saved" from preemption. Therefore, state governments may continue to regulate insurance, which is a traditional state function as described in Chapter 17.

Although states cannot regulate ERISA plans, they can use their power to regulate insurance as an indirect method of controlling those ERISA plans that purchase insurance for their employees and dependents. In effect, state governments can regulate some ERISA plans *indirectly* by regulating the insurance company that provides the group insurance policy for the ERISA plan or by regulating the terms of the group insurance contract. For example, assume that the state legislature has enacted a mandated-benefit law that requires all health insurance companies doing business in the state to include coverage for chiropractic services in all health insurance policies that are issued in the state. Assume further that an employer in the private sector does not want to include coverage for chiropractic services in its employee group health plan under ERISA. When the employer contacts various health insurance companies to inquire about a group policy of health insurance for its employees, it will find that every health insurance company authorized to do business in that state will insist on including coverage for chiropractic services, even though the employer does not want that particular coverage. Although the employer's ERISA plan is not subject to the state insurance law, all insurance companies in the state are subject to that law. In that way, state governments can effectively control the benefits provided by ERISA plans that purchase group policies of insurance.

ERISA plans can avoid the effect of state-mandated benefit laws in one way: by using the mechanism of self-insurance. If the ERISA plan is self-insured, the state cannot use that indirect method of regulation because the ERISA plan will not do business with any insurance company and will not obtain any policy of insurance. Under the third clause of the ERISA statute, which is referred to as the deemer clause, self-insured ERISA plans are *not* deemed to be insurance companies or to be in the business of insurance. In self-insured ERISA plans, therefore, there is no insurance company or insurance contract for the state to regulate, and those self-insured ERISA plans are beyond the reach of state authority.

With regard to state-mandated benefit laws, there is an important difference between *insured* ERISA plans and *self-insured* ERISA plans. State laws that mandate particular health insurance benefits will apply, albeit indirectly, to ERISA plans that purchase insurance. However, those state laws will not apply at all to ERISA plans that are self-insured.

For example, legislatures in many states enacted laws to prevent so-called "drive-through deliveries" by requiring health insurance companies in their states to provide coverage for at least 48 hours of inpatient care after normal delivery and at least 96 hours after caesarean section, subject to certain exceptions.[11] If an ERISA plan purchases a group health insurance policy in a state that has enacted that type of mandated-benefit law, the insured ERISA plan would have to offer extended maternity coverage as required by the law in that particular state. However, if the ERISA plan elects to self-insure, it would not be subject to the state-mandated benefit law on extended maternity coverage.

Under these circumstances, the only way to require self-insured ERISA plans to provide a particular level of maternity coverage is to enact a federal statute, which would not be preempted by the federal ERISA law. That is precisely what Congress did in 1996 when it enacted a federal law to impose specific requirements for maternity coverage on both insurance companies and self-insured ERISA plans.[12]

The foregoing discussion has focused on the differences between insured and self-insured ERISA plans with regard to the issue of state mandated-benefit laws. With regard to other issues, however, all ERISA plans are treated alike, and there are no practical differences between insured ERISA plans and self-insured ERISA plans. For this latter category of issues, the relevant distinction is between ERISA plans and non-ERISA plans. The most important issue in this latter category is the ability of an employee or dependent to assert state-law claims and remedies against the health-care benefit plan. According to the U.S. Supreme Court, ERISA preempts state-law claims and remedies even for insured ERISA plans.[13] Therefore, state-law claims and remedies will be preempted for both insured and self-insured ERISA plans.

Federal courts often recognize that ERISA's preemption of state-law claims and remedies can result in extreme injustice by depriving patients or their families of any effective remedy for serious injury or death.[14] However, courts also recognize that their role in this type of case is limited to interpreting and enforcing the ERISA statute in accordance with the intent of Congress. Even if they considered ERISA to be unfair and unwise as a matter of public policy, many courts have reluctantly concluded that their hands were tied and have strongly urged Congress to amend the statute.

For example, in concluding that a plaintiff's state-law claims were preempted by ERISA, one federal court wrote that, "[t]he tragic events set forth in Diane Andrews-Clarke's Complaint cry out for relief."[15] The court continued:

> Nevertheless, this Court had no choice but to pluck Diane Andrews-Clarke's case out of the state court in which she sought redress (and where relief to other litigants is available) and then, at the behest of Travelers and Greenspring, to slam the courthouse doors in her face and leave her without any remedy.[16]

In some cases, however, courts attempted to provide relief to patients or their survivors by characterizing the claim as a type of medical malpractice. Although ERISA preempts state-law claims for improper denial of benefits, it does not preempt claims for medical malpractice. Patients who are covered by ERISA plans have the same right as any other patients to sue their healthcare providers for medical malpractice, and they may recover compensatory and punitive damages to the extent allowed by the law of the particular state.

Some courts tried to extend that reasoning to the next logical step by allowing patients in ERISA plans to assert medical malpractice claims against their MCOs. Under that theory, the plaintiff would argue that the claim is not based on the MCO's denial of benefits, but rather on the MCO's failure to provide appropriate medical care. In other words, those plaintiffs insisted that they were complaining about the *quality* of care rather than the *quantity* of care. In addition, some state legislatures enacted statutes that provided a cause of action for people to sue MCOs for damages that are caused by the MCO's negligence in making certain types of treatment decisions.[17]

However, in its 2004 decision in *Aetna Health Inc. v. Davila*, the U.S. Supreme Court severely restricted those attempts to circumvent ERISA, by holding that claims under those state statutes were preempted and that plaintiffs' sole remedy was to sue under ERISA for the amount of benefits that had been denied.[18] Thus, a participant in an ERISA plan cannot get around the effect of ERISA preemption by suing under a state managed care law or by trying to recharacterize a claim for denial of benefits as a type of medical malpractice. As the Supreme Court explained, "if an individual, at some point in time, could have brought his claim under ERISA . . . , and where there is no other independent legal duty that is implicated by a defendant's actions, then the individual's cause of action is completely pre-empted by ERISA."[19] The Supreme Court left a small opening to bring state-law claims against those MCOs that employ physicians or are owned and operated by physicians.[20] However, the practical implication of the Supreme Court's opinion in *Davila* is that neither state legislatures nor lower federal courts will be able to solve the problems caused by ERISA preemption; any solution will have to come from the Congress.[21] To achieve a comprehensive solution, therefore, it will be necessary for Congress to amend the federal ERISA statute.

Proposals to Amend ERISA

Many people believe the best way to get around the problems caused by ERISA is for Congress to simply amend the law. In amending ERISA, one alternative would be to eliminate the federal preemption of state law claims and remedies for improper denial of benefits. Another alternative would be to retain the federal remedy under ERISA as the exclusive remedy for denial of benefits, but expand that federal remedy to permit the recovery of damages in excess of the benefits owed under the plan. In addition, it may be possible to compromise by making incremental changes to ERISA. For example, ERISA could be amended to permit the recovery of *some* additional types of damages, such as lost wages and other economic losses, but still retain certain limitations, such as placing a cap on damages for pain and suffering or limiting the recovery of punitive damages.[22]

For several years, an intense debate was waged in Congress over managed care regulation in general and ERISA preemption in particular. However, despite legislative proposals in 1997, 1998, 1999, and 2001, no federal legislation has been enacted at the time of this writing, and the stalemate over ERISA has prevented the enactment of other managed care reforms.

Members of Congress from both political parties have supported various proposals to amend ERISA.[23] In 1999, the Senate and House of Representatives each passed its own bill, but no agreement was achieved between them, and those bills were not enacted into law.[24] In 2001, the Senate and House of Representatives passed their respective bills with provisions to amend ERISA, but again neither bill was ultimately enacted into law.[25] Although each of those bills would have amended ERISA in some way, there were differences in the details that could not be overcome. Subsequently, similar bills were introduced in 2004 and 2005, but yet again no legislation has been enacted.[26]

Part of the difficulty in reaching an agreement on amending ERISA is determining the cost to health plans and society of allowing recovery of additional damages. Those opposed to amending ERISA argue that the change would lead to a significant escalation of healthcare costs. The issue of cost is not merely a question of projecting the total amount of jury verdicts and settlements that ERISA plans would be required to pay under an amended law. Rather, the issue is the extent to which healthcare costs would increase throughout the country if the law were changed to put ERISA plans at risk of substantial damages for improper denial of benefits. If ERISA plans were afraid to deny authorization for care, it is possible they would feel compelled to approve almost every claim and request for authorization, and society would no longer be able to rely on managed care to contain overall healthcare costs.

Experts disagree about the extent to which costs would be likely to increase as a result of amending ERISA. Even if the law were amended, ERISA plans would not have to approve almost every claim or request for authorization. Instead, ERISA plans would probably approve some additional claims, but they would also take other actions to protect themselves against potential liability. For example, they might rewrite the terms of their benefit plans to totally exclude coverage for certain types of treatment, such as bone marrow transplants, rather than making coverage depend on contestable issues such as whether the treatment is experimental or medically necessary in an individual case.

In 1998, the Congressional Budget Office (CBO) issued a cost estimate on a proposal for managed care reform, including a proposed amendment of ERISA to permit state-law claims for damages.[27] With regard to the proposed amendment of ERISA, CBO stated that, "[t]he cost of this provision depends on assumptions for which the supporting data are extremely limited or nonexistent."[28] Nevertheless, CBO estimated that amending ERISA would cause the premiums for employer-sponsored health plans to increase by only 1.2 percent.[29]

At about the same time that CBO issued its report, the U.S. General Accounting Office (GAO), now known as the Government Accountability Office, issued its own report to Congress with regard to the likely consequences of amending ERISA.[30] Following an excerpt from the GAO report. GAO's most significant finding is that there simply are not enough data to determine the effect of amending ERISA on the quality and cost of care.

U.S. GENERAL ACCOUNTING OFFICE. EMPLOYER-BASED MANAGED CARE PLANS: ERISA'S EFFECT ON REMEDIES FOR BENEFIT DENIALS AND MEDICAL MALPRACTICE, GAO/ HEHS-98–154 (JULY 13, 1998), 1–4

The Congress enacted the Employee Retirement Income Security Act (ERISA) nearly a quarter of a century ago to protect employee pension and welfare benefits. Employers often provide healthcare coverage as an employee welfare benefit. While employers have voluntarily provided healthcare benefits for more than 50 years, a major change has occurred in the type of benefits they now offer. By 1995, nearly three-quarters of those who received coverage through private, employer-based plans were enrolled in some form of managed care rather than in traditional fee-for-service plans. Many believe that, given this change, the protections under ERISA for those who have disputes over health care benefits should be reexamined. . . .

Compelling evidence is lacking on the likely effects of amending ERISA to provide either expanded remedies for losses due to disputed benefit denials or the ability to sue managed care plans for medical malpractice or other negligence under state tort laws. Predictions about the effects of amending ERISA differ markedly, depending on the perspectives of the group involved. Consumer groups and others assert that additional remedies could (1) improve health care quality by holding plans accountable for the consequences of their benefit coverage decisions and (2) provide participants with a course of remedies more comparable to state tort laws when injuries result. However, managed care plan and employer groups maintain instead that these additional provisions would result in increased costs or benefit reductions. Some suggest that additional costs could result from defensive measures and increased service use to guard against potential disputes or liability. According to plan and employer groups, managed care plans that experienced higher costs from increased liability would be likely to pass these costs on to employers who, in turn, might increase employee cost-sharing or cut back on healthcare coverage. To date, data are not available to accurately estimate the extent to which the quality of health care would improve or the amount by which the costs of plans, employers, and employees might change if either ERISA's remedies or preemption of state laws were amended. However, many have suggested that an "upstream" approach—that is, one that seeks to address disputed benefit denials at an earlier stage and thus prevent court suits—may also warrant consideration during the debate on ERISA.

In the foregoing report, GAO recognized the potential advantages of using an "upstream" approach in attempting to resolve disputes over healthcare benefits without the need for litigation. The upstream approach would include a realistic opportunity for the patient to appeal the health plan's denial of benefits and receive a prompt and fair reconsideration of the claim. For health plans that are sponsored by private employers under ERISA, the U.S. Department of Labor has adopted rules that require specific procedures for filing claims, providing notice of decisions, and appealing "adverse benefit determinations."[31] These federal rules apply to *all* ERISA plans, regardless of whether they are insured or self-insured. However, these federal rules only apply to internal review-of-benefit decisions within the plan and do not impose any requirement for independent, external review.[32] In its preamble, the U.S. Department of Labor made it clear that, "[t]here is nothing in the regulation, however, that would preclude a claimant from voluntarily submitting a claim for review pursuant to a State-provided external review process."[33]

According to a report prepared for the Kaiser Family Foundation in 2002, more than 40 states have adopted laws that give patients the right to obtain an independent review of their disputes with health plans.[34] In almost all of those states, the external review decision is binding on the health plan. As of the date of that report, patients had won in approximately half of those external reviews, but few patients had exercised the right to external review.[35] It is also important to note that state external-review laws do not apply to participants in self-insured ERISA plans, which are beyond the reach of state authority.[36] In addition, Congress has considered proposed federal legislation to require independent, external review for health insurance companies and group health plans, including self-insured plans,[37] but here again it is unclear whether any legislation will be enacted.

In 2002, the U.S. Supreme Court ruled in *Rush Prudential HMO, Inc. v. Moran*[38] that states may require HMOs and insurance companies to provide a system for external review of benefit denials. The Illinois statute in that case required HMOs to provide a review by an unaffiliated physician with regard to the issue of medical necessity and even required the HMO to abide by the decision of the unaffiliated physician. The HMO argued that the state external-review law was preempted by ERISA, on the ground that the state law created a new remedy for the patient that differs from the exclusive remedy in federal court under ERISA. However, the U.S. Supreme Court held that the state external-review law was not preempted by ERISA, because the state law did not create any new type of claim, and it does not allow the patient to recover damages in excess of the benefits owed under the plan.[39] The court recognized that the external- review decision would be binding on the HMO, but considered that to be similar to the accepted practice of requiring HMOs and insurance companies to obtain a second medical opinion before denying a request for coverage.[40] Under the court's decision in *Moran*, states may use their authority to regulate the business of insurance to require HMOs and insurance companies to provide independent, external review, but those state laws would not apply to self-insured ERISA plans.[41]

External review is a promising upstream approach for handling benefit disputes. As a practical matter, it can be very beneficial for the patient, the health plan, and the healthcare system as a whole. External review does not provide the level of compensation and deterrence that would be provided by a lawsuit for compensatory and punitive damages. Nevertheless, patients might be able to obtain the treatment they desire through the external review process and, at the very least, may think they are finally receiving a fair hearing by an impartial decision maker. In that way, patients may be more satisfied with the healthcare system and less likely to file time-consuming and expensive litigation. For patients to have confidence in external review, however, it is crucial to ensure that the process is truly fair and independent.

External review can also provide significant advantages for a health plan. If the independent reviewer agrees with the patient, the plan would pay for the requested procedure and the patient would have no reason to sue the plan for compensatory and punitive damages. On the other hand, if the independent reviewer agrees that the health plan acted properly in denying the claim, the patient would still be able to sue the plan. However, under those circumstances, it would be very difficult for the patient to show that the plan had acted in bad faith in denying the claim, and the plan would not likely be required to pay punitive damages. Thus, external review can be beneficial for all parties, and it has been an important part of the legislative proposals for patients' rights and managed care reform.

Placing Managed Care Reform and Patients' Rights in Perspective

Most of the principles of healthcare law and ethics were developed under the traditional system of fee-for-service medicine, indemnity insurance, and free choice of provider. In an effort to reduce the spiraling cost of services, however, many third-party payers have adopted the techniques that are collectively referred to as managed care. Under these circumstances, one of the most important and interesting issues in healthcare law and ethics is how to apply the preexisting legal and ethical rules to the new types of problems that arise under cost containment and managed care.

When problems arise, such as a bad medical outcome or a dispute with a third-party payer, we begin to resolve those problems by considering the legal and ethical principles that already exist. The challenge is to figure out the best way to apply those legal and ethical principles to the new system and determine whether those principles need to be changed. In considering whether to apply an old legal rule to a new situation, we need to ask ourselves whether this new application of the rule would be fair, whether it would be effective, and whether it would promote the underlying policy goal on which the rule was originally based.

In some cases, there may be a question of whether a physician should be held liable for a bad medical outcome, such as the death of a patient. In addition, there may be a dispute between a patient or the patient's family and a third-party payer over the payer's refusal to authorize care. Finally, there may be a disagreement between a physician and a third-party payer over the appropriate standard of care and a physician's right to treat patients enrolled in that plan.

On each of these issues, there is a traditional body of rules to which we can turn, but now we have to apply those traditional rules in a very different context. A comprehensive set of legal rules on medical malpractice has been developed and refined for centuries. In addition, long-standing principles of medical ethics govern the doctor–patient relationship. Only in recent years, however, have we had to apply those rules of malpractice law and principles of medical ethics to the new circumstances of managed care. In our new healthcare system, patients may be restricted in their choice of a physician. Moreover, some physicians may have a financial interest in providing less care to each of their patients, and they may be terminated by the payer if they provide what the provider considers to be too many tests or treatments. Under the traditional fee-for-service system, a set of legal rules was developed to regulate financial incentives to provide *more* tests and treatments. However, we have not yet developed a comprehensive and coherent set of rules to regulate financial incentives to provide less care under the new system of managed care.

Similarly, our legal and ethical concepts of informed consent have traditionally been limited to a requirement to disclose the risks of, benefits of, and alternatives to the proposed treatment. Now that we have moved to a different type of healthcare system, we may want to expand the concept of informed consent to require disclosure of a physician's financial interests.

Another example of the need to apply traditional rules in the new context involves disputes between patients and third-party payers. In the past, those disputes were often limited to the financial issue of whether the payer would be required to pay for care that the provider had already rendered to the patient. Thus, the issue was merely whether the payer, the provider, or the patient would be left "holding the bag" after the treatment had already been rendered. In contrast, payers now use managed care techniques, such as preadmission certification and prior approval, to control expenditures by denying authorization for expensive medical care at the outset. The nature of the dispute between patients and payers has fundamentally changed from an issue of financial liability to an issue of access to lifesaving medical care. We need to carefully consider, therefore, whether the traditional legal principles that had been applied to disputes with payers in the past are sufficient to resolve the new types of problems. In fact, that is the issue at the heart of the debate over patients' rights and managed care reform.

For several years, the media reported frequently about denial of care by MCOs. People were outraged to read that MCOs had denied authorization for lifesaving medical care, such as bone marrow transplants for patients who were dying of cancer. A public reaction against managed care resulted, and Congress debated numerous proposals to reform the system. In 1996, President Clinton created the Advisory Commission on Consumer Protection and Quality in the Health Care Industry,[42] which issued its *Consumer Bill of Rights and Responsibilities* on November 20, 1997.[43] As of spring 2007, however, Congress has still not succeeded in enacting legislation on managed care reform.

With regard to most aspects of managed care reform, the various bills considered by Congress have differed very little. The only issue on which there has been strong disagreement is the amount or type of damages that should be recoverable against a health plan for improper denial of benefits or refusal to authorize care. That one issue prevented Congress from enacting any legislation on patients' rights and managed care reform. In the meantime, the public reaction against managed care caused important changes in the competitive market, as some health plans abandoned techniques that consumers found particularly objectionable.

It is also important to remember that managed care arose for a reason. Under the traditional healthcare system, costs were out of control and increasing at an alarming rate. Therefore, third-party payers developed the techniques of managed care to restrain the costs of treating their enrollees or beneficiaries. It is convenient to blame the HMOs and other payers for instituting those cost-control techniques, but the reality is that most members of our society are unwilling to pay the additional taxes or insurance premiums that would be required to provide every person in the country with every type of potentially beneficial care. Many people recognize the need to impose some limitations on care, as long as it does not adversely affect them or any members of their family. In fact, many people recognize the need to control healthcare expenditures, at least for other people, but do not want *their* care to be "managed."

The demand for healthcare services is nearly infinite and continues to increase with advances in medical science and technology. Unfortunately, we do not have sufficient resources to meet all of that demand, and we do not want to devote all of society's resources to healthcare services to the exclusion of all other societal goals. By imposing limits on treatment, the system of managed care forced us to address the legal and ethical issues of rationing, which many people would prefer not to confront.

Under these circumstances, few people are proposing to go back to the largely unrestricted system that existed before managed care. Despite the strong rhetoric against HMOs and other health plans, most of the proposals for reform have been fairly modest and need to be kept in perspective. Generally, those proposals have accepted the continued existence of managed care and its basic techniques of cost containment.

Although differences are seen among the various proposals for reform, none of the proposals would outlaw the practice of selective contracting or require MCOs to accept any willing provider in their managed care networks. None of the proposals would prohibit the use of capitation as a financial incentive. None of the proposals would outlaw the use of prospective UR or prior authorization. Instead, most of the proposed changes would merely modify the system of managed care in specific ways, such as requiring additional disclosure to the enrollee, eliminating the most egregious types of financial incentives, and improving procedures to appeal the denial of benefits. In addition, Congress has considered proposed legislation to require payment for emergency services when a prudent layperson would have considered the condition to be an emergency and to provide additional rights for patients whose physicians are terminated by the plan during the patient's course of treatment. As already discussed, some of the proposals for reform would expand the liability of health plans for damages caused by improper denial of benefits, but that expansion of liability would not mean that managed care would cease to exist.

The U.S. healthcare system may be viewed as alternating between two undesirable extremes. The traditional system was too costly, and, therefore, our society developed the new techniques of cost containment and managed care. Subsequently, many people concluded that the effort to contain costs had gone too far, and we needed to put renewed emphasis on access and quality of care. Hopefully, as the pendulum swings back and forth between these two extremes, we can find the appropriate compromise among all of society's healthcare goals. The Congressional proposals for reform appear to be a step in that direction by permitting the continued existence of managed care while eliminating its most undesirable aspects.

It is also important to remember that managed care reform can only improve quality and access for people who are already covered by some type of healthcare benefit plan. Therefore, reform of the managed care system may lead to better care for the "haves," but would do little or nothing to help the "have-nots." As we consider proposals for managed care reform, we also need to develop ways to increase insurance coverage for the uninsured and underinsured and promote access to care for all members of our society. In Chapter 17, the legal aspects of health insurance and the ongoing effort to achieve universal health insurance coverage are considered.

PROBLEM 16.1: MR. ALBERT CRENSHAW

Mr. Albert Crenshaw, aged 45 years, is employed as a computer specialist. Through his employer in the private sector, he has obtained health coverage with the Happy Family Health Plan, which is an MCO. Happy Family has a network of participating physicians who have agreed to provide services to Happy Family enrollees.

Each enrollee is required to choose a PCP from Happy Family's list of participating physicians. Because Mr. Crenshaw had recently moved to the area, he did not know any doctors. Therefore, he chose Dr. Julia Smith as his PCP because she was on the list for Happy Family's network.

Dr. Smith is a physician in private practice. Happy Family entered into a participating physician contract with her because she was willing to provide services at a discount. In paying Dr. Smith, Happy Family withholds 20 percent of her fee for each visit and puts that 20 percent into a risk pool. At the end of the year, Dr. Smith will share in any money left in the pool.

Happy Family's participating physician agreement is a standard form contract. It specifies that participating physicians are independent contractors, rather than employees or agents of Happy Family. In addition, the contract between Happy Family and Dr. Smith provides that it may be terminated by either party, with or without cause, on 30 days' notice to the other party.

In the community in which Dr. Smith practices, it has been routine medical practice for many years to give an electrocardiogram (EKG) to any patient older than 40 years who complains of chest pains. However, on October 5, 1998, Happy Family sent a bulletin to Dr. Smith and the other participating physicians with regard to Happy Family's new policy on EKGs. Under that new policy, EKGs will only be covered by the plan if the patient is older than 50 years.

Approximately three weeks later, on October 25, 1998, Mr. Crenshaw began experiencing chest pains after working out at his gym during his lunch hour. He immediately went to Dr. Smith's office. She knew Mr. Crenshaw was covered by the Happy Family Health Plan, and she remembered the recent bulletin she had received from the plan. Dr. Smith examined Mr. Crenshaw but did not perform an EKG, even though performing an EKG under those circumstances was the routine practice in the community at that time.

Dr. Smith advised Mr. Crenshaw that it was safe for him to go back to work. Mr. Crenshaw did go back to work, where he died of a heart attack two hours later.

As soon as Dr. Smith heard about the death of Mr. Crenshaw, she called the president of Happy Family Health Plan. Dr. Smith told him that from now on she was going to order an EKG for every patient who needs it, regardless of age. The next day, Happy Family responded by giving Dr. Smith 30 days' notice of termination from the plan, which would effectively prevent her from treating any Happy Family patients.

Subsequently, Mr. Crenshaw's widow sued Dr. Smith for medical malpractice in state court. The plaintiff (Mrs. Crenshaw) had an expert witness who testified that Mr. Crenshaw would *not* have died if he had been given an EKG instead of being sent back to work. Mrs. Crenshaw also claimed that Happy Family gave financial incentives to Dr. Smith to encourage her to provide less care to patients covered by the plan. According to Mrs. Crenshaw and her lawyer, those financial incentives should be illegal and, at the very least, should have been fully disclosed to Mr. Crenshaw.

In response, Dr. Smith denied that she was liable for the death of Mr. Crenshaw. According to Dr. Smith, she satisfied the new standard of care as established by the Happy Family Health Plan. In addition, Dr. Smith's lawyer argued that the financial arrangements between Dr. Smith and Happy Family were entirely lawful and that Dr. Smith had no legal obligation to disclose her financial arrangements to Mr. Crenshaw. Finally, Dr. Smith's lawyer contended that the medical malpractice case should be thrown out of court because of the federal law known as ERISA, which regulates employer-sponsored health plans such as Mr. Crenshaw's plan.

In addition, Mrs. Crenshaw sued the Happy Family Health Plan in state court for damages caused by Happy Family's improper denial of benefits. According to Mrs. Crenshaw, Happy Family's refusal to pay for a necessary diagnostic test was a substantial cause of her husband's death. Therefore, Mrs. Crenshaw claimed that she is entitled to $1 million from Happy Family to compensate her and her children for 20 years of Mr. Crenshaw's lost wages. In addition, she asked the court to make Happy Family pay $10 million in punitive damages to teach them a lesson and encourage them to change their policy for the future. However, Happy Family's defense lawyer responded that the case against Happy Family may only be heard in federal court because of the federal ERISA law on employee health plans. Moreover, according to Happy Family's lawyer, even if Mrs. Crenshaw wins her case, she cannot recover $1 million in lost wages or $10 million in punitive damages from Happy Family. Rather, the most that she can possibly recover against Happy Family is the cost of the EKG exam, which should have been covered by the plan.

Who is likely to prevail on each claim, and why?

Notes

1. *Wickline v. State of California*, 239 Cal. Rptr. 810, 811–812 (Cal. Ct. App. 1986).

2. See *Murphy v. Board of Medical Examiners of the State of Arizona*, 949 P.2d 530, 532 (Ariz. Ct. App. 1997), *cert. denied*, Dec. 15, 1997.

3. See, e.g., *State Board of Registration for the Healing Arts v. Fallon*, 41 S.W.3d 474 (Mo. 2001).

4. See 1999 Ohio Op. Atty Gen. 265 (1999) (citing Attorney General opinions from a number of states).

5. 29 U.S.C. §§ 1001 *et seq.* (2006).

6. 29 Trials Digest 54, 1993 WL 794305 (Cal. Super. Ct. 1993).

7. 11 F.3d 129 (9th Cir. 1993) (per curiam), *cert. denied*, 511 U.S. 1052 (1994).

8. *Travelers Ins. Co. v. Cuomo*, 14 F.3d 708, 717 (2d Cir. 1993), *rev'd. sub nom New York State Conf. of Blue Cross & Blue Shield Plans v. Travelers Ins. Co.*, 514 U.S. 645 (1995).

9. *Metropolitan Life. Ins. Co. v. Massachusetts*, 471 U.S. 724, 739 (1985).

10. See 29 U.S.C. § 1144(a)–(b) (2006).

11. See generally W.H. Dow, D.M. Harris, and Z. Liu, "Differential Effectiveness in Patient Protection Laws: What Are the Causes? An Example from the Drive-Through Delivery Laws," *Journal of Health Politics, Policy and Law* 31(6):1107–1127 (2006); D.A. Hyman, "Drive-Through Deliveries: Is 'Consumer Protection' Just what the Doctor Ordered?" *North Carolina Law Review*, 78 (1999): 5–99.

12. See Newborns' and Mothers' Health Protection Act of 1996, Pub. L. No. 104-204, tit. VI § 711, 110 Stat. 2874, 2935 (1996) (codified at 29 U.S.C. § 1185).

13. *Pilot Life Ins. Co. v. Dedeaux*, 481 U.S. 41 (1987) (state law claim was preempted even with regard to the insurance company that had issued the group policy).

14. See, e.g., *Corcoran v. United Healthcare, Inc.*, 965 F.2d 1321, 1338–39 (5th Cir. 1992), *cert. denied*, 506 U.S. 1033 (1992).

15. *Andrews-Clarke v. Travelers Ins. Co.*, 984 F. Supp. 49, 52 (D. Mass. 1997).

16. *Id*. at 53 (footnote omitted).

17. See, e.g., Texas Health Care Liability Act, Tex. Civ. Prac. & Rem. Code Ann., §§ 88.001–88.003 (West 1998).

18. *Aetna Health Inc. v. Davila*, 542 U.S. 200 (2004).

19. *Id*. at 210.

20. T.S. Jost, "The Supreme Court Limits Lawsuits Against Managed Care Organizations," *Health Affairs* (Web Exclusive) (August 11, 2004): W4-417 at W4-423 to W4-424.

21. *Id.* at W4-425 ("This leads to the final ramification of *Davila*. If anyone is going to permit tort actions to be brought against managed care organizations, it will have to be Congress.").

22. See, e.g., H.R. 2563, 107th Cong. § 402 (2001); S. 374, 106th Cong., tit. III, § 302 (1999).

23. See, e.g., S. 1052, 107th Cong. § 402 (2001); H.R. 2563, 107th Cong. § 402 (2001); H.R. 216, 106th Cong., tit. III, § 302 (1999); H.R. 358, 106th Cong., tit. III, § 302 (1999); H.R. 3605, 105th Cong., tit. III, § 302 (1998); H.R. 1415, 105th Cong. (1997).

24. S.1344, 106th Cong. (1999); H.R. 2723, 106th Cong. (1999).

25. S.1052, 107th Cong. § 402 (2001); H.R. 2563, 107th Cong. § 402 (2001).

26. See E. Barnidge, "What Lies Ahead for ERISA's Preemption Doctrine After a Judicial Call to Action Is Issued in Aetna Health Inc.," *Houston Law Review* 43 (2006): 125–158, at 152–53 (2006).

27. U.S. Congressional Budget Office, *Cost Estimate: H.R.3605/S.1890: Patient Bill of Rights Act of 1998* (July 16, 1998). [Online information; retrieved 2/14/07.] www.cbo.gov/showdoc.cfm?index=667 &sequence=0.

28. *Id.* at 16.

29. *Id.* at 3–4 (Table 2), 18.

30. U.S. General Accounting Office, *Employer-Based Managed Care Plans: ERISA's Effect on Remedies for Benefit Denials and Medical Malpractice*, GAO/HEHS-98–154 (July 13, 1998). [Online document; retrieved 2/14/07.] www.gao.gov/archive/1998/ he98154.pdf.

31. 29 C.F.R. § 2560.503–1(b) (2006).

32. See *id.* at § 2560.503–1(k)(2)(ii) (recognizing that procedures for external review are not encompassed within § 503 of ERISA, 29 U.S.C. § 1133, pursuant to which the secretary of labor adopted the claims procedure rules).

33. U.S. Department of Labor, Employee Retirement Income Security Act of 1974, Rules and Regulations for Administration and Enforcement, Claims Procedure, 65 Fed. Reg. 70,246, 70,254 (November 21, 2000).

34. K. Pollitz, et al., *Assessing State External Review Programs and the Effects of Pending Federal Patients' Rights Legislation* (revised May 2002), at v, vii. [Online document; retrieved 2/14/07.] www.kff.org/insurance/externalreviewpart2rev.pdf.

35. See also Kaiser Family Foundation and Consumers Union, "A Consumer Guide to Handling Disputes with Your Employer or

Private Health Plan, 2005 Update," (2005), at 26–28. [Online document; retrieved 2/8/07.] www.kff.org/consumerguide/upload/7350ConsumerGuidev4_080805.pdf (reviewing the results of external reviews in various states as of 2005).

36. Pollitz, et al., *supra* note 34 at v, viii.

37. See H.R. 2563, § 104, 107th Cong. (2001); S. 1052, § 104, 107th Cong. (2001).

38. 122 S. Ct. 2151 (2002).

39. *Id.* at 2167.

40. *Id.* at 2169 and n.13.

41. See *id.* at 2162 n.6 ("Illinois's Act would not be 'saved' as an insurance law to the extent it applied to self-funded plans.").

42. See Exec. Order No. 13,017, 61 Fed. Reg. 47,659 (1996), amended by Exec. Order No. 13,040, 62 Fed. Reg. 14,773 (1997).

43. See generally President's Advisory Commission on Consumer Protection and Quality in the Health Care Industry, *Quality First: Better Health Care for All Americans.* [Online document; retrieved 2/14/07.] www.hcqualitycommission.gov/final/.

HEALTH INSURANCE AND THE ONGOING EFFORT TO ACHIEVE UNIVERSAL COVERAGE

To ensure that every individual has access to care, we need to adopt laws and regulations to increase the extent of health insurance coverage. In addition, we need to regulate the market for insurance and the business of insurance for the protection of the public.

This chapter addresses the major legal issues with regard to health insurance. First, we discuss the regulation of insurance and the roles played by state and federal governments in regulating insurance. Then, we consider the problems involved in using the law to increase access to health insurance coverage. Finally, this chapter describes the important efforts of state governments to achieve universal health insurance coverage, and considers the way in which federal law may pose a barrier to health reform in the individual states.

State Regulation of Insurance Companies and HMOs

In addition to regulating healthcare providers, governments regulate third-party payers, such as health insurance companies, to protect consumers. After individuals and groups pay for health insurance or health maintenance organization (HMO) coverage, it is important to ensure that the benefits will be available when people become sick or injured. In addition, we can protect consumers by regulating the rates, contract terms, marketing, disclosures, and claims practices of insurance companies and HMOs. Finally, we can try to promote access to coverage for the millions of people who are uninsured and prevent the loss of coverage as a result of a change in employment or family status.

In light of these important policy concerns, it is not surprising that insurance has been one of the most intensively regulated industries in the United States. Because insurance companies operate in interstate commerce, they clearly fall within the regulatory power of the federal government. However, in the McCarran-Ferguson Act of 1945,[1] Congress chose to leave the regulation of the insurance business primarily to the states. For more than 50 years, insurance companies have been regulated by state insurance commissioners in each state. In addition, state officials regulate HMOs as well as Blue Cross and Blue Shield plans. Nevertheless, federal laws may be applied to the insurance industry if those laws specifically relate to the business of insurance or if those laws are consistent with state policies and regulation.[2]

One of the most important goals of state insurance regulation is to ensure that the company is solvent and financially responsible. Under a contract of insurance, individuals and groups pay premiums to the company in advance, and they rely on the company to remain in business and have sufficient assets to pay the claims that arise in the future. Therefore, state insurance laws require companies to demonstrate that they have sufficient assets before they can obtain a license to do business in the state. In addition, state insurance commissioners will audit the companies on a periodic basis and will require the companies to maintain adequate reserves. If an insurance company is at risk of becoming insolvent, the state insurance commissioner may appoint a rehabilitator or receiver to manage the affairs of the company for the protection of the policyholders. As a last resort, claims for benefits may be paid by a state insurance guaranty association, which is funded by all of the other insurance companies that have obtained authority to do business in the state.

In addition to ensuring the solvency of health insurance companies and HMOs, state officials may regulate the rates and terms of the insurance or HMO contract. For example, many states have enacted statutes that require all health insurance contracts to provide coverage for specific services, such as mammograms, Pap smears, and prostate-cancer screening. However, as discussed in Chapter 16, these state insurance laws do *not* apply to self-insured employee benefit plans that are covered by the federal Employee Retirement Income Security Act (ERISA) law.

The Problem of Extending Access to Coverage

Although the estimates vary, it is clear that millions of Americans lack health insurance coverage. Some of the uninsured work for small employers that do not offer health insurance coverage to their employees, and others work on a part-time or seasonal basis and might not qualify for insurance benefits. In addition, some people are unable to purchase individual coverage because of a preexisting medical condition, or they may be limited to inadequate coverage at an exorbitant rate. As a general rule, employers have no legal obligation to offer health insurance benefits to their employees, and insurance companies have no legal obligation to provide coverage to any particular individual. Unfortunately, the solution is not as simple as merely passing laws to require all insurance companies and HMOs to provide coverage to everyone at an affordable rate.

If we enact a law that requires all insurers to charge everyone the same rate, which is referred to as community rating, people who are young and healthy will have to pay higher premiums to subsidize people who are old and sick. Many of the young and healthy may be unwilling or unable to pay the higher community-rated premium and will simply forgo purchasing any health insurance. After all, they are currently young and healthy. However, removing many of the young and healthy people from the risk pool would cause premiums to rise even more for those who remain in the system. Therefore, simply passing a law to require community rating would not be sufficient.

Similarly, merely adding a requirement to cover all applicants, regardless of their health status, would not be sufficient. If we pass a law to require insurance companies and HMOs to cover everyone who applies and prohibit exclusion on the basis of health status, the rates will increase as older and sicker people are brought into the risk pool. Again, many of the young and healthy would drop out of the system and simply go without insurance coverage. If the uninsured young people ever become seriously ill or injured, they could purchase health insurance at that point and could not be denied coverage at that time on the basis of their medical condition. Because healthy people would have no incentive to buy health insurance, the rates for everyone else would increase. That would cause even more people to drop out, and eventually the entire health insurance system would self-destruct in a so-called "death spiral." Thus, reforming the insurance market to extend coverage to the uninsured is not as simple as merely enacting laws to require community rating or prohibit exclusion on the basis of health status.

To accomplish our policy goals, we probably need a system of universal coverage in which the young and healthy people cannot simply choose to drop out. One way to achieve a system of universal coverage is the Canadian-style single-payer system, which is funded by tax revenues. However, universal coverage can be achieved in other ways. The Clinton administration had proposed a system of employer mandates, which would have required all employers to provide health insurance. In addition, some members of Congress had proposed a system of individual mandates in which each person would be legally obligated to purchase health insurance. Of course, employer mandates would have to be accompanied by subsidies for the unemployed, and individual mandates would have to be accompanied by subsidies for those unable to afford coverage.

So far, our society has not been willing to adopt any of these methods of achieving universal coverage. Therefore, Congress has been attempting to reform the health insurance system on an incremental basis. In some ways, incremental reform is more difficult than developing a system of universal coverage, because of the danger that reform will cause young and healthy people to simply forgo coverage. The practical problem of insurance reform, therefore, is to develop ways to improve access to coverage and portability of coverage for as many people as possible without raising premiums so much that healthy people will drop out of the system.

Partially in response to this problem, President Clinton signed the Health Insurance Portability and Accountability Act (HIPAA) of 1996 on August 21, 1996.[3] Sometimes this federal statute is referred to as Kassebaum-Kennedy because it was sponsored by Senator Nancy Kassebaum (R-KS) and Senator Edward Kennedy (D-MA). Among other provisions, HIPAA imposes significant requirements on self-insured employee health plans, as well as on insurance companies that provide coverage to large groups, small groups, and individuals.

In the group insurance market, health plans can only exclude coverage of preexisting conditions for a maximum of 12 months in most cases. Moreover, that 12-month period of exclusion must be reduced by the individual's prior periods of creditable coverage, so long as no break in coverage lasts more than 63 days. For example, a new employee at Company X may be subject to a 12-month preexisting condition exclusion under Company X's employee health plan. However, that employee is generally entitled to credit against that 12-month exclusion period any time that he was covered under a previous employer's plan, provided there was no break in coverage of more than 63 days.

This provision for credit against the new employer's period of exclusion is referred to as group-to-group portability. This type of "portability," however, does not mean employees will take their old insurance coverage with them to their new jobs. Rather, group-to-group portability under HIPAA refers to getting credit against the period of exclusion for preexisting conditions when the employee obtains coverage under the *new* employer's plan. HIPAA portability, therefore, is different from continuation coverage under the federal Consolidated Omnibus Budget Reconciliation Act, in which former employees may elect to continue their *old* coverage for a limited period of time at their own expense.[4]

In the individual insurance market, HIPAA specifies that all health insurers that sell individual policies in the state are required to provide individual coverage, upon request, to all persons who qualify as "eligible individuals." This concept is referred to as group-to-individual portability, because it applies to people who lost their group coverage and wish to buy coverage in the individual market. However, the definition of "eligible individual" in HIPAA is very restrictive and essentially includes only those people who were covered for a substantial period of time before losing their coverage. Moreover, federal law does not limit the premiums that insurers may charge eligible individuals, but those rates may be regulated by state law.[5]

Originally, the proposed legislation had contained a provision for parity of mental health benefits, which would have required a health plan to provide the same level of benefits for mental illness as the plan provided for physical illness. Congress deleted that provision from the final HIPAA legislation. A few weeks later, however, Congress enacted a very limited provision for mental health parity as well as a requirement for maternity coverage of at least 48 hours in the hospital after normal delivery and at least 96 hours after caesarean section.[6] Since that time, Congress has continued to debate the possible continuation and expansion of the federal requirements for mental health parity, but those issues have not been fully resolved. The separate requirements for 48-hour and 96-hour maternity coverage are discussed in Chapter 16.

State Efforts to Achieve Universal Health Insurance Coverage

As already discussed, Congress has taken only incremental steps toward the goal of increasing health insurance coverage. Those steps have included protecting people who already have coverage from losing their coverage when they change jobs or lose their jobs. In addition, federal efforts have included creating the State Children's Health Insurance Program in 1997, as described in Chapter 8. Federal efforts have not succeeded in creating a system of universal coverage, and, therefore, the focus of reform has shifted to the individual states.

A few states have enacted laws in an attempt to create universal or near-universal coverage, and many other states have been considering ways to expand coverage in their respective states. In January 2007, the *Washington Post* described "a wave of experiments at the state level."[7] These state experiments can be very useful by trying alternatives for which a consensus cannot be reached at the national level. In addition, successful experiments at the state level can provide models for subsequent adoption on a national basis. Both Congress and the Supreme Court have recognized that the states can serve as laboratories for experimentation in healthcare reform.[8]

In 2006, Massachusetts adopted a comprehensive law on healthcare reform.[9] Although former Governor Romney vetoed several provisions of that bill, the state legislature overrode all of the governor's vetoes. The new law imposes requirements on employers, and it requires individuals to obtain health insurance coverage if they can afford do so. The law creates a system of subsidies for those whose income is too high to qualify for Medicaid but too low as a practical matter to be able to purchase health insurance. Rather than continuing to use large amounts of public funds to pay hospitals for providing care for the indigent, the new system shifts some of those funds to providing subsidies for uninsured individuals to purchase health insurance coverage.[10] Following is a summary of the new Massachusetts law from the state legislature's Conference Committee, dated April 3, 2006.

HEALTH CARE ACCESS AND AFFORDABILITY
CONFERENCE COMMITTEE REPORT

SUMMARY

This Conference Committee Report contains a comprehensive plan for increasing health insurance coverage for all residents of Massachusetts. This bill is a bridge between principles in the House and Senate bills, H 4479 and S 2282. The bill would redeploy current public funds to more effectively cover currently uninsured low-income populations, and would make quality health coverage more affordable for *all* residents of the Commonwealth. The bill promotes individual responsibility by creating a requirement that everyone who can afford health insurance obtain it, while also responding to concerns about barriers to health care access. Provisions in the bill aim at achieving nearly universal health insurance coverage, but also maintain a strong safety net that has historically distinguished the state. Finally, the bill would ensure that the Massachusetts Medicaid program complies with the terms of the new federal waiver, maintaining continued receipt of annual payments from the federal Medicaid program.

A) COMMONWEALTH HEALTH INSURANCE CONNECTOR

The bill creates the Commonwealth Health Insurance Connector, to connect individuals and small businesses with health insurance products. The Connector certifies and offers products of high value and good quality. Individuals who are employed are able to purchase insurance using pre-tax dollars. The Connector allows for portability of insurance as individuals move from job to job, and permits more than one employer to contribute to an employee's health insurance premium. The Connector is to be operated as an authority under the Department of Administration and Finance and overseen by a separate, appointed Board of private and public representatives.

B) INSURANCE MARKET REFORMS

The bill merges the non- and small-group markets in July 2007, a provision that will produce an estimated drop of 24 percent in non-group premium costs. An actuarial study of the merging of the two insurance markets will be completed before the merger to assist insurers in planning for the transition. The bill also enables HMOs to offer coverage plans that are linked to Health Savings Accounts, reducing costs for those who enroll in such plans. Young adults will be able to stay on their parents' insurance plans for two years past the loss of their dependent status, or until they turn 25 (whichever occurs first), and 19–26 year-olds [sic] will be eligible for lower-cost, specially designed products offered through the Connector. Finally, the bill would impose a moratorium on the creation of new health insurance mandated benefits through 2008.

C) Subsidized Health Insurance
Commonwealth Care Health Insurance
The bill creates a subsidized insurance program called the Commonwealth Care Health Insurance Program. Individuals who earn less than 300 percent FPL and are ineligible for MassHealth will qualify for coverage. Premiums for the program will be set on a sliding scale based on household income, and no plans offered through this program will have deductibles. The program will be operated through the Connector, and retain any employer contribution to an employee's health insurance premium. The subsidized products must be certified by the Connector as being of high value and good quality.

For individuals who earn less than 100 percent of the Federal Poverty Level ($9,600/yr), special protections in this bill provide for subsidized insurance products with comprehensive benefits, and waive any premiums. Currently, most childless adults are not eligible for MassHealth at any income level, unless they are disabled or have very little history of employment.

Insurance Partnership Program
The bill expands eligibility for employee participation in the current Insurance Partnership program from 200 percent to 300 percent FPL, in order to provide another option for small businesses who want to offer health care to their employees.

D) The Medicaid Waiver
By shifting significant federal resources from supporting individual hospitals to funding health insurance coverage for uninsured individuals, and by living within a lifetime spending ceiling for waiver services, the bill meets the terms set by the Centers for Medicare and Medicaid for renewal of our 1115(a) MassHealth Demonstration Waiver.

E) Medicaid Expansions, Restorations, Enhancements
The bill expands Medicaid coverage of the uninsured by providing $3 million for comprehensive community-based outreach programs to reach people who are eligible for Medicaid but not yet enrolled, and by expanding eligibility for children. Currently, children in families who earn up to 200 percent of the Federal Poverty Level (FPL) are eligible for MassHealth. The bill increases eligibility to children in families earning up to 300 percent FPL ($38,500/yr for a family of 2).

The bill also restores all MassHealth benefits that were cut in 2002, including dental and vision services, and creates a 2-year pilot program for smoking cessation treatment for MassHealth enrollees.

In response to concern that Medicaid has underpaid many of its providers in recent years, the bill includes $90 million in rate relief for Fiscal Years 2007, 2008 and 2009. It does this while keeping within the budget neutrality limits of federal financing under the Medicaid waiver. The bill also establishes, for the first time, a process of tying rate increases to specific performance goals related to quality, efficiency, the reduction of racial and ethnic disparities, and improved outcomes for patients.

F) Individual Responsibility for Health Care

The bill requires that, as of July 1, 2007, all residents of the Commonwealth must obtain health insurance coverage. Individuals for whom there are not affordable products available will not be penalized for not having insurance coverage. A sliding "affordability scale" will be set annually by the Board of the Connector.

The purpose of this "Individual Mandate" is to strengthen and stabilize the functioning of health insurance risk pools by making sure they include healthy people (who, if not offered employer-sponsored and -paid insurance, are more likely to take the risk of not having insurance) as well as people who know they need regular health care services (and therefore are more likely to go to great lengths, and expense, to obtain insurance). The financing of the bill is based on redirecting some of the public funds we currently spend on "free care" provided through hospitals, to provide subsidized health insurance to the uninsured. The mandate is another way to make sure people do not rely on "free care" for their health care, but that they get comprehensive insurance.

Beginning in July 2007, Massachusetts residents will be required to have health insurance. Residents will confirm that they have health insurance coverage on their state income tax forms filed in 2008. Coverage will be verified through a database of insurance coverage for all individuals. The Department of Revenue will enforce this provision with financial penalties beginning with a loss of the personal exemption for tax year 2007 and then increasing to a portion of what an individual would have paid toward an affordable premium for subsequent years.

G) Employer Responsibility for Health Care

Fair Share Contribution

The bill creates a "Fair Share Contribution" that will be paid by employers who do not provide health insurance for their employees and make a fair and reasonable contribution to its cost. The contribution, estimated to be approximately $295 per full time employee (FTE) per year, will be calculated to reflect a portion of the cost paid by the state for free care used by workers whose employers do not provide insurance. Currently, a portion of the payments made by employers who do provide health coverage go towards free care costs, and this new contribution will help level the playing field. The Fair Share Contribution requirement will only apply to employers with 11 or more employees who do not provide health insurance or contribute to it, as defined by the Division of Health Care Finance and Policy, and will be pro-rated for employers with seasonal or part-time employees.

Free Rider Surcharge

The Free Rider surcharge will be imposed on employers who do not provide health insurance and whose employees use free care. Imposition of the surcharge will be triggered when an employee receives free care more than three times, or a company has five or more instances of employees receiving free care in a year. The surcharge will range from 10 percent to 100 percent of the state's costs of services provided to the employees, with the first $50,000 per employer exempted. Revenue gained from the surcharge will be deposited in the Commonwealth Care Trust Fund.

Mandatory Offer of Section 125 Plans

Section 125 plans or "cafeteria plans" allow an employer to offer health insurance and other programs such as day care funding to employees on a pre-tax basis. Because of the significant savings which result from pre-tax insurance purchase, employers with more than 10 employees will be required to offer this pre-tax benefit to employees.

H) REDUCTION OF RACIAL AND ETHNIC HEALTH DISPARITIES

The bill aims to reduce racial and ethnic health disparities by requiring hospitals to collect and report on health care data related to race, ethnicity and language. Medicaid rate increases in the bill are made contingent upon providers meeting performance benchmarks, including in the area of reducing racial and ethnic disparities. The bill creates a study of a sustainable Community Health Outreach Worker Program to target vulnerable populations in an effort to eliminate health disparities and remove linguistic barriers to health access. Finally, the bill creates a Health Disparities Council, to continue the work of the Special Commission on Racial and Ethic Health Disparities by recommending appropriate Legislative steps to reduce health disparities.

H) HEALTH SAFETY NET OFFICE AND FUND

Many recommendations of the Inspector General's Office regarding the management of the Uncompensated Care Pool are included in the bill. Effective October 1, 2007, the current Uncompensated Care Pool is eliminated, replaced by the Health Safety Net Fund. The Fund will be administered by a newly-created Health Safety Net Office located within the Office of Medicaid. The HSN Office will develop a new standard fee schedule for hospital reimbursements, replacing the current charges-based payment system. The plan anticipates the transfer of funds to the Commonwealth Care Health Insurance Program as free care use declines.

I) FUNDING

The plan leverages federal dollars to enhance and match state spending, and uses revenue generated by employer contributions to fund health insurance coverage.

Unlike the Massachusetts approach, the Maryland legislature took the approach of requiring large nongovernmental employers in that state to pay at least 8 percent of its employee wages on health insurance, or, alternatively, to pay the shortfall in health insurance costs to the state.[11] The Maryland legislature understood that the only company that would be affected by the new law was Wal-Mart Stores, Inc. ("Wal-Mart").[12] However, a retail trade association, which included Wal-Mart as a member, sued a Maryland state official for declaratory and injunctive relief. The federal district court held that the Maryland law is unenforceable because it is preempted by the federal ERISA. As discussed in Chapter 16, ERISA preempts state laws insofar as they relate to the benefit plans of employers in the private sector. To allow multistate employers to operate a uniform set of benefits for all of their employees in various states, Congress provided that those employers only need to comply with the federal law, and they are exempt from state requirements in developing and operating their employee benefit plans. Although states retain the power to regulate insurance companies, many ERISA plans are self-insured and beyond the reach of state authority. On January 17, 2007, the Court of Appeals for the Fourth Circuit agreed with the district court and held that the federal ERISA law preempts the Maryland law. Following is an excerpt from the opinion of the Court of Appeals.

RETAIL INDUSTRY LEADERS ASSOCIATION V. FIELDER, 475 F.3D 180 (4TH CIR. 2007) (CITATIONS AND FOOTNOTES OMITTED)

On January 12, 2006, the Maryland General Assembly enacted the Fair Share Health Care Fund Act, which requires employers with 10,000 or more Maryland employees to spend at least 8 percent of their total payrolls on employees' health insurance costs or pay the amount their spending falls short to the State of Maryland. Resulting from a nationwide campaign to force Wal-Mart Stores, Inc., to increase health insurance benefits for its 16,000 Maryland employees, the Act's minimum spending provision was crafted to cover just Wal-Mart. The Retail Industry Leaders Association, of which Wal-Mart is a member, brought suit against James D. Fielder, Jr., the Maryland Secretary of Labor, Licensing, and Regulation, to declare that the Act is preempted by the Employee Retirement Income Security Act of 1974 ("ERISA") and to enjoin the Act's enforcement. On cross-motions for summary judgment, the district court entered judgment declaring that the Act is preempted by ERISA and therefore not enforceable, and this appeal followed.

Because Maryland's Fair Share Health Care Fund Act effectively requires employers in Maryland covered by the Act to restructure their employee health insurance plans, it conflicts with ERISA's goal of permitting uniform nationwide administration of these plans. We conclude therefore that the Maryland Act is preempted by ERISA and accordingly affirm.

I

Before enactment of the Fair Share Health Care Fund Act ("Fair Share Act"), 2006 Md. Laws 1, the Maryland General Assembly heard extensive testimony about the rising costs of the Maryland Medical Assistance Program (Medicaid and children's health programs). It learned that between fiscal years 2003 and 2006, annual expenditures on the Program increased from $3.46 billion to $4.7 billion. The General Assembly also perceived that Wal-Mart Stores, Inc., a particularly large employer, provided its employees with a substandard level of healthcare benefits, forcing many Wal-Mart employees to depend on state-subsidized healthcare programs. Indeed, the Maryland Department of Legislative Services (which has the duties of providing the Maryland General Assembly with research, analysis, assessments, and evaluations of legislative issues) prepared an analytical report of the proposed Fair Share Act for the General Assembly, that discussed only Wal-Mart's employee benefits practices. In the background portion of the report, the Department of Legislative Services wrote:

> Several States, facing rapidly-increasing Medicaid costs, are turning to the private sector to bear more of the costs. Wal-Mart, in particular, has been the focus of several states, who are accusing the company of providing substandard health benefits to its employees. According to the *New York Times*, Wal-Mart full-time employees earn an average $1,200 a month, or about $8 an hour.
>
> Some states claim many Wal-Mart employees end up on public health programs such as Medicaid. A survey by Georgia officials found that more than 10,000 children of Wal-Mart employees were enrolled in the state's children's health insurance program (CHIP) at a cost of nearly $10 million annually. Similarly, a North Carolina hospital found that 31 percent of 1,900 patients who said they were Wal-Mart employees were enrolled in Medicaid, and an additional 16 percent were uninsured.
>
> As a result, some States have turned to Wal-Mart to assume more of the financial burden of its workers' health care costs. California passed a law in 2003 that will require most employers to either provide health coverage to employees or pay into a state insurance pool that would do so. Advocates of the law say Wal-Mart employees cost California health insurance programs about $32 million annually. Washington state is exploring implementing a similar state law.
>
> According to the [*New York*] *Times*, Wal-Mart said that its employees are mostly insured, citing internal surveys showing that 90% of workers have health coverage, often through Medicare or family members' policies. Wal-Mart officials say the company provides health coverage to about 537,000, or 45 percent of its total workforce. As a matter of comparison, Costco Wholesale provides health insurance to 96 percent of eligible employees.

In response, the General Assembly enacted the Fair Share Act in January 2006, to become effective January 1, 2007. The Act applies to employers that have at least 10,000 employees in Maryland, and imposes spending and reporting requirements on such employers. The core provision provides:

> An employer that is not organized as a nonprofit organization and does not spend up to 8 percent of the total wages paid to employees in the State on health insurance costs shall pay to the Secretary an amount equal to the difference between what the employer spends for health insurance costs and an amount equal to 8 percent of the total wages paid to employees in the State.

An employer that fails to make the required payment is subject to a civil penalty of $250,000.

The Act also requires a covered employer to submit an annual report on January 1 of each year to the Secretary, in which the employer must disclose: (1) how many employees it had for the prior year, (2) its "health insurance costs," and (3) the percentage of compensation it spent on "health insurance costs" for the "year immediately preceding the previous calendar year." The Act defines "health insurance costs" to include expenditures on both healthcare and health insurance to the extent that they are deductible under § 213(d) of the Internal Revenue Code.

Any payments collected by the Secretary are directed to the Fair Share Health Care Fund, which is held by the Treasurer of the State and accounted for by the State Comptroller like all other state funds. The funds so collected, however, may be used only to support the Maryland Medical Assistance Program, which consists of Maryland's Medicaid and children's health programs.

The record discloses that only four employers have at least 10,000 employees in Maryland: Johns Hopkins University, Giant Food, Northrop Grumman, and Wal-Mart. The Fair Share Act subjected Johns Hopkins, as a nonprofit organization, to a lower 6 percent spending threshold which Johns Hopkins already satisfies. Giant Food, which employs unionized workers, spends over the 8 percent threshold on health insurance and lobbied in support of the Fair Share Act. Northrop Grumman, a defense contractor, was subject to the minimum spending requirement in an earlier version of the Act, but the General Assembly included an amendment that effectively excluded Northrop Grumman. Because Northrop Grumman has many high-salaried employees in Maryland, the General Assembly was able to exclude it by an amendment that permits an employer, in calculating its total wages paid, to exempt compensation paid to employees in excess of the median household income in Maryland. The parties agree that only Wal-Mart, who employs approximately 16,000 in Maryland, is currently subject to the Act's minimum spending requirements. Wal-Mart representatives testified that it spends about 7 to 8 percent of its total payroll on healthcare, falling short of the Act's 8 percent threshold.

The legislative record also makes clear that legislators and affected parties assumed that the Fair Share Act would force Wal-Mart to increase its spending on healthcare benefits rather than to pay monies to the State. For example, one of the Act's sponsors, Senator Thomas V. Mike Miller, Jr., Maryland Senate President, described the Act during a floor debate: "It takes people who should be getting health benefits at work off the [State's] rolls and *it requires those employers to provide it.*"

Shortly after enactment of the Fair Share Act, the Retail Industry Leaders Association ("RILA") commenced this action against the Maryland Secretary of Labor, Licensing, and Regulation to declare the Act preempted by ERISA and to enjoin the Secretary from enforcing it. RILA is a trade association whose members are major companies from all segments of retailing, including Wal-Mart, as well as many of Wal-Mart's competitors, such as Best Buy Company, Target Corporation, Lowe's Companies, and IKEA. Many of these competitors are represented on RILA's board, which voted unanimously to authorize RILA to prosecute this action.

RILA's complaint alleged that the Fair Share Act was preempted by ERISA. It also alleged that the Fair Share Act violated the Equal Protection Clause of the Fourteenth Amendment to the United States Constitution and the "special law" prohibition of the Maryland Constitution, art. III, § 33.

Shortly after filing its complaint, RILA filed a motion for summary judgment on its ERISA-preemption claim and its equal-protection claim. In response, the Secretary filed a motion to dismiss RILA's complaint for lack of jurisdiction, arguing (1) that RILA lacked standing; (2) that its claims were not ripe; and (3) that its complaint was barred by the Tax Injunction Act, which prohibits federal courts in most cases from enjoining, suspending, or restraining a State's collection of taxes. In the alternative, the Secretary filed a cross-motion for summary judgment addressing all three of RILA's claims.

The district court rejected the Secretary's jurisdictional arguments and concluded that ERISA preempted the Fair Share Act because the Act effectively mandated that employers spend a minimum amount on healthcare benefit plans. The court also found that the Fair Share Act did not violate the Equal Protection Clause because the Act's classifications were not irrational. Each party appealed, challenging the rulings adverse to it.

II

We address first the Secretary's jurisdictional challenges based on standing, ripeness, and the Tax Injunction Act. . . .

In sum, we hold that RILA has standing; that RILA's claim is ripe for adjudication; and that RILA's complaint is not barred by the Tax Injunction Act.

III

On the merits of whether ERISA preempts the Fair Share Act, the Secretary contends that the district court misunderstood the nature and effect of the Fair

Share Act, erroneously finding that the Act mandates an employer's provision of healthcare benefits and therefore "relates to" ERISA plans. The Secretary offers a different characterization of the Fair Share Act—one with which ERISA is not concerned. He describes the Act as "part of the State's comprehensive scheme for planning, providing, and financing health care for its citizens." In his view, the Act imposes a payroll tax on covered employers and offers them a credit against that tax for their healthcare spending. The revenue from this tax funds a Fair Share Health Care Fund, which is used to offset the costs of Maryland's Medical Assistance Program.

To resolve the question whether ERISA preempts the Fair Share Act, we consider first the scope of ERISA's preemption provision, and then the nature and effect of the Fair Share Act to determine whether it falls within the scope of ERISA's preemption.

A

ERISA establishes comprehensive federal regulation of employers' provision of benefits to their employees. It does not mandate that employers provide specific employee benefits but leaves them free, "for any reason at any time, to adopt, modify, or terminate welfare plans." Instead, ERISA regulates the employee benefit plans that an employer chooses to establish, setting "various uniform standards, including rules concerning reporting, disclosure, and fiduciary responsibility."

The vast majority of healthcare benefits that an employer extends to its employees qualify as an "employee welfare benefit plan," which ERISA defines broadly as:

> any *plan, fund, or program* which . . . was established or is maintained for the purpose of providing for its participants or their beneficiaries, through the purchase of insurance or otherwise, . . . *medical, surgical, or hospital care or benefits, or benefits in the event of sickness, accident, disability,* death or unemployment, or vacation benefits, apprenticeship or other training programs, or day care centers, scholarship funds, or prepaid legal services. . . .

. . . Because the definition of an ERISA "plan" is so expansive, nearly any systematic provision of healthcare benefits to employees constitutes a plan.

The primary objective of ERISA was to "provide a uniform regulatory regime over employee benefit plans." To accomplish this objective, § 514(a) of ERISA broadly preempts "any and all State laws insofar as they may now or hereafter *relate to* any employee benefit plan" covered by ERISA. This preemption provision aims "to minimize the administrative and financial burden of complying with conflicting directives among States or between States and the Federal Government" and to reduce "the tailoring of plans and employer conduct to the peculiarities of the law of each jurisdiction."

The language of ERISA's preemption provision—covering all laws that "relate to" an ERISA plan—is "clearly expansive." The Supreme Court has focused judicial analysis by explaining that a state law "relates to" an ERISA plan "if it has a *connection with* or *reference to* such a plan." But even these terms, "taken to extend to the furthest stretch of [their] in determinacy," would have preemption "never run its course." Accordingly, we do not rely on "uncritical literalism" but attempt to ascertain whether Congress would have expected the Fair Share Act to be preempted. To make this determination, we look "to the objectives of the ERISA statute" as well as "to the nature of the effect of the state law on ERISA plans," recognizing that ERISA is not presumed to supplant state law, especially in cases involving "fields of traditional state regulation," which include "the regulation of matters of health and safety,"

Through application of these principles, the Supreme Court has held that not all state healthcare regulations are equal for purposes of ERISA preemption. States continue to enjoy wide latitude to regulate healthcare *providers*. And ERISA explicitly saves state regulations of *insurance companies* from preemption. But unlike laws that regulate healthcare providers and insurance companies, "state laws that mandate[ ] employee benefit structures or their administration" are preempted by ERISA. Such state-imposed regulation of employers' provision of employee benefits conflict[s] with ERISA's goal of establishing uniform, nationwide regulation of employee benefit plans. . . .

B

We now consider the nature and effect of the Fair Share Act to determine whether it falls within ERISA's preemption. At its heart, the Fair Share Act requires every employer of 10,000 or more Maryland employees to pay to the State an amount that equals the difference between what the employer spends on "health insurance costs" (which includes any costs "to provide health benefits") and 8% of its payroll. As Wal-Mart noted by way of affidavit, it would not pay the State a sum of money that it could instead spend on its employees' healthcare. This would be the decision of any reasonable employer. Healthcare benefits are a part of the total package of employee compensation an employer gives in consideration for an employee's services. An employer would gain from increasing the compensation it offers employees through improved retention and performance of present employees and the ability to attract more and better new employees. In contrast, an employer would gain nothing in consideration of paying a greater sum of money to the State. Indeed, it might suffer from lower employee morale and increased public condemnation.

In effect, the only rational choice employers have under the Fair Share Act is to structure their ERISA healthcare benefit plans so as to meet the minimum spending threshold. The Act thus falls squarely under *Shaw*'s prohibition of state mandates on how employers structure their ERISA plans. Because the Fair Share Act effectively mandates that employers structure their employee healthcare plans to provide a certain level of benefits, the Act has an obvious "connection with" employee benefit plans and so is preempted by ERISA.

This view of the Fair Share Act is reinforced by the position of the State of Maryland itself. The Maryland General Assembly intended the Act to have precisely this effect. As we noted in Part I, the context for enactment of the Act, including the Department of Legislative Services' official description of it, shows that legislators and interested parties uniformly understood the Act as *requiring* Wal-Mart to increase its healthcare spending. If this is not the Act's effect, one would have to conclude, which we do not, that the Maryland legislature misunderstood the nature of the bill that it carefully drafted and debated. For these reasons, the amount that the Act prescribes for payment to the State is actually a fee or a penalty that gives the employer an irresistible incentive to provide its employees with a greater level of health benefits.

It is a stretch to claim, as the Secretary does, that the Fair Share Act is a revenue statute of general application. When it was enacted, the General Assembly knew that it applied, and indeed intended that it apply, to one employer in Maryland—Wal-Mart. The General Assembly designed the statute to avoid applying the 8 percent level to Johns Hopkins University; it knew that Giant Food was unionized and already was providing more than 8 percent; and it amended the statute to avoid including Northrop Grumman. Even as the statute is written, the category of employers employing 10,000 employees in Maryland includes only four persons in Maryland and therefore could hardly be intended to function as a revenue act of general application.

While the Secretary argues that the Fair Share Act is designed to collect funds for medical care under the Maryland Medical Assistance Program, the core provision of the Act aims at requiring covered employers to provide medical benefits to employees. The effect of this provision will force employers to structure their recordkeeping and healthcare benefit spending to comply with the Fair Share Act. Functioning in that manner, the Act would disrupt employers' uniform administration of employee benefit plans on a nationwide basis. As Wal-Mart officials averred, Wal-Mart does not presently allocate its contributions to ERISA plans or other healthcare spending by State, and so the Fair Share Act would require it to segregate a separate pool of expenditures for Maryland employees.

This problem would not likely be confined to Maryland. As a result of similar efforts elsewhere to pressure Wal-Mart to increase its healthcare spending, other States and local governments have adopted or are considering healthcare spending mandates that would clash with the Fair Share Act. For example, two New York counties recently adopted provisions to require Wal-Mart to spend an amount on healthcare to be determined annually by an administrative agency. Similar legislation under consideration in Minnesota calculates total wages, from which an employer's minimum spending level is determined, with reference to Minnesota's median household income. If permitted to stand, these laws would force Wal-Mart to tailor its healthcare benefit plans to each specific State, and even to specific cities and counties. This is precisely the regulatory balkanization that Congress sought to avoid by enacting ERISA's preemption provision.

The Secretary argues that the Act is not mandatory and therefore does not, for preemption purposes, have a "connection with" employee benefit plans because it gives employers two options to avoid increasing benefits to employees. An employer can, under the Fair Share Act, (1) increase healthcare spending on employees in ways that do not qualify as ERISA plans; or (2) refuse to increase benefits to employees and pay the State the amount by which the employer's spending falls short of 8 percent. Because employers have these choices, the Secretary argues, the Fair Share Act does not preclude Wal-Mart from continuing its uniform administration of ERISA plans nationwide. . . .

In contrast, . . . the Fair Share Act *directly* regulates employers' structuring of their employee health benefit plans. . . .

The Fair Share Act likewise would deny Wal-Mart the uniform nationwide administration of its healthcare plans by requiring it to keep an eye on conflicting state and local minimum spending requirements and adjust its healthcare spending accordingly.

. . . . [T]he Secretary relies most heavily on its argument that the Fair Share Act gives employers the choice of paying the State rather than altering their healthcare spending. The Secretary contends that, in certain circumstances, it would be rational for an employer to choose to do so. It conceives that an employer, whose healthcare spending comes close to the 8 percent threshold, may find it more cost-effective to pay the State the required amount rather than incur the costs of altering the administration of its healthcare plans. The existence of this stylized scenario, however, does nothing to refute the fact that in *most* scenarios, the Act would cause an employer to alter the administration of its healthcare plans. Indeed, identifying the narrow conditions under which the Act would not force an employer to increase its spending on healthcare plans only reinforces the conclusion that the overwhelming effect of the Act is to mandate spending increases. This conclusion is further supported by the fact that Wal-Mart representatives averred that Wal-Mart would in fact increase healthcare spending rather than pay the State.

In short, the Fair Share Act leaves employers no reasonable choices except to change how they structure their employee benefit plans.

Because the Act directly regulates employers' provision of healthcare benefits, it has a "connection with" covered employers' ERISA plans and accordingly is preempted by ERISA.

IV

On its cross-appeal, RILA contends that the district court erred in finding that the Fair Share Act does not violate the Equal Protection Clause. Because we have concluded that the Fair Share Act is preempted by ERISA, we need not consider RILA's equal-protection claim.

V

The Maryland General Assembly, in furtherance of its effort to require Wal-Mart to spend more money on employee health benefits and thus reduce Wal-Mart's employees' reliance on Medicaid, enacted the Fair Share Act. Not disguised was Maryland's purpose to require Wal-Mart to change, at least in Maryland, its employee benefit plans and how they are administered. This goal, however, directly clashes with ERISA's preemption provision and ERISA's purpose of authorizing Wal-Mart and others like it to provide uniform health benefits to its employees on a nationwide basis.

Were we to approve Maryland's enactment solely for its noble purpose, we would be leading a charge against the foundational policy of ERISA, and surely other States and local governments would follow. As sensitive as we are to the right of Maryland and other States to enact laws of their own choosing, we are also bound to enforce ERISA as the "supreme Law of the Land."

The judgment of the district court is
AFFIRMED.

It is possible that the U.S. Supreme Court will agree to consider the Maryland case or a case involving a similar state law. In the meantime, the Maryland law cannot be enforced, and state governments need to search for other ways to expand health insurance coverage in their individual states.

The decision of the Fourth Circuit in the Maryland case is not binding on federal courts in other circuits, but other courts might find that reasoning to be persuasive. Even if other courts decide to follow the reasoning of the Fourth Circuit, each state law is different and each case might be distinguishable on its facts. It is unclear, therefore, whether courts would be likely to uphold or strike down the healthcare reform laws of other states, such as the Massachusetts law described. In the event that ERISA ultimately presents an insurmountable barrier to healthcare reform, the focus necessarily will shift back to Congress to do what is needed at the federal level to achieve the goal of universal health insurance coverage throughout the country.

Notes

1. 15 U.S.C. §§ 1011–1015 (2006).
2. See *Humana, Inc. v. Forsyth*, 525 U.S. 299, 302–306 (1999) ("[w]hen federal law is applied in aid or enhancement of state regulation, and does not frustrate any declared state policy or disturb the State's administrative regime, the McCarran-Ferguson Act does not bar the federal action.").

3. Pub. L. No. 104-191, 110 Stat. 1936 (1996) (codified at 29 U.S.C. §§ 1181 *et seq.*).

4. 29 U.S.C. – 1162 (2006).

5. See U.S. General Accounting Office, *Private Health Insurance: Progress and Challenges in Implementing 1996 Federal Standards*, GAO/HEHS-99–100 (May 1999): 12.

6. See The Department of Veterans Affairs and Housing and Urban Development and Independent Agencies Appropriations Act of 1997, Pub. L. No. 104-204, § 711, 110 Stat. 2874, 2935–36 (1996) (codified at 29 U.S.C. § 1185).

7. C. Lee, "Universal Health Coverage Attracts New Support," *Washington Post*, January 22, 2007, at A03.

8. *New York State Conference of Blue Cross & Blue Shield Plans v. Travelers Insurance Company*, 514 U.S. 645, 667 n.6 (1995) (analyzing the legislative history of the federal Medicare program).

9. Chapter 58 of the Acts of 2006. [Online information; retrieved 2/10/07.] www.mass.gov/legis/laws/seslaw06/sl060058.htm.

10. See E.F. Haislmaier and N. Owcharenko, "The Massachusetts Approach: A New Way to Restructure State Health Insurance Markets and Public Programs," *Health Affairs* 25(6) (2006): 1580–1590.

11. Fair Share Act, Md. Code. Ann., Lab. & Empl. § 8.5-103(a)(1) (2006).

12. *Retail Industry Leaders Association v. Fielder*, 435 F. Supp. 2d 481, 485 and n.3 (D. Md.), *aff'd*, 475 F.3d 180, 2007 U.S. App. LEXIS 920 (4th Cir. 2007).

TABLE OF CASES

TABLE OF STATUTES

15 U.S.C. § 1 (2007),
15 U.S.C. § 2 (2007),
15 U.S.C. § 18 (2007),
15 U.S.C. § 18a (2007),
15 U.S.C. §§ 34–36 (2007),
15 U.S.C. §§ 1011–1015 (2006),
21 U.S.C. §§ 801 *et seq.* (2006),
29 U.S.C. § 794 (2006),
29 U.S.C. §§ 1001 *et seq.* (2006),
29 U.S.C. § 1144 (2006),
29 U.S.C. § 1162 (2006),
31 U.S.C. §§ 3729 *et seq.* (2006),
42 U.S.C. § 274e (2006),
42 U.S.C. §§ 291 *et seq.* (2006),
42 U.S.C. § 1320a–7a(b) (2006),
42 U.S.C. § 1320a–7b (2006),
42 U.S.C. § 1320a–7b(a) (2006),
42 U.S.C. § 1320a–7b(b)(1)–(2) (2006),
42 U.S.C. § 1320b–8 (2006),
42 U.S.C. § 1395 (2006),
42 U.S.C. § 1395a(a) (2006),
42 U.S.C. § 1395bb (2006),
42 U.S.C. § 1395dd (2006),
42 U.S.C. § 1395dd(a) (2006),
42 U.S.C. § 1395nn(b) (2006),
42 U.S.C. § 1395w–22j(4)(A)(i) (2006),
42 U.S.C. § 1395w–111(1) (2006),
42 U.S.C. § 1396a(a)(30)(A) (2006),
42 U.S.C. § 1396d(a)(4)(B) (2006),
42 U.S.C. § 1396p(c) (2006),
42 U.S.C. § 1397aa(c) (2006),
42 U.S.C. § 1397bb(b)(4) (2006),
42 U.S.C. § 2000d (2006),
42 U.S.C. §§ 11101–52 (2007),

42 U.S.C. §§ 12181 *et seq.* (2006),

42 U.S.C. § 12181(7)(F) (2006),

42 U.S.C. § 12182(a) (2006),

710 Ill. Comp. Stat. 45/405 (2005),

Assisted Suicide Funding Restriction Act of 1997, Pub. L. No. 105-12, 111 Stat. 23 (1997) (codified as amended at 42 U.S.C. §§ 14401 *et seq.*),

Balanced Budget Act of 1997, Pub. L. No. 105-33, 111 Stat. 251 (1997),

Balanced Budget Act of 1997, Pub. L. No. 105-33, § 1852(j), 111 Stat. 251, 295–96 (1997),

Balanced Budget Act of 1997, Pub. L. No. 105-33, § 4314, 111 Stat. 251, 389 (1997) (codified at 42 U.S.C. § 1395nn),

Balanced Budget Act of 1997, Pub. L. No. 105-33, § 4641, 111 Stat. 251, 487 (1997) (codified as amended at 42 U.S.C. § 1395cc(f)(1)(B)),

Balanced Budget Act of 1997, Pub. L. No. 105-33, §§ 4901(a) *et seq.*, 111 Stat. 251, 552 (1997) (codified at 42 U.S.C. §§ 1397aa *et seq.*),

Cal. Civ. Code § 3333.2 (West 1997),

Death with Dignity Act, Or. Rev. Stat. §§ 127.800–.897 (1997),

Deficit Reduction Act of 2005, Pub. L. No. 109-171, § 6036 (effective July 1, 2006),

Department of Veterans Affairs and Housing and Urban Development and Independent Agencies Appropriations Act of 1997, Pub. L. No. 104-204, § 711, 110 Stat. 2874, 2935 (codified at 29 U.S.C. § 1185),

Emergency Medical Treatment and Active Labor Act (EMTALA), 42 U.S.C. § 1395dd (2006),

Employee Retirement Income Security Act of 1974 (ERISA), 29 U.S.C. §§ 1001 *et seq.* (2005),

Ethics in Patient Referrals Act, Pub. L. No. 101-239, § 6204, 103 Stat. 2106, 2236 (1989) (codified at 42 U.S.C. § 1395nn),

Fair Share Health Care Fund Act, Md. Code. Ann., Lab. & Empl. § 8.5-103(a)(1) (2006),

False Claims Act, 31 U.S.C. § 3729 (2000),

Fla. Laws ch. 418 (2003),

Health Care Quality Improvement Act of 1986, Pub. L. No. 99-660, §§ 421–27, 100 Stat. 3743, 3788–92 (1986) (codified as amended at 42 U.S.C. §§ 11131–37 (2005)),

Health Insurance Portability and Accountability Act of 1996 (HIPAA), Pub. L. No. 104-191, 110 Stat. 1936 (1996) (codified at 29 U.S.C. §§ 1181 *et seq.*),

Health Insurance Portability and Accountability Act of 1996, Pub. L. No. 104-191, § 205, 110 Stat. 1936, 2000 (codified at 42 U.S.C. § 1320a–7d),

Health Insurance Portability and Accountability Act of 1996, Pub. L. No. 104-191, §§ 241–250, 110 Stat. 1936, 2016–21 (codified in scattered sections of 18 U.S.C.),

TABLE OF REGULATIONS

63 Fed. Reg. 1,659, 1,661 (January 9, 1998),

63 Fed. Reg. 1,659 (January 9, 1998) (proposed rule) (to be codified at 42 C.F.R. pts. 411, 424, 435, 455),

63 Fed. Reg. 8,987 (February 23, 1998),

63 Fed. Reg. 8,998 (February 23, 1998),

63 Fed. Reg. 67,486 (December 7, 1998),

64 Fed. Reg. 37,985 (July 14, 1999),

64 Fed. Reg. 59,918 (November 3, 1999) (proposed rule),

64 Fed. Reg. 61,353, 61,356 (November 10, 1999) (Special Advisory Bulletin),

64 Fed. Reg. 63,518 (November 19, 1999),

65 Fed. Reg. 18,434 (April 7, 2000),

65 Fed. Reg. 70,246, 70,254 (November 21, 2000),

65 Fed. Reg. 82,462, 82,465 (December 28, 2000),

66 Fed. Reg. 856 (January 4, 2001) (final rule),

66 Fed. Reg. 56,607, 56,607–08 (November 9, 2001),

67 Fed. Reg. 14,776 (March 27, 2002) (proposed rule; modification),

67 Fed. Reg. 31,404 (May 9, 2002) (proposed rule),

67 Fed. Reg. 31,471 (May 9, 2002) (proposed rule),

67 Fed. Reg. 31,506 (May 9, 2002),

67 Fed. Reg. 31,507 (May 9, 2002) (proposed rule),

67 Fed. Reg. 53,182 (August 14, 2002) (final rule),

68 Fed. Reg. 47,311 (August 8, 2003),

68 Fed. Reg. 47,314 (August 8, 2003),

68 Fed. Reg. 53,222–53,264 (September 9, 2003),

68 Fed. Reg. 53,244–53,245 (September 9, 2003),

69 Fed. Reg. 16,054 (March 26, 2004) (interim final rule),

70 Fed. Reg. 4,858 (January 31, 2005),

71 Fed. Reg. 4,5110 (August 8, 2006),

71 Fed. Reg. 4,5140 (August 8, 2006) (final rule),

N.C. Admin. Code tit. 10, r. 3R.1700 (2002).

INDEX

ABOUT THE AUTHOR

Dean M. Harris, JD, is a clinical associate professor in the Department of Health Policy and Administration, School of Public Health, University of North Carolina (UNC) at Chapel Hill, and adjunct associate professor in the UNC School of Law. In addition, he serves as adjunct professor in the Department of Health Economics and Management in the Guanghua School of Management at Peking University, Beijing, China. He previously taught in an executive MBA program at The Fuqua School of Business at Duke University.

At the UNC School of Public Health, Professor Harris teaches courses on health law, ethics, and comparative health systems. In addition, he taught a course on healthcare antitrust law for several years at UNC School of Law.

Professor Harris received his B.A. degree from Cornell University in 1973, and received his J.D. degree with high honors from UNC School of Law in 1981. His current research interests include healthcare law and regulation in developing countries, comparative law of medical malpractice, and ways to regulate the privatization of healthcare facilities.

In addition, Professor Harris is a licensed attorney in North Carolina. He practiced law from 1981 to 1999, with a primary focus on representation of healthcare organizations and providers. In his work in the healthcare field, he provided legal advice and representation in areas such as antitrust, certificate of need and other regulatory matters, mergers and acquisitions, joint ventures and corporate reorganization, medical staff membership and clinical privileges, Medicare and Medicaid, professional licensure, and patient care issues.